Writing World History
1800–2000

Studies of the German Historical Institute London

GENERAL EDITOR: Peter Wende

Writing World History
1800–2000

EDITED BY

BENEDIKT STUCHTEY
AND
ECKHARDT FUCHS

GERMAN HISTORICAL INSTITUTE LONDON
OXFORD
UNIVERSITY PRESS

This book has been printed digitally and produced in a standard specification in order to ensure its continuing availability

OXFORD
UNIVERSITY PRESS

Great Clarendon Street, Oxford OX2 6DP

Oxford University Press is a department of the University of Oxford.
It furthers the University's objective of excellence in research, scholarship,
and education by publishing worldwide in

Oxford New York

Auckland Cape Town Dar es Salaam Hong Kong Karachi
Kuala Lumpur Madrid Melbourne Mexico City Nairobi
New Delhi Shanghai Taipei Toronto
With offices in
Argentina Austria Brazil Chile Czech Republic France Greece
Guatemala Hungary Italy Japan South Korea Poland Portugal
Singapore Switzerland Thailand Turkey Ukraine Vietnam

Oxford is a registered trade mark of Oxford University Press
in the UK and in certain other countries

Published in the United States
by Oxford University Press Inc., New York

Reprinted 2007

ISBN 978-0-19-925557-3

Cover illustration: 'Clio', medal by Sir Edward Poynter, 1889.
© The British Museum

Printed and bound by CPI Antony Rowe, Eastbourne

Foreword

The writing of world history has changed immensely over the last fifty years in Western and non-Western historiographies. It is increasingly taking a comparative perspective and, at present, American scholars are dominating a field that has hitherto been largely in the hands of European historians. Although the questions and problems of world history, in particular of different civilizations, were addressed in Ancient Greece by Herodotus and in early medieval Persia by Rashid al-Din, to give but two of numerous examples, the subject as such was really shaped in the European Enlightenment, and especially by Voltaire. Later, Karl Marx articulated an approach that set the writing of world history on to important new paths. However, neither Voltaire nor Marx, nor the best-sellers of their age, the philosophers of history Oswald Spengler, Arnold Toynbee, and H. G. Wells, who presented grand syntheses for whose generalizations they were so strongly criticized, were prepared to exchange their established Eurocentric views for a really critical global perspective. The same applies to projects such as Lord Acton's *Cambridge Modern History* and the later German *Propyläen Weltgeschichte*, which required a substantial number of authors, necessarily resulting in a lack of coherence. A considerable shift took place in the 1950s, when American historians approached the subject under the influence of cultural anthropology and other neighbouring disciplines. One of the key texts at his time and to the present is William McNeill's *The Rise of the West* (1963). A student of Toynbee's, McNeill believed in large-scale patterns of change, but he began to distrust the concept of 'civilizations'. Many highly successful and influential world historians with the same genealogy could be named who helped to shape our understanding of a world that is itself marked by constant change.

It is a particular merit of this volume, which grew out of an international conference held by the German Historical Institute London in spring 2000, that among the contributors are historians actively engaged in the writing of world history. Thus the essays profit by bridging theory and practice. Controversies remain on a number of issues such as, for example, periodization, the balance between Western and non-Western approaches, and the relationship between global and national histories, given that the authors of the present volume come from American, European, and non-European universities. The conference participants and those authors who unfortunately could not be present but kindly agreed to provide an essay make clear what a lively and steadily growing field of research world history and the writing of it remains. This collection is a timely contribution covering a broad spectrum of topics and questions on which further studies may build. It is the second volume on this subject produced by the same editors. The first was published early in 2002 as *Across Cultural Borders: Historiography in Global Perspective* (Lanham, Boulder, New York, and Oxford: Rowan & Littlefield Publishers).

The German Historical Institute London owes thanks to many individuals and institutions. The conference itself was co-sponsored by the German Historical Institute Washington, and we thank its then Acting Director, Dr Christof Mauch, for his willingness to co-operate. A number of people gave expert advice and critical comments during the planning phase. We are also grateful to those who chaired the discussions with great discretion and stimulated the debate during the conference, and later helped with their advice on editorial problems. We should like to mention especially Professor John Burrow and Professor Georg G. Iggers as well as Professor Michael Bentley, Professor Jürgen Osterhammel, Professor Roxann Prazniak, Professor Ernst Schulin, Professor Hagen Schulze, and Professor Eduardo Tortarolo. Many thanks must go to Anne Ashby of Oxford University Press for all her help in publishing this volume. We would also like to thank Dr Angela Davies who, as usual, provided indispensable help in the process of editing the present volume. The main credit, however, for conceiving and organizing the conference, as well as for editing the present volume, must go to Dr Benedikt Stuchtey and Dr Eckhardt Fuchs, and I should like to take this opportunity to express my thanks to them.

Peter Wende

Frankfurt/Main
July 2002

Contents

1

Introduction
Problems of Writing World History: Western and Non-Western Experiences, 1800–2000

BENEDIKT STUCHTEY AND ECKHARDT FUCHS

I

In attempting to define the place of world history in the curriculum of high school students, Edwin M. Pahlow described a cartoon published in the journal *Life*. It pictured a woman in a book shop. '"I want to buy a globe," she said. "I'd like a small one. If you have a globe of the United States, I'll take that."'[1] This is not the place to comment on Pahlow's interpretation of this cartoon but to investigate his argument that teaching world history reflects a general view of what constituted the world. For Pahlow, world history meant widening the geographical scope of a 'globe of the United States' for practical moral reasons that aimed to link the history and culture of the USA with a European heritage. From this perspective, world history was the addition of Euro-American history to the history of the USA.

This view of world history that attempted to overcome American exceptionalism had an equivalent in 'Western Civ' courses at American colleges. These originated in a course on 'Contemporary Civilization' at Columbia College in 1919. Before the First World War, English history had been at the centre of American and European studies and only a few world histories had appeared. One was William Swinton's *Outlines of the World's History*,[2] published as a textbook in 1874, and another was Philip

[1] Quoted from Edwin M. Pahlow, 'Why World History', *Education*, 53 (1932), 133–99, at 193.

[2] William O. Swinton, *Outlines of the World's History Ancient, Medieval, and Modern, with Special Relation to the History of Civilization and the Progress of Mankind* (New York, 1874).

V. N. Myers's *A General History for Colleges and High School* published fifteen years later in Boston. 'General History' was taught at high schools and colleges, but was soon rejected by professional historians because it was seen as amateurism. After the First World War, the curriculum change at Columbia College was a response to America's efforts during the war, to the new complexity of international affairs, and to the increasing diversity of the population. World history courses aimed to instruct American students in democratic citizenship during a period of cultural unification and growing internationalism in the USA.[3] The rapid spread of the courses all over the USA reflected a growing interest in European and international affairs, but textbooks and historical accounts did not overcome a Eurocentric perspective whose origin lay in nineteenth-century European studies of world history. Nevertheless, 'Western Civ' was, in Peter Novick's words, 'a war baby',[4] and it became an integral part of the history curriculum after the Second World War.

The growing interest in world history after 1945 was caused by the emergence of the two superpowers and the Cold War. In the USA a modernization analysis defined by economics interpreted Western democracies—and especially the USA—as a universal model of development that would prevent young nations from joining the communist bloc. 'Western Civ', now an obligatory introductory course for history students at American universities, was actually world history with the ideological and political mission of putting the USA at the top of historical development. World history courses were not incorporated into curricula as an alternative to 'Western Civ' until the 1970s. By then, research on world history had already started establishing the concepts of large and complex civilizations and of 'total history'. Its institutionalization began in the 1980s with the founding of the World History Association and the *World History Bulletin*.[5]

[3] See Lawrence W. Levine, 'Looking Eastward: The Carrier of Western Civ' [1996], in Ross E. Dunn (ed.), *The New World History: A Teacher's Companion* (Boston, 2000), 18–25; Gilbert Allardyce, 'Toward World History: American Historians and the Coming of the World History Course' [1990], ibid. 29–58, at 34 f.; William McNeill, 'The World History Survey Course', in Joe C. Dixon and Neil D. Martin (eds.), *1982 World History Teaching Conference* (ERIC document).

[4] Peter Novick, *That Noble Dream: The 'Objectivity Question' and the American Historical Profession* (Cambridge, 1988), 312.

[5] Recently many books and articles have been published on the history of world history in the last twenty years and its present stage. Since 1990 the *Journal of World*

In Germany, the rise of world history as a subject followed a different course. In the USA world history courses in the form of 'Western Civ' arose out of two world wars and preceded the writing of academic accounts. In Germany, by contrast, world history courses have not entered the history curriculum at universities to the present day.[6] However, the writing of world and universal history can be traced back to Enlightenment historiography and earlier. Universal historians of this era, such as Isaak Iselin, Johann Christoph Gatterer, August Ludwig Schlözer, and Friedrich Schiller, based their histories of mankind on travel reports, linked historical with anthropological and ethnological data, and rejected traditional historiography as a history of kings and dynasties.[7] Johann Gottfried Herder's

History has been the main forum for discussion in this new field. See, among others, Dunn, *The New World History*; Philip Pomper, Richard H. Elphick, and Richard T. Vann (eds.), *World History: Ideologies, Structures, and Identities* (Malden, Mass., 1998); Jerry H. Bentley, *Shapes of World History in Twentieth-Century Scholarship: Essays on Global and Comparative History* (Washington, DC, 1996).

[6] However, there were also textbooks for high-school courses and for a popular audience. See, among others, Ernst Alexander Schmidt, *Grundriß der Weltgeschichte für Gymnasien und andere höhere Lehranstalten zum Selbstunterricht für Gebildete* (2nd edn.; Berlin, 1835); Johann G. Kutzner, *Die Weltgeschichte in zusammenhängenden Einzelbildern nach schul- und volkspädagogischen Grundsätzen für Volkslehranstalten und zur Selbstbelehrung für Jedermann aus dem Volke* (Berlin, 1858); Theodor Flathe, G. F. Hertzberg, Ferdinand Justi, Julius von Pflugk-Harttung, and M. Philippson (eds.), *Allgemeine Weltgeschichte*, i (Berlin, 1884); Julius von Pflugk-Harttung (ed.), *Weltgeschichte: Die Entwicklung der Menschheit in Staat und Gesellschaft, in Kultur und Geistesleben*, 6 vols. (Berlin, 1910). It should also be mentioned that world history in the shape of 'Western Civ' was part of the curriculum in East Germany, within Marxist theory and with different ideological aims. But it was as Euro/American-centric as American courses.

[7] Isaak Iselin, *Philosophische Muthmaßungen über die Geschichte der Menschheit*, 2 vols. (Frankfurt, 1764); Johann Christoph Gatterer, *Abriß der Universalhistorie in ihrem ganzen Umfange* (Göttingen, 1773); August Ludwig Schlözer, *Vorstellung seiner Universal-Historie*, 2 vols. (Göttingen, 1772–3); Friedrich Schiller, 'Was heißt und zu welchem Ende studiert man Universalgeschichte?' [1789], in Karl-Heinz Hahn (ed.), *Schillers Werke: Nationalausgabe*, xvii (Weimar, 1970), 359–76. For general information see Jürgen Osterhammel, 'Neue Welten in der europäischen Geschichtsschreibung (ca. 1500–1800)' in Wolfgang Küttler, Jörn Rüsen, and Ernst Schulin (eds.), *Geschichtsdiskurs*, ii: *Anfänge modernen historischen Denkens* (Frankfurt am Main, 1994), 202–15; Horst Walter Blanke and Dirk Fleischer (eds.), *Theoretiker der deutschen Aufklärungshistorie*, 2 vols. (Stuttgart, 1990); Peter Hanns Reill, *The German Enlightenment and the Rise of Historicism* (Berkeley, 1975); Michael Harbsmeier, 'World Histories before Domestication: Writing Universal Histories, Histories of Mankind and World Histories in 18th-Century Germany', *Culture and History*, 5 (1989), 93–131; Harald Kleinschmidt, 'Japan im Welt- und Geschichtsbild der Europäer: Bemerkungen zu europäischen Weltgeschichtsdarstellungen vornehmlich des 16. bis 18. Jahrhunderts', *Bochumer Jahrbuch zur Ostasienforschung*, 3 (1980), 137–207; Edwin J. Van Kley, 'Europe's "Discovery" of China and the Writing of World History', *American Historical Review*, 76 (1971), 358–85.

concept of world history was the most ambitious because he took the position that every culture deserved an equal place in human history. He saw the ideal for other cultures neither in the enlightened civilization of Europe nor in a progressive process of perfectibility. Rather, he emphasized the singularity of other peoples, that is, a cultural diversity that could not be understood with European normative concepts and teleology.[8] For these cosmopolitan philosophers and historians who based their accounts on centuries-old traditions of Oriental studies and travel reports, the Orient was part of a universal world view.[9]

However, the idea of the difference between 'primitive' and 'civilized' peoples, or, more accurately, that other cultures were inferior to Indo-European ones, can be found as early as Christoph Meiners's *History of Mankind* published in 1785.[10] In general, the global aproach to history was abandoned in the course of the nineteenth century. The development of history as an academic discipline in the nineteenth century encouraged a geographical narrowing of its subject matter. Jürgen Osterhammel, referring to the scholarly reception of Asia, has described this process, which took place between 1780 and 1830, as a transformation from the 'inclusive Eurocentrism' of the Enlightenment that considered the superiority of Europe as a heuristic hypothesis, to an 'exclusive Eurocentrism' that took the hypothesis for granted.[11] The Eurocentric claim to represent human civilization had its philosophical justification in Hegel's *Philosophy of History* and its historiographical foundation in Leopold von Ranke's concepts of world history.[12] European history was elevated to the level of world history.

[8] Johann G. Herder, *Ideen zur Philosophie der Geschichte der Menschheit* [1784–91] (= vol. vi of *Werke in zehn Bänden*, ed. M. Bollacker) (Frankfurt am Main, 1989). For a philosophical perspective see Immanuel Kant, 'Idee zu einer allgemeinen Geschichte in weltbürgerlicher Absicht' [1784], in *Kants gesammelte Schriften*, ed. Prussian Academy of Sciences, viii (Berlin, 1923), 15–31.

[9] See Jürgen Osterhammel, *Die Entzauberung Asiens: Europa und die asiatischen Reiche im 18. Jahrhundert* (Munich, 1998); id., 'Neue Welten in der europäischen Geschichtsschreibung (ca. 1500–1800)', 202–25; id., '"Peoples without History" in British and German Historical Thought', in Benedikt Stuchtey and Peter Wende (eds.), *British and German Historiography 1750-1950: Traditions, Perceptions, and Transfers* (Oxford, 2000), 265–87.

[10] Christoph Meiners, *Grundriß der Geschichte der Menschheit* (Lemgo, 1785).

[11] Osterhammel, *Die Entzauberung Asiens*, 380.

[12] For German historiography see Andreas Pigulla, *China in der deutschen Weltgeschichtsschreibung vom 18. bis zum 20. Jahrhundert* (Wiesbaden, 1996); Christoph Marx,

The universalization of European historical thought coincided with a nationalistic and Eurocentric historiography that barely took non-European peoples into account or, with the exception of the classical civilizations, condemned them as 'stagnant' or 'without history'. There was a close connection between modernity, the modern historical discipline, and Eurocentrism. This Eurocentrism found its initial historiographic expression in the European national histories. When the new discipline began to fragment in the course of the professionalization of history during the nineteenth century, the universal approach was lost and non-European history—with the possible exception of the work of the historian and geographer Carl Ritter—became the domain of other disciplines from folklore, anthropology, and ethnology, to archaeology, American, and Oriental studies. World history itself played a minor role in German historiography for most of the nineteenth century. Early world histories, such as those by Friedrich Christoph Schlosser and Carl von Rotteck, were written in the universalist tradition of the Enlightenment and, in Schlosser's case, were based on Kant's philosophy of history.[13] With the exception of Ranke's seven-volume world history, which was published between 1880 and 1886, world history was written outside the realm of historical scholarship. In these works world history did not mean the universal history of mankind, but the history of cultivated peoples that is embedded in the state.

Two decades later the situation changed. Around 1900 professional historians turned towards world history. On the one hand historical events such as the Civil War in the USA, the reformation of Russia after 1861, and the Meiji Revolution in Japan, to name just a few, drew attention to the fact that there was a real general development in the world. World history became relevant to the imperial politics of the great powers, and the colonial empires needed knowledge about their colonized people. On the other hand, new archaeological,

'Völker ohne Schrift und Geschichte': Zur historischen Erfassung des vorkolonialen Schwarzafrika in der deutschen Forschung des 19. und frühen 20. Jahrhunderts (Stuttgart, 1988); Osterhammel, 'Peoples Without History'.

[13] Friedrich Christoph Schlosser, *Weltgeschichte in zusammenhängender Erzählung*, 4 vols. (Frankfurt am Main, 1815–41); id., *Weltgeschichte für das deutsche Volk*, 19 vols. (Frankfurt am Main, 1844–57); Carl von Rotteck, *Allgemeine Geschichte vom Anfang der historischen Kenntniß bis auf unsere Zeiten: Für denkende Geschichtsfreunde*, 11 vols. (Freiburg, 1813–18).

ethnological, and anthropological discoveries supplied historians with many new historical facts about the so-called 'primitive peoples' and non-Western societies. However, the world histories of professional historians became even more limited than the preceding world histories with their assumption of a universal spread of Western Christian culture. As early as 1864, Georg Weber wrote in the introductory remarks to his world history that 'the German people more than any other is called upon to give world history its real shape. Its position in the centre of Europe, its aspiration for universal education, its inborn cosmopolitan inclination, which also applies the standard of humanity, justice, and philanthropy to the strange and hostile, seems to enable the Germans to act as the guardians and managers of the treasures of history.'[14] This statement indicates a shift from a world history written from the Enlightenment perspective of a universal mankind and Ranke's European view of world history to the perception of the world through German eyes that occurred in the course of nineteenth-century German historiography. Around the turn of the century, professional historians such as Dietrich Schäfer and Hans Delbrück published world histories that were founded on political aspects of the state and served the imperialistic aims of the German Empire.[15] They not only restricted world history to the history of the cultured peoples of Europe as Ranke did, but also moved Germany to the centre of human history. Whereas for Ranke German history was part of European history, Schäfer placed the German people at the peak of human civilization.[16] Theodor Lindner, a student of Ranke's and a professor at the University of Halle, took a middling position. In his *World History* he called for the integration of non-Western cultures into his philosophy of history. He went further than Ranke and the German nationalist historians in trying to apply the historicist theory of historical writing to non-European cultures.[17]

[14] Georg Weber, *Geschichte des Morgenlandes: Nach dem neuesten Stande der orientalischen Geschichtswissenschaft bearbeitet* (Leipzig, 1882), 16 f.; id., *Allgemeine Weltgeschichte*, 19 vols. (Leipzig, 1857–81), p. xiii.

[15] See Hans Delbrück, *Weltgeschichte: Vorlesungen, gehalten an der Universität Berlin 1896/1920*, pt. 1: *Das Altertum* (Berlin, 1924).

[16] Heinrich von Treitschke, *Politik: Vorlesungen gehalten an der Universität zu Berlin*, ed. M. Cornicelius, vol. i (Leipzig, 1897), 121.

[17] Pigulla, *China*, 244. Pigulla analyses Linder's concept of world history from the latter's perspective on Chinese history.

One might explain this nationalism and Eurocentrism among historians in terms of a general *Zeitgeist* in the imperial age. But there was a subversive discourse in Germany. A few cultural historians, such as Karl Lamprecht and Kurt Breysig, as well as academic outsiders, such as Hans Helmolt, opposed the one-sided political history of historicism and tried to introduce a non-nationalistic world history. Helmolt rejected the Eurocentric world view and called for the incorporation of all peoples, even those 'without history', into a general world history. His scheme was not based on historical chronology or the development of various stages but on ethno-geographical criteria. Helmolt began his world history with America and the Pacific Ocean, continued with Oceania, the Indian Ocean, and West Asia, before moving on to the Mediterranean and south-eastern Europe. The final volumes dealt with the German and Latin peoples, western Europe, and the Atlantic Ocean. Since for him it was not possible to separate nature from history, geography became the basis for world history.[18]

Apart from Karl Lamprecht and his socio-psychological theory of 'ages of cultures' (*Kulturzeitalter*) that he applied not only to his German history in twelve volumes, but also to his conception of universal history,[19] the most prominent historian pursuing universal history before the First World War was Kurt Breysig, a professor at Berlin University. He stated that world history, based on the idea of the unity of humanity, is a sequence of conditions or phases that are the same for all peoples but that different peoples pass through them at different times.[20] In the first volume of his *Geschichte der Menschheit* (History of Mankind), published in 1907, Breysig elaborated his thesis that the 'primitive peoples' of his time reflected the original stage which the so-called 'cultural peoples' had already been through. His evolutionary model of history was based on universal comparison.[21] But Breysig faced strong resistance among

[18] Ibid., pp. vi, 19 f.

[19] Karl Lamprecht, 'Zur universalgeschichtlichen Methodenbildung' [1909], in Hans Schleier, *Karl Lamprecht: Alternative zu Ranke: Schriften zur Geschichtstheorie* (Leipzig, 1988), 374–404; Karl Lamprecht, 'Universalgeschichtliche Probleme', in id., *Moderne Geschichtswissenschaft: Fünf Vorträge* (Freiburg im Breisgau, 1905), 103–30. On Lamprecht's concept of world history see Roger Chickering, 'Karl Lamprechts Konzeption einer Weltgeschichte', *Archiv für Kulturgeschichte,* 73 (1991), 437–52.

[20] Kurt Breysig, *Der Stufenbau und die Gesetze der Weltgeschichte* (Stuttgart, 1927).

[21] Kurt Breysig, *Die Geschichte der Menschheit: Die Völker ewiger Urzeit. Die Amerikaner des*

historians. It is not surprising that a few years after the German debates on the scientific character of history—the *Methodenstreit* (controversy on methodology), which had ended in Lamprecht's cultural history being defeated by the historicists, mostly from Berlin, in 1899—Breysig's ideas and works were rejected by his colleagues in the Berlin faculty, as was his plan to create an interdisciplinary institute for comparative historical research in Berlin ten years later. Their in some ways justified critique addressed Breysig's construction of historical laws, his renunciation of empirical work, and the exceedingly broad scope of his approach.[22] Behind this rejection, however, lay ideological prejudices that had already shaped the debates on Henry Thomas Buckle's historical approach in the 1860s and 1870s, and that erupted again during the Lamprecht controversy in the 1890s.[23] Political and ideological antagonism divided the combatants. By and large, it was the historicist tradition with its focus on individuality in history and the centrality of the state and foreign policy that reduced universal history to the political history of the European powers and banished alternative approaches from the discipline. The exclusion of 'primitive peoples' from history not only served the political purpose of cultural superiority and colonial imperialism. It must also be seen as an attempt to close off the historical discipline from other disciplines such as anthropology, ethnology, and the social sciences, which professional historians viewed as a major threat.[24]

A quick review of German world histories in the twentieth century reveals that until the 1970s the Eurocentric picture had changed little since the time of Leopold von Ranke. Even if early twentieth-century philosophers of history and historians

Nordwestens und des Nordens (Berlin, 1907). On Breysig's concept of universal history see Bernhard vom Brocke, *Kurt Breysig: Geschichtswissenschaft zwischen Historismus und Soziologie* (Lübeck, 1971), 268 ff.

[22] Brocke, *Kurt Breysig*, 87 ff.

[23] On Buckle and his reception in Germany see Eckhardt Fuchs, *Henry Thomas Buckle: Geschichtsschreibung und Positivismus in England und Deutschland* (Leipzig, 1994). On Lamprecht and the Lamprecht controversy see Roger Chickering, *Karl Lamprecht: A German Academic Life* (Atlantic Highlands, 1993); Luise Schorn-Schütte, *Karl Lamprecht: Kulturgeschichtsschreibung zwischen Wissenschaft und Politik* (Göttingen, 1984); Brocke, *Kurt Breysig*, 62 ff.

[24] See Andrew Zimmerman, 'Geschichtslose und schriftlose Völker in Spreeathen: Anthropologie als Kritik der Geschichtswissenschaft im Kaiserreich', *Zeitschrift für Geschichtswissenschaft*, 47 (1999), 197–210.

tried to develop a more professional world historiography that abandoned the theoretical framework of the nation-state in favour of a broader approach to history, most of them nevertheless emphasized the superiority of European history and culture. With the exception of Oswald Spengler and Otto Franke, whose *Geschichte des Chinesischen Reiches* (History of the Chinese Empire, 1930–52) brought Asia back into historiographical scholarship,[25] from Hans Freyer to Karl Jaspers and Alfred Heuß the Eurocentric view of world history in the vein of Ranke, Jacob Burckhardt, and Ernst Troeltsch—not the German-centred view of Schäfer and Delbrück—prevailed. The title of Freyer's book, *Weltgeschichte Europas* (World History of Europe), published in 1948, shows that Troeltsch's phrase of 1922, 'For us there only exists a universal history of European culture', was still the credo after 1945.[26] Although in the 1960s and 1970s this began to change, Germany did not catch up with the USA's development of world history as a separate subdiscipline.

II

This volume contributes to the topical discipline of world history by addressing the subject comparatively and by concentrating on its theoretical and methodological foundations. Under the heading of 'Mapping the Subject', the first three essays deal with *theory*, while the other ten essays are concerned with its *application* under the heading 'Rethinking and Writing World History'. While independent in concept and design, this volume follows an earlier work in which the editors invited various contributors to reflect upon the possibility of transcending a Eurocentric approach in terms both of the individual historiographies that were assessed and of the methodologies that were used for the

[25] See Osterhammel, 'Peoples without History', 268 f.

[26] See Ernst Troeltsch, *Der Historismus und seine Probleme*, vol. i: *Das logische Problem der Geschichtsphilosophie* (= *Gesammelte Schriften*, vol. iii) (Tübingen, 1922), 710. On critique of this tradition see Franz Hampl, 'Universalhistorische Betrachtungsweise als Problem und Aufgabe: Ihre Bedeutung in Theorie und Praxis der modernen Geschichtswissenschaft', in id., *Geschichte als Kritische Wissenschaft*, vol. i: *Theorie der Geschichtswissenschaft und Universalgeschichte*, ed. Igomar Weiler (Darmstadt, 1975), 132–81; Peter Rassow, 'Nationalgeschichte und Universalgeschichte', *Geschichte in Wissenschaft und Unterricht*, 2 (1951), 513–21.

comparative analysis.[27] Both projects aim to move beyond the traditional national focus of historiography by exploring the utility and the limits of conceptions that fundamentally differ from the (Eurocentric) understanding of the nation-state and that call for a world historiography by equally taking into account Western and non-Western cultures of history-writing. The opportunities for, and limitations placed on, intercultural historiographical exchange and transfer can be better investigated when indigenous traditions are seen in light of their independence rather than merely in their relation to Western thought. Building on the current academic as well as public interest in world history in the Western and non-Western world, the editors have now attempted to link the critical investigation of the traditions of world history-writing with the most recent theoretical and ideological debates on this subject. From a transcultural perspective the volume offers an analysis of the historical traditions of world history over the past 200 years. In a further step it demonstrates different ideas about the world and the relationship between 'periphery' and 'centre' in various geographical areas such as the USA, France, Britain, Russia, Germany, Africa, India, China, and Japan.

It goes without saying that a *comprehensive* picture of Western and non-Western historiographies could be achieved only with great difficulty, and it would not be advisable for a single volume to attempt this. Indeed, quite the opposite has been the objective of this volume. It concentrates on a small but representative sample of selected case studies that can convey an impression of the state of the art in their respective fields. The essays try to make clear that interpretations of the world reflect perceptions of one's own culture, and that the notion of the world can be used to legitimize political aims. In sum, the volume presents different modern approaches to contemporary world history and its debates. As this field emerged most prominently in the USA in the twentieth century and developed into a separate subdiscipline, American concepts of world history have dominated the discourse in recent years. The aim is to go beyond the comparison of these concepts by offering a critical evaluation of their theoretical foundations, ideological implications, and moral

[27] Eckhardt Fuchs and Benedikt Stuchtey (eds.), *Across Cultural Borders: Historiography in Global Perspective* (Lanham, 2002).

connotations. To this extent *Writing World History* offers a critique of an ethnocentric world history. If we look at past and present discussions on world history, five problems are central to new approaches to the subject in the future: the development of criteria for the relevant problems of world history; the question of 'good' or 'bad' world history; intellectual and institutional prerequisites; the question of whether comparative history is world history; and space and time as the units of world history.[28]

In the first three essays theoretical questions and the advantages and supposed disadvantages of world history writing are discussed. In 'World History and Grand Narrative' Jerry H. Bentley asks why and how grand narratives of modern historiography have come under attack by postmodern and postcolonial critics, and why there is no doubt that Eurocentric grand narratives make an unstable scaffolding for historical scholarship. Yet, according to the author, counter-narratives advanced by postmodern and postcolonial scholars, usually in the form of micro-narratives, basically invert grand narratives deriving from the Enlightenment, even if they make some cogent corrections to them in doing so. The purpose of Bentley's essay is to move beyond unrelated micro-narratives towards an understanding of the larger world and the place of individual societies within it, while avoiding the mostly Eurocentric ideologies of grand narratives. The understanding of world history, then, is not a triumphalist vision celebrating progress in general or contempo-ray global capitalism in particular. All too often rising populations, expanding technological capacity, and increasing cross-cultural interaction have exacted a high price in human suffering and environmental pressures that may well prove to be unsustainable over a long term. Nor is this view of world history a teleological model like those deriving from the Enlightenment. It leaves the end of history open and recognizes the capacities of human actors to organize their societies and conduct relations with others in unpredictable ways.

Patrick K. O'Brien's essay on 'The Deconstruction of Myths

[28] These points were proposed by Jürgen Osterhammel for the final discussion at the conference on which this volume is based. See Eckhardt Fuchs and Benedikt Stuchtey, 'Conference Report: Writing World History, 1800–2000. Conference of the German Historical Institute London and the German Historical Institute Washington, held at the GHIL, 30 March–1 April 2000', *Bulletin of the German Historical Institute London*, 22/2 (2000), 80–5, at 85.

and Reconstruction of Metanarratives in Global Histories of Material Progress' studies parameters for historical investigations into the global history of economic growth. O'Brien looks at the paradigms set up by Karl Marx and Max Weber and their work on non-European economies, and discusses the models and explanations which they gave for long-term economic developments. In this context he also asks questions about the role of Weber's study of non-Western civilizations and his comparative methodology in order to understand why capitalism arose in the West and not in the East. While the Marxist approach has been concerned with 'modes of production' and, more recently, with processes of international and inter-state rivalry and colonial exploitation, the Weberian programme is directed either at a comparison of hegemonic systems of belief, or at an empirical analysis of the political, legal, and institutional frameworks within which economic activity has operated historically around the world. Further, a 'Marxian' paradigm that has been elaborated by the World Systems School of Historical Sociology is addressed. The central hypothesis of the World Systems School is that the transition to capitalism (or commercial society) and eventually to successful industrial market economies occurred first in Western Europe because Europeans reaped timely and crucial gains from intercontinental trade and the colonization of the Americas for some three or more centuries before the onset of the French and Industrial Revolutions. Max Weber's erudition looks more impressive because his approach, questions, and topics for investigation effectively set the agenda for the construction of global histories of material progress in recent decades. At the end of the twentieth century a modern generation of economic historians attempted to relocate the now highly visible scientific, technological, and economic achievements of Western societies in a global context. Weber left them with an approach, a vocabulary, and several suggestive hypotheses that have been taken forward, modified, or rejected by two generations of post-war and postcolonial research.

This crossing of cultural and geographical borders is all the more welcome as it sets out to offer evidence to affirm what Eric Jones had observed in an earlier study on world economics and the historical role of the Industrial Revolution.[29] Here Jones

[29] Eric Jones, *Growth Recurring: Economic Growth in World History* (Oxford, 1988).

suggests that in principle, world economies did grow and that, contrary to the widely held belief in the stagnation of material progress until the eighteenth century, rising populations and the improvements in agriculture provoked their growth. If compared with the economic advances as simultaneously experienced in Japan in the Tokugawa period, or even economic growth in Song China preceding both the European and Japanese experiences, it can clearly be concluded that material progress could best be achieved when obstacles such as hierarchical political structures and disparities of wealth were removed: an experience applicable to Western and non-Western societies alike. Therefore the (British) Industrial Revolution was not unique in its relevance to world history, and short-term perspectives do not seem to be helpful for the writing of world history.

While Bentley and O'Brien are convinced of the relevance and importance of conceptualizing a new writing of world history, Arif Dirlik is more sceptical as regards both the academic and the political implications. What is its justification and what is its point, he asks, so long as it essentially reflects 'world-making' and cannot separate itself from the continuing dominance of Eurocentrism? In 'Confounding Metaphors, Inventions of the World: What is World History For?' he argues that world history is ultimately about 'world-making', which requires world historiography to be confronted not just in terms of technical historical questions, but, more importantly, in terms of the metahistorical assumptions that guide it. Dirlik addresses questions that arise from a presumed connection in contemporary world historiography between 'globalization' and world history writing, and the associated problem of overcoming Eurocentrism. Arguing that most discussions of world history do not account for globalization as a contradictory (and hegemonic) concept, one can also question the ability of world history to overcome Eurocentrism, as this is built into our very conceptions of the world and of history. While not questioning the legitimacy or even the necessity of world history, which may be inevitable given our histories, Dirlik queries a tendency to privilege world history over other histories and to rehearse Western globalization. The consequence would be to caution against positivism in practising it and to call for greater critical awareness of the discourse on the past. Whereas world history once underwrote the triumph of Western civilization, it is argued that it is now to be rewritten to bear witness to the triumph of globalization. Dirlik's warning is directed at the ease with which globalization is taken as something novel and unproblematic, raising the old questions concerning the relationship of history to its cultural context, which is itself inseparable from the material context, perhaps more explicitly in the present than ever before.

From a global perspective, of course, a Grand Narrative as suggested by Jerry Bentley could hardly be written without taking account of the American past's special path, as Michael Adas emphasizes in his essay. 'Out of Step with Time: United States Exceptionalism in an Age of Globalization' is an exploration of the uneasy relationship between mainstream narratives of US history and recent scholarship that attempts to situate the American experience within broader comparative or global frames of reference. Adas starts from the disconcerting juxtaposition of assumptions of exceptionalism with convictions that the American historical trajectory ought to serve as a model for the rest of mankind, which have coexisted uneasily from the early decades of colonization along the Atlantic coast. He argues that both positions are problematic. The first has led to overspecialization and scholarly myopia, and has also made for considerable resistance on the part of professional historians in the USA to serious comparative analysis or attempts to conceptualize key developments in American history as variants of broader global processes. Cross-cultural studies have been undertaken to identify differences in foreign societies that might act as barriers to civilizing, developmentalist, or modernizing influences from the USA. From a global perspective, the full integration of the American experience into the broader history of mankind has been shown to be vital to understanding key themes in early modern history, and essential for unravelling the complexities of the modern era, particularly the long twentieth century. Here historical comparisons and the establishment of common experiences such as, for example, the frontier and the impact of scientific and technological change, have again proved to be important preconditions. However, Adas also indicates that world history achieved academic respectability relatively late in the USA, having first had to distance itself from the dominance of the specialized disciplines as well as from the impact of European historiography.

Most strikingly, German historicism made a great impact on historiographies such as the Chinese.[30] And by recognizing the arbitrary nature of the chronological and regional boundaries of traditional historiography, the French *Annales* school created important foundations for modern world historiography, without, of course, defining itself as such. As Lutz Raphael shows in his contribution on 'The Idea and Practice of World Historiography in France: The *Annales* Legacy', French world historiography received a new impetus from the reformers who criticized the somewhat narrow historical practice which French historians had established since the 1880s, centred on politics, biography, and political institutions. Among the first reformers was the philosopher Henri Berr. A study of Berr's editorial project, *L'évolution de l'humanité*, and his programme of world historiography as inspired by evolutionism and the history of civilization makes clear that for Berr, 'mankind' was the emerging outcome of converging developments in religion, society, art, and science. This evolution can be observed in the different histories of civilizations, culminating in the Western model. The eclectic blend of contemporary Western ideas on progress and its causes encompassed ideas of vitalistic philosophy, classical idealism, and materialistic approaches. At its centre was the concept of the growing unity of world history interpreted as a process of integration. By enlarging the number of disciplines that participated in his enterprise, Berr integrated the different approaches of sociology, philosophy, and linguistics, etc. into history. However, the intellectual programme and its practical realization should be distinguished, as in contrast to the systems of Spengler or Toynbee, the French project was more open to experimentation, attempting to be a kind of work-in-progress in writing world history. By the time of his death in 1954, Berr had edited about sixty volumes, some with such outstanding scholars as Marc Bloch and Lucien Febvre.

Febvre's and Bloch's critical distance towards world history and their comparative approaches before the Second World War also need to be put into this context, as is the case with Fernand Braudel's global history and his idea of geohistory, the history of the *longue durée*, the history of globalization by European capital-

[30] See e.g. Q. Edward Wang, 'German Historicism and Scientific History in China, 1900–1940', in Fuchs and Stuchtey (eds.), *Across Cultural Borders*, 141–61.

ism, and the history of civilizations ('Grammaire des civilisations'). With Braudel, world historiography became an integral part of the *Annales* programme. According to Raphael, Braudel's three books on the Mediterranean world can be described as his vision of a global history. Studying the major works Braudel published since the 1940s, in particular his famous book *La Méditerranée et le monde méditerranéen à l'époque de Philippe II* (1949), one can discover the threefold programme, of first, immovable geographical time; secondly, the *longue durée* of social, demographic time; and thirdly, the short time-span of events. The study of the impact of the *Annales* on the West and the non-West has itself now become an important part of the history of historiography. To name but a few, from Carol Fink's highly stimulating biography of Marc Bloch and Peter Burke's *tour d'horizon* of the school of the *Annales*, to the works of Olivier Dumoulin, André Burguière, and Hervé Coutau-Bégarie, the historicizing of this school has been well under way for almost twenty-five years.[31] This was documented some years ago by François Dosse, who stressed the intellectual and institutional power-politics of the *Annales*, which he regarded as a particular feature of French academia.[32] Another characteristic is probably the unsurpassed French art of reflecting on one's own subject for which the history of the *Annales* seems to be most suitable. As the editors of a volume on the most important twentieth-century methodological trends in history suggest, for the last seventy years the *Annales* have provoked innovations in the theory of history that were more far-reaching and radical than any other.[33] Whether one day historiography will have a new Braudel is quite a different matter. In any case, in his time and until recent years, his impact has been enormous. 'La nouvelle histoire' caused what Burke called a 'historical revolution'. The historians had taken over what had hitherto been the prerogative of the philosophers—the lead in the intellectual life of the nation.[34] As regards Braudel, this was rightly seen in global dimensions.[35]

[31] See in particular Peter Burke, *The French Historical Revolution: The Annales School 1929–89* (Oxford, 1990).

[32] François Dosse, *New History in France: The Triumph of the 'Annales'* (Urbana, 1994).

[33] Jean Boutier and Dominique Julia (eds.), *Passés Recomposés* (Paris, 1995).

[34] Pierre Daix, *Braudel* (Paris, 1995).

[35] For a recent evaluation see R. Bin Wong, 'Entre monde et nation: les régions braudéliennes en Asie', *Annales: Histoire, Sciences Sociales*, 56/1 (2001), 5–42.

The contrast with what Michael Bentley calls the 'The Singularities of British *Weltgeschichte*' could hardly be bigger. Addressing the works and ideas of British historians such as Wells, Toynbee, and Barraclough, and discussing the distinction between historical writing and historiography as relevant to the evaluation of world history in Britain, Bentley shows that in this context German historiography, which was not very relevant to the *Annales*, became a prominent model for British historians again in the later nineteenth century. The role of the historians Gooch, Butterfield, Collingwood, and Oakeshott is of particular significance. Yet, taking into account that the only grand narrative produced in Britain was the Whig conception of history, the influence of evolutionism instead of historicism on British world history becomes clearer.[36] Consequently, the assumption that British world historiography was modelled only on the German experience needs to be challenged. The British impetus toward universalism in historiography did not appear in conventional histories. Rather, it became part of a profound Victorian tradition of evolutionary social theory, as John Burrow has also shown elsewhere.[37] It is of special interest, therefore, to set up what Michael Bentley understands as a model of what world history intrinsically requires from any national style of historiography. Five preconditions for generating effective world history can be identified: (1) cultural sustenance for an inclusive global metanarrative; (2) receptivity to the spatial dimension of historical explanation; (3) commitment to an epistemology and method that validate a global field; (4) a scholarly infrastructure that positively valorizes a global conceptualization of historical problems; and (5) weak or absent counter-presuppositions that could render (1)–(4) inoperable.

It may not, however, be easy to apply these categories to the world-historical traditions of other countries. For example, Italian historiography in the nineteenth century, itself strongly influenced by German works, was dominated by the national

[36] Cf. Benedikt Stuchtey, 'Literature, Liberty, and Life of the Nation: British Historiography from Macaulay to Trevelyan', in Stefan Berger, Mark Donovan, and Kevin Passmore (eds.), *Writing National Histories: Western Europe since 1800* (London, 1999), 30–46.

[37] John Burrow, 'Historicism and Social Evolution', in Stuchtey and Wende (eds.), *British and German Historiography*, 251–64.

problem.[38] Universal history was still largely seen as the history of the development of European civilizations, economic domination, and imperial expansion. Only one important Italian work was dedicated to world history, the thirty-five-volume *Storia Universale* by Cesare Cantù, published between 1838 and 1846. The Italian readership for history was not broad, but there was a relatively strong interest in world history as shown by the large number of translations, especially of German works (Johannes von Müller, Gabriel Gottfried Bredow, Georg Weber, and Heinrich Leo). When foreign works were translated, pages on Italy were often added, focusing on the Middle Ages. The *Storia Universale*, on the other hand, was used as a source for the compilation of school-books. The reorganization of the school system in the Kingdom of Italy produced a new need for text-books and the writing of general history became, at least in part, an editorial activity. Cantù was a Catholic historian, and the history of Christianity played a central role in his vision of universal history. In fact, in his eyes universal history was the history only of Christianity. From this perspective, the Middle Ages occupied a privileged place in Cantù's pages, while the legacy of the classical world in the history of European civilization was played down. Cantù actually wrote a history of European and Christian civilizations, and of the spread of this tradition; a history of Western 'action' opposed to Eastern 'stillness'. But this reduction of world history to the history of European preponderance was rejected by other Italian historians such as, for example, Carlo Cattaneo, and not only on the grounds that the *Storia* was too conventional.[39]

The case of 'Writing World History in Tsarist Russia and in the Soviet Union', as Thomas Bohn demonstrates, differs sharply from the findings we have in western and southern Europe, also as regards the political function of historiography. Here the historian is concerned with the history of an empire or a superpower. Russia's long path in finding its place in Europe, the tension between looking backwards and modernization,

[38] The paper on the case of Italy given at the conference by Mauro Moretti unfortunately could not be made available for publication.

[39] H. Hearder, *Italy in the Age of the Risorgimento 1790–1870* (London, 1983); Clara M. Lovett, *Carlo Cattaneo and the Politics of the Risorgimento, 1820–60* (The Hague, 1972); Martin Thom, 'Unity and Confederation in the Italian Risorgimento: The Case of Carlo Cattaneo', in Berger, Donovan, and Passmore (eds.), *Writing National Histories*, 69–81.

society and state, professional works and popular syntheses, and, finally, between Eurocentric models on the one hand and the construction of a patriotic Russian *Sonderweg* on the other: all these issues were to be dealt with when considering the country's place between its colonial periphery and Europe. The main topic of eighteenth-century Russian historiography was the significance of the Vikings as founders of the first Russian dynasty. In the nineteenth century Russian historians focused on the reforms of Peter the Great and the modernization of state and society on European patterns. Finally, twentieth-century Russian historical writing concentrated on the Bolshevik seizure of power and the introduction of the socialist system. In the Russian language 'General History' and 'World History' are often used synonymously. While the first as a subject refers to all countries apart from Tsarist Russia and the Soviet Union, 'World History' as a scholarly term implies the gradual progress of all nations of the world. There were, of course, alternatives to professional historiography. The Slavophiles in the 1840s, the Panslavists in the 1870s, and the Eurasians in the 1920s tried to undermine the dominance of the German–Latin peoples and to avoid the Eurocentrism of professional historiography by describing a specific Russian civilizatory path.[40]

As regards size, the only other European empire with which the Russian could be compared is the British, although the former defined itself as continental while the latter was seen primarily as a maritime power. Between the later nineteenth century and the end of the Second World War a substantial number of books and articles, both scholarly and popular, on the past and present of the British Empire were published in Germany. Understanding British imperial history as a kind of world history, these studies looked at the historical, economic, social, and cultural dimensions of the Empire, partly against the relative insignificance of Germany's colonial ventures. Given that imperial history and world history are certainly not synonymous, they none the less saw an overlap between these fields, in particular as regards the exchange of institutions and ideas. After 1918 these were not all simply revisionist attempts to regain an empire for Germany; they also included academic

[40] See also Hans Hecker, *Russische Universalgeschichtsschreibung: Von den 'Vierziger Jahren' des 19. Jahrhunderts bis zur sowjetischen 'Weltgeschichte' (1955–1965)* (Munich, 1983).

investigations by authors such as the above-mentioned Dietrich Schäfer or Erich Marcks. In his essay 'World Power and World History: Writing the British Empire, 1885–1945', Benedikt Stuchtey looks at scholarly and popular publications in Germany, not only books, handbooks, and atlases, but also some of the more influential journals, such as *Deutsche Kolonialzeitung* and *Preußische Jahrbücher*. What criteria allowed German authors to see the history of the British Empire as part of world history? To what extent could colonial history and the history of decolonization act as agents for a global history?

The liberal-conservative historians, still clinging to the strong tradition of German historical idealism, interpreted the idea of great powers as carrying with themselves the 'world idea'. No empire was as well placed as the British Empire to embody the power of Western civilization, its unique colonial expansion, and its exceptional impact on the course of world history. The concept of a strong nation-state as the backbone of empire may have been most impressively developed by historians such as Treitschke and Sybel, but undoubtedly a generation later German academia profited equally from intellectual transfer from Britain in establishing concepts of empire that were reminiscent of John Robert Seeley and Charles Dilke and their successors Newton and Egerton.[41] Fascination with the British Empire derived from admiration for colonial endeavours, but mainly from its power and control over foreign territory. Although the British nation was, in contrast to the French and German, an imperial nation *sui generis* and therefore difficult to imitate, a substantial number of German authors interpreted Britain's particular qualification for imperial expansionism as an example of the Western world's right of conquest and later duty of decolonization. If the close relationship between writing world history and writing (British) imperial history was perceived by German authors as embodying the superiority of Western civilization, they also saw it as symbolizing the British intellectual traditions of evolutionism and utilitarianism, not to mention what was termed the 'British philosophy of life' of individualism and materialism, two aspects that were constantly addressed.

[41] Cf. Benedikt Stuchtey, '"Westward the course of empire takes its way": Imperialism and the Frontier in British and German Historical Writing around 1900', in Stuchtey and Wende (eds.), *British and German Historiography*, 289–334.

But what about the non-Western and, in part, former colonial world? This volume offers case studies of Africa, India, China, and Japan.[42] In most parts of these continents or countries, Europe's economic, cultural, political, and military decline after two world wars and the break-up of European colonial empires was reflected in the worldwide rise of the influence of the USA. One of the aims of this volume is to show that the traditions, perceptions, and possibly transfers of both Western and non-Western historiographies can be understood only by a multiple perspective. It is fascinating to see where the differences are between our examples from the non-Western world, from which also follow the differences in the impact of the West. In any case, as one certainly cannot speak of a uniform picture either in the West or in the East, it seems more appropriate to investigate the different degrees of dependence. This is strongest in the case of Africa, with an official history still strongly dominated by Western-educated Africanist historians, less so in India, especially since independence, when the central topic became the Indian nation-state, and least in China with a Chinese historiography that did not pick up European ideas and methods, but maintained the status of a closed country, a status which was even enhanced after the Communists came to power in 1949. Japan is quite different from the other examples. Politically independent, it never experienced a European power on its islands. Indeed, Japan was a colonial power itself. On the other hand, Japanese historiography more than that of any other Asian country orientated itself by European models and innovations. Thus European or Western influence and the emancipation from it was interpreted very differently in each case, and each country found its own path to modernity and to an individual understanding of the world.

While there were many differences, the parallel tendencies and similiarities between the case studies are also instructive. In their essays the authors show that the countries they present all

[42] A publishable version of Jochen Meissner's paper on South America was not available when we were finally obliged to go to press, but see the very useful article by Alan Knight, 'Latin America', in Michael Bentley (ed.), *Companion to Historiography* (London, 1997), 728–58. Unfortunately, there is no essay on the Islamic world in this volume, but see the pioneering essays by Marshall G. S. Hodgson on Islam in a global context in his important volume *Rethinking World History: Essays on Europe, Islam, and World History* (Cambridge, 1993), 97–243.

experienced an increase in the estimation of the value of their own history after 1945, distinguishing themselves from the Western interpretation of history. This went along with the concepts of ethnicity in Africa and modernity in India, stronger consciousness of the indigenous historiographical tradition in China, and Japan's interpretation of its past as peace-loving. Despite their different viewpoints, all these examples also show that the awareness of the need for a multi-perspectival historiography in an increasingly multi-polarized world has become ever more accepted. S. N. Eisenstadt's theses of 'multiple modernities' are especially fruitful in this context. And as far as a theoretical background to this new field of research is concerned, Jörn Rüsen's reflections on comparative historiography as a multinational or transnational business must certainly be taken into account.[43]

Compared with the other case studies in this volume, South America does not form a historiographical world of its own. Its historians mostly saw themselves as part of a wider transatlantic cultural context and of its different national historiographical traditions. Nevertheless, a series of historical problems related to the specific historical constellations of the region have concerned historians from and of South America more than others. These were, for example, the consequences of unequal exchange between highly industrialized and less industrialized regions, the encounter between European, African, and Amerindian cultures, and the historical interpretation of race relations, European expansion, colonialism, and imperialism. South America challenged Eurocentric perspectives on World History in these fields in various ways and contributed to questioning naïve conceptions of universal history. In 1933 Gilberto Freyre published his *Casa grande e senzala* (The Masters and the Slaves). Fernand Braudel and Thomas Mann took note of this work, and it went through twenty-five editions. Freyre underlined the importance of the Black (and Amerindian) heritage for the social history of Brazil. In this book he interpreted the deplorable state of affairs in Brazil and the country's apparent inability to match

[43] See Jörn Rüsen, 'Some Theoretical Approaches to Intercultural Comparative Historiography', *History and Theory*, 35 (1996), 5–22; id., 'Comparing Cultures in Intercultural Communication', in Fuchs and Stuchtey (eds.), *Across Cultural Borders*, 335–47.

the development of other countries not in the usual racist terms, but with the help of social patterns of explanation. One of Freyre's teachers had been Franz Boas, and he took a particular interest in anthropological and transcultural approaches. Freyre was probably one of the most important popularizers of a radical change of perspective: the miscegenation of races and cultures, long considered to be one of the reasons why Brazil had not been able to follow the path of 'northern development', now became an important asset of Brazilian history. In this view, Brazil's problems were of a social, not a racial character. It is interesting to see this interpretation in light of what the political scientist Anthony W. Marx has called Brazil's 'exceptionalism'. In his recent comparative study of the USA, South Africa, and Brazil, Marx argues that these three countries' policies of race relations and discrimination did not necessarily derive from their past as settler societies. Rather, the crucial point was a major conflict such as the Civil War and the South African War, which were essentially intra-white ethnic conflicts resulting in intolerant racial policies, and, as a consequence of this, Black mobilization for political liberty. By contrast, the Brazilian state experienced much weaker ethnic antagonisms thanks to an established hierarchy and a strongly centralized state, although neither was more tolerant in racial terms.[44]

The case of Africa was very different, forming a much less coherent picture, as suggested by Andreas Eckert in his essay on 'Fitting Africa into World History: A Historiographical Exploration'. To the present day, the majority of 'mainstream' historians probably hold the view that, all in all, Africa had little relevance for the emergence of world history. Conversely, world history in the strict sense of the word is not a major preoccupation of historians in sub-Saharan Africa, and, in fact, very few Africanist historians outside the continent, such as Philip Curtin and Patrick Manning, promote or are part of the 'world history movement'. Eckert demonstrates that during the second half of the twentieth century historians *of* Africa (in most cases non-Africans) tried to fit African history more closely into world history without necessarily labelling their efforts 'a contribution to world history'. Three wider historiographical fields serve as examples. First, the author looks at the works of the Senegalese

[44] Anthony W. Marx, *Making Race and Nation* (New York, 1998).

scholar Cheikh Anta Diop, who employed a multi-disciplinary approach to argue that Ancient Egypt, which he considered part of 'Black Africa', was the model for Western civilization. The second part of the essay addresses the question of migration and diaspora. Phenomena such as the globalization of capital and culture, the technological revolution, and the breakdown of information boundaries have necessitated a rethinking of the African diaspora and its changing meanings as well as, for instance, the role of Africans in the making of the Atlantic world. Since the days of the Atlantic slave trade, Africans have established global networks, supposedly through migration and diasporas, culminating in the idea of the birth of 'the original' African who straddled continents and cultures. Finally, one needs to draw attention to the connection between Africa and the world economy by discussing interpretations of the World Systems/dependency school and the works of Ralph Austen and Frederick Cooper. As Eckert has also shown elsewhere, the historiography *about* Africa is a good example of a multicultural project, with African, American, British, German, and French historians and historians from other countries involved. The turning away from the idea of the nation-state goes with a turning towards the concept of ethnicity. However, for obvious reasons, *in* Africa the subject is much less powerful.[45]

Through the African example two questions are addressed that play an important role in late twentieth-century reflections on world history: the problem of migration, and the problem of slavery. Both are closely connected. Human migration, both in its form as refugee displacement, and as a constant flow of peoples leaving their native countries and crossing borders to new political, economic, cultural, and religious worlds, has always constituted an element in the history of the world, from prehistory to the present. Voluntary mobility, migratory movements, and flight from persecution similarly manifest themselves as perennial realities in the history of the Western and non-Western world alike. Despite their differences and contingencies one can even speak of a universal phenomenon that formed the patterns and processes of human migration: according to the

[45] Andreas Eckert, 'Ethnizität und Nation in der Geschichtsschreibung zu Afrika seit 1960', in Hartmut Kaelble and Dietmar Rothermund (eds.), *Nichtwestliche Geschichtswissenschaften seit 1945*, Theme Issue 11/4 of *Comparativ* (2001), 17–30.

findings of a volume on the universality of migratory movements, there have always been and always will be certainties in these patterns and processes suggesting the possibility of general laws. In other words, migration as a global feature contained, among others, exiles, slaves, refugees, settlers, migrant labourers, and diasporic communities. Their sites of movement, from camps to cities of migration, the crossing of borders and the technologies of their control and regimentation, and finally, of course, the implications of the transnationalization of labour, must be set in context.[46] Wang Gungwu, a foremost specialist on China, contributes to the growing field of global history in his edited volume, *Global History and Migrations*. While he does not claim that this needs to be differentiated from world history, the value of his book lies in the *longue durée* with which the contributors treat their topics, thus demonstrating continuity rather than historical breaks. The case of migration in Africa, for example, is portrayed by Philip Curtin in a lengthy analysis showing that almost all parts of this vast continent had gone through similar experiences over the past centuries, from the Bantu diaspora to the Atlantic slave trade and contemporary migration as a result of the changing labour market. As Curtin suggests, no other part of the world possesses such a heritage of an ever mobile population which makes it exemplary for larger issues in writing the world history of migration, whether intercontinental or intracontinental. And what are the changing economies of human migration over the centuries?[47]

Both migration and slavery have attracted a substantial body of scholarship in recent decades. Put into the context of world history, slavery has been a central issue in the history of America since 1500, contributing to the dichotomy of freedom and unfreedom that can both be closely associated with the emergence of the New World. Between the early sixteenth and the early nineteenth century about two African slaves arrived for each European immigrant, but the latter took the voyage as the starting point for a life free of the dependencies they faced in Europe. Moreover, as David Brion Davis has recently argued, the unfreedom of the slaves who contributed to making the

[46] Wang Gungwu (ed.), *Global History and Migrations* (Boulder, 1997).

[47] In fact, the long perspective is of particular value in this context. Unfortunately it is not taken in Robin Cohen (ed.), *The Cambridge Survey of World Migration* (Cambridge, 1995), which concentrates only on the time after 1945.

American economy dynamic, helping to build up international markets for mass consumer goods such as cotton and sugar, encouraged those who enjoyed freedom to fight for the abolition of slavery. Thereby they reinvented their own tradition of a public discourse on freedom with which the nation identified so strongly.[48] In Davis's view, however, the academic profit to be gained from studying the history of slavery lies in its international dimension. He understands it as a global phenomenon that spanned the continents of Africa, America, and Europe and that was an important, yet momentous aspect of the process of modernizing the world. And it was far-reaching. Although the North American Civil War eventually led to liberty for most slaves, the new emancipation, it is argued, to the present day has still not overcome the most visible consequences of slavery—poverty, insufficient education and medical care, racism, and limited opportunities for social advancement. To this extent, the dimensions of the histories of migration and slavery are global in both space and time. What matters, then, is to broaden the scope of our questions, if possible beyond Eurocentrism, but certainly and first of all beyond the usual perspective that is directed towards the nation-state. In his study of the impact of slavery on the history of the Western world, Jürgen Osterhammel has proposed a more problem-orientated historiography as follows:

> There are questions—and they are becoming increasingly important—which can be neither posed nor answered within the usual framework of national historiography. Nor does attaching geographical labels to continents address these questions. The frontiers between Europe and not-Europe, seemingly taken for granted, become indistinct; they themselves become the subject of investigation. Contexts become as important as what is connected, especially when connections give rise to something new. Among the many such problems of transgression there is a smaller number of questions which are not touched by academic trends and fashions, but at most by changing sensitivities and value judgements about what is important. These questions, constantly unsettling in their significance for the present, resist any attempt to answer them validly once and for all. Among them is that of the interplay between freedom and unfreedom in modern history.[49]

[48] David Brion Davis, *In the Image of God: Religion, Moral Values and Our Heritage of Slavery* (New Haven, 2001).

[49] Jürgen Osterhammel, *Sklaverei und die Zivilisation des Westens* (Munich, 2000), 15–16.

The history of migration and slavery in Africa can be studied from the African or the Western viewpoint, or, ideally, from a comparative perspective. The history of European contact with Africa, however, is usually not separated from the history of European colonialism, whether in the form of slavery, forced migration, missionary activities, or other forms of cross-cultural interactions. It was, as the doyen of the history of European expansion and world history, Felipe Fernández-Armesto, has suggested, a global *and* a European opportunity that opened the gates for expanding societies, both Western and non-Western, to enter the multi-continental and multi-oceanic dimensions of their histories. Chinese maritime expansion can be compared with colonial techniques from the Mediterranean to the Atlantic as used by the Europeans. In order to overcome nationalistic patterns, it is necessary to formulate a common mode of socio-economic analysis that allows a comparative understanding of Western and non-Western colonial politics.[50] The same author explains in the preface to his massive history of the world over the last thousand years that 'Western world domination, which books on world history usually try to describe or "explain", is seen in what follows as neither foreordained, nor enduring; I argue that it was later, feebler, and briefer than is commonly supposed. Therefore more space is given to the rest of the world . . . according to a novel bias in favor of the unusual, which helps to even the score.'[51] But, as the Oxford historian Terence Ranger has shown for the case of Africa, the study of European contact with Africa before and after the time of imperialism can help to understand a 'white' history on a 'black' continent without the agencies of Western supremacy, power, and the alleged right of colonial conquest: 'there could be a history of whites in Africa that is not also a history of colonialism.'[52] This history of whites, as Ranger suggests, is the history of a more peaceful ethnic, social, and cultural interaction, bearing the possibility of a new periodization of African history and putting less stress on the division of

[50] Felipe Fernández-Armesto (ed.), *The Global Opportunity* (Brookfield, 1995); id. (ed.), *The European Opportunity* (Brookfield, 1995).

[51] Felipe Fernández-Armesto, *Millennium: A History of the Last Thousand Years* (New York, 1995), 13.

[52] Terence Ranger, 'Europeans in Black Africa', *Journal of World History*, 9/2 (1998), 255–68, at 261.

pre-colonial, colonial, and postcolonial ages that, after all, clearly reflects the Western perspective.

The case of India is similar as even in the nineteenth century there was no historiographical tradition to speak of, although some reflections on the historical craft, and attempts at writing history, can be found in the later nineteenth century, particularly in Bengal. Thereafter, because of the cosmopolitan nature of many Indian intellectuals, the writing of world history began to emerge. It is a striking fact that Jawaharlal Nehru, India's first prime minister, was himself something of a world historian. His *Glimpses of World History* makes for illuminating comparison with the works of Wells and Toynbee, who were themselves more ecumenical than many others. Nehru's conception of world history was crucially shaped against the background of the tension India experienced between Western colonialism and incipient political emancipation. Other, predominantly Marxist, writers such as Rajne Palme Dutt and Kosambi also offer a certain conception of the 'world' in their writings, and it is certainly worth exploring what conception of the 'world' they might have had. This is the task of Vinay Lal's reflections on 'Provincializing the West: World History from the Perspective of Indian History'. There are also the entirely forgotten works of writers such as K. M. Pannikar, who produced histories of Africa and South-East Asia. Even the present discourse on 'globalization' still works with a largely unitary conception of the 'world', but according to Lal one ought to probe whether the notion of 'world' is not itself more elastic than many have imagined. This is the point he pursues, since one can be sharply critical of histories that are tethered to the nation-state (as they mainly are) and yet also be critical of 'world history'. What idea of the 'world' does world history inhabit?

Lal asks how Indians were thinking of the world, if they were doing so at all, in the period of colonialism. He then moves on to an exploration of the emergence of 'world history' in twentieth-century India, the conception of the world shared by historians and other social scientists, and the tensions between 'world history' and the notions of the world held by such Indians as Gandhi and Rabindranath Tagore. It also needs to be discussed how the world outside looked to Indian thinkers and cosmopolitan inhabitants of India's colonized cities, how colonial and postcolonial notions of 'world history' were contested, evaded, and defied by Indian intellectuals, and also how these notions are still prevalent in India. However, although 'world history' has acquired greater resonance again in recent years with the emergence of multiculturalism, this version of world history, however ecumenical, is still conducted within the framework of European history, and almost entirely from the perspective of the Euro-American world. There are few, if any, truly comparative studies of world history, and the current globalization discourse still operates with a unitary concept of the world that does not perceive the variety of interpretative possibilities which it contains.

Vinay Lal's highly critical overall impression not only confirms Arif Dirlik's reservations, but also suggests the need to investigate other Asian historiographical traditions, in particular China and Japan. Both Ricardo King Sang Mak in 'The "Middle Kingdom" Struggles to Survive: The Chinese Worldview in the Nineteenth Century' and Julia Adeney Thomas writing on 'High Anxiety: World History as Japanese Self-Discovery' concentrate on the nineteenth and early twentieth centuries, while Sebastian Conrad's essay 'The Opened and the Closed Country: Conflicting Views of Japan's Position in the World' leads us to the later twentieth century and to more recent questions. The timeframe of these three essays is deliberately not set earlier in order to address the question of China's and Japan's perceptions of the world, or world history, when both countries were already in close contact with the rest of the world. How was their perception reflected by Western imperial politics, and did traditional Chinese and Japanese historical thinking evolve new modern world views in the societies?[53]

In recent years both countries have received much scholarly attention and, again, comparative studies are particularly fruitful. Akira Iriye's work on China and Japan, for example, focuses on the issues of power and culture, and gives a great deal of space to the international dimension of the transnational relationship. While Chinese cultural and religious concepts of the

[53] For an investigation of earlier historiographical perceptions and transfers see Q. Edward Wang, 'History, Space, and Ethnicity: The Chinese Worldview', *Journal of World History*, 10/2 (1999), 285–305; further see Hartmut Kaelble, 'Nichtwestliche Geschichtswissenschaften seit 1945: Afrika, Indien, Japan, China', in Kaelble and Rothermund (eds.), *Nichtwestliche Geschichtswissenschaften*, 7–16.

universe and humanity in general had a temporary influence upon Japanese thinking, Chinese perceptions of the West were often translated through the Japanese input.[54] It is interesting, however, that although the cultural dimension which Iriye rightly emphasizes played an important role in viewing the other country, it was initially military power, so demonstratively exercised in the war of 1894–5, and later economic and trade relations that became central to Sino-Japanese relations.

Despite China's booming trade with South-East Asia and the continuous inflow of Western science and technology since the late Ming, Chinese monarchs and official scholars still embraced the traditional world order in which most nations outside the orbit of Chinese civilization had but marginal significance. The factors that contributed to the formation of the Chinese worldview were very diverse, and included an understanding of the dichotomous, yet dynamic relationship between centre and periphery. Han ethnic culture centred around the ideas of 'zhongguo' and 'tianxia', meaning the capital of all states and referring to the central geographical position in the world that China occupied according to this view. There was still a separation from the outside world in the first half of the nineteenth century. After the Opium War, which Mak interprets as a turning-point, Chinese intellectuals first began to update their understanding of the world outside China, becoming more open to the West. Having looked at the outer world with fear, hope, and anxiety, Chinese thinkers now attempted to redefine their country's position in the world. Whereas the first generation still believed in the possibility of a Chinese *Sonderweg* which was independent of the rest of the world, the second generation recognized the shortcomings of Chinese civilization and aspired to at least partial integration into world society. In the age of High Imperialism, finally, Social Darwinism was a crucial factor in the perception of the country and its relations with other nations. Another factor, as recognized in one of the classic historical works of the twentieth century, Joseph Needham's multi-volume *Science and Civilization in China* (1954–94), was the envisaged synthesis of China and the West which he believed was possible through the modes of science and civilization. In order to realize what Needham termed the 'world cooperative

[54] Akira Iriye, *China and Japan in the Global Setting* (Cambridge, Mass., 1992).

commonwealth', the dialectic between East and West would be overcome by perceiving science as a universal force, a power within the development of world history.

Julia Adeney Thomas's essay suggests that the various modes of world history in Japan can best be understood not as attempts to comprehend others, or the non-Japanese world, but rather as forms of self-discovery and self-definition of the Japanese nation. Whether Chinese culture was magnificent or corrupt, whether Western science was properly ethical or not, these places were cast as intelligible, while Japan remained a mystery to itself. Other places influenced global interchange and thus world history, while Japan sought to find and defend itself within their systems. In Japan, world history, from the Tokugawa period (1600–1868) to the post-Second World War era, was shaped by high anxiety and uncertainty in dealing with the country's national identity and defence. Dialogue with the world outside Japan had the primary function of a dialogue with the Japanese nation itself. Thomas sketches the development of Japanese world history through four stages, beginning with the *kokugaku* and the Mito school histories at the end of the Tokugawa period (1600). Unable to visit the world outside Japan because of government restrictions, these writers imagined world orders of various types in order to bolster Japan's (and the Emperor's) status. By the late nineteenth century, with the Tokugawa *bakufu* overthrown and the establishment of regular diplomatic and trading relations, various 'scientific' modes of understanding world history had left the Japanese pondering their place in global evolutionary progress or in the Marxian dialectic. The third wartime stage, a revolt against modes of temporal world history, insisted that in essence Japan was without history, preserved from the fractured, relentless temporality of the non-Japanese world by the unbroken Imperial lineage. After the defeat, world history and the question of Japan's place in it were central again, as they had been at the end of the nineteenth century.

Finally, Sebastian Conrad, looking at the development of Japanese world historiography after 1945, discusses the efforts made in Japan to define the country's position between Asia and Europe, as well as between Asian and Western history. World history was popular, firmly anchored in school syllabuses, and had the function of placing Japan's past into a universal historical context. Two concepts were especially influential for Japan's relationship with the world. The contradictory notions of 'opening the country' and 'national seclusion' not only denote different periods in Japanese history, but have come to be used metaphorically to denote different ways of situating Japan within world history. The enthusiasm for universal history resulted in the production of a number of handbooks and surveys delineating historical developments around the globe. More common, however, was the use of the term as a reference point to interpret the Japanese past. 'World history' was invoked in order to situate Japan *vis-à-vis* the other Asian nations or the 'West'.

The shift from a unified and universal paradigm of world history to a theory of national seclusion and distinct civilizations was accompanied by a tendency to replace the leading temporal metaphors with spatial categories. World history appeared as a matter not of chronology and periodization, but of separation and demarcation. Finally, at the end of the twentieth century, world history was depicted as evolving differently in different regions, each 'civilization' carving out a space of its own. As Conrad shows, the interpretation of the *sakoku* period since the 1990s also looked for a comparison with Europe. Europe, like Japan, became increasingly dependent on Asian goods such as sugar and cotton, but while Europe reacted by finding substitutes for these and other products and searching for new markets, Japan's answer was isolation and seclusion, and what could be understood as a Japanese version of the Industrial Revolution. This, finally, produced an alternative to Western standards constructing a 'better', if separatist path towards modernity that was reached by peaceful means of co-operation and transfer.[55]

III

A number of questions arise from these studies. Are there essential differences between 'universal history', 'world history', and 'global history', and, if so, what are they? What are the relations

[55] Sebastian Conrad, 'Die Politik der nationalen "Abschließung": Die Überwindung des "westlichen Geschichtsbildes" in Japan?', in Kaelble and Rothermund (eds.), *Nichtwestliche Geschichtswissenschaften*, 40–52.

between world history on the one hand and local, regional, and national history on the other? As we have already said above, universal history possesses a long historiographical tradition, especially in Germany. Institutionally based since the sixteenth century, universal history was studied at Protestant German universities in particular in order to provide a vision of unity, given that the country was not united in political, territorial, or ecclesiastical respects. With the 'secularization of the universal-historical idea',[56] that is, a gradual emancipation from the biblical narrative, came an opening for the non-European, especially the Asian world. This phenomenon,[57] as well as the philosophical concepts of individual thinkers such as, to name but a few, Kant and Schiller, Hegel and Lord Acton, has attracted major scholarship.[58] It is, however, the twentieth century that is most interesting to our investigation, as the majority of the essays in this volume concentrate on developments in this century which witnessed colonization and decolonization, two devastating world wars and hundreds of regional wars with international involvement, nuclear threats, and fundamental, rapid changes in our lives.

Arnold Toynbee, more than the optimistic Wells and the pessimistic Spengler, was the first scholar since the late Enlightenment really able to present a picture of the world beyond Eurocentrism, for which 'he deserves a place of honour in the history of modern historiography'; moreover, he differentiated between the various parts of Europe itself, thereby refuting the idea of a homogenous West.[59] Compared with parallel enterprises such as, for example, the multi-volume *Propyläen-Weltgeschichte*,[60] Toynbee's work is certainly attractive for its

[56] Adalbert Klempt, *Die Säkularisierung der universalhistorischen Auffassung: Zum Wandel des Geschichtsdenkens im 16. und 17. Jahrhundert* (Göttingen, 1960), esp. 106 ff.

[57] See Osterhammel, *Die Entzauberung Asiens.*

[58] Ernst Schulin's important overview, *Universalgeschichte* (Cologne, 1974) is still unsurpassed. On the 'troubled' tradition of universal history and new perceptions of the world see also Ernst Breisach, *Historiography: Ancient, Medieval and Modern* (Chicago, 1994), 177–95, and the highly stimulating essay on Western historiography since the Enlightenment by Michael Bentley in id. (ed.), *Companion to Historiography*, 395–506.

[59] See Jürgen Osterhammel, '"Höherer Wahnsinn": Universalhistorische Denkstile im 20. Jahrhundert', in Horst Walter Blanke, Friedrich Jaeger, and Thomas Sandkühler (eds.), *Dimensionen der Historik: Geschichtstheorie, Wissenschaftsgeschichte und Geschichtskultur heute. Jörn Rüsen zum 60. Geburtstag* (Cologne, 1998), 277–86, quotation at 280.

[60] Walter Goetz (ed.), *Propyläen-Weltgeschichte: Der Werdegang der Menschheit in Gesellschaft und Staat, Wirtschaft und Geistesleben* (Berlin, 1929–33).

homogeneity, bearing the stamp of one author's hand only. It seems that, at least in Anglo-American scholarship, Toynbee represents something of a watershed—to be admired, rejected, or taken as starting point for the analysis of twentieth-century concepts of writing world history.

William H. McNeill's history of the world in one volume, *The Rise of the West: A History of the Human Community* (1963), is in many respects among the most influential contributions to this field. It reflects Toynbee's inspirations in emphasizing, for example, large-scale patterns of change.[61] The author of a biography of Toynbee had collaborated for a while with the subject of his investigation.[62] And none other than McNeill's *magnum opus* was introduced to the readers of a newly established journal on the first pages of its first issue.[63] While he took up the Toynbeean challenge at a time when most of his colleagues were increasingly critical of the grand design, McNeill also distanced himself from the claims that were and often still are associated with the universal perspective: that it possessed a deeper insight into the past than other historical approaches; that it had the ability to draw historical laws from the past; and that it could possibly see the future as a consequence of the synthesis of history. Instead, suggested McNeill, universal history, here synonymous with world history, was neither superior to other disciplines nor prophetic.[64] According to Jürgen Osterhammel, McNeill thus crucially demythologized world history and brought it back into the everyday world. It became one among other university subjects, and McNeill called for close contact with the other historical disciplines while mistrusting meta-theories.[65] At the beginning of the twenty-first century, the writing of world history as reflected in this volume has profited enormously from McNeill, whose hand can be detected in a number of the sources quoted in the footnotes. Few if any universities (in the USA) could today do without teaching world history, and few

[61] See the entries on 'McNeill' and on 'world history' in Kelly Boyd (ed.), *Encyclopedia of Historians and Historical Writing* (London, 1999), 753–4 and 1330–5.

[62] William H. McNeill, *Arnold J. Toynbee: A Life* (Oxford, 1989).

[63] William H. McNeill, '*The Rise of the West* after Twenty-Five Years', *Journal of World History*, 1 (1990), 1–21.

[64] William H. McNeill, 'The Changing Shape of World History', in Philip Pomper, Richard H. Elphick, and Richard T. Vann (eds.), *World Historians and Their Critics*, Theme Issue 34 of *History and Theory: Studies in the Philosophy of History*, (1995), 8–26.

[65] Osterhammel, 'Höherer Wahnsinn', 282.

world historians would nowadays accept the claim made by Spengler, Wells, and Toynbee that they possessed the knowledge and analytical skill to explain past and present. Many, however, might feel a debt to the modern tradition of world historiography that changed dramatically from the 1960s.[66]

According to Bruce Mazlish and Ralph Buultjens, the aim of global history in contrast to universal and world history is not to sum up the past, but to find themes with global significance. In the modern world, in which global consciousness has become increasingly prevalent while our knowledge is more and more fragmented, Mazlish argues that global history has the potential to picture the world more coherently.[67] This naturally implies, first, that more attention should be paid to the history of the so-called Third World; secondly, that more research should be undertaken on multinational, cross-cultural, and interdisciplinary levels; and, thirdly, that the image of a multiple Western world and, for instance, a single world such as East Asia, needs to be reversed, questioning the alleged uniqueness of either part, but especially so of the West.[68] Otherwise the danger would remain that both world history and global history were predominantly of interest to Western intellectuals. In that case, 'dialogues across civilizations' would be only a dream and no real communication would take place.[69]

Do we still need to pursue the distinction between micro-history and macro-history? Which discipline's methods are more appropriate for the writing of world history?[70] The French historian and sometime co-editor of *Annales*, Emmanuel Le Roy

[66] Cf. the major overviews by Ernst Schulin, 'Universalgeschichtsschreibung im 20. Jahrhundert', in id., *Traditionskritik und Rekonstruktionsversuch: Studien zur Entwicklung von Geschichtswissenschaft und historischem Denken* (Göttingen, 1979), 163–202; R. I. Moore, 'World History', in Bentley (ed.), *Companion to Historiography*, 941–59; Edoardo Tortarolo, 'World Histories in the 20th Century and Beyond', *Storia della Storiografia*, 38 (2000), 129–37; Gale Stokes, 'The Fates of Human Societies: A Review of Recent Macrohistories', *American Historical Review*, 106/2 (2001), 508–25.

[67] Bruce Mazlish and Ralph Buultjens (eds.), *Conceptualizing Global History* (Boulder, 1993); Bruce Mazlish, 'Comparing Global History to World History', *Journal of Interdisciplinary History*, 28/3 (1998), 385–95; id., 'Crossing Boundaries: Ecumenical, World, and Global History', in Pomper *et al.* (eds.), *World History*, 41–52.

[68] For this argument cf. Jack Goody, *The East in the West* (New York, 1996).

[69] Roxann Prazniak, *Dialogues across Civilizations: Sketches in World History from the Chinese and European Experiences* (Boulder, 1996).

[70] For an instructive overview cf. Jürgen Schlumbohm, 'Mikrogeschichte-Makrogeschichte: Zur Eröffnung einer Debatte', in id. (ed.), *Mikrogeschichte, Makrogeschichte: Komplementär oder inkommensurabel?* (Göttingen, 1998), 7–32.

Ladurie, once declared that the present was better served by the truffle collectors than the parachutists. Is the historical discipline likely to fragment further as the result of the advent of ever more specialists, or will this be averted with the help of world history? A veteran world historian like Andre Gunder Frank would regard the potential of world history as specifically to avoid a fragmentation in so far as the totality of the overview guarantees a better understanding of its parts. Not a subdiscipline, but the leading discipline in the social sciences, world history provides a framework that makes global interconnections visible and conceivable.[71]

If, however, this is taken for granted and our present world is experienced as witnessing an emerging global and multinational culture in which knowledge and communication are widely diffused and no longer possess a centre, the writing of world history needs as little justification as its rethinking and conceptualization. It is an experience that almost everybody has every day.[72] Consequently, therefore, publishers are currently announcing new world or global history titles in almost all their lists. The market is growing, with numerous conferences planned and new journals being established, reflecting a widespread interest in world history across the academic disciplines. This is not the place to attempt an overview of the recent literature.[73] It seems more appropriate to draw attention to some of the characteristic features that are different from, or reminiscent of, the works of the times of Spengler and Toynbee.

1. Naturally, modern works have heavier methodological trappings to carry in their intellectual rucksacks than their predecessors did. Few world historians would today write with a similar innocence as regards the theoretical background of the grand design of their books. To engage in such a project entails the study of how others have coped with the problem of the architecture of writing world history, something neither Spengler nor his contemporaries paid much attention to. But forty years ago, Fritz Wagner had already called for closer exchange and co-operation between Eastern and Western

[71] Among his numerous studies see e.g. Andre Gunder Frank, *ReORIENT: Global Economy in the Asian Age* (Berkeley, 1998).

[72] See 'World History Today—Chimera or Necessity?', Special Theme Issue of *Storia della Storiografia*, 35 (1999).

[73] Cf. Stokes, 'The Fates of Human Societies'.

historians. He saw the danger that European historians could be too influenced by the break-up of the Western colonial empires, the contemporary anti-colonial movements, and what he called a 'Marxist eschatology', which was not favourable for a balance between East and West. To achieve this balance meant to overcome a 'spiritual imperialism' that prevailed all over the globe.[74]

2. The purpose of 'World Civilization' courses, discussed at the beginning of this introduction and a key university subject in the USA more than in any other part of the globe, is cross-disciplinary research. Thus 'World Civ' actually challenges the hitherto dominant 'Western Civ' as it moves in line with the postmodern dethronement of the canon of Western literature, which was taken for granted for understanding the world. A 'new perspective', as Clive Ponting claims in his textbook, needs, among other things, to be able to envisage the transmission of culture.[75] But interrelating the different modes, discovering relations between them, and looking across cultural borders, has often been suspected of too easily becoming a somewhat dubious, if not superficial, project. Yet, as a bestselling volume by Jacques Barzun shows, cultural history can take up this challenge as long as it is firmly rooted in historical method.[76]

3. On the other hand Felipe Fernández-Armesto, author of the highly praised books *Millennium: A History of our Last Thousand Years* (1995); *Truth: A History* (1997); and *Civilizations* (2000), has become more sceptical as to the feasibility of patterns and methods. 'Global history', he writes in a book review,

> is a discipline in search of a method. Recent attempts to teach it and write it have used grand narrative as an organizing device, or the juxtaposition of civilizations, or comparative case studies, or multiple perspectives, or an imaginary perpective. The subject still seems elusive. For a historian to see the world at once—as a system of interconnections, the way a meteorologist sees it—is, some students conclude, impossible, vitiated by a basic falsehood. For most of the past, there have been no genuinely worldwide themes, no global stretch of connections.[77]

[74] Fritz Wagner, *Der Historiker und die Weltgeschichte* (Freiburg, 1965), 146–51.

[75] Clive Ponting, *World History: A New Perspective* (London, 2000).

[76] Jacques Barzun, *From Dawn to Decadence: Five Hundred Years of Western Cultural Life: 1500 to the Present* (London, 2000).

[77] Felipe Fernández-Armesto in his review of John E. Wills, *1688: A Global History* (2000), in *Times Literary Supplement*, 2 Mar. 2001, 27.

This scepticism, however, may earn world historians the criticism of writing less for an academic than a social purpose, more for an after-dinner speech than in the interests of knowledge. Style, which is undoubtedly the strength of authors from Toynbee to Fernández-Armesto, wins over substance, the sketchy anecdote over the detailed footnote.

4. The affinity with literature: Fernández-Armesto's design of dividing the few grand narratives of history into many smaller ones identifies the dilemma that the modern world no longer possesses a single coherent system as conceived intellectually by Enlightenment historians. Instead, a number of 'histories' take its place. They may be informative and well formulated, but run the risk of lacking context and a strong argument, and thus being close to the literary imagination. Is world history a story at all? And what kind of story? Is it open-ended, or has it become redundant? In order to answer these questions we need not philosophies of history but modern universal interpretations of world history. What matters is rethinking and rewriting world history, and possibly finding a common agenda, if we want to understand what Spengler at his time called the decline of the West, and what the historian of South Asian Studies at the University of Chicago, Dipesh Chakrabarty, has termed 'Provincializing Europe'.[78]

5. According to Robert Moore world history 'need not, and indeed must not, aim to be encyclopedic—that can be left to encyclopedias. . . . It can only be defined as a perspective, one of many in which any particular event, structure or process may be viewed.'[79] World historians are generally regarded as better qualified than any other historians or specialists in their field to integrate the research of neighbouring disciplines and put their findings into a larger perspective. This is connected with their ability to pose new questions on a grand scale, to identify problems for new research and investigation, and prevent the

[78] Dipesh Chakrabarty, *Provincializing Europe: Postcolonial Thought and Historical Difference* (Princeton, 2000); see also Jörn Rüsen (ed.), *Westliches Geschichtsdenken: Eine interkulturelle Debatte* (Göttingen, 1999); Philip D. Curtin, *The World and the West: The European Challenge and the Overseas Response in the Age of Empire* (Cambridge, 2000); and in particular the thought-provoking introduction by Philip Pomper, 'The Theory and Practice of World History', in id. *et al.* (eds.), *World History*, 1–17, and William H. McNeill, 'The Changing Shape of World History', ibid., 21–40.

[79] Robert I. Moore, 'World History', in Bentley (ed.), *Companion to Historiography*, 948–9.

growing fragmentation of history as a university subject by making their colleagues more aware of what happens in areas other than their own. In other words, world historians face no lesser challenge than to make history more coherent again. Yet Lord Acton, who engaged more than one hundred authors for the *Cambridge Modern History* (1902–10), already saw the difficulty of this task when, in his famous letter to the contributors, he wrote that he understood universal history, in contrast to combined history, as 'a continuous development', a succession of the different parts of history 'in reference and subordination to a higher series, according to the time and the degree in which they contribute to the common fortunes of mankind'.[80] Whether world historians of the twenty-first century can display the same optimism remains a matter of debate, or a matter of definition. Increasing interrelatedness could also be called 'globalization'. Another Cambridge historian, A. G. Hopkins, now Professor of History at the University of Texas in Austin, has recently presented this in his division of the period after 1600 into the categories of archaic, modern, and postcolonial. In sum, however, any such project could easily be criticized for primarily attempting to systematize existing research into the broader framework of international relations, or of imperial history, or of both. Yet Hopkins's claim that he is providing a new perspective on globalization must rightly be given a special place in modern research in the field.[81]

What is the social and political relevance of world history? Can a 'soft' Eurocentrism be advocated for epistemological purposes, as a way of exploring new paths in the history of historiography through transcultural comparison and transfer? The problem of unevenness in the state of knowledge remains, an issue we have already addressed in the introduction to our earlier volume, *Across Cultural Borders*.[82] Can a balanced world history ever be written while the West is much better researched than the world outside Europe? What opportunities does a comparison offer, and what are its limitations? In the nineteenth century universal history was still largely seen as the history of

[80] Lord Acton, 'Letter to the Contributors to the *Cambridge Modern History*', in Fritz Stern (ed.), *The Varieties of History: From Voltaire to the Present* (London, 1956), 247–9, at 249.

[81] A. G. Hopkins, 'The History of Globalization—and the Globalization of History?', in id. (ed.), *Globalization in World History* (London, 2002), 11–46.

[82] Fuchs and Stuchtey (eds.), *Across Cultural Borders*, 1–26.

the development of European civilization, economic domination, and imperial expansion. The current debates on Eurocentrism and postcolonialism play a major role in this context. What implications do they have for the teaching of history, in particular world history, given that, for example, the politics, economics, and culture of Asia have gained increasing attention in US colleges and universities in recent years?[83] What constituted the rise and eventual fall of the West if put into the wider dimensions of world history?[84] This is a problem that also becomes interesting with regard to the opening of other spaces and the awareness of playing a political, economic, and cultural role in the world, when its centre gradually moved away from Europe. Such could be the case, for example, with the Pacific, which, as a region, built up an identity in response to the emerging process of economic integration. Japan had already coined the term 'Pacific Age' more than a hundred years ago. Finally, the significance of and (debatable) need for a theory of world history needs to be addressed, a clear terminology found, and a distinction drawn between the work of a professional body of historians traditionally orientated by the nation-state and amateur history-writing on world history. Since Edward Said's comments on 'Orientalism' in Western scholarship, the history of civilization has also been criticized. As Michael Geyer and Charles Bright write, modern world historiography has by no means freed itself of Western stereotypes.[85] A reorientation of the subject would throw up many theoretical and practical questions, and confirm the potential of 'Writing World History'. This is also the argument of Arif Dirlik's paper in this volume.

Discussing the case of slavery as a world-historical problem and listing a number of pragmatic points which are helpful in setting criteria for the writing of world history, Jürgen Osterhammel draws attention to one particular question: that of a world-historical *problem*.[86] Other considerations are relevant, of

[83] See Ainslee T. Embree and Carol Gluck (eds.), *Asia in Western and World History: A Guide for Teaching* (Armonk, 1995).

[84] Cf. William H. McNeill, 'World History and the Rise and Fall of the West', *Journal of World History*, 9/2 (1998), 215–36.

[85] Michael Geyer and Charles Bright, 'World History in a Global Age', *American Historical Review*, 100/4 (1995), 1034–60; see also Paul Costello, *World Historians and Their Goals: Twentieth-Century Answers to Modernism* (Illinois, 1993).

[86] See Jürgen Osterhammel, 'Aufstieg und Fall der neuzeitlichen Sklaverei. Oder: Was ist ein weltgeschichtliches Problem?', in id., *Geschichtswissenschaft jenseits des*

course, for example that world history need not necessarily span long periods of time, but could equally cover what Braudel termed 'epochs', that is the synchronic description of civilizations. Yet, it seems most attractive to look at Osterhammel's statement that the world historian particularly needs to be aware of the perspective and to formulate the problem, both of which he takes from the diversity of existing theories and methods. It follows that intelligent world history must not give the impression of being able to convey a complete picture of the world. Rather, it should ask what is a problem of the past with a world-wide dimension.

Overcoming the dominance of Eurocentrism is less a problem of substance than one of method that seems, for many past and possibly future years, to be placed at the centre of the debate on writing world history. The title of Freyer's book, *Weltgeschichte Europas*, referred to above is difficult to understand today except as irony. Similar difficulties apply to the periodization of world history. Generations of historians have constantly asked whether it is still dominated by the Western timeframe.[87] Revisionist historians, looking at comparative world-historical projects such as those of William McNeill, Eric Wolf, Immanuel Wallerstein, and Eric Hobsbawm, still discover a focus on Western societies and their cultures. Indeed, Hobsbawm's master narrative in *The Age of Extremes* is essentially informed by a Western chronology and Eurocentric examples of history, set against the background of the decline of European dominance over the globe and the following transformation of the world into what he terms a 'single operational unit' as a consequence of the twentieth-century revolution in transportation technologies and communication.[88] This is the criticism of Peter Gran,[89] and a volume of essays by Goudsblom, Jones, and Mennell.[90] The latter makes clear that a Eurocentric perspective on human history no longer

Nationalstaats: Studien zu Beziehungsgeschichte und Zivilisationsvergleich (Göttingen, 2001), 342–69, at 343–4.

[87] See H. Spangenberg, 'Die Perioden der Weltgeschichte', *Historische Zeitschrift*, 127 (1923), 1–49; William Green, 'Periodizing World History', in Pomper, Elphick, and Vann (eds.), *World Historians*, 99–111.

[88] Eric Hobsbawm, *The Age of Extremes: A History of the World, 1914–1991* (New York, 1994), 14.

[89] Peter Gran, *Beyond Eurocentrism: A New View of Modern World History* (Syracuse, 1996).

[90] Johan Goudsblom, Eric Jones, and Stephen Mennell, *The Course of Human History: Economic Growth, Social Process, and Civilization* (Armonk, 1996).

leads to new concepts and interpretations that are necessary for the understanding of the complex problems of the late twentieth-century world system. The authors plead for closer co-operation between historians and sociologists. This, they hope, would result in what Goudsblom presents as five major sociohistorical trends that are interrelated and common to all parts of the world: an increase in the number of people, their concentration, the specialization of social functions, social organization, and, finally, social stratification. A study of these factors may help in formulating 'a common theory of human history and social evolution'.[91]

In his book *Beyond Eurocentrism*, Gran develops the idea of four different 'hegemonic logics', which can be identified as ideologically based class conflict, regionalism, gender, and race. These categories are exemplified by individual cases ('roads'), for example, Russia, Italy, Albania, the Congo, Great Britain, and the USA. According to Gran, these cases bridge world history and domestic history and lead to a modern version of world history 'beyond Eurocentrism' when applied to Western and non-Western countries alike. As George Fredrickson has suggested in his cross-national works comparing white and black ideologies in the USA and South Africa respectively, comparative history has the potential to undermine an illusion of uniqueness, the historical *Sonderweg*: 'Cross-national history, by acquainting one with what goes on elsewhere, may inspire a critical awareness of what is taken for granted in one's own country, but it also promotes a recognition that similar functions may be performed by differing means.'[92] However, Gran still emphasizes examples from the Western world, and, as he acknowledges, his model certainly profits from the earlier ideas only of European (!) intellectuals such as Antonio Gramsci, Michel Foucault, and Karl Marx. Marx's ideas on world history, above all, still play a role in reflections on world historiography to the present day. However, this is probably less the case in German scholarship, which, since the 1960s, has regarded Max Weber as one of the most striking intellectual forces in Western life. Not only in this volume but also elsewhere, Patrick O'Brien

[91] Ibid. 30.

[92] George Fredrickson, *The Comparative Imagination: On the History of Racism, Nationalism and Social Movements* (Berkeley, 1997), 65.

has drawn attention to the significance of Marx the cosmopolitan, and especially the great source of inspiration in the field of writing world history, if not as the result of Marx's intention of conceptualizing universal history, then for his Eurocentric worldview.[93] Marx's philosophy was fundamentally Eurocentric, hence he developed his model of the evolution of distinct stages in history based on the experience of Europe. But this allowed him and subsequent generations of Marxist thinkers to take a comparative perspective showing that neither Asia nor those societies which Marx and his contemporaries dismissed as 'peoples without history' followed the path taken by Europe.[94] Other disciplines such as ethnology and anthropology stepped in to widen our knowledge of the 'peoples without history', and they have contributed significantly to a new global view which, as the English historian Geoffrey Barraclough once suggested, should direct itself beyond the borders of national and regional narratives.[95]

Barraclough, whom *The Times* in its obtituary called 'one of the foremost and one of the most complete all round historians and scholars of his generation',[96] was indeed one of the few British historians of his time to be interested in the questions of world history. In the eyes of his contemporaries, he rightly succeeded Toynbee as Research Professor of International History at the Royal Institute of International Affairs in 1956. The more the historian freed himself from the preconceptions of national history and the nation-state, the more he developed a general concept of the past that established legitimacy and value for the present. This was Barraclough's conviction when he spoke of 'a larger view of history', responding to the constantly 'changing world', the title of one of his best-known books.[97] In this view universal history was an attitude, a methodological approach that distinguished itself not only by rejecting Eurocentrism, but also by overcoming one of the strongest

[93] Patrick O'Brien, 'The Reconstruction, Rehabilitation and Reconfiguration of the British Industrial Revolution as a Conjuncture in Global History', *Itinerario*, 24, nos. 3–4 (2000), 117–34; id., 'Metanarratives in Global Histories of Material Progress', *International History Review*, 23/2 (2001), 345–67.

[94] Cf. Shlomo Avineri, *The Social and Political Thought of Karl Marx* (Cambridge, 1980).

[95] See Kenneth C. Dewar, 'Geoffrey Barraclough: From Historicism to Historical Science', *The Historian*, 56/3 (1994), 449–64.

[96] *The Times*, 31 Dec. 1984, 14.

[97] Geoffrey Barraclough, *History in a Changing World* (Oxford, 1955).

heritages of Western historiography, that of historicism. In sum, world or universal history in the later twentieth century was a response to a need generally felt in the specialized disciplines for a new, coherent, and comprehensive view on established facts. In Barraclough's words: 'World-history cuts into reality at a different angle from other types of history; and because its angle is different, it cuts across the lines they have traced.'[98] It is these lines the present volume sets out to investigate.

[98] Quoted from Dewar, 'Geoffrey Barraclough', at 457.

PART I
Mapping the Subject

2

World History and Grand Narrative

JERRY H. BENTLEY

Grand narrative has come under siege in the postmodern, postcolonial environment of contemporary times.[1] Critics have lambasted the received Eurocentric grand narratives of the Enlightenment, scientific, nationalist, liberal, democratic, capitalist, industrial, Marxist, modernization, technological, and other varieties—and rightly so. Among historians, critics have most often attacked these grand narratives because they badly misrepresent the experiences of peoples beyond Europe. Gyan Prakash, for example, has repudiated all grand narratives—including those of Indian nationalist and Marxist historians—that force Indian experience into Eurocentric moulds, calling instead for a historical vision 'that is neither inside nor outside the history of western domination but in a tangential relation to it'.[2] Similarly, Steven Feierman has argued that European categories foredoom any effort to understand African societies, which he holds are comprehensible only in African terms. Thus

Many thanks for helpful critiques and suggestions offered by Robert Borofsky, David A. Chappell, David Christian, Andre Gunder Frank, Peter H. Hoffenberg, and Rachel Laudan.

[1] For some thoughtful reflections on the current status of grand narrative, see Allan Megill, ' "Grand Narrative" and the Discipline of History', in Frank Ankersmit and Hans Kellner (eds.), *A New Philosophy of History* (Chicago, 1995), 151–73; and Kerwin Lee Klein, 'In Search of Narrative Mastery: Postmodernism and the People Without History', *History and Theory*, 34 (1995), 275–98. Robert F. Berkhofer, Jr., also addresses the issue of grand narrative in *Beyond the Great Story: History as Text and Discourse* (Cambridge, Mass., 1995).

[2] Gyan Prakash, 'Postcolonial Criticism and Indian Historiography', *Social Text*, 31/32 (1992), 8–19, at 8; and 'Writing Post-Orientalist Histories of the Third World: Perspectives from Indian Historiography', *Comparative Studies in Society and History*, 32 (1990), 383–408, where Prakash rejects all totalizing approaches in favour of postmodern and postfoundational historical analysis. See also Rosalind O'Hanlon and David Washbrook, 'After Orientalism: Culture, Criticism, and Politics in the Third World', *Comparative Studies in Society and History*, 34 (1992), 141–67; and Gyan Prakash, 'Can the "Subaltern" Ride? A Reply to O'Hanlon and Washbrook', ibid. 168–84.

African historical experience undermines all the received grand narratives, leading to 'the dissolution of world history' and 'the end of universal narratives'.[3] Apart from historians, other postmodern critics have rejected Eurocentric grand narratives because the historical record has so often mocked their universalizing visions and their promises of reason, progress, prosperity, freedom, liberation, equality, and justice. Jean-François Lyotard reflected this line of attack succinctly when he asserted that the defining characteristic of the postmodern era is 'incredulity toward metanarratives'.[4]

It is not difficult to understand disenchantment with the received Eurocentric grand narratives, which clearly make unstable scaffolding for historical scholarship. Yet the effort to construct historical meaning implies some larger vision of the past, whether it takes the form of grand narrative or some other architectural framing device. Otherwise, history would become an incoherent collection of infinite unrelated and unrelatable micro-narratives, and scholars would find themselves in the condition of William James's famous infant, who for lack of conceptual and discriminatory faculties experiences the world as 'one great blooming, buzzing confusion'.[5] Worse, by refusing to recognize the larger world and the links connecting human societies, unrelated micro-narratives entail a vision of history driven *de facto* by local cultural determinisms: the reduction of history to unrelated micro-narratives precludes the identification or analysis of historical dynamics transcending individual societies.[6]

[3] Steven Feierman, 'African Histories and the Dissolution of World History', in Robert H. Bates, V. Y. Mudimbe, and Jean O'Barr (eds.), *Africa and the Disciplines: The Contributions of Research in Africa to the Social Sciences and Humanities* (Chicago, 1993), 167–212. See also a shorter version of the same essay, 'Africa in History: The End of Universal Narratives', in Gyan Prakash (ed.), *After Colonialism: Imperial Histories and Postcolonial Displacements* (Princeton, 1995), 40–65.

[4] Jean-François Lyotard, *The Postmodern Condition: A Report on Knowledge*, trans. G. Bennington and B. Massumi (Minneapolis, 1984), p. xxiv. See also Lyotard's essay 'Universal History and Cultural Differences', in Andrew Benjamin (ed.), *The Lyotard Reader* (Oxford, 1989), 314–23.

[5] William James, *The Principles of Psychology*, ed. Frederick H. Burkhardt *et al.*, 3 vols. (Cambridge, Mass., 1981), i. 462.

[6] The costs of this approach are dear. Fernando Coronil has made the point quite well: 'This current, directed against metanarratives of history, produces disjointed mini-narratives which reinforce dominant worldviews; reacting against determinisms, it presents free-floating events; refusing to fix identity in structural categories, it essentializes identity through difference; resisting the location of power in structures or institutions, it diffuses it throughout society and ultimately dissolves it. Ironically, this popular trend

In fact, however, most recent critics of grand narrative have not retreated to the nominalism of unrelated micro-narratives. Indeed, they have not rejected grand narrative *per se* so much as certain kinds of grand narrative. While they have not often acknowledged the point, postmodern and postcolonial critics have generally assumed some alternative to the received Eurocentric grand narratives. Usually the alternatives have taken the form of inversions of Enlightenment-derived narratives that make history not a story of reason, progress, prosperity, freedom, liberation, equality, or justice, but rather a record of imperialism, colonialism, racism, sexism, subjection, domination, self-interest, exploitation, and in some cases also resistance on the part of the oppressed.[7] These counter-narratives basically invert the Enlightenment story: they are derivative reactions, and as such they lack the power to escape the Enlightenment's gravitational field. They offer some cogent critiques and make some sorely needed corrections to the Enlightenment story, to be sure, but they offer visions of the larger past that are no more complete or compelling than the Eurocentric narratives that they seek to displace.

Is it possible to construct more useful alternatives to the received Eurocentric grand narratives that can serve as framing devices for historical scholarship? Is it possible to move beyond

leaves us facing a world of disjointed elements at a time when the globalization of space—marked by integrative and exclusionary processes—makes it intellectually compelling and politically indispensable to understand how parts and whole hang together.' See Fernando Coronil, 'Can Postcoloniality Be Decolonized? Imperial Banality and Postcolonial Power', *Public Culture,* 5 (1992), 89–108, at 99–100. Marxist critics have often argued that the rejection of grand narrative dissolves the basis for historically grounded politics. See e.g. Aijaz Ahmad, *In Theory: Class, Nation, Literatures* (London, 1992); Madan Sarup, *An Introductory Guide to Post-Structuralism and Postmodernism* (2nd edn.; Athens, Ga., 1993); and Arif Dirlik, *The Postcolonial Aura* (Boulder, 1997).

[7] See e.g. Michel Foucault, *Madness and Civilization: A History of Insanity in the Age of Reason,* trans. R. Howard (New York, 1965); *The History of Sexuality,* trans. R. Hurley (New York, 1978); and *Discipline and Punish: The Birth of the Prison,* trans. A. Sheridan (New York, 1979). See also scholarship from the subaltern school: Gayatri Chakravorty Spivak, 'Can the Subaltern Speak?', in Cary Nelson and Lawrence Grossberg (eds.), *Marxism and the Interpretation of Culture* (Urbana, 1988), 271–313; Ranajit Guha and Gayatri Chakravorty Spivak (eds.), *Selected Subaltern Studies* (New York, 1988); Gyan Prakash, 'Subaltern Studies as Postcolonial Criticism', *American Historical Review,* 99 (1994), 1475–90; Florencia E. Mallon, 'The Promise and Dilemma of Subaltern Studies: Perspectives from Latin American History', *American Historical Review,* 99 (1994), 1491–1515; and Frederick Cooper, 'Conflict and Connection: Rethinking Colonial African History', *American Historical Review,* 99 (1994), 1516–45.

unrelated micro-narratives towards an understanding of individual societies, the larger world, and their relationships? These questions are especially crucial for the field of world history, which seeks large-scale explanations while rejecting partial or centric grand narratives as inappropriate by definition: it goes without saying in these latter days that any vision of the past making global claims cannot simply universalize the experience of any single society and foist it on all the rest of the world's peoples.

But both the received Eurocentric grand narratives and the counter-narratives assumed by postmodern and postcolonial scholars direct attention towards themes of cultural distinctiveness, exclusive identities, local knowledge, and the experiences of individual societies that are ostensibly distinct and coherent—the principal concerns of professional historical scholarship from the mid-nineteenth century to the present. So long as historians take these themes as their principal concerns, there probably is no way to avoid Eurocentrism or some other kind of equally partial centrism.[8] Moreover, these themes encourage historians to overlook or deny processes of cross-cultural interaction, even though these processes have played prominent roles in the production of individual societies themselves.

Any effort to construct a larger framework of world history will therefore need to move beyond the inherited thematics of historical scholarship. This essay suggests that several long-term patterns of human experience have potential to yield a vision of the past that helps make sense of history on a global scale. The kind of framing device proposed here does not take the form of grand narrative as usually conceived so much as what feminist critics Nancy Fraser and Linda Nicholson have called large-scale

[8] Consideration of multiple voices and inclusion of different narratives might enable historians to avoid the worst effects of centric analyses in tightly focused studies. But it plainly would be impossible to implement this approach on a global scale by making a place for every voice and every narrative in all of world history. Yet this is the only alternative to Eurocentric grand narrative that Feierman and Lyotard entertain in their works cited above. For two especially persuasive studies that take multiple voices seriously when dealing with focused historical experiences, see Patricia Nelson Limerick, *The Legacy of Conquest: The Unbroken Past of the American West* (New York, 1987); and Richard Price, *Alabi's World* (Baltimore, 1990). For some reflections on efforts to incorporate multiple perspectives, see Robert F. Berkhofer, Jr., 'A Point of View on Viewpoints in Historical Practice', in Frank Ankersmit and Hans Kellner (eds.), *A New Philosophy of History* (Chicago, 1995), 174–91; and *Beyond the Great Story*, esp. 170–201.

empirical narratives, as opposed to totalizing ahistorical metanarratives.[9] The approach here begins with empirical experience—rather than ideological preferences or convictions—in search of perspectives valuable for purposes of constructing an architectural framework of human history on the large scale. The point is not to universalize the experience of any particular society, no matter how influential, but rather to entertain the possibility that beyond cultural distinctiveness, exclusive identities, local knowledge, and the experiences of individual societies, there might be some larger human stories, or at least larger contexts to serve as meaningful frameworks for thinking about the world's past.

One last caveat: in taking this approach, this essay does not deny, dismiss, or ignore the problems of language, representation, and narrative that scholars have drawn attention to since the linguistic turn. Rather, it aims to bring focus to some dimensions of human reality that historians have rarely examined. Historical processes unfold on different levels—local, national, regional, continental, hemispheric, oceanic, global, and perhaps others as well. In practice, however, professional historians have focused their analyses almost exclusively on local and national experiences, and they have taken national communities as the almost exclusive framework of historical scholarship. Granting that language and narrative are imperfect tools, there is a real need to move beyond the assumption that history is a property attaching principally to national communities, and further to explore ways of understanding the dynamics of large-scale historical processes.

The following essay offers one perspective on the global past—one out of many that surely are conceivable—that draws on global human experience rather than projecting the preferences or experiences of some single people or society on all the others. This view of the past stands on three realities of global human experience and the relationships among them. The three realities are rising human population, expanding technological capacity, and increasing interaction between peoples of different societies. The argument is that they worked like a triple helix to

[9] Nancy Fraser and Linda Nicholson, 'Social Criticism without Philosophy: An Encounter between Feminism and Postmodernism', *Theory, Culture, and Society*, 5 (1988), 373–94.

reinforce one another with powerful effects throughout history.[10] All three of these realities are highly problematic, so each needs some clarification.

To stretch a point, the population of human species—including *Homo erectus* as well as *Homo sapiens*—has been rising for about the past 1.5 million years. But human population has risen much more clearly and for more identifiable reasons for the past 200,000 years or so, since the evolution of *Homo sapiens*. It certainly has not increased at a constant rate. Rather there have been long periods of slow to moderate growth interrupted briefly by eras of demographic decline and spurts of extremely rapid increase. But the unmistakable trend over the long term is up. Only rarely have diseases, natural disasters, human catastrophes, or Malthusian crises seriously reduced human population—as in the case of pandemic plague in the fourteenth century or epidemic smallpox in the Americas and Oceania after the sixteenth century—and so far, those demographic retreats have been both temporary and short-lived.

Population has increased because of different reasons at different times. The large story is that there have been three big demographic surges associated with different forms of economic organization. The first surge began about 1.5 to 2 million years ago with the emergence of *Homo erectus* as an effective hunter who also migrated to most parts of the eastern hemisphere. The transition to agriculture launched a second round of rapid population increase beginning about 10,000 years ago. The third demographic surge accompanied the process of industrialization beginning in the eighteenth century. Historical demographers often disagree on the details of population history and the dynamics that drove them, but they uniformly agree on these large outlines of human population history.[11] Within this big

[10] For a brilliant and sophisticated argument, very congenial to my own view, that sketches a model of social evolution based on interaction, see Andrew Sherratt, 'Reviving the Grand Narrative: Archaeology and Long-Term Change', *Journal of European Archaeology*, 3 (1995), 1–32. See also Johan Goudsblom, E. L. Jones, and Stephen Mennell, *Human History and Social Process* (Exeter, 1989).

[11] United Nations, 'History of World Population Growth', in *The Determinants and Consequences of Population Trends* (New York, 1973), 10–31; John D. Durand, 'Historical Estimates of World Population: An Evaluation', *Population and Development Review*, 3 (1977), 253–96; Colin McEvedy and Richard Jones, *Atlas of World Population History* (Harmondsworth, 1978); Jean-Noël Biraben, 'Essai sur l'évolution du nombre des hommes', *Population*, 34 (1979), 13–25; Massimo Livi-Bacci, *A Concise History of World*

story of three demographic surges, there are several smaller stories. First, following each of the demographic surges, there have been incremental increases associated with new technologies or better crops. Second, different rates of development and change in different societies have resulted in considerable regional variation in demographic experiences. Third, irregular but serious crises have caused dramatic demographic decline. Fourth, however, population has always recovered from decline (thus far) and resumed the path of increase.[12]

Demographic expansion is thus certainly not an unproblematic reality. Population has risen at different rates in different lands, and it has been subject to numerous constraints, including climate, disease, human or natural catastrophe, land resources, and agricultural technology. Moreover, human population will not continue to grow forever. On the basis of current trends, demographers predict that human population will grow until about the middle of the twenty-first century CE, then stabilize at 10 to 12 billion, or possibly even decline.[13]

Nevertheless, varying local patterns to the contrary notwithstanding, it remains clear that since the evolution of *Homo sapiens* and especially since the invention of agriculture, there has been a global human demographic history. Despite occasional demographic crises, for any given thousand-year period since the invention of agriculture, population has been higher at the end than at the beginning.[14] Moreover, population has fluctuated not simply because of the choices made by individual local communities, although these choices have played important roles, but also because of interactions between peoples of different societies and relationships between local communities, their neighbours, and the larger world.

While human population has been rising for more than a million years, albeit inconsistently, human history is also a story of expanding technological capacity. The point here is not to advance a triumphalist vision of technological progress. Indeed,

Population, trans. Carl Ipsen (2nd edn.; Oxford, 1997). For prehistoric population see Fekri A. Hassan, *Demographic Archaeology* (New York, 1981).

[12] Livi-Bacci, *Concise History of World Population.*

[13] Max Singer, 'The Population Surprise', *Atlantic Monthly* (Aug. 1999), 22–5.

[14] Johan Goudsblom, 'Human History and Long-Term Social Processes: Towards a Synthesis of Chronology and "Phaseology" ', in Goudsblom, Jones, and Mennell, *Human History and Social Process*, 22–5.

I personally do not regard progress as a useful category of historical analysis. Expanding technological capacity has certainly increased human power, comfort, and safety in many ways, but it has also made possible appalling cruelty, suffering, and environmental damage that leave the term 'progress' with a hollow ring. Rather my point is that human societies have devised increasingly effective tools over time and thus have accumulated a huge storehouse of devices and techniques that facilitate both manipulation of the natural world and organization of human societies. Over the long term, human groups have mostly extended rather than cut back on their technological capacities.

As in the case of demographic increase, the story of expanding technological capacity is anything but unproblematic. For one thing, there are many local histories of technology, and they differ from one another even more than local histories of population. Beyond Eurasia and north Africa, where technological innovations spread widely and rapidly even in ancient times, human societies devised radically different tools and techniques before a process of relative technological homogenization began to take effect in modern times. Technological homogenization, of course, has not been a one-way street: while many influences and innovations travelled from Europe and North America to the larger world, especially after about 1800 CE, many also originated in other world regions and spread widely in modern as well as premodern times.[15]

A second and perhaps more difficult complication for the story of expanding technological capacity is the fact that local histories of technology all reflect political, social, economic, cultural, and ecological influences on technological development rather than some sort of Faustian drive towards technological mastery.[16] Indeed, there have been cases in which human societies have voluntarily abandoned established technologies without their replacement by alternatives. For the most part, when human groups have abandoned effective technologies,

[15] Arnold Pacey, *Technology in World Civilization: A Thousand-Year History* (Cambridge, Mass., 1990).

[16] See esp. two spirited essays: Peter C. Perdue, 'Technological Determinism in Agrarian Societies', in Merrit Roe Smith and Leo Marx (eds.), *Does Technology Drive History? The Dilemma of Technological Determinism* (Cambridge, Mass., 1994), 170–200; and Richard W. Bulliet, 'Determinism and Pre-Industrial Technology', ibid. 202–15.

they have done so either involuntarily, because circumstances such as the general collapse of a society have forced them to do so,[17] or because they replaced earlier technologies with alternatives that at least seemed more effective, even if they really were not. Cases in which humans have voluntarily abandoned established technologies without their replacement by alternatives generally reflect the influence of powerful political, social, economic, cultural, or ecological considerations.

A few examples illustrate the possibilities:

- The aboriginal inhabitants of Tasmania lost the arts of fishing and sewing as well as the technology of making bone tools, presumably because their population (about 4,000) was too small to support specialist craftsmen.[18]
- Austronesian inhabitants of Pacific islands abandoned the production of Lapita pottery about 500 BCE. Islanders did not use pottery for cooking, and they were able to rely on durable coconut shells and carved wooden bowls for storage. Islanders used pottery mostly for exchange, and the end of ceramic production coincided with decline of the widespread Lapita trading network.[19]
- Some Polynesian mariners gave up their long-distance navigational skills after about the fourteenth century, most likely because they had no need to undertake expensive and dangerous long-distance voyages after organizing productive agricultural societies in the Pacific islands.[20]
- In the early fifteenth century, rulers of Ming China ordered an end to ambitious voyages of reconnaissance throughout the Indian Ocean basin and suppressed knowledge of shipbuilding technologies that had supported the voyages. Explanations for their decision include military threats in

[17] General collapses, such as those of Harappan society, the western Roman empire, the lowland Maya, and others, have indeed forced societies to abandon complex technologies on a large scale. But the general collapse of a society (as distinguished from periodic crises, military defeat, and the fall of states or ruling dynasties) is a fairly rare historical phenomenon. For a sophisticated analysis of collapse, see Joseph A. Tainter, *The Collapse of Complex Societies* (Cambridge, 1988).

[18] Jared Diamond, *Guns, Germs, and Steel: The Fates of Human Societies* (New York, 1997), 256–8, 311–13.

[19] Patrick Vinton Kirch, *The Lapita Peoples: Ancestors of the Oceanic World* (Cambridge, Mass., 1997), 159–61.

[20] Ben Finney, *Voyage of Rediscovery: A Cultural Odyssey through Polynesia* (Berkeley, 1994), 292–304.

central Asia that demanded financial resources, political pressures arising from factional disputes at the Ming court, and the high expense of the expeditions themselves.[21]

- Tokugawa shoguns abolished the production and use of firearms in Japan in the seventeenth century largely for political reasons—to reduce the possibility of threats to their rule.[22]
- At least for the moment, the world community is shying away from the use of nuclear weapons for political and moral reasons, although it may be too early to declare this case closed.

From these and other cases that could be cited, it is clear that compelling political, social, economic, cultural, and ecological considerations have sometimes persuaded peoples to abandon technologies that they had previously found valuable. The world's peoples have mostly chosen to maintain and enhance their technological inheritances, but their decisions represent choices rather than destinies.

Of course, even when they have abandoned some individual technologies, human societies have generally continued to refine other technologies, so that general technological regression has been extremely rare in human history, except temporarily in the wake of human or natural catastrophe that has caused the general collapse of a society. Thus terms such as 'technological regression' and 'technological stagnation' have little if any use for purposes of historical analysis. Indeed, their use often reflects ideological interests, such as a concern to construct an image of a dynamic, inventive, innovative Europe in a world of technological lethargy.[23]

For the most part, then, human beings have constructed increasingly effective technologies of production, transportation, and communication—not to mention destruction—even if the pace of innovation in most eras was slow by the standards of the past two centuries. Innovation and increasing technological

[21] Louise Levathes, *When China Ruled the Seas: The Treasure Fleet of the Dragon Throne, 1405–1433* (New York, 1994).

[22] Noel Perrin, *Giving up the Gun: Japan's Reversion to the Sword, 1543–1879* (Boston, 1979).

[23] For just such an ideological deployment of these and similar concepts, see David S. Landes, *The Wealth and Poverty of Nations: Why Some Are So Rich and Some So Poor* (New York, 1998), esp. 54–9.

capacity have been common characteristics of human societies not just since the industrial era or the period since the invention of agriculture, but for the past 200,000 years and especially the past 40,000 years. The earliest stone tools brought to light by archaeologists date to three million years before the present. *Homo habilis* began to fashion Oldowan hammers, choppers, and scrapers some two million years ago, and *Homo erectus* produced more sophisticated Acheulian handaxes, picks, and cleavers beginning about 1.7 million years ago. Acheulian technology persisted for more than a million years with little significant innovation. About 200,000 years ago, however, the finely crafted Mousterian tools of early *Homo sapiens* suddenly displaced Acheulian implements. About 40,000 years ago, modern *Homo sapiens* inaugurated a technological explosion involving the crafting of blades and the use of new materials such as bone, antler, and ivory. About 20,000 years ago came the production also of altogether new types of tools such as needles, spear throwers, harpoons, and bows and arrows.[24]

Just as population grew dramatically after the introduction of agriculture and mechanized industry, technological capacity expanded rapidly under conditions that favoured both specialized craft production and the spread of technological expertise. After 5000 BCE new techniques of production generated increasing quantities of agricultural crops and manufactured goods. After 4000 BCE sails, wheels, animal traction, and other technologies of transportation made it possible to convey peoples, goods, and messages over long distances in relative safety. After 3000 BCE new techniques of social, political, and military organization made it possible to establish large states. After 1500 BCE iron metallurgy made effective tools and weapons widely available. After 1750 CE steam power, electricity, fossil fuels, and nuclear energy vastly increased the tempo of production and transportation, while electronic signalling liberated the communication of messages from physical transport. Thus, from the palaeolithic era to the present, especially for the past 40,000 years, and dramatically for the past 7,000 years, the trend is

[24] Kathy D. Schick and Nicholas Toth, *Making Silent Stones Speak: Human Evolution and the Dawn of Technology* (New York, 1993). See also John E. Pfeiffer, *The Creative Explosion: An Inquiry into the Origins of Art and Religion* (New York, 1982); and François Bordes, *The Old Stone Age*, trans. J. E. Anderson (London, 1968).

towards the development and diffusion of technologies that expand human capacity for production, transportation, communication, and organization.

With rising population and expanding technological capacity, human groups have constructed thousands of distinctive societies. Indeed, the organization of societies that are more or less distinctive and coherent is a global historical process of profound significance for all humanity, and almost all historical scholarship has focused precisely on the formation, development, integration, historical experiences, and sometimes dissolution of these societies. Since the earth is a finite space, however, it follows almost inevitably from rising population and expanding technological capacity that human history is not only the collective record of these many individual societies and their experiences, but also a story of increasing interaction between peoples of different societies. More precisely, human history is a story of increased intensity of cross-cultural interaction over longer and longer distances and larger and larger spaces.

What does 'cross-cultural interaction' mean? Even more than demographic growth and increasing technological capacity, cross-cultural interaction is a problematic category, partly because it assumes the existence and stability of coherent cultural and social configurations. Traditional, postmodern, and postcolonial scholars all quite properly interrogate the integrity of reified analytical units such as 'Asia' and 'Europe', and even more specific units such as 'China' and 'France'. Lacking coherent cultural and social configurations, how can there be cross-cultural interaction? My view is that it would be pointless to formulate general, universalizing definitions of cultural configurations and their interactions. The diversity of human behaviour and experience bedevils in advance any such *faux*-scientific project. Allowing for disagreements on the margins, it is very clear that several kinds of historical processes have linked the fates and fortunes of peoples from different societies. The most important of these historical processes include large-scale migrations, campaigns of imperial expansion, long-distance trade, the spread of biological species, and encounters and exchanges of religious and cultural traditions (including transfers of technological skills and expertise). In combination, these processes have left quite a mark on the world's past, and they draw attention to some dimensions of human experience that traditional, postmodern, and postcolonial historians have all largely ignored, given their concern with cultural distinctiveness, exclusive identities, local knowledge, and the experiences of individual societies.

Like rising population and expanding technological capacity, the intensity and range of cross-cultural interactions have not increased at a regular or consistent rate. Processes of cross-cultural interactions are not independent, autonomous, sovereign historical agents. To the contrary, they are fruits of human agency, and as such they are subject to political, economic, technological, and cultural influences. For much of history, productivity levels and technologies of transportation limited possibilities for cross-cultural interaction. But even in the absence of material constraints, cross-cultural interaction is not an autonomous force. During much of the twentieth century, for example, political and ideological barriers obstructed cross-cultural dealings that were fully feasible on economic and technological grounds. Throughout history, the world's peoples (or their rulers) have made choices about the extent to which they participate in processes of cross-cultural interaction or disengage from them. In many cases they have been unable to implement their preferred choices, but they have always determined to some greater or lesser extent the terms on which they have participated in processes of cross-cultural interaction. Those terms have variously facilitated, promoted, accelerated, obstructed, discouraged, or retarded processes of cross-cultural interaction. Yet human beings have such strong interests in dealing with peoples from other societies that they have tended over time to overcome hindrances and obstacles to cross-cultural interactions. As a result, generally speaking, the intensity and range of cross-cultural interactions have increased throughout history, albeit at irregular and inconsistent rates.[25]

[25] See Philip D. Curtin, *Cross-Cultural Trade in World History* (Cambridge, 1984); Alfred W. Crosby, *Ecological Imperialism: The Biological Expansion of Europe, 900–1900* (Cambridge, 1986); Jerry H. Bentley, *Old World Encounters: Cross-Cultural Contacts and Exchanges in Pre-Modern Times* (New York, 1993); id., 'Cross-Cultural Interaction and Periodization in World History', *American Historical Review*, 101 (1996), 749–70; and id., 'Hemispheric Integration, 500–1500 C.E.', *Journal of World History*, 9 (1998), 237–54. Some world-system analysts see trade and other interactions as cyclical: Andre Gunder Frank and Barry K. Gills (eds.), *The World System: Five Hundred Years or Five Thousand?* (London, 1993); Christopher Chase-Dunn and Thomas Hall, *Rise and Demise: Comparing World-Systems* (Boulder, 1997).

Just as they have increased inconsistently in their intensity and range, processes of cross-cultural interaction have touched the world's peoples differentially, since some peoples have had greater opportunities than others to participate in processes of cross-cultural interaction. It is certainly not the case that all or most individuals participated directly in processes of cross-cultural interaction before recent times—by engaging in a campaign of imperial expansion, for example, or by travelling abroad as a merchant, or by dying from a disease introduced from afar, or by converting to a foreign religious faith. Nevertheless, processes of cross-cultural interaction have profoundly influenced the development of almost all societies, and by defining, shaping, or transforming the conditions of existence, they have at least indirectly touched the lives of most human beings who have lived on planet earth.

One implication of this point is that the theme of cross-cultural interaction needs to figure prominently on the agenda of historians in general and world historians in particular. Indeed, cross-cultural interaction emerges as perhaps the principal theme of global historical analysis. Networks of cross-cultural interaction, communication, and exchange are defining contexts of human historical experience just as surely as are the myriad ostensibly distinct societies and ostensibly coherent national communities that scholars have taken by convention as the default categories of historical analysis. Thus, attention to processes of cross-cultural interaction is quite simply indispensable for purposes of understanding the trajectories of individual societies as well as the development of the larger world as a whole.

The three realities of global human experience presented here are not isolated or static pieces of information. Just as important as the realities themselves is the point that they have intertwined in helix fashion and reinforced one another with powerful effects. Both rising population (reality number 1) and increasing production leveraged by expanding technological capacity (reality number 2) have served as foundations for commercial exchanges between peoples of different societies (an aspect of reality number 3). Meanwhile, increasingly effective technologies of transportation and communication (reality number 2) have expedited cross-cultural interactions of all kinds (reality number 3). Cross-cultural trade (an aspect of reality number 3) has facilitated transfers of technology and biological exchanges, which in turn have supported rising population (reality number 1) and enhanced technological capacity among interacting societies (reality number 2).[26] These three realities of global human experience therefore do not represent isolated, unrelated, independent processes, but rather shifting constellations of intertwined processes that fuel and mutually reinforce each other, giving rise to a powerful complex of global historical dynamics.

Some concrete examples might help to clarify this point. After the introduction of agriculture, densely populated societies emerged in China, India, south-west Asia, and the Mediterranean basin. Dense populations fostered specialization of labour, which resulted in efficient agricultural and craft production as well as technological innovation. After about 500 CE these societies produced vast quantities of textiles, porcelain, iron, steel, and bullion, alongside agricultural products and other goods. Transportation technologies involving horses, wagons, camels, and ocean-going ships made it possible to trade these products throughout the eastern hemisphere. Dense populations and concentrations of wealth generated demand for products from distant lands. The result was a thriving trading world extending from the islands of south-east Asia to the Mediterranean basin—including also sub-Saharan east Africa and west Africa—that influenced the organization of almost all societies in the eastern hemisphere for more than a millennium, until at least the eighteenth century CE.[27] The mutual reinforcement of dense and growing populations, expanding technological capacities, and increasing intensity of cross-cultural interactions thus helps to explain the emergence of a hemispheric network of communication and exchange.

Another example arises from Ester Boserup's famous argument about dynamic relationships between population and

[26] To cite only a few studies that support this view implicitly, if not explicitly, see William H. McNeill, *The Rise of the West: A History of the Human Community* (Chicago, 1963); K. N. Chaudhuri, *Trade and Civilisation in the Indian Ocean: An Economic History from the Rise of Islam to 1750* (Cambridge, 1985); id., *Asia before Europe: Economy and Civilisation of the Indian Ocean from the Rise of Islam to 1750* (Cambridge, 1990); Andrew M. Watson, *Agricultural Innovation in the Early Islamic World, 700–1100* (Cambridge, 1983); Richard W. Bulliet, *The Camel and the Wheel* (Cambridge, Mass., 1975); and Bentley, *Old World Encounters*.

[27] Chaudhuri, *Trade and Civilisation in the Indian Ocean*; Chaudhuri, *Asia before Europe*; Bulliet, *The Camel and the Wheel*; Bentley, *Old World Encounters*; and Mark Elvin, *The Pattern of the Chinese Past* (Stanford, 1973).

technology: in some cases, population pressures have encouraged technological innovation, which then supported increased production and further demographic increase. Less well known is Boserup's point that the more important phenomenon is the transmission rather than the invention of technologies.[28] Indeed, from the dawn of agriculture to the nineteenth century CE, the spread of food crops, domesticated animals, and related agricultural technologies unquestionably accounted for the bulk of human population growth. Many of these diffusions took place over very long distances, as in the cases of the so-called Islamic green revolution in the postclassical era and the Columbian exchange of early modern times, both of which fuelled rapid population growth.[29] These cases reveal the dynamic relationships between population, technology, and cross-cultural interactions as well, since cross-cultural travel, trade, and communication facilitated the spread of agricultural crops and technologies.

For a final example, consider the process of industrialization in modern times. The role of technology was obviously crucial for industrialization, and it has accordingly loomed large in all historical analyses of the process. The tools of industrialization were largely European inventions, as were many industrial products, such as railways. Yet industrialization was by no means an exclusively European affair. The first big industry, cotton textile production, depended on raw cotton imported from India, Egypt, and the southern United States. While providing raw materials in abundance, European colonies in Asia, Africa, and the Americas served as markets for European manufactures, and some of them also supplied labour for European agricultural and industrial interests. Indeed, in the absence of European colonies, especially those in the Americas, industrialization is inconceivable. Meanwhile, a demographic surge fuelled further industrial development from the nineteenth

[28] Ester Boserup, *Population and Technological Change: A Study of Long-Term Trends* (Chicago, 1981), esp. 3–5. See also Ester Boserup, *The Conditions of Agricultural Growth: The Economics of Agrarian Change under Population Pressure* (London, 1965); and Ronald Demos Lee, 'Malthus and Boserup: A Dynamic Synthesis', in David Coleman and Roger Schofield (eds.), *The State of Population Theory: Forward from Malthus* (Oxford, 1986), 96–130.

[29] Watson, *Agricultural Innovation in the Early Islamic World*; Alfred W. Crosby, *The Columbian Exchange: Biological and Cultural Consequences of 1492* (Westport, 1972); and id., *Ecological Imperialism: The Biological Expansion of Europe, 900–1900* (Cambridge, 1986).

into the twenty-first century. Once again, then, population, technology, and cross-cultural interaction intertwined like the strands of a triple helix to reinforce one another as they generated a powerful dynamic driving historical development.[30]

The vision of world history sketched in this essay certainly does not represent a cure-all either for history in general or for world history in particular. It has little to say about the experiences or historical dynamics of individual communities, which obviously are crucial contexts for understanding the world's peoples, except in so far as they have participated in large-scale historical processes. Another problem is that by taking the long-term perspective, this vision of the past could easily overlook the hurly-burly and contingency of world history, even if it brings some large-scale processes into clearer focus. Some might charge, too, that this vision of history stops just where historical analysis usually begins, with political contests and conflicts of will, although it would be a simple matter to take these issues into account in any analysis of individual processes of cross-cultural interaction.

Granting that it does not capture some important dimensions of historical experience, the view of the global past sketched here nevertheless might enable historians to deal usefully with some other significant issues. Most importantly, it establishes a framework that permits historians to move beyond the cultural distinctions, exclusive identities, local knowledge, and experiences of individual societies (most of them in fact national communities) that have been the principal concerns of professional historical scholarship from Leopold von Ranke to the present. This framework provides a context for a properly historical analysis to complement analyses of large-scale processes that economists, sociologists, anthropologists, and others have offered from different disciplinary perspectives. It also facilitates the construction of alternatives to the received Eurocentric visions of world history. The postmodern and post-

30 From the vast literature dealing with industrialization, here I cite only a few works that clearly place industrialization in a larger global context, and do so from very different perspectives: Immanuel Wallerstein, *The Modern World-System*, 3 vols. to date (New York, 1974–); E. L. Jones, *The European Miracle: Environments, Economies and Geopolitics in the History of Europe and Asia* (2nd edn; Cambridge, 1987); Andre Gunder Frank, *ReORIENT: Global Economy in the Asian Age* (Berkeley, 1998); and Kenneth Pomeranz, *The Great Divergence: China, Europe, and the Making of the Modern World Economy* (Princeton, 2000).

colonial strategy of going local is not the only way—and indeed may not even be a particularly good way—to move beyond Eurocentrism. Genuinely global and comparative analyses are also necessary and perhaps more effective correctives to Eurocentric mythologies.[31]

As I see it, then, the understanding of world history sketched here is not a triumphalist vision celebrating progress in general or contemporary global capitalism in particular. All too often rising population, expanding technological capacity, and increasing cross-cultural interaction have exacted a high price in the coin of human suffering and environmental pressures that may well prove to be unsustainable over a long term. Nor is this view of world history a teleological model like those deriving from the Enlightenment. It leaves the end of history open and recognizes the capacities of human actors to organize their societies and conduct relations with others in unpredictable ways. Nor again is it a totalizing device that forces inappropriate standards on individual societies. It holds that barring demographic or technological collapse, some level of cross-cultural interaction is inevitable rather than optional, but it recognizes that different peoples and societies have followed very different historical trajectories and have participated in global processes in very different ways because they determine or at least influence the terms on which they interact with others.

Rather than a triumphalist or teleological or totalizing conception, this view of world history might serve best as a framing device offering one way—out of many that are no doubt conceivable—to contextualize the experiences of most if not all human societies. It does not by any means represent the only useful approach to the past: different and more fine-grained visions will be more appropriate for purposes of understanding many historical problems, including the historical experiences of individual peoples and societies. But it offers several advantages for efforts to understand large-scale historical processes. It avoids ethnocentrisms and essentialisms by recognizing that from palaeolithic times to the present, the world's peoples have participated in cross-cultural interactions that have profoundly influ-

[31] For spirited efforts along this line see Frank, *ReORIENT*; Pomeranz, *The Great Divergence*; and Timothy Brook and Gregory Blue (eds.), *China and Historical Capitalism: Genealogies of Sinological Knowledge* (Cambridge, 1999).

enced the development of their societies. It registers a clear improvement over invidious or tendentious alternatives that view some regions as sites of dynamism and progress, while regarding others as sinks of stagnation and regression. It offers a perspective on the course of global historical development, seeking to understand how the earth's peoples have interacted with one another to fashion a world that transcends individual societies. In doing so it acknowledges the roles of all peoples in the making of a world inhabited by all. For these reasons it might have some value as an alternative to Enlightenment and other Eurocentric grand narratives as well as their postmodern and postcolonial inversions.

3

The Deconstruction of Myths and Reconstruction of Metanarratives in Global Histories of Material Progress

PATRICK KARL O'BRIEN

I. *Smith, Marx, and Weber*

Along with histories of hegemony and power, histories of material life and economic growth are the most popular of metanarratives currently published in the growing field of global history. Indeed, no surprise will be occasioned by the appearance in our times, marked by 'globalization', of histories seeking to encompass a 'world economy', dealing with chronologies going back millennia and written to expound upon the disparate levels of material progress achieved by tribes, societies, communities, and national economies located on all continents. Such concerns continue to be the litmus test of the mission of global economic history to keep 'humanity in view'. After all, most people, in most places for most of history have been preoccupied with obtaining food, shelter, clothing, and other manufactured artefacts that they required to sustain either a basic, a comfortable, and, only latterly, an agreeable standard of living.

Traditions of historical enquiry into the wealth and poverty of nations began with Herodotus but modern paradigms for investigation need be traced no further back than to the towering intellects of two cosmopolitan, but perhaps equally 'Eurocentric' Germans: Karl Marx and Max Weber. Both scholars maintained a serious interest (admittedly as a counterpoise to Europe) in the evolution of the Indian, Chinese, American, and Russian economies, although Weber's investigations into Oriental religions, philosophies, cities, and states look far more serious than anything written by Marx or Engels.

The vocabularies and concepts borrowed by generations of historians from the corpus of writings left by Marx and Weber can no longer be presented as coherent theory. Nevertheless, it is still useful—when trying to understand material progress and relative decline across continents over long spans of time—to distinguish Marxian from Weberian approaches. The former has classically been concerned to investigate the potential for material progress embodied in distinctive 'modes of production' observed for different parts of the world, while the Weberian 'research programme' can be divided into two major strands of enquiry: first, a comparison of hegemonic systems of belief, operating to promote or constrain personal and group behaviour in economic life; and secondly, an empirical analysis of the political, legal, and institutional frameworks within which economic activity has operated historically around the world.

In classical Marxian thought, the only mode of production capable of generating sustained material progress, 'capitalism', is based upon wage labour and the accumulation of capital. Marx found that the first transition from pre-capitalist to capital modes of production occurred in Western Europe. Thereafter global historians (working within a Marxian tradition) have addressed his question of when and why the transition occurred there before considering the obverse question: what sorts of 'pre-capitalist' modes of production prevailed throughout Africa, Asia, and the Amerindian Americas that delayed or arrested comparable transitions to capitalism upon other continents?

Recently a 'deviant' (or supplementary) Marxian paradigm has been elaborated in an impressive volume of research conducted by the World Systems School of Historical Sociology. This 'School' maintains that the transition to capitalism (or commercial society) that led eventually to the establishment of successful industrial market economies occurred first in Western Europe because Europeans reaped timely and decisive gains from intercontinental trade and the colonization of the Americas for some three or more centuries before the onset of the French and Industrial Revolutions. Europe's economic benefits from participation in *intercontinental* commerce and imperialism are broadly conceived to encompass positive externalities as well as a range of favourable political, institutional, and cultural feedbacks and spin-offs connected to ever increasing flows of commodities shipped into European ports from all over the world, and especially from across the Atlantic.

Unsurprisingly, the World System School's emphasis upon the extension of markets for European exports to Asia, Africa, and the Americas, and, above all, its insistence on the pervasive significance of imports (embodying productive knowledge) from other continents has been contested. Classical Marxist scholars defend canonical texts concerned with progressive and non-progressive modes of production and thereby implicitly join forces with neo-classical economic historians who continue to regard the particularities of Europe's own history as the motor of its earlier transition to capitalism or commercial society. Parenthetically, and for this particular debate, neither of these representations, nor that other unresolvable discussion about continuous versus discontinuous transformations from one kind of traditional economic system to another, and ultimately more progressive, system seem to matter. What is now at issue is to specify and measure the significance of endogenous compared to exogenous forces promoting economic growth in one part of the world economy (Europe) and restraining a similar momentum on the continents of Asia, Africa, and Southern America.

Unfortunately, Marxian scholarship concerned with Asiatic modes of production and with the presence, or absence, of peculiar forms of 'feudalism' found outside Europe now looks more theoretical than historical. Furthermore, and perhaps because the tradition was ostracized and ossified during the Cold War, classical Marxism seems less influential than its Weberian counterpart in establishing the parameters, structure, and vocabulary of a discourse concerned with 'restraints' which for several centuries operated to prevent Asiatic economies from following *the* 'European trajectory' which was leading towards divergent standards of living between the West and the Rest that became conspicuous over the course of the nineteenth and twentieth centuries. Unfortunately, the *ad hoc* comments made by Marx on Asian societies are now regarded as little more than typical Eurocentric speculations of his time, which led generations of his followers down a blind alley in search of supposedly ubiquitous and unchanging Asiatic modes of production.

Max Weber's erudition is more impressive. His approach, questions, and topics for investigation have effectively set the parameters for the construction of global histories of material progress written in recent decades. He dealt with long spans of time, read widely about classical and Oriental civilizations, and used comparative methods in order to comprehend why capitalism arose in the West and not in the East. Reading, as he did, over chronologies covering millennia, he recognized that the economies of India and China displayed impressive scientific and technical precocity. Weber appreciated that Arabs and Asians had established sophisticated systems and efficient institutions for the conduct of internal and overseas trade long before European ships and merchants began to sail regularly into and around the Indian Ocean and China Seas during the sixteenth and seventeenth centuries.

Weber remained less impressed than Adam Smith and Karl Marx with the economic significance for European development of the discovery and colonization of the Americas. He was not inclined to rank the gains from transatlantic trade and colonization above endogenous forces, operating over centuries of history to promote economic growth within Europe. Along with Marx, Weber retained an appreciation of how and why the accumulation of capital and the evolution of slavery, through feudal to free markets for labour mattered as 'proximate' determinants of material progress in Western Europe.

For scholars, concerned to include an analysis of intra- and intercontinental trade in metanarratives about the long-run history of material progress, Weber elaborated upon themes that have exercised a powerful impact on modern stories told about the economic success of the West and the relative failures of the East over the past millennium. Along with Montesquieu and other thinkers of the Enlightenment, Weber and Weberians believe that discernible contrasts in the institutional, ideological, and legal frameworks within which economic activities, including trade, were embedded in Europe compared to Asia had prevailed for several centuries and that marked differences in religious beliefs, cultural conditioning, family life, and political systems promoted divergent paths of economic growth that eventually produced a clear divide within the world economy into affluent and poor nations.

II. *The New Global History of 'Surprising Resemblances'*

In recent decades, a modern generation of economic historians has carried forward the Weberian tradition of attempts to reconfigure the now highly visible economic achievements of Western societies in a global perspective. Weber left them with an approach, a vocabulary, and several suggestive hypotheses that have been modified and rejected by two generations of post-war and postcolonial research. There are now libraries of books and articles dealing with 'Eastern' agricultures, industries, towns, commercial networks, communications, trade, science, technologies, cultures, business organization, taxation, state systems, government policies, and economic cosmologies covering the last millennium and written in large part by historians from universities not long emancipated from imperial rule. This impressive but still far from comprehensive volume of historical research has, moreover, been communicated to the West by specialists in area studies from North American, European, Australian, and Japanese universities. Not long after the Second World War and during the era of decolonization, historians were offered an opportunity—provided by the accumulation of a large and sophisticated body of knowledge long available about Europe and North America but emerging on Asia, the Middle East, Africa, and Latin America—to re-position their hitherto disconnected histories of wealth and poverty one against another in order to construct global histories of material progress that might have satisfied the aspirations of Montesquieu, Voltaire, Smith and their 'enlightened' followers, and pleased Max Weber.

Clearly, and as a prelude to analysis and explanation, it will be necessary to date that divergence in living standards between the western and eastern ends of the Eurasian landmass because the assumption that unmistakable gaps in real incomes per capita and labour productivities (measured for the decade preceding the Great War) must have prevailed for centuries prior to that time cannot be supported with hard economic data. Indeed, recent historical research on Asia has produced some partial, regionally specific and still inconclusive evidence to suggest that standards of living in Western Europe and *maritime* provinces of China and South India may not have differed perceptibly much before the late eighteenth century.

That contestable suggestion has led global historians, labelled as 'Eurocentric' by their opponents, to fall back upon unquantified 'Weberian' (and 'Marxist') assertions that the economies of 'North-Western' Europe were surely on potentially more promising trajectories for early transitions to efficient industrial market economies for 'several' centuries before even the most developed regions of Asia. Europe's cultures, political systems, property rights, legal frameworks, regimes for the discovery and diffusion of reliable knowledge, commercial and financial organizations, trading networks, markets for commodities, labour and capital are conventionally represented as being altogether more likely than anything discernible in Asian systems of production to have generated preconditions for factories, mechanized industry, and steampower, transportation by land and sea; for the generation of inanimate forms of energy; for the mechanization and reorganization of agriculture, manufacturing, and commerce into concentrated locations and functional firms.

More than three decades ago, Marshal Hodgson (one of the godfathers of modern global history) opined that 'all attempts to invoke pre-modern seminal traits in the Occident to account for the divergence in living standards can be shown to fail under close historical analysis'. Two generations of postcolonial research on India, China, and South-East Asia (synthesized in the recent writings of Fernand Braudel, Kirty Chaudhuri, Gunder Frank, Jack Goody, Ken Pomeranz, Kaoru Sugihara, and David Washbrook) concur. From his own impressive and detailed comparisons of levels and types of economic development achieved by European and Asian economies during the early modern period, Braudel inferred that 'the populated regions of the world faced with demands of numbers seem to us to be quite close to each other'. But there is, he observed, 'a historiographical inequality between Europe and the rest of the world. Europe invented historians and made good use of them. Her own history is well lit and can be called as evidence or used as claim. The history of non-Europe is still being written. And until the balance of knowledge and interpretation has been restored, the historian will be reluctant to cut the Gordian knot of world history.' One distinguished historian of Europe, David

Landes, displays no such reluctance and his celebrated book, *The Wealth and Poverty of Nations*, elaborates over some 600-odd pages on a 'historical record' of 'Weberian' preconditions which he claims demonstrates why 'for the last thousand years Europe (the West) has been the prime mover of development and modernity'.

Modern historical research has, however, virtually 'degraded' (or at least severely qualified) repetitions of Marxist and Weberian assertions that the political, institutional, and cultural frameworks within which economic activities in Asia were embedded for centuries before the Industrial Revolution differed from Europe in ways that clearly and *significantly impeded* the evolution and integration of commodity and factor markets, the development of financial intermediation, the spread of private property rights, the operations of mercantile networks, proto-industrialization, and, above all, commercialization within agriculture. What recent but different syntheses of whole libraries of historical research on the economies of Asia (as well as Europe) observe and document are not only a range of advanced and less developed regions across Western Europe, but also a 'world of surprising resemblances' across Eurasia. Surveys of monographic literature have effectively rendered a whole corpus of Marxian and Weberian interpretations redundant. It can no longer be taken for granted that for centuries before the Industrial Revolution, European economies experienced virtually exceptional transitions to capitalism; evolved discernibly more efficient legal, behavioural, institutional, and political frameworks for the formation, integration, and operation of markets, and thereby allowed for progress (albeit at a slow rate and with limited help from new technologies) down a path prescribed for in models of Smithian growth. Furthermore, historians of pre-industrial Asia have also located and analysed 'cultures' that encouraged industrious and ambitious households to transform their extra earnings into displays of possessions and luxuries. Their work reveals that, contrary to the expectations of Werner Sombart (and his modern European followers), common attributes of material life appeared in too many cities, towns, and villages across the Eurasian landmass for anyone to single out the 'rise of material culture' as something peculiar to the 'acquisitive' households of Western Europe.

Before the era of liberal capitalism, 1856–1914, states everywhere placed impediments in the path of Smithian growth; but that endlessly repeated (endemic but always implausible) notion that dynastic and territorial rivalries among European states consistently provided more favourable (less unfavourable) conditions for the spread and integration of markets during the early modern era of mercantilism and warfare has also been undermined. More simplistic versions of that hypothesis conflate virtuous circles and cycles for development flowing from 'competition' with the destructive violence and rivalries of early modern European power politics. Furthermore, notions (that have been floating around since Montesquieu) that the emperors and bureaucracies of despotic eastern empires ruled over the economies (and ergo their fiscal bases) in irrational ways that can be represented as more predatory, arbitrary, and consistently and peculiarly malign towards Smithian growth now look increasingly obsolete as historical scholarship.

In the recently reconstructed economic histories of a 'world of surprising resemblances', canonical accounts of Smithian growth—of European economies growing up gradually but inexorably on distinctive trajectories within their restricted and relatively underdeveloped promontory of Eurasia—look untenable simply because too many of Hodgson's 'seminal' traits of the Occident turn out to be not only ubiquitous, but prior features of the Orient. Perhaps such Weberian (and/or Marxian) perceptions will be revived and underpinned by more research and debate. Future research (or even a renewed search among extant histories) might *delineate* and perhaps measure unmistakable/incontestible differences in the scale, scope, and intensity of Smithian growth across time and space. Meanwhile, and as recent reconfigurations of Asian economic history become known and acceptable, and debate moves on from the realm of acrimony towards conversation, we may well witness a revival of more nuanced and carefully specified long-run historical explanations for divergencies in productivity and living standards between East and West that historians have long agreed became unmistakable over the nineteenth, and stark during the twentieth century.

III. *Europe Strikes Back*

Meanwhile to suggest (as anti-Weberian revisionists do) that an unexpected and unpredictable conjuncture between East and West appeared quite suddenly in the late eighteenth century also remains fragile as a core hypothesis about long-run global economic development. That is so because revisionism offers three contested explanations for both the 'late' and the 'great divergence', and to each there are counter-arguments.

The first contention is that in different ways, for different reasons, and along different chronologies, imperial governmental structures in the Orient became increasingly inefficient and incapable of providing their subject populations and territories with the good order, protection against external aggression, and other public goods required to maintain satisfactory levels of private economic activity, market integration, and innovation. In short, strategic and administrative defects afflicting the Safavid, Ottoman, Mughal, and Ming-Qing Empires intensified through time and thereby made space for the rise of the West. Investigations into the nature, extent, and significance of the political crises clearly affecting all three Oriental empires in the eighteenth century and China by 1800 continue, and may well lead to the kind of insights now coming on stream from comparative histories of early modern European states, concerned to contrast the evolution of political arrangements and policies conducive or obstructive towards economic growth and innovation within Western Europe. This debate about the constitution of government and behaviour of states will only be taken forward by historians who know something about the foundation and evolution of political and other subordinate institutions, their diverse forms, and the precise ways they interconnected with the economic activities of households, farms, and firms not only in early modern Europe, but in Asia as well. As the literature now stands, repetition of recycled Enlightenment equations between republicanism, liberty, and parliamentary forms of governance on the one hand, and transitions to industrial market economies on the other, seem less and less satisfactory. Furthermore, the import of elastic theory, vacuous vocabularies, and opaque taxonomies from neo-institutional economics adds very little to the comprehension to be derived from careful study, and proper historical investigations into specific political, legal, and institutional frameworks for national, regional, and sectoral rates and patterns of economic growth across Eurasia.

Secondly, and at the heart of the key revisionist explanation for divergence between East Asia and Western Europe, is a quintessentially classical growth story which is based upon an impressive array of historical scholarship investigating connections and mechanisms derived ultimately from the writings of Smith, Malthus, and Ricardo. For example, Pomeranz represents cultivable land as a relatively fixed factor of production and suggests that additions to the stocks of useful and reliable knowledge allowed only for incremental and limited technological progress. Upswings in population growth led (only *in extremis* and in some regions) to Malthusian crises, but more commonly both in Western Europe and in the Ming-Qing Empire to constricting shortages of land-intensive crops and agrarian raw materials, including basic foodstuffs, timber utilized for manufacturing and construction, wood converted into fuel and energy for both industrial and domestic purposes, and fibres derived from plants and animals for purposes of transformation into textiles.

Over some two or more centuries, before 1750, when population growth rates in Europe and China advanced at comparable rates, the Chinese economy coped with the 'pressure of numbers' basically by intensifying labour in order to relieve shortages of food and agrarian raw materials. For Pomeranz and other scholars (who reject Eurocentric explanations for the great divergence cast in terms of Smithian growth), the problem is to explain how and why European economies did not proceed down the same path as China, but instead avoided diminishing returns to labour engaged in agricultures and proto-industries and gradually diffused mechanized techniques of production across manufacturing and transportation. Pomeranz re-posed a key question very cogently. 'Why', he enquired, 'did England's economy not continue to develop like the economy of the Yangzi Delta?' In other words, modern revisionism insists, as Marc Bloch advised long ago, on carefully specified and *reciprocal* comparisons.

The answers offered by Pomeranz are carefully supported with a reflexive reading of modern scholarship, and refer to contrasts between endogenous and exogenous potential for the avoidance of diminishing returns to land and other natural resources available to China and to Europe. After millennia of successful land management, Chinese agriculture stood closer to its production possibility boundary than European agriculture. Possibilities for coping with population pressures by extensions to margins of cultivation and cropping, through tenurial reform, investments in the infrastructure for intra-regional trade and specialization, by re-allocating pasture to arable, improving the control of water supplies, implementing efficient food stabilization policies, etc. had already been carried further in China than Europe.

Europe not only enjoyed some discernible (alas, unmeasurable) opportunities for taking up 'slack' within the agrarian system, but the potential gains from trade and specialization in foodstuffs and raw materials within northern and southern, eastern and western parts of our continent remained greater than the long-exploited patterns of intra-regional trade within the Chinese Empire. Indeed (and as demographic pressures intensified over the eighteenth century), the potential for trade diminished because, unfortunately, rates of population increase became faster among China's poorer, less urbanized provinces of primary production. The empire's northern and inland regions then adjusted by re-allocating surplus agricultural labour into proto-industry, consuming higher proportions of both the food and agrarian raw materials produced within their boundaries, and by importing less manufactured goods. Thus China's precocious Smithian growth, high levels of trade and path dependency upon a mix of labour-intensive crops (particularly rice), rendered the imperial economy more 'ecologically vulnerable' than Europe to population pressures when they intensified over the century before the Industrial Revolution.

Nevertheless, revisionists insist (and have adduced a not entirely sufficient or convincing body of evidence to support their view) that Britain and other European economies were also on a similar trajectory of diminishing returns and rising costs for the production of food, fuel, and fibres, but the West *postponed* the onset of more severe ecological problems and shortages during the early phases of industrialization in the eighteenth century and *circumvented* them over the nineteenth century by exploiting two 'windfalls' of massive significance, namely, endowments of cheap and accessible energy in the form of coal, and the fecund soils and abundant natural resources of the Americas. In bringing to the foreground the contribution of the Americas, revisionists have in effect returned the attention of historians to exogenous (overseas) sources of Western Europe's economic advance, underlined by Adam Smith and Karl Marx and reified in recent decades into a *primus mobile* by Wallerstein, Chase-Dunn, Blaut, Frank, Gills, and others in the World Systems School of Historical Sociology.

But Wrigley and an earlier generation of British economic historians had already explored the profound significance and widespread ramifications of endowments of cheap fossil fuels in allowing Britain to escape (before the rest of Europe) from potential 'Malthusian traps'. Although precise calculations are difficult to make and several figures (including revised estimates from Pomeranz) jostle for recognition, the tradition of energy accountancy as a way of explaining increasing and decreasing returns goes back to the nineteenth century. And it is not difficult to accept that school's major conclusions, namely, that the substitution of coal and steam power to provide for the heat supplied to Britain (and other European economies) by oxen, horses, wood, and manpower for various benchmark decades after the Napoleonic Wars would (counterfactually) have absorbed ever-increasing and implausibly large shares of Europe's virtually fixed supplies of agricultural land. Furthermore, all forms of heat and energy-intensive industry and transportation (metallurgy, glass, pottery, beer, sugar and salt, refining soap, starch, railways, and ships) benefited from the substitution of coal for other more costly and less efficient organic forms of energy. Feedbacks and spin-offs from the mining, transportation, and utilization of coal, including the construction of canals, precision engineering, and, above all, the impetus provided by coal for the development, improvement, and diffusion of engines for the provision of energy from steam, remain impossible to calculate. They became central for Europe's aptly named 'age of steam'. Yet that age (1846–1914) remained imminent rather than dominant during the first stages of the Industrial Revolution, which occurred decades before that particular golden age of liberal capitalism.

Furthermore (and to revert to Bloch's reciprocal mode of comparative history), the question of why China failed to exploit its known and very considerable deposits of coal, and thus become more like England, Belgium, and Westphalia, is, perhaps, not pursued in the depth that such a salient contrast demands. Chinese coal may well have been more combustible and less well located than European deposits, but it stayed below ground as an abundant and presumably as a potentially more efficient source of energy, compared to the manpower, wind, and water that the Chinese, Japanese, and other Asian economies continued to utilize throughout the nineteenth century. References to geology, geography, and transportation problems do not seem to be sufficient to explain why China remained virtually an outsider throughout the age of steam.

Finally, to return to Adam Smith and overseas expansion, Europeans (not Chinese, Arabs, or Indians) discovered, conquered, infected, plundered, colonized, and eventually established mutually beneficial, commercial relationships with the Americas. That protracted enterprise should not be designated as 'peripheral', nor reified (as it continues to be in the writings of Immanuel Wallerstein, James Blaut, and the World Systems School of Historical Sociology) as the 'motor' driving Europe's benign transformation towards successful industrial market economies over the course of the nineteenth century.

Material benefits from the rediscovery of the Americas did not come on stream for a long time after 1492, and accrued disproportionately to two latecomers and free riders—the Netherlands and England. No doubt quantitative exercises in national accountancy designed to measure the macro-economic significance of transatlantic commerce for either the development of Europe as a whole, or even for particular countries such as the Netherlands or Britain, most persistently and profitably involved with expansion overseas, are fraught with conceptual and statistical difficulties. No economic historian could deny that the establishment of colonies regulated along mercantilist lines together with slave plantations in the New World turned the terms and conditions for transatlantic trade in favour of Europe; compared, that is, to commerce with Asia and certainly to a counter-factual scenario, whereby the settlement and the build-up of viable and independent economies in the Americas depended upon unregulated but unprotected private investment and the immigration of free labour from Europe rather than the enslavement of Africans. Furthermore, recent research into world trade in bullion has clarified the importance of the complex and multifaceted role played by Chinese, Indian, and South-East Asian demand for New World silver in maintaining the profitability and momentum of European investment in the Americas for some two centuries before the Industrial Revolution. That investment also promoted an entirely gradual movement towards the integration and growth of an embryonic global economy, within which the separated maritime towns and regions of Europe, Africa, Asia, and the Americas interacted—usually with positive effects for both European and Asian development.

Nevertheless, a national accounts framework continues to be the only viable perspective available to historians who wish to specify and quantify the overall significance of variables such as intercontinental exports and imports for national (and European-wide) rates of capital formation and structural change and innovation from 1492 to 1815. If, as Paul Bairoch's imperfect and badly referenced data suggest, European exports to other continents and imports from the Americas, Asia, and Africa are but 'small' percentages of the total value of European output, then inferences that either the Americas (or the non-European world as a whole) continued, as late as the end of the eighteenth century, to play a comparably minor role for the advance of the West could only be meaningfully challenged in two ways. First (and this logic could be compelling), in early modern Europe, economic growth took place at specific margins and *if* a large share of the annual *increment* to total European or to particular national products can be connected directly or indirectly to intercontinental commerce, then that over-publicized and glamorous subsector of several maritime economies might indeed be plausibly represented as 'highly significant' for the continent's economic advance. Quantitative tests could then relate the gains from intercontinental trade to 'net' capital formation and to aggregated volumes of potentially 'tradable outputs' in order to manufacture ratios that are more relevant for locating, dating, and comprehending the sources of economic growth from, say, 1500 to 1800. Revisionists, who take their perceptions from

Adam Smith, will prefer to shift the focus for concentration to Britain, which over time became more involved than any other European economy with intercontinental commerce and colonization. That is all too understandable, simply because the 'ratios of significance' for a quintessentially 'British' Industrial Revolution (diffused as traditional and contested stories would have us believe with lags on to the mainland) will become that much larger and rhetorically more persuasive as numbers designed to represent the importance of the Americas for Europe's transition to modern industrial economies.

Another route that can be followed in order to make the case in a less parsimonious way, but which comes closer to the details of micro-dynamism favoured by historians like Fernand Braudel, Immanuel Wallerstein, and Ken Pomeranz, is to construct narratives built around the array of imports that Europeans transhipped from the New World and Asia back into their famous maritime ports (Lisbon, Seville, Cadiz, Antwerp, Amsterdam, Bordeaux, and London). Imports represented tangible manifestations of the 'bounty' that Europe eventually obtained from investments in commerce and colonization in the Americas and (by way of extension and linkages) to gains from trade with Asia as well. American and Asian imports included bullion, foodstuffs, manufactured goods, industrial inputs, and raw materials. Imports, obtained in very large part through the exercise of coercion designed to secure favourable terms of trade, increased in volume with the incorporation of maritime Atlantic economies into global commerce, slowly at first, but more rapidly as the infrastructure and organizations required for long-distance trade were built up over the sixteenth and seventeenth centuries. Histories of spin-offs and externalities have been woven around most of the major imports from other continents carried into European ports. Their connections to the maintenance and extension of benefits from long-established patterns of intra-European trade, to the foundation of new food processing industries, to geo-political rivalry and state formation, to the growth in the wealth and powers of merchant oligarchies, to the rise of maritime cities, to changes in science, technology, and the arts; indeed, to almost all aspects of European economic, political, and urban life, have been elaborated in numerous histories of sugar, tea, coffee, cocoa, maize, rice, tobacco, tropical fruit, tomatoes, beans, chillies, potatoes, timber hardwoods, dyestuffs, wax, fish, oils, cotton fibres; quinine, curveé sarsaparilla, pecal, laxatives; porcelain, silk and cottons, textiles, and, above all, to silver and gold. That bibliography is long. Volumes imported fluctuated but increased on trend. Points of entry and distribution for Asian and American imports changed through time from city to city and from country to country. The problem is how to connect imports from other continents to narratives (or models) of early modern European development in which national economies are carried forward to plateaux of possibilities from where transitions to industrial market economies became probable.

Fernand Braudel, Giovanni Arrighi, and Charles Kindleberger find the key mechanisms they wish to underline in a geopolitical matrix of dynamic circuits between maritime cities, big merchants, and nation-states. Pomeranz devotes his research and analysis to two possible macro-economic connections. One operates through a recently elaborated thesis about Europe's premodern 'industrious' revolution, which emanated from decisions by myriads of households to work harder and to allocate more of the labour time and other resources under their control to production for markets. Behind such decisions made by households are shifts in tastes or propensities to consume, stimulated by the availability of 'exotic' and 'addictive' foodstuffs—such as sugar, tea, coffee, cocoa, tobacco, tropical fruit, tomatoes, and spices; pharmaceuticals and luxurious but affordable Asian manufactures such as silks, cottons, jewels, and porcelain, imported from the Americas as well as the East. In brief, the rise of material culture in Europe has been linked, in carefully specified ways, to intercontinental trade and colonization, to changes in consumption and investment, and to the patterns of work by European households.

Nothing comparable occurred in Asia because the consumption of tropical groceries, porcelain, silks and cotton textiles, and other indigenous products had already diffused down the social scale. In the Orient, imperial states had virtually no fiscal or other interest in the promotion of commerce and colonization that might in the fullness of time pay for itself in the form of imported and taxable luxuries. At the same time, Chinese and Indian demands for foodstuffs and manufactures produced in

Europe remained limited in volume and scope, although the New World silver that European merchants exchanged for Asian foodstuffs, manufactures, and raw materials presumably promoted monetary transactions and internal trade in China and India in the same way that American bullion did within Europe.

Revisionists make the most of a not unconvincing case for symbiotic linkages between the luxurious, exotic, addictive, and desirable characteristics embodied in imports from Asia and the Americas to the Industrious Revolution, the maintenance of European commitments to intercontinental trade, and the enslavement of Africans and flows of investment into colonization and plantations in the New World. They cite literature which locates the impetus to development from urban processing industries (sugar refining, coffee roasting, tea and tobacco blending, etc.) in maritime cities, heavily engaged in transoceanic commerce. They are familiar with histories that explain how the manufacture of cotton textiles in Britain developed over the eighteenth century within a matrix of trade with India, the import of cotton fibres from plantations in the Americas, state involvement with its East India Company, and the promotion of a functional process of import substitution by English Parliaments from 1660 to 1721.

Nevertheless, it will be heuristic to confront this new and stimulating narrative which foregrounds the role of Asian and American imports in bringing about divergent economic developments between Western Europe and East Asia. First, the share of the calorific intake supplied by sugar, tea, and other tropical groceries could only have been small. Growing proportions of British merchant ships were indeed built in North American colonies (and in Asia) even before the French blockades cut off supplies of Baltic timber and other naval stores (pitch, tar, and hemp) during the Napoleonic Wars. Nevertheless, that established patterns of East–West and intra-European trade in timber reverted to normal after that war, and iron rather than American forests seriously alleviated European shortages of wood for construction and for shipbuilding in the nineteenth century.

A statistically more compelling case for the substitution of cotton fibres grown on slave plantations in the Americas for supplies of flax, hemp, silk, and wool grown in Europe can be made. Once again, the *scale* of imports in relation to total consumption of indigenous fibres becomes important later rather than earlier in the nineteenth century. The suggestion that supplies of cotton wool from the Americas had long been 'virtually indispensable' for the development of mechanized cotton textile production in Europe is not convincing because an equally plausible counterfactual scenario can be formulated to suggest that the accumulating and steadily improving capacity to produce mechanized cotton yarn and cloth first in Britain, and then elsewhere on the Continent, would have stimulated other primary producers in Asia (even China) and the Middle East to respond to European demand for cotton fibres.

New economic history consigned axioms of indispensability to the realms of improbability more than three decades ago. Yet there is certainly a more nuanced but less dramatic argument to be made for the importance of supplies of slave-produced cotton fibres, namely that cheap raw materials promoted the growth of one major manufacturing industry in Europe and that the engineering problems involved in the mechanization of spinning and weaving cloth were more easily solved with fibres with the tensile properties of cotton than thrown silk (not so clear!), wool, flax, and hemp. Nevertheless, in rather short compass the problems of mechanizing all major processes in the production of cloth made from the entire range of natural fibres were solved. By then supplies of cheap flax from Russia and wool from Australia, Argentina, and other primary producers come on stream to supply Europe's textile industries with all the fibres that they could process mechanically.

IV. *Divergence and Convergence*

The problem of 'the Great Divergence' between Western Europe and East Asia is important for historians to address because it is still with us. We can agree that the early shift from organic to inorganic forms of energy provided Europe (particularly Britain) with an early start. Nevertheless, and for several reasons, the other leg of the revisionist explanation (which follows the line taken by Adam Smith, Karl Marx, and the

World Systems School) that the discovery, conquest, and exploitation of the Americas also generated comparably large windfall gains and allowed Western Europe to circumvent the problems of diminishing returns afflicting Oriental empires carries far less conviction.

First of all, classical diminishing returns to land seem less applicable to India and South-East Asia than to China. Furthermore, the convergence of Japan (despite a poor endowment of natural resources) undermines histories based on classical growth models. Secondly, and on any recasting and reconfiguration of the data now available to measure the significance of intercontinental commerce, standard exercises in national income accountancy are unlikely to provide persuasively large ratios. Meanwhile the now fashionable postmodern retort that large outcomes could flow from small changes to exogenous variables simply destroys any claims that economic history might have to precision. We might rhetorically enquire whether small outcomes could flow from large changes to endogenous variables.

Thirdly, it is not at all clear that the arable land, pastures, forests, and seas of Western Europe, together (and through trade) with its periphery to the East could not have sustained the rates of population growth, industrialization, and urbanization experienced, say, down to the mid-nineteenth century without massive imports of primary produce from the Americas. To hark back to the central point of Mark Elvin's classic book, was it not the case that China had exhausted more of the potential gains from intra-regional trade, intensification of labour inputs, and agrarian improvements well before the growth of its population accelerated in the eighteenth century? Elvin's thesis can, moreover, be reformulated in the language of classical economics. Compared to Western Europe, just how far were China (and other regions of Asia) away from their (technologically constrained) production possibility boundaries before 1750? Classical economists (Smith and Malthus) both perceived that China had proceeded further and had continued to move faster down the path of diminishing returns.

Leaving coal aside, the intercontinental trade data suggest that Europe possessed the foodstuffs and agricultural raw materials required to persist with Smithian growth and the urbanization and industrialization of the workforce without recourse to massive imports of primary produce from the Americas until well into the nineteenth century. Meanwhile, the accumulation, testing, and application of a body of reliable knowledge required to carry the mechanization and transformation of industry and transport, the deployment of steam power, urbanization, and reorganization of finance and commerce had proceeded a long way and perhaps beyond a point of no return—or what historians of China refer to as involution.

This observation, which is concerned with the unavoidable and important demarcation of relevant chronologies, is intended to underline a distinction that has perhaps not been made clearly enough throughout the modern debate about interconnections between 'The Industrial Revolution' and 'The Great Divergence'. The Industrial Revolution owed something—but probably not a lot—to the incorporation of the Americas into global commerce. That remains clear if we look again at the volume and array of imports entering European ports before 1846. On the whole (and with the conspicuous exceptions of maize, potatoes, and cotton fibres) imports merely 'supplemented' supplies of the Continent's own basic foodstuffs and raw materials. The cargoes carried by ships into European ports were dominated for centuries by tropical groceries and manufactured luxuries. At most they embodied attributes that scholars (who 'represent' the 'rise of material culture', 'industrious revolutions', and the multifaceted role of grand merchants engaged in oceanic commerce as 'preconditions' for Western Europe's early industrialization) find appealing to place at the centre of their narratives about the origins of the North–South divide.

Agreed the Great Divergence and the Industrial Revolution form part of an interconnected narrative, and that the degree of divergence in labour productivities and real incomes between Europe and China which had so clearly appeared by 1914 looks inconceivable without the massive supplies of basic foodstuffs and raw materials imported from the Americas and other primary producers. But since those supplies came on stream over the second half of the century, questions of what started and what sustained the Industrial Revolution should not be conflated.

In most of its essentials, the Industrial Revolution which

demarcates the beginnings of divergence had appeared several decades earlier. During its early stages tenuous and not highly significant connections can be constructed between intercontinental commerce on the one hand and the substitution of coal-based forms of heat and power for traditional forms of energy derived from wood, wind, water, animals, and human muscles on the other. Some elements of early and gradual mechanization of industrial processes (particularly for textiles) can be linked to trans-oceanic trade, but again the connections still seem more tangential than central. There are missing elements in current explanations for divergence which would be concerned with 'regimes' for the production and diffusion of useful and reliable knowledge in Europe and China. Technology really mattered for the Industrial Revolution and *if* the English and follower economies on the mainland might well (but for coal and close involvement with the Americas) have gone the way of the Yangzi Delta, then why has even that commercialized and advanced region of the Manchu Empire taken such a long time to regain the economic rank and status it held in the world economy in the mid-eighteenth century?

SELECT BIBLIOGRAPHY OF SECONDARY SOURCES

ALDCROFT, DEREK H. and SUTCLIFFE, ANTONY, (eds.), *Europe in the International Economy 1500–2000* (Cheltenham, 1999).

AMSDEN, ALICE H., *The Rise of the Rest: Challenges to the West from Late Industrializing Economies* (Oxford, 2001).

ARNDT, HANS W., *Economic Development: The History of an Idea* (Chicago, 1987).

ARRIGHI, GIOVANNI, *The Long Twentieth Century* (London, 1994).

BAIROCH, PAUL, *Victoires et déboires: Histoire écononomique et sociale du monde du xvie siècle a nos jours*, 2 vols. (Paris, 1998).

BENDIX, REINHARD, *Max Weber: An Intellectual Portrait* (New York, 1962).

BENTLEY, JERRY, *Old World Encounters: Cross-Cultural Contacts and Exchanges in Pre-Modern Times* (Oxford, 1993).

BLACKBURN, ROBIN, *The Making of New World Slavery* (London, 1997).

BLAUT, JAMES, *The Colonizers Model of the World* (New York, 1993).

——*Eight Eurocentric Historians* (New York, 2000).

BRAUDEL, FERNAND, *Civilization and Capitalism: 15th to 18th Century*, 3 vols. (London, 1984).

BROOK, TIM and BLUE, GEOFFREY, (eds.), *China and Modern Capitalism* (Cambridge, 1999).

CAIN, PETER and HARRISON, MARK, (eds.), *Imperialism: Critical Concepts in Historical Studies*, 3 vols. (London, 2001).

CHASE-DUNN, CHRISTOPHER and HALL, THOMAS, *Rise and Demise: Comparing World Systems* (London, 1997).

CHAUDHURI, KIRTI N., *Asia before Europe* (Cambridge, 1990).

COSTELLO, P., *World Historians and their Goals* (De Kalb, 1993).

CROSBY, A. W., *Ecological Imperialism: The Biological Expansion of Europe 900–1900* (Cambridge, 1986).

CROUZET, F., *A History of the European Economy 1000–2000* (Charlottesville, 2001).

CURTIN, P., *Cross Cultural Trade in World History* (Cambridge, 1984).

DENG, GANG, *Chinese Maritime Activities and Socioeconomic Development c. 2100 B.C.–1900 A.D.* (London, 1997).

——*Development Versus Stagnation: Technological Continuity and Agricultural Progress in Pre-modern China* (London, 1993).

DE VRIES, JAN, 'The Industrial Revolution and the Industrious Revolution', *Journal of Economic History*, 54 (1994), 249–70.

ELVIN, MARK, *The Pattern of the Chinese Past* (Stanford, 1973).

EPSTEIN, LARRY, *Freedom and Growth: The Rise of States and Markets in Europe 1350–1750* (London, 2000).

FLINN, MICHAEL, *The History of the British Coal Industry 1700–1830* (Oxford, 1984).

FLYNN, DENIS and GIRALDEZ, ARTURO, (eds.) *Metals and Monies in an Emerging Global Economy* (Aldershot, 1997).

FRANK, ANDRE GUNDER, *ReORIENT: Global Economy in the Asian Age* (London, 1998).

GOODY, JACK, *The East in the West* (Cambridge, 1996).

HARRIS, JOHN R., *Essays on Industry and Technology in the Eighteenth Century* (Aldershot, 1992).

HELD, DAVID *et al.*, *Global Transformations* (Oxford, 1999).

HODGSON, MARSHAL, *Rethinking World History* (Cambridge, 1993).

HOSELITZ, BERT, *Theories of Economic Growth* (New York, 1960).

JONES, ERIC, *Growth Recurring: Economic Change in World History* (Oxford, 1988).

KINDLEBERGER, CHARLES P., *World Economic Primacy 1500–1990* (Oxford, 1996).

LANDES, DAVID, *The Wealth and Poverty of Nations* (London, 1998).

LIVI-BACCI, MASSIMO, *A Concise History of World Population*, trans. Carl Ipsen (Oxford, 1992).

MACFARLANE, ALAN, *The Riddle of the Modern World: Of Liberty, Wealth and Equality* (Basingstoke, 2000).

MOKYR, JOEL, *Technological Creativity and Economic Progress* (Oxford, 1990).
NEF, JOHN U., *The Rise of the British Coal Industry* (London, 1932).
NISBET, ROBERT, *History of the Idea of Progress* (London, 1980).
O'BRIEN, KAREN, *Narratives of Enlightenment* (Cambridge, 1997).
O'BRIEN, PATRICK K., 'The Britishness of the First Industrial Revolution and the British Contribution to the Industrialization of "Follower Countries" on the Mainland', *Diplomacy and Statecraft*, 7 (1997), 48–67.
——and PRADOS DE LA ESCOSURA, LEANDRO, (eds.), *The Costs and Benefits of European Imperialism from the Conquest of Ceuta (1415) to the Treaty of Lusaka (1974)*, special issue of *Revista de Historia Economica*, 1 (1998).
O'ROURKE, KEVIN and WILLIAMSON, JEFFREY, *Globalization and History* (London, 1999).
POMERANZ, KENNETH, *The Great Divergence: China, Europe and the Making of the Modern World Economy* (Princeton, 2000).
——and TOPIK, STEVEN, *The World that Trade Created* (London, 1999).
RAUDZENS, GEORGE, *Empires: Europe and Globalization, 1492–1788* (Stroud, 1999).
ROSTOW, WALT W., *Theorists of Economic Growth from David Hume to the Present* (Oxford, 1990).
SANDERSON, STEPHEN K., *Social Transformation: A General Theory of Historical Development* (Oxford, 1995).
SKOCPOL, THEDA (ed.), *Vision and Method in Historical Sociology* (Cambridge, Mass., 1984).
SMIL, V., *Energy in World History* (Boulder, 1994).
SOGNER, S. (ed.), *Making Sense of Global History* (Oslo, 2001).
SOMBART, WERNER, *Luxury and Capitalism* (Ann Arbor, 1967).
SUGIHARA, KAORU, 'The European Miracle and the East Asian Miracle. Towards a New Global History', *Osaka University Economic Review*, 12 (1996), 27–48.
SWEDBERG, RICHARD, *Max Weber and the Idea of Economic Sociology* (Princeton, 1998).
THOMPSON, WILLIAM R., *The Emergence of Global Political Economy* (London, 2000).
TRACY, JAMES (ed.), *The Political Economy of Merchant Empires* (Cambridge, 1991).
TUNZELMAN, G. NICK VON, *Steam Power and British Industrialization to 1860* (Oxford, 1978).
WALLERSTEIN, IMMANUEL, *The Modern World System*, 3 vols. (New York, 1974, 1980, and 1981).
WASHBROOK, David, 'From Comparative Sociology to Global History:

Britain and India in the Pre History of Modernity', *Journal of the Economic and Social History of the Orient*, 40 (1997), 410–43.

WEBER, MAX, *General Economic History* (New York, 1961).

WONG, ROY BIN, *China Transformed: Historical Change and the Limits of European Experience* (Ithaca, 1997).

WRIGLEY, E. ANTHONY, *Continuity, Chance and Change: The Character of the Industrial Revolution in England* (Cambridge, 1988).

ZEITLIN, IRVING M., *Ideology and the Development of Sociological Theory* (Englewood Cliffs, 1999).

4

Confounding Metaphors, Inventions of the World: What is World History For?

ARIF DIRLIK

This essay addresses a question that is crucial to a critical appreciation of the writing and teaching of world or global histories.[1] Is world history about explaining the world, and how it came to be what it is, historically, or is it, to use the felicitous term of a historian of China, about 'world-making'?[2] This question, pertinent to all history, helps distinguish a constructivist approach to the past from the historicist assumption that history is about the recovery of the truth of the past. It is especially important for world history, since the latter, in claiming as its scope the world or the globe, inevitably requires conceptualization and empirical generalization at a very high level of abstraction, and must of necessity rely on data mediated by a prolific range of particular histories. It is also important because, for these very reasons, any world historian worthy of the name must be uncommonly aware of the constructedness of the past, if only because of an awareness of the variety of world histories that have been constructed at different times and in different places. I am referring here not only to changes in the conceptualization of the world in

A slightly different version of this essay was published under the same title in the *Review of Education/Pedagogy/Cultural Studies*, 22/4 (2001), 323–67.

[1] I will use these terms interchangeably below, as it seems to me that the distinction between world and global history is a rather vacuous one that suppresses the relationship between globalization as process and globalization as outcome, which may be divorced therefore from globalization as process to be rendered into a paradigm without any grounding in the history that produced it. It should be evident from my argument below that the two are intimately related, and the advocates of globalization as paradigm have little to show in demonstrating their difference from world historians, except by ignoring history. For a plea for globalization over world history, see Bruce Mazlish and Ralph Buultjens (eds.), *Conceptualizing Global History* (Boulder, Colo., 1993).

[2] Richard J. Smith, *Chinese Maps* (Hong Kong, 1996), 64.

EuroAmerican contexts that have been described by Jerry Bentley,[3] but also to the different meanings attached to the terms 'world' and 'history' in different societal contexts.

If there is nothing transparent about a concept such as 'world history', if it indeed derives its changing meanings from different understandings of the world and of history, it raises questions that go far beyond technical questions of historiography that are usually the focus of attention among historians, such as how to organize the data of the past intelligibly without losing sight of concrete phenomena at the level of abstraction required by world history. Jerry Bentley, for example, concedes the constructedness of the past in most world histories, but goes on to offer the prospect of ever better world histories as the writing of world history becomes more professional, and past parochialisms are overcome with greater inclusiveness of other cultures and cultural perspectives in the understanding of the world.[4] In other words, the constructedness of the world is not a necessary condition of history, but a matter of past limitations that may be overcome with greater progress in historical practice. However, this focus on technical historiographical problems may distract attention from fundamental questions that are metahistorical in their implications. The latter invite the consideration that at the level of abstraction required by world and global histories (in contrast, say, to national and local histories, where closeness to the data mitigates the sense of distance), history appears nakedly as an interpretative undertaking, with all the cultural, ideological, and political burdens that such an undertaking implies.

World history, then, is inevitably about 'world-making', which leads to the second question that is of interest in this discussion. What is world history for? This is a question that we may ask of all history, and there is no reason why world history should be exempted from it, especially given the ambitious scope of its claims. We may answer the question in a number of ways that range from the simply pedagogical to the abstractly ideological. But however we may answer it, the answer needs to be

[3] Jerry H. Bentley, *Shapes of World History in Twentieth-Century Scholarship: Essays on Global and Comparative History* (Washington, DC, 1996). Bentley's very use of the word 'shapes' is indicative of his grasp of this problem.

[4] Ibid. 2–3, 21–6.

historical; it needs to account, in other words, for the different meaning and significance attached to world history in different historical contexts, not just the historiographical, but the political and cultural meaning and significance. The latter obviously also has something to do with the way world history is written or taught—its very substance, in other words, as well as the ideological functions assigned to it.

World history in our day displays an urge not only to overcome a nation-bound historiography that seems to be incapable of addressing possibly the most important phenomena of the contemporary world which transcend national and even regional boundaries, but also to do so by overcoming the Eurocentrism of past world histories. This is justified, more often than not, by reference to 'globalization', which not only characterizes a contemporary condition but also, in its paradigmatic role, casts the past in a new light. Roland Robertson states cogently this connection between a contemporary consciousness of globalization and the resurgent interest in a new kind of world history:

> On the one hand, the fact and the consciousness of rapidly increasing interdependence across the world has sharpened the concern with an understandable trajectory of the whole of humanity. On the other hand, whereas earlier writing in that vein consisted, and to some extent still consists, in variations on one 'grand narrative' depicting the rise and the 'triumph' of the West, there has been an increasing tendency for world history to be written with respect to heretofore unheard 'voices.'[5]

There is something intellectually and culturally radical about these aspirations, which may be a reason for the attraction world history exerts on historians of a culturally progressive bent.[6] On the other hand, the very idea of 'globalization' is laden with cultural and political contradictions, and how a globalization-driven world historiography accounts for such contradictions, or fails to do so, bears closer scrutiny, as do its claims,

[5] Roland Robertson, 'Globalization as a Problem', in id., *Globalization: Social Theory and Global Culture* (Thousand Oaks, Calif., 1994), 8–31, at 30.

[6] For a discussion of the idealistic motivations underlying world and global histories, and an excellent discussion of conflicts over world history within the USA, see Gilbert Allardyce, 'Toward World History: American Historians and the Coming of the World History Course', *Journal of World History*, 1/1 (1990), 23–76.

therefore, to overcome the Eurocentrism of a past historiography. At a time when political and economic élites in First World locations, especially in the USA, have endowed terms such as 'globalization' and 'multiculturalism' with the status of cultural and political slogans, there is nothing to be taken for granted in the radical claims of world history. As Raymond Grew has put it:

> Few statements today provoke so little controversy as the claim that human beings today are more in touch with their fellow beings around the world than ever before in history. The list of examples—instant communication of information, a culture of universal styles and experiences, the world-wide reach of markets and trade, the products composed of parts from several continents—has become a litany, and reference to the global village is a cliché that conference-going professors can hardly afford to challenge: 'Historians no longer have to invent the world in order to study world history.'[7]

The 'litany', we might add, is not just the doing of 'conference-going professors', but derives its power from the ideological and institutional privileging of globalization among certain sectors of US society at large. 'World historians', in turn, justify their undertaking by referring to a globalized world 'without borders' that needs a different kind of history. To quote Bentley and Ziegler:

> Our purpose in this book is to offer a global perspective on the past—a vision of history that is meaningful and appropriate for the interdependent world of contemporary times. During an era when peoples from all parts of the earth meet, mingle, interact, and do business with each other, a global perspective has become an essential tool for informed and responsible citizenship. Because global interactions profoundly influence the fortunes of peoples in all lands, it is impossible to understand the contemporary world by approaching it exclusively from the viewpoint of western Europe, the United States, Japan, or any other individual society. And it is equally impossible to understand the world's history by viewing it through the lenses of any particular society.[8]

[7] Raymond Grew, 'On the Prospect of Global History', in Mazlish and Buultjens, *Conceptualizing Global History*, 227–49, at 228. The quotation is from Michael Geyer and Charles Bright, 'For a Unified History of the World in the Twentieth Century', *Radical History Review*, 39 (Sept. 1987), 69–91.

[8] Jerry H. Bentley and Herbert F. Ziegler, *Traditions and Encounters: A Global Perspective on the Past* (Boston, Mass., 2000), p. xxvii.

Where world history once underwrote the triumph of Western Civilization, it is now to be rewritten to bear witness to the triumph of globalization. Essentially celebratory, such a statement seems to fail, in my opinion, not only to account for the complexities of the concept and processes of globalization, but also to suggest any critical awareness of the possibility that from perspectives other than those of its promoters, globalization may well appear to be a contemporary substitute for earlier paradigms of modernization—and even Westernization.[9] The ease with which the authors take globalization as something novel and unproblematic raises age-old questions concerning the relationship of history to its cultural context, which itself is inseparable from the material context, perhaps more explicitly in the present than ever before. All the more need to enquire, therefore, whether world history, for all its radical claims, represents a counterpart in the conceptualization of the past to contradictory impulses in the globalization paradigm at once to recognize the diversity of the world, and to contain it in a manner consistent with inherited premisses of political and cultural hegemony.

I. *World History and World-Making*

A fundamental problem with world history as a historical genre is an inability to define its boundaries. World history at its most transparent is about writing histories of the world as a whole, dealing with processes that involve, and have implications for, the formation of the world. Also included in world history, however, are histories of specific phenomena, events, and cultural artefacts that trace the unfolding of the latter across numbers of geographical and political boundaries. A quick perusal of a journal such as the *Journal of World History* reveals that world history may also include, at the other extreme, concrete local phenomena so long as they are accounted for in

[9] To some, it also represents an expression of US cultural imperialism. See Pierre Bourdieu and Loic Wacquant, 'The Cunning of Imperialist Reason', *Theory, Culture and Society*, 16/1 (1999), 41–58, at 42. We need hardly remind ourselves, in the wake of the WTO protests in Seattle, of the close association of globalization in many minds with corporate imperialism.

an extra-local context, or with attention to their extra-local implications and repercussions.

There is nothing wrong with bringing a global perspective or a global context to the understanding of historical phenomena, and more often than not they enable historical explanations that are broad in vision and rich in possibilities. But whether or not every historical approach that seeks to transcend local, national, or regional perspectives belongs under a genre of world or global history is highly problematic, and *prima facie* evidence of the uncertainties implicit in those terms. This essay restricts itself to world histories proper; that is, those histories that take as their scope the whole world. Such histories as they are understood by the most progressive among contemporary world historians seek to be as inclusive of the world as is humanly possible, and as even-handed in their recognition of different peoples' contributions to the history of humankind as the prevailing state of knowledge will permit. The goal here is not to question the practical or the intellectual motivations that inform world history writing, but rather to enquire into the narrative possibilities of fulfilling their intended goals.

Questions of scope and boundary remain even in the specific version of world history taken up here, which call for greater agency on the part of the historian in constructing the past, and making sense of it. In a different, and perhaps contradictory, sense, the very global scope of the undertaking places severe limitations on the ability of historians to question in any serious depth the many narratives out of which they construct the grand narrative that is world history. Moreover, to the extent that those narratives are products in the first place of an earlier tradition of world historiography, they rule out the possibility of any serious break with that tradition. To quote Bentley and Ziegler again:

> At first glance, *Traditions and Encounters* might look similar to several other books that survey the world's past. Like the others, *Traditions and Encounters* examines the historical development of societies in Asia, Europe, Africa, the Americas, and Oceania. But *Traditions and Encounters* differs from other works in two particularly important ways. First, in addition to charting the development of individual societies, it focuses attention systematically on interactions between peoples of different societies. And second, it organizes the human past into seven

eras that represent distinct and coherent periods of global historical development.[10]

While the authors stress that their account of world history differs from others, they do not tell us why *Traditions and Encounters* still 'might look similar to several other books that survey the world's past'. The periodization of the past into seven eras is questionable, though we might take note that rather than a certain mode of organizing the past, these eras to the authors 'represent distinct and coherent periods'.[11] More important in my opinion is the first claim, the systematic stress on 'interactions between peoples of different societies'. Why, with this important new emphasis, the end product should still seem similar to other surveys is worth a closer look.

Two questions seem to be especially relevant: (1) What is it that we mean when we speak of world history? (2) What are the 'units' of world or global history? The answers to these questions are obvious to the point of being trivial. Taken literally, world history is an impossibility, since no 'world' or 'global' history can aspire to cover the surfaces so implied, or all the activities and phenomena that constitute history even in the domains and areas within its coverage. The 'world' in world history is at best metaphorical, referring not so much to the world of concrete existence, but to a concept of the world through which the historian seeks to grasp the world of reality, or, less idealistically, metonymic, as the 'world' the historian uncovers stands in for a larger world of which it serves as a representation. The problem lies not with the rhetoric but in the confounding of rhetoric with reality, which in the one case erases other possible conceptions of the world and, in the other, erases alternative representations with their own claims on the realities of the world. World history, like all history, may sustain its claims only by foregrounding certain conceptions or aspects of the world and of its

[10] Ibid.

[11] The periodization here is quite similar to that adopted by another text also motivated by global concerns, Peter N. Stearns, Michael Adas, and Stuart B. Schwartz, *World Civilizations: The Global Experience* (New York, 1992). The authors of this text divide world history into six periods that are quite similar to those in Bentley and Ziegler with one exception: the 'post-Classical era' that appears as one period in the former (from the fall of the Roman Empire to the 15th century) is divided in the latter into two periods (the 'Post-Classical Era', 500–1000 CE, and an 'Age of Cross-Cultural Interaction', 1000–1500 CE).

history at the expense of other possible conceptions or aspects, in the process marginalizing and erasing the latter.

Phrased in this manner, the problem with world history appears not as a matter of whether or not we should write world history, or think of the past in world-historical terms, but the claims of a world history conceived positivistically.[12] Three such problems are worthy of special note. First is an imperial claim, based on the scope of vision or coverage, that world history offers a more comprehensive understanding of the world than histories of less ambitious breadth, which 'privilege[s] any evidence of interconnectedness, no matter how bland, over distinctiveness, no matter how creative'.[13] Underlying this problem is a question of what it is that we seek to understand about the world. Implicit in the privileging of world history is an assumption that processes of world-historical nature offer us a better understanding of the world and its becoming. What this assumption ignores, however, is that world-historical processes, in their actualization, are refracted through concrete circumstances and, if they are to be grasped in their historicity, depend for their historical significance and consequence in their processing at a multiplicity of levels, including the level of microhistory, which also have the power, therefore, to redefine and redirect those processes.

Secondly, so long as scope of historical oversight serves to privilege one kind of history over another, it follows that those world histories that claim the greatest scope may claim the greatest promise of understanding the world; in which case world history would be expected to offer a progressively more comprehensive and accurate understanding of the world, as Jerry Bentley suggests in the discussion above. As this issue almost immediately raises the issue of Eurocentrism, I will leave it aside for the moment, except to raise two qualms about it. The first concerns its implicit suggestion, for instance, that the colonizer must of necessity have a better grasp of the world than the colonized. The second, once again, concerns what we

[12] Stearns, Adas, and Schwartz, for example, acknowledge their undertaking explicitly as an 'interpretive undertaking'. They stress as the analytical distinguishing feature of their text the goal of relating 'fact to interpretation, while leaving ample room for classroom exploration. Analytical emphasis is evident in the attention to periodization, which presents strands of interpretation amid the parade of facts' (*World Civilizations*, p. xxii).

[13] Grew, 'On the Prospect of Global History', 233.

understand by the terms 'world' or 'globe'. If breadth of vision is a significant criterion, which conception of the world can claim greater breadth: one that stops with the physical world or globe, or one that incorporates the world within a cosmological scheme, a question that is not asked very often because it goes against the tenets of a positivistic historiography.[14]

Finally, along more methodological lines, a positivistic historiography that confounds its rhetorical invention of the world with the world's reality is vulnerable to the tautology of a teleological functionalism. Recognition of the inventedness of the world allows for critical reflectiveness on the cultural and ideological moments that go into the invention, and a simultaneous recognition that the connections that we establish between the past and the present are only one possible set of connections among others; that our perceptions of historical development are products also of 'forgetting' other possible paths of development that were suppressed and/or marginalized so that the present could come into existence. When the invention is substituted for reality, however, we end up once again with a pre-critical, tautological, evolutionism that can do no better than discover in history an alibi to the present. Bentley states that 'scholars increasingly recognize that, through their interactions, all the world's peoples have contributed to the making of history, and world history represents a particularly appropriate means of recognizing the contributions of all peoples to the world's common history'.[15]

Similar questions may be raised concerning the 'units', both temporal and spatial, around which world history is organized. The former refers to the periodization of world history around temporalities united by common characteristics across widely different spaces, which justify, therefore, the division of history into periods; either because comparable phenomena seem to be replicated across widely different spaces, or because of identifiable connections between different parts of the world. But the temporalities themselves are subdivided into spatial units that range in their scope from the geographical to the historical.

[14] It is raised nevertheless from alternative perspectives. For an uncompromising attack on positivistic history that also affirms alternative cosmologies, see Vine Deloria, Jr., *Red Earth, White Lies: Native Americans and the Myth of Scientific Fact* (New York, 1995).

[15] Bentley, *Shapes of World History*, 2–3.

Hence the world is divided into 'natural' units such as continents or oceans, and then into historical ones that take civilizations, cultures, or nations as the bases upon which to speak of processes that transcend these units. But are these 'units' the points of departure for, or the products of, world or global history?

'World history', as a historical project, must of necessity privilege time over space; for to do otherwise—to give priority to space over time—would necessitate a recognition of the dividedness, or even the 'splinteredness' of time, which would make history impossible. The temporality that is privileged is not just any temporality but what Fernand Braudel has described as 'a type of time experienced on a world scale: *world time*', adding that this temporality 'is not . . . and never can be the sum total of human history. This exceptional time-scale governs certain areas of the world and certain realities depending on period and place. Other areas and other realities will always escape it and lie outside it.'[16] The privileging of this temporality comes at a heavy price. On the one hand, it abolishes all local temporalities, including those of entire societies, whose realities do not fall within its realm. On the other hand, it requires the reification of spatial entities (from the natural to the historical) which serve as the units of world or global interactions. It may be a Heisenberg principle in history that you cannot disorganize time and space at the same time and still come up with a coherent account of the past. In this case, the coherence is achieved by the erasure not only of many temporalities but also the complex and shifting arrangements that characterize the spatialities that serve as the units of history.

We are all aware these days that there are no stable configurations and no essences that can define a society, and that everything is invented: from continents to oceans, from traditions, civilizations, cultures, and nations to histories. At a certain point, the inventedness of these various entities does not matter because it is arguable that once they have been invented, and have entered our consciousness of the world, they acquire at the very least a historical reality with the power to shape the world and its history. It may matter even less because the invention of

[16] Fernand Braudel, *The Perspective of the World*, vol. 3 of *Civilization and Capitalism: 15th to 18th Century*, trans. from the French by Sian Reynolds (New York, 1979), 17–18.

the world is not just an intellectual process but one that goes hand in hand with the reconstruction of the world through very material processes, be they economic, political, or technological. That the geography of the world as we know it is a product of European expansion and ordering of continents and oceans is a reminder of the historicity of geography, but no less of a fact for those, including those inhabiting the various regions of the world, who now map their own places in the world acccording to that geography. That myths and traditions are products of civilizational imaginings or nationalist historiographies, even when we may be able to pinpoint their exact historical origins, does not detract from the powerful part they play in claims to identity or claims on history. That world history as we know it, in its assumptions concerning both the world and history, is a product of a Eurocentric ordering of the world's spatialities and temporalities does not extinguish an urgency nevertheless to write world history, and to write it in ever new ways to come closer to the truth of the world.

On the other hand, mindfulness of the inventedness of all these things is crucial to any critical appraisal of the formation of the world; not just intellectually but also in understanding its processes. We know that the past has been periodized in different ways at different times and places not as a matter of empirical temporalities but more importantly as a matter of social meanings attached to different ways of conceiving time. We know that the very notion of the world is not just a matter of what we know of the world, but also a matter of judgement on what is at stake in different conceptualizations of the world.[17] Mindfulness of the historicity of our conceptions of time and space is crucial above all to a critical historiography that seeks to

[17] In other words, the world that matters. Richard Smith observes that 'traditional' maps with their mixture of empirical geography and imagined cosmologies did not go out of fashion during the Qing Dynasty in China until the 19th century, when the new geography (introduced first by the Jesuits two centuries earlier) won out in response to a new political situation. See Smith, *Chinese Maps*, 59. A similar point is made by James Romm with reference to the ancient Greeks when he states that 'we who have seen the whole earth, either as represented on maps and globes or as reproduced in satellite photographs, find it difficult to adopt the perspective of those who have not . . . the most fundamental act by which the archaic Greeks defined their world was to give it boundaries, marking a finite stretch of earth from the otherwise formless expanse surrounding it.' James S. Romm, *The Edges of the Earth in Ancient Thought* (Princeton, 1992), 1–2. Of course, it also takes enormous conceit to assume that because we have seen the globe as a whole, we have therefore acquired an omniscience concerning what it contains.

distinguish the concretely historical from history governed by teleologies.

It is remarkable then that a world historiography that seeks to overcome its legacy of Eurocentrism should persist in organizing the past around temporalities and spatialities that are very much products of a Eurocentric ordering of the world. That the teleology is no longer that of a EuroAmerican end to history, or EuroAmerican notions of historical versus non- or pre-historical societies, does not make this historiography any the less teleological. As history retains a temporal direction, this time toward 'globalization', past temporalities are reorganized according to their compliance with, or contributions to, principles of globalization; principles that derive their organizational power not from the very complex concrete temporalities of the past (or the present, for that matter), but the cultural expectations of the present, at least the cultural expectations of certain groups in the present. This also means, almost inevitably, that a history organized along such a temporal dimension requires that certain societies are better equipped to move from one temporality to the next because they have embedded in them the dynamics of change, while others do not. There would be no reason for criticism of this perspective if change were to be understood in a multi-dimensional sense; but this is not the sense in which it is understood. To the extent that the notion of change retains any kind of teleology, both materially and ethically, change (and, therefore, time) has direction, and certain spatialities indicate greater potentiality for movement toward this kind of change than others, which means that it is stilll possible to rank them hierachically for their potential for progress. For all its claims to break with the past, contemporary 'world history' bears upon it the stamp of the past fundamentally because it cannot seem to shed either its notion of the 'world' or of 'history'.

This is equally the case with the spatial units around which world history is organized, from continental or oceanic units, to civilizations, cultures, and nations. Bentley's and Ziegler's world history looks 'similar' not just 'to several other books that survey the world's past', but to most world histories because ultimately it organizes the world according to the same geographies, physical and political, that provide the units of most world history texts. This is not very surprising because those units were products to begin with of a certain modern ordering and naming of the world's geography and politics. In other words, the text takes as the point of departure for its organization of the world and of its past, temporal and spatial units that were products of the very same history that it seeks to break with.[18] The physical locations for the history, from Africa and Europe to Asia and the Americas, are all inventions of a modern geography. So are the political or cultural units that interact with one another in the formation of world history. To take one concrete example, a China that begins in the third millennium BC and then proceeds through subsequent centuries to serve as a unit of 'cross-cultural encounters' is a China not of the third millennium BC, but a China that is projected back into the third millennium BC through modern nationalist imaginings that share a good bit in common with the legacies of Orientalism. One could extend the argument through subsequent centuries, almost all the way to the present, when it is possible to speak not of China, but of re-inventions of China; re-inventions that owed much to participation in a changing world, but also to the progressive colonization of a complex area by powers emanating from the Yellow River area in an ongoing dialectic between civilization and barbarism.

Most world history undertakings, including contemporary ones, take for granted in their organization of the world separate political or culture areas that then interact with one another to produce 'world-times' and 'world-spaces', ignoring that it is the interactions that produced the world-times and world-spaces; in some ways getting history backwards. And they presuppose for these areas the same kind of evolutionary development that they do for the world as a whole. Thus a 'China', a potential China, leads inexorably from the Xia Dynasty to the China of the present,

[18] This is not to say that geographers have done much better, as is evident in a recent study of cartography that offers a sustained critique of Eurocentrism in the mapping of the world. The authors challenge a mapping of the world in terms of continents, and offer instead a scheme that they describe as 'world regional'. Not only are the world regions superimposed upon the same old continents, they also look suspiciously like the regions of area studies. Even more revealing is the admission of the authors that 'the world regional system has some serious flaws . . . it is contaminated both by the myth of the nation-state and by geographical determinism . . . though less Eurocentric than the standard continental scheme, it still bear[s] traces of its origin within a self-centered European geographic tradition . . . where we part company from textbook geography is less in cartographic depiction than in conceptual procedure.' See Martin Lewis and Karen Wigen, *The Myth of Continents: A Critique of Metageography* (Berkeley, 1997), 186.

without the fundamental question being raised of the different worlds occupied and envisaged by the Xia and the modern Chinese, or even contemporary Chinese and their Qing Dynasty predecessors. For a society to draw upon the past to define itself in the present (any present) is neither novel nor suprising. But what enables a society to make different pasts into its own is a historical problem. When Koreans, Japanese, and Vietnamese drew upon Confucian texts in their own self-definitions, they did not think that they were drawing upon 'Chinese' texts, but Zhou Dynasty texts that were part of a common legacy of sacred texts in that area that we now call East Asia or, politically, China. *Zhongguo* itself carried a different meaning then from what it does now. There is a huge difference between 'central kingdoms' that define themselves *vis-à-vis* outlying 'barbarians', and a central kingdom that conceives of itself as a civilization or a nation.

This is obviously not just a modern or Eurocentric assumption. On the other hand, there is something Eurocentric about an evolutionary temporality that identifies a society with its origins, assuming a geographical progression if not a cultural essence. In the world of the people we call the Chinese, it was possible until late in the nineteenth century to think temporalities in alternative ways; as regressions from times past, as circularities, as change without progress, and progress. And this is speaking of temporalities at the high-élite level, without speaking of the population at large, or regional differences. These alternative temporalities have been erased by a nationalist reconstruction of the past, obsessed with the question of progress; so it is possible to say that the reification of Chineseness is a product of a modern Chinese national consciousness, itself a product of a forced modernity. It is the same modernity, viewed in global perspective, that is responsible for placing 'China' in a world-historical scheme that not only erases these temporalities, but also the spatialities of a society so named. It does no less, of course, with respect to other societies, including European societies, which are presently haunted by the 'resurgence of history'[19] in the form of different localities reasserting their cultural prerogatives against official ideologies of European and/or national culture.

[19] I owe the term to Jean-Marie Guehenno, *The End of the Nation-State*, trans. Victoria Elliott (Minneapolis, 1995), p. x.

Interestingly, like the multiculturalism which is its unavoidable partner in liberal circles, globalization, and its urge to recognize the contributions to world history of diverse peoples, reinforces the reification of spaces but also cultural reification. After all, you cannot recognize a Chinese or Indian contribution to world history unless you recognize Chinese or Indians to begin with, which identifies entire pasts of a complex nature with their contemporary nationalist representations. Ironically, the most severe critics of Eurocentrism partake with seeming ease in this very product of a Eurocentric ordering of the world.

II. *The Location of Eurocentrism: Does Globalization Signal the End or the Victory of Eurocentrism?*

William McNeill, a distinguished student of 'world history',[20] and an inspirational force behind much of contemporary world historiography, has remarked recently that 'the expansion of readily available information has been spectacular, and academic historians can no longer, as they did in my youth, remain cheerfully indifferent to what happened among the four-fifths of humankind that did not inhabit Western Europe and the United States. This strikes me as an obvious advance, even at the price of cacophonous confusion.'[21] If Eurocentrism could be overcome by bringing Europe's many 'others' into history, or even by a recognition of historicity to 'peoples without history', as McNeill's statement suggests, then our times could be celebrated as heralding a new, post-Eurocentric age. It seems, at least within a US context, that all one needs to be admitted into history is to ask for it, and sometimes even that is not necessary, for it is possible to be included in history these days without even knowing it. It is possible even to challenge 'the view that American people shared a precious and unique "Western civilization" with parts of

[20] I will put this term in quotation marks below when I refer to 'world history' as an approach, in order to distinguish it from references to the history of the world. The distinction is necessary for two reasons. First, 'world history' as an approach does not necessarily cover the history of the world as a whole, which most 'world' or 'global' historians concede readily. Second, it is my opinion that much of history is world history, even when the focus may be narrow, and authors do not necessarily identify themselves with the approach so designated.

[21] William H. McNeill, 'History and the Scientific World View', *History and Theory*, 37/1 (Feb. 1998), 1–13, at 7.

Europe' on the grounds that 'the historical heritages of every people of the earth are of equal value, even if, or especially if they were mistreated by European imperialists in the recent past'.[22]

The crowding of history, and a recognition in at least some quarters that the crowds have a right to be there, not only de-centres 'Western civilization', but calls into question the temporalities of a Eurocentric conceptualization of the world, where the particular historical trajectory of EuroAmerican societies served as a teleology worldwide in marking time. It was this teleology, empowered by claims to the present as well as the future, that provided the yardstick for determining stagnation in history as well as exclusion from it. There is certainly a widespread feeling at present that since different historical heritages have equal claims on history, the future, too, is up for grabs—at least among the societies that now make their own claims to the centre. At its extreme, the criticism of a EuroAmerican teleology, in its bourgeois as well as Marxist formulations, takes the form of denying to Europe and North America a significant part in history, portraying them as unwanted intruders who managed for a brief while to hijack time, as they had colonized space.

Probably few of us would agree that any of this signals the imminent demise of Eurocentrism. We may feel more critically self-conscious, or even guiltier, than in the past about excluding others from history, and do our best to adopt world or global history perspectives that not only enable us to accommodate as many peoples and perspectives as technically possible, but help us transcend our own parochialisms; at the extreme, we may even deny to Europe (and North America) a special place in the shaping of history. And yet none of this alleviates a sense of unease that Eurocentrism persists against all efforts to overcome it. It seems often enough that the very preoccupation with Eurocentrism perpetuates it by endlessly re-turning attention to EuroAmerica. No matter how hard we try to de-centre, re-centre or ex-centre[23] history, Eurocentrism persists as a frame of reference. Critics of Eurocentrism inspired by cultural studies spend more time on what EuroAmerican writers and theorists

[22] Ibid. 6.

[23] This term is Janet Lippman Abu-Lughod's. See 'The World-System Perspective in the Construction of Economic History', *History and Theory*, 34/2 (1995), 86–98, esp. 94–5.

have had to say about the rest of the world than they do speaking of the societies at hand, which further displaces the latter from the historian's attention. Aside from area specialists who have long sought to bring the societies they study to the centre of their disciplines (with considerable irony, given the origins of area studies in a Eurocentric paradigm of the world), world or global historians are particularly prominent in our day in efforts to open history to others, and to search for explanations that eschew the centrality of EuroAmerica to historical development. As a sympathetic critic observes, however, the 'central question' of most world history writing is still 'to explain why European civilization outshone all others'.[24] Inclusion of others in history is by no means inconsistent with a Eurocentric teleology. As the same author writes:

> world history offers the framework for a continuous narrative, one that starts with the pulse of civilization beating to the rhythm of riparian agriculture along the Tigris and Euphrates, then moves through the classical world and across two millennia until Europe's power and influence extend across the globe. The civilizations not in this direct line, however much admired, are presented initially as separate stories but differ most from the main narrative in always coming to an end, each giving way to the next until all become part of the world the West has won.[25]

Beyond textbook histories, influential works by Francis Fukuyama and David Landes respectively have in recent years reaffirmed EuroAmerican political models as 'the end of history', and EuroAmerica as the dynamic force of the last millennium.[26] Landes's work, in particular, is addressed to critics of Eurocentrism, whom he lambasts as bad historians, 'Europhobes', and 'anti-intellectuals', and argues against 'multicultural, globalist, egalitarian history' to affirm the centrality of 'Western civilization and its diffusion' to historical progress over the last millennium.[27] His explicitly critical stance against anti-Eurocentrists is also an indication that Eurocentrism is not

[24] Raymond Grew, 'Paul Costello, *World Historians and Their Goals: Twentieth Century Answers to Modernism*', Review Essay, *History and Theory*, 34/4 (1995), 371–94, at 372.

[25] Ibid. 371.

[26] Francis Fukuyama, *The End of History and the Last Man* (New York, 1992), and David S. Landes, *The Wealth and Poverty of Nations: Why Some Are So Rich and Some So Poor* (New York, 1998).

[27] Landes, *The Wealth and Poverty of Nations*, 513.

merely a residue of past habits (as might be the case with world history textbooks), but continues to function as an important component of thinking about the past.

If inclusion of others in history does not in and of itself negate Eurocentrism, then neither does the repudiation of a Eurocentric teleology, as is evident in the case of Samuel Huntington's *Clash of Civilizations*, which is not a historical work *per se*, but freely draws upon history.[28] What is relevant about Huntington's argument in the present context is his disavowal of the 'West' as either the end of history, or as a model to be emulated by other 'civilizations', which retain immutable characteristics against all historical change. Under the circumstances, 'the concept of a universal civilization helps justify Western cultural dominance of other societies and the need for those societies to ape Western practises and institutions'.[29] Huntington's, too, is a 'multicultural' world but, unlike in liberal versions of multiculturalism, he views it not as a product of, but as an insurmountable obstacle to, globalization; civilizations in this view will go their separate ways in the foreseeable future. What qualifies his argument as Eurocentric is neither exclusion of other societies from history, nor their subjection to a Eurocentric teleology, but his normative evaluation of the 'West', with its unique values—from democracy to human rights—which others simply will not get.

To reiterate, Eurocentrism persists not just as a residue of the past. These various reaffirmations of Eurocentrism are as much a response to contemporary circumstances as the repudiation of Eurocentrism. There is little in this persistence of Eurocentrism that is surprising. After all, if history is important in the construction of identity, there should be nothing unexpected about the centring of history around a real or imagined identity. Much of the current discussion of history in relation to identity seeks to abolish identity by denying to it a centre, by stressing the fluidity or instability of identity, or its constructedness and inventedness; which issues in the replacement of settled with hybrid identities, and of centres by borderlands. However

[28] Samuel P. Huntington, 'The Clash of Civilizations?', *Foreign Affairs* (Summer 1992), 22–49; 'The West Unique, Not Universal', *Foreign Affairs* (Nov./Dec. 1996), 28–46; and *The Clash of Civilizations and the Remaking of World Order* (New York, 1996).

[29] Huntington, *Clash of Civilizations*, 66.

appealing this dethroning of identity may be under current circumstances (more in some societies than in others, and more for some groups in those societies), it does not, as Lewis Wurgaft argues, abolish the concern for identity *per se*.[30] In fact, one of the ironies of the current ferment over identity is its simultaneous questioning of the possibility of stable identities, and its demand for the recognition of identities suppressed in the past; which in the realm of history takes the form of demands for the recognition of the historical presence of those groups that earlier had been left out of history. Globally, the questioning of civilizational, cultural, or national identity coincides with the reaffirmation of such identities. What we seem to have at present is not the abolition of centres, but the crowding of the centre to history by proliferating claims to it, on the one hand, and a proliferation of centres, on the other hand.

It is problematic under the circumstances to expect that a reflexive awareness of Eurocentrism should lead to abolition of a Europe- or US-centred history. This is especially the case if we recognize that European and US power still dominates the world, and that the economic, social, political, and cultural products of Europe and the USA continue to play a transformative role globally. One may not like the way world histories are written at present, or the way Landes and Huntington deal with the relationship between culture and history, but that is no reason for rejecting off-hand the issues that they raise.

The goal of this essay, however, is not to justify the Eurocentrism of these works, but to return through these explicit reaffirmations of Eurocentrism to the question at hand: the location of Eurocentrism. What these works reveal is that the inclusion of others in history, or even the repudiation of Eurocentric teleology, does not exhaust the question of Eurocentrism. In fact, the persistence of Eurocentrism in spite of inclusiveness and a multi-directional approach to history reveals that there may be something quite misleading about the problem of Eurocentrism framed in those terms—especially if we recall that there is little that is new in EuroAmerican historiographies about either inclusiveness or the recognition of civilizational diversity. Eurocentrism goes much deeper. Kerwin Klein reminds us that even

30 Lewis D. Wurgaft, 'Identity in World History: A Postmodern Perspective', *History and Theory*, 34/2 (1995), 67–85.

anti-Eurocentrism in some of its versions may be very much part of a Western tradition.[31]

The distinguishing feature of Eurocentrism is not its exclusiveness, which is common to all ethnocentrisms, but rather the reverse: its inclusiveness. From books to television, and now the internet, peoples of the world, their cultural practices and their experiences, are inventoried, organized, and recorded into history in ways that are mostly beyond their imagination and control—unless they are participants in the activity. It is this activity, and its organizing principles, that at the most fundamental level constitute Eurocentrism. Since this activity coincided in its origins with a new scientific classification and explanation of the world, moreover, it claims access to truths that are not available to the people so classified themselves, and priority over *their* self-perceptions and perceptions of the world. History, along with other social sciences systematized in the nineteenth century, articulates a new mastery over the world. This history is no longer a history of states, or the church, or of moral exemplars, that serves the present by offering to it the mirror of the past. It is a history that takes entire societies and the whole world in all its aspects as its domain, and seeks to classify and explain them holistically and systematically. History as we know it—with its truth claims based on its methods, with its spatial and temporal assumptions, its units of analysis, and its analytical categories—is ultimately the most fundamental location of Eurocentrism. This is not to say that there is only one way of doing history, that history (or Eurocentrism) is free of contradictions, or that it is itself immune to historicity. On the contrary, the very claim to universality, and the effort to encompass the world as a whole, generates its own contradictions. Efforts to resolve these contradictions, however, are circumscribed by their own context in history, and intensify its domination of modern consciousness.

To rehearse a few well-known facts, historically, Eurocentrism as we confront it now is the product of an unprecedented urge and effort to organize the knowledge of the world, including other ways of knowing, into one systematic whole. Appearing at the origins of European modernity, both the urge and the effort

[31] Kerwin Lee Klein, 'In Search of Narrative Mastery: Postmodernism and the People Without History', *History and Theory*, 34/4 (1995), 275–98.

still characterize our present. Over the centuries others than Europeans have come to participate in the effort, but it is still EuroAmericans—by now, most prominently, the Americans of the USA—who are driven by the urge, and disseminate it across the globe. The participation of others, on the other hand, does not signal the dissolution of Eurocentrism, but *their* incorporation in a Eurocentric modernity.

The urge to inventory the world is already visible in the *Travels of Marco Polo*, which reads in many of its parts as a mapping of the world, and a catalogue of its peoples and commodities. The inventorying of both the natural and the human worlds intensifies with overseas explorations. Daniel Boorstin has documented that the inventories included not only what Europeans observed of the world, but also what others knew of it; in other words, European knowledge grew also by incorporating local knowledges.[32] By the eighteenth century both the accumulation and the organization of this new knowledge became more systematic, issuing in the nineteenth century in the social sciences of which we are heirs. McNeill writes:

> A flood of information about the Americas and other formerly unknown parts of the earth assaulted European consciousness . . . European learning reaffirmed (or at least paid lip service to) Christian truths, explored new fields of knowledge, accumulated more and more information about the past, and about far parts of the earth, and dodged the question of how to fit all the new data together. This remained the case until the eighteenth century when radical efforts to organize empirical knowledge systematically (stimulated partly by Newton's spectacular success in physics and astronomy) began to meet with apparent success in such fields as botany. . . In these same centuries, the Chinese, Moslem and Indian traditions of learning were far more successful in resisting challenge from without, improving upon the Europeans by refusing to pay attention to new and discrepant information. When a few self-styled 'Enlightened' thinkers, located mainly in France, began to abandon the inherited Christian framework of knowledge entirely, guardians of inherited truth in Asia were not impressed. Instead, serious efforts to come to grips with what eventually became undeniably superior European knowledge and skills were delayed until almost our own time.[33]

[32] Daniel Boorstin, *The Discoverers* (New York, 1983).

[33] William H. McNeill, 'The Changing Shape of World History', *History and Theory*, 34/2 (1995), 8–26, at 10.

This remarkable passage, coming from the most prominent world historian of our times, is noteworthy for dodging the question of agency. It also illustrates cogently the point that the accumulation of knowledge is central to distinguishing European from other civilizations in the modern world. In this development, history played the part of cataloguing human societies and reordering the past in order to account for their diversity. Before societies could be assigned their places in this new order, or excluded from it for being without history, they first had to be included in the new account of the past.

This accumulation of knowledge, and its organization, became not just the context but also the formative moment of Eurocentrism. It is curious that critics of Eurocentrism have little to say about these well-known developments that could come out of any textbook on Western civilization; or perhaps it is not very curious, for the very reason that this account of developments has a Eurocentric sound to it. The price to be paid for ignoring these developments, however, is to endow the concept of Eurocentrism with a transparency that it does not have, mostly by dehistoricizing it.

John Elliott argued nearly three decades ago that it was the discovery of human societies around the globe that forced a revision of the past, and ultimately inspired a new narrative which placed Europe at the centre and the end of history.[34] It matters little whether a sense of Europe-centredness or European (Christian) superiority preceded these developments. Such a sense, possibly a universal feature of all ethno-centrisms, does not suffice to distinguish Eurocentrism as a historical phenomenon. Neither does it help explain why the 'centring' of history emerges as a problem in the first place. We may observe from our contemporary persepective that Eurocentrism and Sino-centrism, to take just two examples, coexisted for centuries blissfully unaware of their respective claims to the centre of the world because in an ideological sense, if not *just* an ideological sense, they inhabited different 'worlds', as did most of the populations inhabiting the globe. It was their incorporation into a single world that was to raise the question of the centre which persists to our day.

[34] John H. Elliott, *The Old World and the New 1492–1650* (Cambridge, 1970).

The consequence in a *European* perspective, at least in the long run, was the disappearance of the outside. The 'wild' men and curious peoples outside Europe were now brought within the boundaries of Europe,[35] calling forth a new narrative that ordered 'civilizations' as well as the 'timeless' others in a new temporal hierarchy; history itself became possible only in relationship to other civilizations 'vegetating in the teeth of time', to cite a well-known phrase of Marx's, or in relation to these timeless others, which in the nineteenth century would become the domain of anthropology. Eurocentrism and history, in other words, coincided in their emergence. We might add to them the new spatialization of the world, which was a condition of their emergence. When by 1768 James Cook had completed his explorations of the Pacific, Europeans could claim a new global vision to which there was no outside; the task that remained was to explore regions that remained in the interstitial shadows of this new world. As they mapped and named this world, so did they assign its inhabitants into natural and temporal categories, newly designed to account for the diversity of the world. This global vision was the justification ultimately for the hubris towards other peoples and their knowledges; that Europeans could know them and their knowledges better than they did as they could claim a global oversight. What was suppressed in the process was the possibility of other ways of knowing the world—and the past.

We need to be cautious here not to reify either Europe or Eurocentrism, but to view them in their historicity. Eurocentrism in contemporary discourse is understood primarily in its relationship to the rest of the world. It was equally important, as Samir Amin points out, in the invention of Europe. Amin has argued convincingly that it was the discovery of a world crowded with peoples that in the end culminated in the invention of a European tradition that continues to inform textbook accounts such as the one quoted above. Medieval Europeans, he suggests, had much more in common with their contemporaries outside Europe than they did with their predecessors or their

[35] This argument has been inspired by Hayden White, who has written of the implications for the European psyche of the internalization of the 'wild man'. See Hayden White, 'The Forms of Wildness: Archaeology of an Idea', in id., *Tropics of Discourse: Essays in Cultural Criticism* (Baltimore, 1978), 150–82.

successors on the Continent. It was modern Europe that invented a linear history that proceeded from origins in Greece and Rome, through the medieval period, to the modern.[36] Europe itself had to be invented as Europeans reinvented the world. What was suppressed in the process was the part European expansion, and European appropriation of other knowledges, played in the formation of Europe. A product of these developments, history, was rendered into their cause.

The argument is highly suggestive in pointing to a fundamental contradiction within Eurocentrism: the abolition of the outside by bringing the world within Europe, while at the same time insisting on an outside in the invention of Europe; Europe unique, but universal, to recall the claim to which Huntington objects. Eurocentrism as a vision directed within as much as without calls attention to other possible contradictions as well: that the claims to universality may have led to contestations over its meaning within a Europe that experienced fragmentation into nation-states even as a secular vision emerged of Europe as a whole *vis-à-vis* the outside. The problems of Eurocentrism on a global scale that we encounter today, in other words, may have been played out first on a European scale, pointing to the possibility that due to its internal contradictions, Eurocentrism must remain an unfinished project, because its very claims to universality, its very efforts to contain the outside by bringing it within, generates new particularities that refuse to be so contained. The particularities may be marked by the Eurocentrism of their origins, however, complicating the location and meaning of Eurocentrism.

Parallels between intra-European relations and European relations with the outside world in the emergence of Eurocentrism are revealing in more ways than one. In historicizing Eurocentrism, one should not assign causal priority to developments internal to Europe as a continent versus European interactions with others beyond the continent, as the two were part of the same process (the separation of the two in many ways is crucial to, and characteristic of the Eurocentrism/anti-Eurocentrism debate). Fernand Braudel, employing world system analysis, has argued that the formation of Europe from

[36] Samir Amin, *Eurocentrism*, trans. from the French by Russell Moore (New York, 1983).

the eleventh century on was very much entangled in the relations of various European societies with one another *and* with the outside world.[37] As Amin would suggest, there was no clear delineation early on of an inside and an outside to Europe. The 'wild men' inhabited the interstices of European societies, as they inhabited the world outside Europe; which should make us wonder if, in spite of assumptions of a common world of Christianity, to a Venetian in the twelfth century the colonization of locations within Europe differed substantially as political or ideological projects from colonization of locations outside of Europe.

This question is interesting for two reasons. The first is to underline the reification of the idea of 'Europe' that informs dehistoricized uses of the term 'Eurocentrism' by its critics no less than by its defenders. Such reification suppresses the fact that the invention either of Europe or of Eurocentrism was not a 'European' project *per se*, but the product of initiatives that emanated from shifting locations within Europe temporally, in which the collaboration between states and capital played a dynamic part, as Giovanni Arrighi has analysed recently, and which was accompanied by intense conflict between various European states.[38] Class and gender status played an important part in determining participation in these projects, as well as the distribution of their rewards and punishments. There were, in other words, close parallels between colonization at home and abroad. The paradigm of colonialism may have much to tell us about state-building projects, especially with the emergence of the nation-state: in the state monopolization of the instruments of violence, in the use for the control of the population of new techniques of surveillance and inventory, and in the efforts to create homogeneous national cultures that erased local differences, to cite some of the most important.[39] Most relevant for the purposes here may be the erasure of local knowledges, whether place-based or women's knowledges, as feminist critics

[37] Fernand Braudel, *Civilization and Capitalism: 15th to 18th Century*, esp. vol. 3: *The Perspective of the World.*

[38] Giovanni Arrighi, *The Long Twentieth Century: Money, Power and the Origins of Our Times* (London, 1994).

[39] For the use of the paradigm of colonialism in the analysis of nation-building in a more positive sense than here, see Eugen Weber, *Peasants Into Frenchmen: The Modernization of Rural France, 1870–1914* (Stanford, 1976).

of science have argued. Scholars in recent years also have pointed to parallels between the 'civilizing mission' of imperial states in the colonies and the 'civilizing mission' they employed with regard to women and the working classes at home.[40]

The second reason is to complicate further the relationship between Eurocentrism and history. Here, too, history had a crucial role to play, but with rather different results for its boundaries, identified in this context with the nation, which may be the reason for the close association between history and the emergence of the nation-state: to absorb into one narrative diverse local histories, to order the latter in temporal hierarchies that presupposed the nation as the centre and the end of history, and to erase 'alternatives' to history that did not fit in with the teleology of the nation. History conceived in terms of the nation is not necessarily inconsistent with universalism; but at the very least it renders the nation into the medium for the articulation of universal ideals, raising the possibility of national claims to universality, which is no longer to be taken for granted as it serves now as the grounds for contestation between a variety of national claims. State-building and nation-making within Europe was subject to much contestation and conflict both between and within states, and so were the ideologies that articulated them, including history. Assertions of universal history were accompanied by contending claims to the centre, and to the spirit of universality. Hegel, whose name comes up regularly in discussions of Eurocentrism, was not simply a European philosopher but also a German one, who held forth Germanic claims to universality. On the other hand, Herder, also an Enlightenment product whose name comes up less often, insisted on locating universality in the characteristics particular to each nation, that derived from different historical (and geographical) legacies. The neglect of Herder in contemporary discussions of Eurocentrism is rather surprising (and, perhaps, revealing). While Herder was a product of the Enlightenment in his universalism, and may have introduced a linear history of Europe (from Babylon to his present) by the back door, the

[40] Susan Thorne, ' "The Conversion of Englishmen and the Conversion of the World Inseparable": Missionary Imperialism and the Language of Class', in Frederick Cooper and Ann Laura Stoller (eds.), *Tensions of Empire: Colonial Cultures in a Bourgeois World* (Berkeley, 1997), 238–62.

editor of the English edition of his historical reflections, Frank E. Manuel, wrote three decades ago in very contemporary sounding words:

> Herder, the outstanding representative of a new German philosophical history that ran counter to the French current of linear, rationalist progression, altered the traditional historical perspective and the universe of historical discourse in a revolutionary manner . . . Reading the French philosophical histories from Turgot through Comte, one is still impressed with their fundamental Eurocentrism, and the finiteness, even narrowness, of their historical appreciation of 'otherness.' Herder believed in the individuality of each *Volk*, or agglomeration of people, wherever and whenever it had appeared and its equivalent (or almost equivalent) status in the history of mankind.[41]

The relationship between nation, history, and Eurocentrism is important for at least three reasons. First, Eurocentrism is not an undifferentiated term, but should be qualified in terms of the ways in which it has been expressed through different national articulations. Most relevant in this context may be its complication over the last two centuries by the emergence of states that are the products of the European diaspora, most notably the USA, whose relationship to Europe is immensely complicated; a product of European colonialism, the US image in European eyes would seem to vary over time from a degenerate version of Europe, at the one extreme, to a cultural colonizer of Europe at the other. On the US side, the practice of Eurocentrism is complicated by simultaneous assertions of American 'exceptionalism'. It is this complicated relationship that accounts for my use of the term 'EuroAmerica' in this discussion, by which I seek to convey both a unity and a difference. At any rate, given the complex relationship between the USA and Europe, it seems too simplistic to endow them with a common outlook toward the world that may be encompassed by the term 'Eurocentrism'. Such a qualification, needless to say, should be applicable also to differences between European societies. The goal here is not to abolish Eurocentrism, but to make it more precise.

The stress on the nation is necessary, secondly, because while history conceived in terms of the nation contradicts the notion

[41] Frank E. Manuel, 'Editor's Introduction' to Johann Gottfried von Herder, *Reflections on the Philosophy of the History of Mankind*, abridged and with an Introduction by Frank E. Manuel (Chicago, 1968), pp. ix–xxv, esp. xiv, xv–xvi.

of a universal history or, therefore, an undifferentiated Eurocentrism, in its emergence within the context of a European history with its universalistic assumptions, the nation-form itself is endowed with universal relevance and legitimacy. The nation, and history written around the nation, may be the most cogent articulations of the contradictions of a universalism that generates its own particularisms. At the same time, given its entanglement in the history of a Eurocentric universalism, the nation-form serves as a prime location for Eurocentrism, and a medium for its global diffusion.

Finally, the nation is important because the particular composition of the nation shapes the understanding of the problematic of Eurocentrism, and the means to overcome it. As noted above, within the particular US context, for example, the question of Eurocentrism is tied in with other issues—such as those of gender, race, and ethnicity—which once again abolish the distinction between the inside and the outside. The writing of non-Eurocentric histories globally becomes indistinguishable under the circumstances from writing histories free of white male domination. There is little reason to assume that this version of Eurocentrism points to the way the problem of Eurocentrism is understood globally, least of all in non-EuroAmerican societies that have been the historical objects of a universalist Eurocentrism.

One more dimension needs to be added to these considerations of the location of Eurocentrism, most importantly, to question the domination by a geographical or spatial bias of both the issue of Eurocentrism, and the problem of de-centring history. To speak of Europe or of the nation as locations for history and, therefore, Eurocentrism, is to remain in largely spatial, or spatially identifiable categories. But what of categories that are not spatial *per se*, or spatial only in a metaphorical sense, in the sense of social and political spaces? Class, gender, race, ethnicity, religion, and culture, among others, are such categories. These categories, which cut across national and even continental boundaries, have provided alternative ways of centring history since the nineteenth century, often in explicit opposition to notions of Europe or the nation. Could they nevertheless serve as locations for Eurocentrism, and media for its dissemination, since they, too, are entangled in the history of

Europe, and have been introduced into other histories through the agency of European historiography? Each one of them, moreover, has been proposed at different times and by different people as a candidate around which to rewrite the history of the world.

Where class is concerned, the verdict seems to be clear. Critics of Eurocentrism these days readily include Marxist historiography among the perpetrators of Eurocentrism. This may well be the case, but could not the same be said of histories written around those other categories, which are equally products of European historiography and social science, very much rooted in EuroAmerican cataloguing of the world, and its theorization? It seems that separating these categories out of considerations of Eurocentrism is informed by the limited understanding of Eurocentrism against which I have argued above: on the basis of absences and exclusions from Eurocentric histories. Viewed from this perspective, that is, Eurocentrism as a principle for reordering the world's evidence and reorganizing the past, however, they are very much complicit in a Eurocentric conceptualization of the world, as the world in its historical unfolding called forth new categories for its comprehension. That much of the opposition to Eurocentrism these days is conducted in the name or with the aid of such categories does not prove that they stand in opposition to Eurocentrism. On the contrary, the employment of such categories may be an indication of the depth to which even opposition to Eurocentrism is by now entangled within a Eurocentric conception of the world.

This is the final question which this essay raises with regard to the location of Eurocentrism. Is there an outside to Eurocentrism in our day? Is Eurocentrism just a European or American thing, or is it part of a consciousness that is by now global? The answer seems obvious: Eurocentrism is internal to societies worldwide, if not explicitly, then in the internalization of history, of its spatial and temporal assumptions, and its categories. Eurocentrism is crucial to understanding the spatialities and temporalities of modernity, not just in EuroAmerica but globally, from at least the nineteenth century. The spatial conceptualizations around which we have organized history, from nations to areas to continents and oceans to the Three Worlds and beyond to globalization, are in a fundamental sense implicated in a Eurocentric modernity. Even more fundamental may be the reworking of temporalities by a Eurocentric conceptualization of the world, which in the end has come to serve as the temporality around which to rewrite the pasts of widely different societies. For the last century, but especially since the Second World War, Eurocentrism has been the informing principle in the constructions of history, not just in EuroAmerican historiographies, but in the spatial and temporal assumptions of dominant historiographies worldwide. EuroAmericans conquered the world, renamed places, rearranged economies, societies, and politics, and erased or drove to the margins premodern ways of knowing space, time, and many other things as well. In the process, they universalized history in their self-image in an unprecedented manner. EuroAmericans did not do all this themselves, however, but with the participation and complicity of those in other societies who perceived in Eurocentric history and its categories new ways of grasping the present and the past, and resolving the problems inherited from the past, or thrown up by the challenges of the present. There may still be peoples untouched by history, but they are fewer and more marginal by the day.

A further, perhaps even more profound, consequence of the global internalization of Eurocentrism is that Eurocentric history provides the medium through which societies around the globe know one another. This is partly a matter of the continued economic, political, and cultural power of EuroAmerica which enables the historians of European and American societies to play an intermediary role in the organization and practice of history everywhere. But more fundamental are the conceptualizations of space and time that are the legacies of the last few centuries of EuroAmerican domination of the world with the consequence that the EuroAmerican writing of the world, and of its past, mediates the comprehension of the world globally. This raises the question of whether or not there could be, for example, a Chinese or Indian history of the world that is not mediated by Eurocentrism? Probably not, is the likely answer. To the extent that the Chinese may be interested in Indian conceptions of the past, or even in Indian history, that interest would seem to lie primarily in placing China and India within a history the standards of which have been laid down already in

Eurocentric temporalities.[42] Even if EuroAmerica were to be taken out of history, so that history could be written around non-EuroAmerican societies, and their interactions, the spatial and temporal legacies of Eurocentrism would still be there, as those societies as they now exist are themselves the products historically and conceptually of the EuroAmerican writing of the world.

Here we need to turn to the question of agency, raised above with reference to the quotation from McNeill. McNeill states there that 'a flood of information . . . assaulted European consciousness', without telling the reader where this information came from, as if it simply rained down on Europeans from the skies above. It is also curious that the quotation seems to privilege Chinese, Muslims, and Indians for their ability to resist this 'assault', for which, however, they seem also to have paid a price when confronted later on with Europeans with their 'undeniably superior knowledge'. The argument seems convoluted, possibly because it seeks in words to escape Eurocentrism while reaffirming its ultimate victory. The contradiction may characterize a great deal of current anti-Eurocentrist arguments. The immediate question it raises, however, is whether or not Eurocentrism may be grasped without reference to the structures of power that propelled it globally. It is a question that is ignored in most discussions of Eurocentrism that treat it as simply an intellectual or cultural issue. Indeed, to even raise the question opens one to the charge of Eurocentrism. Nevertheless the question needs to be raised not only because it is relevant to grasping the global victory of Eurocentrism in the midst of its renunciations at the level of culture, but also because it enables a critique of the contradictions that characterize currently popular globalist alternatives to Eurocentrism.

[42] An example of this historicization of China and India is to be found in the influential book by Liang Shuming, which arranged historically Chinese, Indian, and Western civilizations, each with its defining civilizational characteristic, so that the past belonged to India, the present to the West, and the future to China. See Liang Shuming, *Dongxi wenhua ji qi zhexue* (Eastern and Western Cultures and Their Philosophies) (n.p., 1921). This kind of thinking persists, and not just in China. Little comment is needed on views of 'less advanced' or 'primitive' societies. In light of what I say below, it is important to note that Liang's book was pre-Marxist. For a similar preoccupation with the 'West' on the part of Indians, see Vinay Lal, 'Discipline and Authority', *Futures*, 29/10 (1997), 985–1000, esp. 993–4.

III. *End of History or A New Beginning?*

'History', Nicholas Dirks once observed, is 'a sign of the modern.'[43] The emergence of a historical consciousness in Europe was inseparable from the emergence of a consciousness of modernity that called for a new ordering of the past as Europeans encountered a multitude of new peoples and new phenomena that called for inclusion in the account of humanity, which in turn called for a revisioning of the European past. 'In discovering America', J. H. Elliott has written, 'Europe discovered itself.'[44] Eurocentrism was as much about the invention of Europe as it was about the ordering of the peoples of the world in a temporal scheme in which Europe represented the pinnacle of progress. And history was to bear witness to the European achievement. By the second half of the century, at the hands of German historians, history was rendered into the organizing principle of all the natural and the human sciences. As Georg Iggers writes of German historicism (which would spread subsequently throughout Europe and North America):

> the new outlook, later often referred to by the term historicism, was hailed as an intellectual advance. Historicism was more than a theory of history. It involved a total philosophy of life, a unique combination of a conception of science, specifically of the human or cultural sciences, and a conception of the political and social order. It assumed, as Ortega y Gasset formulated it, that 'Man, in a word, has no nature; what he has is . . . history.' But it also firmly believed that history revealed meaning and that meaning revealed itself only in history. Seen in this way, history became the only way of studying human affairs.[45]

The late nineteenth century may have been the high point in the dominance of history. The historicist confidence in history brings into relief the contemporary crisis of historical consciousness. There is little doubt about a current crisis in history, if more in the cultural meaning than in the professional practice of history.[46] It is commonplace, especially from the perspective of

[43] Nicholas Dirks, 'History as a Sign of the Modern', *Public Culture*, 2/2 (1990), 25–32.

[44] Elliott, *The Old World and the New, 1492–1650*, 53.

[45] Georg G. Iggers, *Historiography in the Twentieth Century: From Scientific Objectivity to the Postmodern Challenge* (Hanover, 1997), 28–9.

[46] I have discussed this problem in a number of places. See the collection *Postmodernity's Histories: The Past as Legacy and Project* (Boulder, Colo., forthcoming).

cultural studies, to associate this crisis with postmodernism and postcolonialism. This crisis is rooted most fundamentally in the intellectual consequences of a consciousness of globality. Indeed, there is much to be gained from viewing postmodernism and postcolonialism themselves as intellectual manifestations of an increasingly globalized consciousness since the 1960s. Postmodernism and postcolonialism, both residual concepts that derive their meaning from their relationship to the past, do not present themselves as viable candidates for a new paradigm that might enable us to grasp the present in its novelty. On the other hand, they make quite good sense as concepts of a transitional period when viewed from the perspective of globalization, which has a good bit to say about the present, but also illuminates the past in new ways. It offers the possibility also, if only as a possibility, to shift our vantage point from the First World to other locations—which are difficult to specify because of their multiplicity. Globalization is especially pertinent to understanding postcolonialism, as the latter is in many ways representative of the resurgence of the formerly marginalized.

The contradictions incorporated into globalization as a paradigm as it seeks to comprehend a contradictory world are visible in the conflicting visions of the past to which it has given rise. These range from renewed efforts to grasp the past in its totality that also overcome the Eurocentrism of an earlier world historiography, to declarations of the 'end of history', to the fragmentation of the past into mutually irreconcilable narratives. What they all share in common might be described, in Guehenno's terms, as 'the resurgence of history'. Globalization is in many respects about a surfeit of history, both as its constituent and its product.

This essay has already referred to the explicit connections drawn by various authors between globalization, and the contemporary surge of interest in world history. Others have gone even further, declaring 'world history' to be insufficient to the tasks at hand, calling instead for 'global history'.[47] However we might wish to name it, calls for a total history of humanity that corresponds to the requirements of globalization are motivated by an urge to accord historical presence to all the peoples

[47] Bruce Mazlish and Ralph Buultjens (eds.), *Conceptualizing Global History* (Boulder, Colo., 1993).

of the world. This concern provides eloquent testimonial to the differences between a contemporary consciousness of globalization, and earlier conceptions of globality in which, as Robertson observes, history was rendered into an account of the 'triumph' of the West, and the Others of EuroAmerica were rendered into 'voiceless' remnants of the past without any claims on history; the 'people without history', as Eric Wolf put it in his seminal critique of EuroAmerican historiography.[48] Contemporary world or global histories seek to redress this suppression of other pasts in an earlier historiography, but they also seek to address a contemporary situation, which is at once national and international in the questions it raises. Nationally, it addresses the concerns of those groups (from ethnic minorities to women) who had been left out of history earlier; internationally, it seeks to bring back into history peoples whose presence on the global scene can no longer be rendered invisible in a Eurocentric teleology. It is arguable nevertheless that for all its pretensions to a greater even-handed comprehensiveness than earlier, contemporary world or global historiography is no more comprehensive in its coverage of the world than the globalization it claims as its inspiration—and legitimacy. It is also based on a partial understanding of globalization, stressing its integrative aspects against the fragmentation that is also built into the very concept of globalization. In both these respects, world or global historiography still represent inventions of the world, something that is recognized at least tacitly in Bentley's reference to the 'shapes of world history'.

I have no objections to either the writing or the teaching of world history, as I believe that a knowledge of the world is a courtesy that both students and the general public in an imperial society owe to the rest of the world. But this is not to be confounded either with an end to Eurocentrism, or even-handedness in the representation of the past. On the first issue, merely to substitute globalization for the 'triumph' of the West in the 'grand narratives' of history is insufficient to overcome Eurocentrism, as globalization as we have known it is inseparable from EuroAmerican integration of the world, which is not going to disappear simply because it is disavowed in a globalist

[48] Eric R. Wolf, *Europe and the People Without History* (Berkeley, 1982).

historiography. Secondly, Eurocentrism is built into the very idea of a world history with global aspirations, as historically the emergence of world history, as of history in general, was a product of EuroAmerican expansion over the world, which called forth new ways to contain and order the world's peoples as well as knowledges. We still need to keep in mind that such histories are produced in Europe and the USA, and if others are now included in the historical process, the inclusion is by invitation.[49] To the extent that this historiography leaves out of the picture pasts that were erased in the process—including pasts that militated against the forces of capitalist globalization, that might have provided alternatives to the contemporary outcome of things—it reproduces the teleological functionalism of an earlier historiography.

Indeed, without an account of the relationship between Eurocentrism and the enormous power of capitalism that enabled European expansion, the criticism of Eurocentrism may perpetuate Eurocentric assumptions in new guises. The preoccupation with Eurocentrism pervades not just cultural studies, but the rewriting of history, most visibly in efforts to produce a new 'world history', which, too, may be above all a EuroAmerican preoccupation, that perpetuates earlier hegemonies in new form. The epistemological concerns of world history proponents can overcome the restrictions of national units in the writing of history. On the other hand, the representation as Eurocentrism of the stress on modern capitalism promises not only to erase the distinctiveness of modern history, but also to eliminate the capitalist mode of production as a distinct mode with its own forms of production and consumption, oppression and exploitation, and ideology. This is the case with Andre Gunder Frank's '5,000 year world-system' which, in the name of erasing Eurocentrism, universalizes capitalist development in much the same way as classical economics; that is, by making it into the fate of humankind, rather than the conjunctural product of a particular history. Gunder Frank does not explain either why a 'China-centered' history constitutes more of a world-history than a EuroAmerican centred one.[50]

[49] Thinking on world history has been accompanied all along with considerations of national power and its relationship to the world.

[50] Andre Gunder Frank, *ReORIENT: Global Economy in the Asian Age* (Berkeley, 1998).

Even more revealing is a recent report on the status of world history writing in China. Ironically, the report observes that, contrary to what one might expect, Chinese historians continue to write modern world history around capitalism, and, it follows for the author, a Eurocentric paradigm. This to the author is, of course, a product of the continued domination of Chinese historical thinking by the 'ideological framework' of 'a European-centered, Marxist-imbued world history'.[51] 'We are scientific and they are ideological, so we know better', might be the conclusion, which perpetuates the same hegemonic attitudes as in earlier days. No wonder that the author can also state that the large place given to Chinese history in the curriculum (autonomously of world history) issues 'from an ethnocentric view not unfamiliar to Western historians. China's self-perception as *Zhongguo*, or the "Central Kingdom," is well-known.'[52] Not only does the author erase Chinese historians as contemporaries instead of raising questions about her own version of world history, but she also proceeds to erase Chinese history by falling back upon the authority of long-standing clichés in the 'Western' historiography of China. Apart from the fact that this Chinese 'self-perception' has its own history, other societies, too, teach their national histories separately from world history, which has more to do with nationalist education in the modern world than some Chinese 'ethnocentrism'. Whose 'ethnocentrism' is the question that jumps to mind once again. World history as an undertaking is not to be held responsible for this kind of obscurantism, but the latter is a reminder nevertheless of the need for continued intellectual vigilance in an undertaking that is highly vulnerable to producing the opposite of what it intends. One way to do so is to distinguish Eurocentrism from recognition of the historical role that EuroAmerica, empowered by capitalism, played in the shaping of the modern world. Without capitalism, Eurocentrism might have remained just another parochial ethnocentrism.

The very dialectic of globalization, the dialectic of integration/fragmentation, is resolved in the globalization paradigm by

[51] Dorothea A. L. Martin, 'World History in China', *World History Bulletin*, 14/1 (Spring 1998), 6–8, at 6.

[52] Ibid. For a more sophisticated discussion of the problems of centring history within Chinese world historiography, see Leif Littrup, 'China and World History', in Yu-ming Shaw (ed.), *Reform and Revolution in Twentieth Century China* (Taipei, 1987), 16–29.

incorporating difference within a global unity. This is, in fact, what world or global history seeks to do with reference to the past, to play up those integrative tendencies against tendencies to fragmentation, and erase in the process what may be irreconcilable differences. World historiography as it appears at present is an instance of what Wallerstein has described as 'anti-Eurocentric Eurocentrism' that denies the uniqueness of EuroAmerica, and its centrality to the historical process of globalization, but still imposes upon the past the outcomes of that very globalization, rendering globalization itself into a mystical force without an agency.[53]

The problems that world history presents are not just ideological; they are also narrative problems. World history persists ultimately because of a conviction that differences that mark the world and its past may be contained within a single grand narrative. It has yet to confront the problem that the very crowding of diverse peoples (not their contributions to civilization in the abstract) into history may in fact mean the end of history as we have known it because, if those people are recognized genuinely in their differences, they are not to be contained within a single narrative. The problem of narrative has become apparent in a range of historiographies, but the example that is most pertinent to the issue of globalization may be that of different 'cultures' being incorporated into a single narrative of world history, which may end up exploding the whole notion of world history and, with it, history itself. Fredric Jameson, who sees in such crowding of the world the impossibility of narratives, and, therefore, a state akin to schizophrenia when meaning dissolves into 'a rubble of distinct and unrelated signifiers', writes:

> The apparent celebration of Difference, whether here at home or on the global scale, in reality conceals and presupposes a new and more fundamental reality. Whatever the new liberal tolerance is, it has little to do with the exotic range of the emblematic Family of Man exhibit, in which the Western bourgeoisies were asked to show their deeper human affinity with Bushmen and Hottentots, bare-breasted island women and aboriginal craftsmen, and others of the anthropological type who are unlikely to visit you as tourists. These new others, however, are at least as likely to visit us as immigrants or *Gastarbeiter*, to

[53] Immanuel Wallerstein, 'Eurocentrism and Its Avatars: The Dilemmas of Social Science', in id., *The End of the World As We Know It* (Minneapolis, 1999), 168–84, at 178.

that degree they are more 'like' us, or at least the 'same' in all kinds of new ways, which new internal social habits—the forced social and political recognition of 'minorities'—help us to acquire in our foreign policy.[54]

Jameson here is clearly describing a novel predicament for EuroAmericans, especially EuroAmerican élites, who have lost control of historical narratives, and of the guarantees they provided for present identity and future direction. The dilemma he poses is a very real one; it confronts all the descendants of nineteenth-century World Fair organizers and museum-makers who now face the prospect of returning to the 'savages' the skeletal remnants that were supposed to preserve savagery in historical memory, but who must now meet the very same savages as political and legal equals. But what he has to say applies not only to what he loosely describes as liberals, but to radicals as well, including the left radicals with whom he identifies and dis-identifies almost in the same breath. As he puts it further on: 'We need to explore the possibility that there exists, in what quaintly used to be called the moral realm, something roughly equivalent to the dizziness of crowds for the individual body itself: the premonition that the more people we recognize, even within the mind, the more peculiarly precarious becomes the status of our own hitherto unique and "incomparable" consciousness or "self".'[55] What he does not recognize, however, is that this has been the condition for a majority of the world's peoples, especially those peoples who had earlier been left out of history, who have now re-entered history to disturb the First World élites' complacency about self and history.

The pertinent question here may be: does the end of history for one serve as the beginning of history for others and, if so, what does that say about history? It may help demonstrate further the power of globalization as a paradigm, a paradigm at once of integration and disintegration, that what appears as the dissolution of history from one perspective apears as its recovery from another. It is possible, indeed, that globalization appears to a Western intellectual as a radical break with the past in its repudiation of a Eurocentric teleology, that nevertheless retains

[54] F. Jameson, *Postmodernism: Or, The Cultural Logic of Late Capitalism* (Durham, NC, 1994), 357.

[55] Ibid. 358.

in its most basic assumptions the vision of a world of unity, while from other perspectives globalization means release from a hegemonic ideology of global unity, that allows a choice once again of entry into a global stream of history on one's own terms, scrambling in the process the meaning of exactly what such a stream might mean.

In either case, globalization from Third World perspectives at its most radical presently entails a repudiation not just of a Eurocentric mapping of modernity, but of history itself as a fundamental expression of Eurocentrism. The Indian psychologist Ashis Nandy is one such critic who has subjected history to harsh criticism as one corner of the triangular ideology of a Eurocentric modernity along with science and developmentalism. Nandy's critique takes us far beyond the limited questions of who is to be included in history, and how to confront history and historical thinking as the problem. The argument is deceptively simple, as perhaps a radical critique should be: history, as one mode of thinking about the past, present, and future, has been established in the modern world as the *only* way to think them, consigning all other ways of thinking, along with those who thought in those ways, to the realm of the non-historical. The dominance of history 'is derived from the links the idea of history has established with the modern nation-state, the secular worldview, the Baconian concept of scientific rationality, nineteenth-century theories of progress, and, in recent decades, development . . . once exported to the nonmodern world, historical consciousness has not only tended to absolutize the past in cultures that have lived with open-ended concepts of the past or depended on myths, legends, and epics to define their cultural selves, it has also made the historical worldview complicit with many new forms of violence, exploitation and satanism in our times and helped rigidify civilizational, cultural, and national boundaries.'[56] Most available criticisms of history are themselves historical. As in the case of colonial nationalism which assimilates Orientalism in its own self-definition, to be historical in the non-EuroAmerican world is to rewrite the past under the hegemony of an epistemology that has Eurocentrism built into its

[56] Ashis Nandy, 'History's Forgotten Doubles', *History and Theory*, 34/2 (1995), 44–62, at 44 (abstract).

very structure.[57] On the other hand, from this same perspective, contemporary efforts in the West to globalize history by writing everyone into it, even in all their differences, appear as little more than an effort to contain genuine difference by rendering all societies historical. Nandy concedes that 'at one time not long ago, historical consciousness had to coexist with other modes of experiencing and constructing the past even within the modern world. The conquest of the past through history was still incomplete in the late nineteenth century, as was the conquest of space through the railways . . . As long as the non-historical modes thrived, history remained viable as a baseline for radical social criticism. That is perhaps why the great dissenters of the nineteenth century were the most aggressively historical.'[58] But such is no longer the case, as the historical way has become the only way of knowing the past, when a critical epistemology has turned into a means of dominance. The point at present is not to find alternative *histories*, but *alternatives* to history.[59]

We may or may not agree with Nandy's indictment of history, or with the possibility of 'alternatives to history' in a post-historical age. What is most important about his critique, and with other critiques along a similar vein, is that it is the expression of an alternative presence in the dialogue over the past, that no longer waits upon a First World liberal accommodation of other histories, but declares its presence in opposition to the latter—much the same as those native Americans who, against pleas for the preservation of history and science, demand the return of skeletal remains from museums into the safe-keeping of their descendants.[60] Globalization, ultimately, consists of the prolifer-

[57] This, of course, may be even more of a problem in Marxist than in liberal historiography. For a discussion see Arif Dirlik, 'Marxism and Chinese History: The Globalization of Marxist Historical Discourse and the Problem of Hegemony in Marxism', *Journal of Third World Studies*, 4/1 (Spring 1987), 151–64. As this journal is not easily accessible, the essay was also published as 'Marxisme et histoire chinoise: la globalisation du discourse historique et la question de l'hegemonie dans la référence marxiste à l'histoire', *Extreme-Orient Extreme-Occident*, no. 9 (Aug. 1987), 91–112.

[58] Nandy, 'History's Forgotten Doubles', 46.

[59] Ibid. 53. For further discussion of some of these problems, see Vinay Lal, 'History and the Possibilities of Emancipation: Some Lessons from India', *Journal of the Indian Council of Philosophical Research* (June 1996), 97–137, and Arif Dirlik, 'History without a Center? Reflections on Eurocentrism', in Eckhardt Fuchs and Benedikt Stuchtey (eds.), *Across Cultural Borders: Historiography in Global Perspective* (Lanham, 2002), 247–84.

[60] While world historiography has sought to claim for itself any open-minded accommodation of alternative histories, there is a world of distance between world history as

ation of subjects who declare their presence, their *contemporary* presence, against the erasures of the past, or the assimilations of the present. In this very concrete sense, it is, at least from a EuroAmerican perspective, 'the end of the world as we have known it'. From other perspectives, however, the 'end' may well signal a new beginning.

IV. *Concluding Comments*

The subtitle of this essay is borrowed from the title of a book by a French historian of China, Jean Chesneaux's *Pasts and Futures: Or What Is History For?*[61] The questions raised about world history above are not intended to deny the legitimacy or the necessity of writing world history, which may be inevitable given our own histories. Rather, the essay questions a tendency to privilege world history over other histories, cautions against positivism in its practice, and calls for greater critical awareness of the discourse on the past of which world historiography is a moment. In every history is buried a multiplicity of histories. The greater the scope of the history, the greater the number of histories erased. It is up to the historian to decide what histories to bring to the surface of consciousness, and what histories to bury under different conceptualizations of space and time. The criterion of truth does not help, because all these histories have their claims to truth; the way to erase them is usually through the criterion of significance, which determines what histories are relevant to the stories at hand, and which are not.

It is also the case that history with too many narratives would cease to be history, and disintegrate into a multiplicity of stories which, in their very proliferation, would mean the end of history.

history of the world, and accounting for different visions of the past, which is exactly the point of Nandy's criticism. If the latter were taken seriously, as it should be, world history would be an impossibility. See Vine de Loria, Jr., *Red Earth, White Lies*, for a radical repudiation of all 'white' history. Needless to say, these alternatives to history also involve different conceptualizations of 'the world'. Closer to the writing of world history are those historians who do not necessarily take the world as their subject, but try to account nevertheless for the different worlds that human beings bring to their encounters even at their most local and concrete. One example that comes to mind immediately is the Pacific historian Greg Dening, who has articulated his orientation most explicitly in *The Death of William Gooch: A History's Anthropology* (Honolulu, 1995).

[61] Trans. from the French by Schofield Coryell (London, 1978).

In this sense, the predicament of history presently is not very different from the predicament of globalization. Globalization is a contradictory concept. At one extreme, it is the most complete expression of a Western (especially American) imperialism, as it asserts through certain commonalities of everyday life that the world is becoming a place where people are not just increasingly in contact with one another, but are on their way to some kind of homogenization brought about by common practices of consumption—of which the most advanced instances are to be found in the USA. But globalization also entails the admission of an end to a EuroAmerican-centred history, because, unlike in an earlier modernization paradigm (socialist or capitalist) that rested the end of history on EuroAmerican models of history, it admits the possibility of heterogeneity; that universal phenomena, from consumption to social science, are absorbed in local contexts, and refracted through them, so that the transformers have to be transformed in the process of transformation to achieve their goals.

Globalization thus conceived is at once the fulfilment of a teleology, and an admission of its impossibility. History, similarly, has to account for the past not just in terms of a progressive homogenization of human societies through contact, but also in terms of heterogenization, which takes different forms in different periods. History may be written as an account of globalization through 'inter-societal' contacts of one kind or another, which produces an evolutionary representation of the past. It could also be told as an unceasing history of colonization, where people appear not just as colonizers of new lands, but themselves are the objects of colonization, whose local differences are erased progressively as they are brought within the confines of power of one kind or another. Finally, it may be written in terms of its many contradictions that produce both globalization and localization as different aspects of the same processes that nevertheless produce different results according to different historical circumstances. The problem with world history is that it can never adequately account for these processes, which it must contain within recognizable temporal and spatial categories. These are decided not by the recognition of complexity to human pasts, but their subjection to the exigencies of power. That is why we will never see, not as a popular text anyway, a world history that is written as a history of colonialism, because that would constitute an inexcusable breach with the claims of the present to be the latest phase in the liberation of humankind.

The meaning of history lies elsewhere, if it is even possible these days to speak of something so mundane as meaning to history. If global history, or a world history that is global in intention, is to become a reality, there are two things that are not to be ignored: (*a*) that any such history is of necessity post-Eurocentric, however that is understood, and, therefore, post-historical, and (*b*) that a human vision of history, that serves everyday life rather than corporate needs or the marketing needs of corporations, requires that human connections derive their significance from everyday interactions, and not just the needs of abstract, and ideological, arguments for globalization that simply replicate the slogans of their corporate sponsors. This requires recognition of different temporalities and spatialities, in other words, different views of the world that persist in spite of powerful forces of homogenization. The ultimate challenge may be to write the world with due recognition of these differences—which may mean also the end of history as we know it.

PART II
Rethinking and Writing World History

5

Out of Step with Time: United States Exceptionalism in an Age of Globalization

MICHAEL ADAS

The paradox has been there from the early years of settlement along the north Atlantic coast. The Pilgrims, and the Puritans soon after them, had migrated to the 'howling wilderness' of New England out of a determination to build a utopian community that transcended history, a New Zion that was free of the corruption and oppression that they sought to leave behind in Europe. In his metaphor of 'a city upon the hill', John Winthrop captured the Puritans' sense of the exceptional nature of their undertaking, which they believed both divinely ordained and without precedent, at least since biblical times. But while Winthrop underscored the exceptional nature of the Puritan experiment in political, social, and religious development, he also stressed its lessons for the rest of humanity; lessons, he believed, that would be regarded as 'a story and by-word through the world'. The city, after all, was on high ground with the 'eyes of all people' upon it.[1]

Winthrop's metaphor proved to be foundational for the American nation that emerged in the following centuries from a scattering of tiny settler enclaves in New England and along the shores of Chesapeake Bay. Additional images and beliefs—such as the rugged individualism exemplified by the frontiersman, the rags-to-riches ascent of the hardworking entrepreneur, and the

A longer version of this essay was published under the title 'From Settler Colony to Global Hegemon: Integrating the Exceptionalist Narrative of the American Experience into World History', in *American Historical Review*, 106/5 (2001), 1692–720.

[1] Winthrop's expectations were conveyed to his Puritan followers in a lay sermon delivered on their arrival in the New World. See 'A Model of Christian Charity', in Alan Heimert and Andrew Delbanco (eds.), *The Puritans in America: A Narrative Anthology* (Cambridge, Mass., 1985), 71–4.

non-imperialist nature of American expansion—subsequently reinforced exceptionalist formulations of the American experience and national identity on the part of historians and politicians alike. But Winthrop's city on the heights has been among the most enduring and frequently evoked symbols of a national experience that has been seen to be so distinctive that it defies comparison with or incorporation into the history of the rest of humanity. And the discordant internal contradictions of Winthrop's formulation have persisted through centuries of ideological oscillation between exceptionalism and America's variant of a global civilizing mission. Though a number of European historians have drawn attention to 'the basic incompatibility of the exceptionalist claim with political messianism, of singularity with universalism',[2] this fundamental tension in Americans' thinking about themselves and others has gone largely unnoticed, or at least it has rarely been seriously addressed in the now substantial historiographic discourse on American exceptionalism. It is heartening to find in a recent review of Seymour Martin Lipset's *American Exceptionalism*, Mary Nolan's succinct summary of the predicament of peoples—in this case the Germans—who have sought to emulate selectively American ways:

> The [German] goal was to become Americanized while remaining oneself. American exceptionalism, which proclaims the moral and material superiority of the United States, denies the possibility of such emulation and negotiation. The ideology of exceptionalism thus stands in sharp and ironic contrast to much of American foreign and economic policy, from modernization theory to structural adjustment programs, which are premised on America as the only economic and political model.[3]

[2] Quoted passage from Serge Ricard, 'The Exceptionalist Syndrome in U.S. Continental and Overseas Expansionism', in David K. Adams and Cornelis A. van Minnen (eds.), *Reflections on American Exceptionalism* (Kiel, 1994), 73. Some decades earlier, in her work *Les Mythes fondateurs de la nation américaine* (Paris, 1976), Elise Marienstras provided numerous examples of these opposing visions (pp. 90–8), but did not explicitly address their paradoxical juxtaposition.

[3] Mary Nolan, 'Against Exceptionalisms', *American Historical Review*, 102/3 (1997), 773. A quarter of a century ago, William Appleman Williams listed among a number of key themes in American history 'an intense consciousness of *uniqueness*' and 'a hyperactive sense of *mission*' (italics his), but he offered no commentary on their apparent opposition. See *America Confronts a Revolutionary World* (New York, 1976), 27.

Over the centuries, a variety of sometimes overlapping, but often quite distinct, claims for exceptionalism have been made by American thinkers, social commentators, and politicians. Winthrop's metaphor exemplifies the cosmic teleology version of exceptionalism that has dominated both political rhetoric and popular convictions. In this view, the emergence of the USA as a global power represents the working out in the mundane realm of a larger, divinely inspired plan. This sentiment can be found in American readings of their history from the Puritans' conviction that the epidemics that ravaged the Indian population of New England were God's way of preparing the New World for their settlement to Seymour Lipset's recent admission that he believed the 'hand of providence' responsible for the strong leaders who have emerged in times of crisis in the USA's history.[4] Though in some ways a variant of the 'Gott mit Uns' impulse that has been a component of the ideological baggage of most societies throughout history, the divinely ordained vision of the American experience has been both more comprehensive and more extreme than its counterparts elsewhere. It has also proven a good deal more impervious than most other national variants of divinely inspired mission to the unsettling excesses of human folly and cruelty that have abounded in most of human history.

Alternative versions of American exceptionalism are more amenable to empirical testing. They have also had, particularly in the 'American (half) century' of the post-Second World War decades, a much greater impact on thinking and writing about US history as well as approaches to foreign policy in the Cold War era and the first decade of the 'new world order'. Though divine imperatives are often implicit, and at times explicit, in these alternative formulations of exceptionalism, they emphasize the uniquely progressive and socially capacious character of American institutional and material development. The decidedly Whiggish thrust of progressivist variations on the exceptionalist theme owes much to expectations regarding the young American republic held by eighteenth-century European intellectuals.[5] Their fascination with the American experiment

[4] Peter N. Carroll, *Puritans and the Wilderness: The Intellectual Significance of the New England Frontier, 1629–1700* (New York, 1967), 13–14, 37–8; and Seymour Martin Lipset, *American Exceptionalism: A Double-Edged Sword* (New York, 1996), 14.

[5] On these connections, see esp. Joyce Appleby, 'Recovering America's Historic Diversity: Beyond Exceptionalism', *Journal of American History*, 79/2 (1992), 419–21.

appeared to validate the vision of the city on a hill. In the nineteenth century, both Winthrop's metaphor and the acclaim of the *philosophes* informed interpretations of US history that privileged it as the culmination of the evolutionary advance of human civilization. Whether grounded in the bounty of what was seen to be an undeveloped New World environment or the unique mixture of attributes that made up the American 'character', or both, progressivist exceptionalism has celebrated—in varying blends of attributes and emphases —the unprecedented extent to which democracy, individualism and social mobility, civil society, free enterprise, ingenuity and inventiveness, and material well-being have flourished in the USA. In these areas of human endeavour, which are seen to be definitive in terms of human development, progressivist exceptionalists insist that American achievements have not simply surpassed those of any other society in degree, they have reached quite distinctive levels of enactment and refinement.[6]

From a global perspective, these claims to American uniqueness would not have mattered very much if the United States had remained the geographically remote, rather isolated outlier of western European civilization that it was at least well into the nineteenth century. But the nation's rise to the status of a world power by the late 1800s, and its emergence after the Second World War as the epicentre of the process of globalization, meant that both Americans' self-images and the way they represented other peoples and cultures would have increasingly significant repercussions for all of humanity. These transformations gave new salience and intensity to the longstanding contradictions between exceptionalism in its varying guises and visions of America as a model for the rest of humankind. As Joyce Appleby has argued, over the course of the nineteenth century, the antithesis of the exceptionalist vision took on increasing importance in American thinking and policy making aimed at both those who were considered aliens within the republic and foreigners who were increasingly encountered overseas:

[6] The basic tenets of progressivist exceptionalism, which peaked in historical circles in the 1950s and early 1960s, were perhaps the most fully explicated in David Potter's *People of Plenty: Economic Abundance and the American Character* (Chicago, 1954) and Daniel Boorstin's three-volume, essentialist portrait, *The Americans* (New York, 1958–73).

The propagandists of American democracy breached the geographic isolation of their country by universalizing what was peculiar to Americans; their endorsement of natural rights, their drive for personal independence, their celebration of democracy. What might be construed elsewhere as uninterestingly plebeian was elevated by the national imagination to a new goal for mankind.[7]

The persisting conviction that the American experience, despite its unprecedented nature, could serve as a template for the future of less fortunate peoples and less developed cultures not only justified increasing interventionism in the outside world, it often promoted a predisposition to denigrate the worth and viability of foreign, particularly non-Western, cultures.

At times, these negative assessments remained implicit, even unconscious. More often, American policy-makers, missionaries, and bureaucrats were openly disdainful of cultures and peoples deemed to be beyond the pale of Western (or increasingly American) civilization. Though not necessarily racist but decidedly ethnocentric, their approach to these alien societies was premissed on the presupposition that their ways of thinking and doing were diametrically opposed to those of an exceptionally progressive and highly developed USA. From missionary tracts on the plains Indians to the journals of American ambassadors overseas, such epithets as savage and barbaric were standard fare in writings on non-Western peoples from the first years of colonization until well into the twentieth century. Chinese or Japanese leaders who resisted United States inroads into their societies in the late 1800s were caricatured as effete, reactionary, or xenophobic, while Muslim revivalists at the end of the twentieth century are indiscriminately lumped together as irrational fanatics bent on fomenting violent opposition to American-inspired efforts to promote economic and cultural globalization.[8]

Although often conceived in ignorance, these dismissive representations played a significant role in shaping policies

[7] Appleby, 'Recovering America's Historic Diversity', 424.

[8] The most wide-ranging treatment of these responses to the American Indians can be found in Roy Harvey Pearce, *The Savages of America* (Baltimore, 1953). For China, see Peter Buck, *American Science and Modern China, 1876–1936* (London, 1980), and for Japan, Walter LaFeber, *The Clash: U.S.–Japanese Relations Throughout History* (New York, 1997). Recent reactions to Muslim 'fundamentalism' range from Samuel Huntington's strident prognostications in 'The Clash of Civilizations', *Foreign Affairs*, 72/2 (1993), 22–49, to the more muted strictures in Benjamin Barber's *Jihad vs. MacWorld: How the Planet is both Falling Apart and Coming Together and What this Means for Democracy* (New York, 1992).

aimed at promoting the Westernization or Americanization of non-Western peoples and societies. This pattern of denigration, or outright dismissal, also led American agents, overseas advisers, and colonial administrators to conclude that alien cultures were *tabulae rasae* on which they could inscribe their own values and institutions with impunity. This approach to domination across cultures was manifested in early Anglo-American policies towards the indigenous Indian peoples of coastal North America, and it persisted in the centuries of settler frontier expansion and Indian dispossession. As recent historians of these processes have concluded, in these circumstances Americanization literally meant 'cultural erasure' for the Indians. And there is perhaps no more revealing measure of the low regard that Anglo-Americans had for Indian culture than the fact that, with rare exceptions, even the most sympathetic missionary educators and government agents made no effort to learn the languages of the Indians among whom they worked.[9]

From the nineteenth century, the highly ethnocentric and increasingly racist assumptions of the superiority and universal applicability of Euro-American ways that informed American policies towards the Indians were increasingly deployed in encounters with overseas peoples and cultures. In the 1890s and early 1900s, these presuppositions were worked into a distinctive (but by no means unprecedented or unique) American version of the civilizing mission, and some decades later they undergirded the central tenets of modernization theory. Both ideologies were used to justify social engineering projects designed to transform foreign, and again mainly non-Western, societies whose cultures were essentialized as tradition-bound, materially underdeveloped, and hopelessly backward.[10]

Any meaningful attempt to integrate the history of the USA into the analysis of broader global developments over the last

[9] The concept of cultural erasure is explored by Priscilla Wald in her provocative essay on 'Terms of Assimilation: Legislating Subjectivity in the Emerging Nation', in Amy Kaplan and Donald E. Pease (eds.), *Cultures of United States Imperialism* (Durham, NC, 1993), 59–84. See also Robert Berkhofer, *The White Man's Indian* (New York, 1978), esp. 137, 150; and William G. McLoughlin, *Cherokees and Missionaries, 1789–1839* (New Haven, 1984), 51, 63–4, 70–1, 143, and 151.

[10] Michael Adas, 'Improving on the Civilizing Mission? Assumptions of United States Exceptionalism in the Colonisation of the Philippines', *Itinerario* 22/4 (1998), 44–66; and Dean Tipps, 'Modernization Theory and the Comparative Study of Societies: A Critical Perspective', *Comparative Studies in Society and History*, 15/2 (1973), 199–226.

half millennium requires comparative or world historians to grapple with the foundational and enduring paradox that I have argued runs through the historiography of the USA and informs the myths and discourses that have shaped the Americans' sense of national identity and purpose. The exceptionalist side of the opposing readings of the meanings of the American experience had much to do with what Raymond Grew could still characterize, as late as 1985, as 'The Comparative Weakness of American History'.[11] There was, of course, considerable merit in Grew's contention that the indifference, suspicion, or outright hostility that many, if not most, historians of the USA still evinced towards comparative, much less world history, could in large part be traced to the nature of the American historical profession and the ways in which promotions and plaudits were earned within that community. As Grew observed:

> For historians of the United States—who can hardly launch two full careers before beginning to publish, who are already burdened by the need to master an enormous literature and to meet high standards of expertise within the chronologically limited framework of a single nation—it can seem merely prudent to look the other way when the call for comparison is made.[12]

But as Grew also recognized, the very kinds of history and ways of approaching historical issues that the profession privileged were perhaps even more important sources of resistance to serious comparative work or even more ambitious studies of broader global patterns.

For those who held that key processes in US history were unprecedented and unique, it followed that they were so significant that they must be studied in and of themselves. From this perspective, it was also not unreasonable to conclude that these processes could not be meaningfully compared to what more cross-culturally minded or globally orientated scholars deemed to be similar developments in other peoples' history. These convictions appeared to most practitioners of American history to be well-founded, given the sheer size of the USA (and the corresponding bulk of its historical production), its relative isolation well into the twentieth century, and, conversely thereafter—

[11] Raymond Grew, 'The Comparative Weakness of American History', *Journal of Interdisciplinary History*, 16/1 (1985), 87–101.

[12] Ibid. 96.

particularly in the post-Second World War decades—its preponderant influence in international affairs. Again Raymond Grew succinctly captures these contextual buttresses of exceptionalism:

> Our nation . . . spreads across a huge and essentially monolingual continent where daily experience involves less frequent contact than most nations enjoy with neighbors who speak different tongues, look to very different traditions, and claim distinctive cultures. Concerned to root their analysis in the full context of the society they study, historians may even in their most formal work be especially subject to the society and culture that shaped them, which can become a constricting circle for those studying their own society.[13]

Despite this confluence of constraints, it has long been acceptable, at times even fashionable, for historians of the United States to include explorations of the European roots of the new nation's beliefs, institutions, or patterns of colonization as vital components of, and even partial explanations for, the exceptional trajectory of American history.[14] But until the last couple of decades there have been few serious attempts to compare the discovery and settlement of the Atlantic littoral to similar processes in Australia, Argentina, or South Africa—the history of American frontier expansion to these areas and others exhibiting obvious parallels in many parts of the globe—or the nature of American empire-building overseas to imperial expansion by other industrial powers, including Japan. On the contrary, American historians have generally confined their narratives and analyses of these and other defining aspects of the American experience to the USA itself. If they attempted to set that history in a broader transnational framework, they were likely to stress, for example, the ways in which industrialization produced a peculiarly 'American system' of manufacturing; the fundamental distinctions between America's exercise of informal influence overseas and the oppressive empires ruled by its rivals; and the incomparable magnitude and impact of the European immigrant flow to the USA in the late nineteenth and early twentieth centuries. Implicit, but also at times quite conscious,

[13] Ibid. 90.

[14] As long as the American side of this interaction was privileged, an imperative underscored by Carlton Hayes's reproach in the mid-1940s that few who specialized in US history shared his view that the American experience was best studied in the context of a broadly defined, expansive European civilization. See id. 'The American Frontier—Frontier of What?', *American Historical Review*, 51/2 (1946), 199–216, at 200.

comparisons appeared to confirm the exceptionalist nature of central features of American history, ranging from what were seen to be distinctive modes of labour organization and agitation and the absence of significant socialist parties to the weakness of the state and what were assumed to be higher levels of mobility and material prosperity relative to other industrial societies.[15]

As numerous commentators have observed, the predominance of a national frame of reference for thinking and writing about US history has reinforced notions of American exceptionalism in major ways.[16] Because national units as a whole are difficult to compare successfully, reliance upon them has discouraged systematic analysis of trans- and cross-cultural historical patterns. And nation-centric history has often reduced comparisons inserted into narratives focused on developments within the USA to 'one-shot, brief analogies',[17] that have often proved more misleading than informative. Until the past two or three decades, this preoccupation with national history had also marginalized both comparative and world history within the profession. As William H. McNeill, who as early as the 1960s defied these trends by producing widely read and cited cross-cultural studies, has observed, for much of the twentieth century professional historians in the USA have had little regard for world perspectives. These were assumed to yield little more than poorly documented generalizations and deeply personal commentaries on the human condition, such as those authored by Toynbee and Spengler in the decades of global crisis following the First World War.[18]

In an extended critique of American exceptionalism, Ian Tyrrell has also deplored the neglect, and often the outright dismissal, of cross-cultural research by historians of the USA. In Tyrrell's view, the Americans' preoccupation with their own history has not only discouraged serious scholarship with a

[15] For a superb exploration of these issues, despite conclusions that may prove unsettling for comparativists and globalists, see Michael Kammen, 'The Problem of American Exceptionalism: A Reconsideration', *American Quarterly*, 45/1 (1993), 1–43.

[16] For an early and thorough critique of these connections, see Laurence Veysey, 'The Autonomy of American History Reconsidered', *American Quarterly*, 31/4 (1979), 455–77.

[17] The apt phrasing is Carl Degler's. See 'Comparative History: An Essay Review', *Journal of Southern History*, 34/3 (1968), 426.

[18] William H. McNeill, 'A Defense of World History', in id., *Mythistory and Other Essays* (Chicago, 1986), 82–95.

transnational frame of reference, it has skewed much of the comparative work that has been undertaken in recent decades. His contention that comparative work undertaken by American scholars has usually begun with questions or patterns discerned in US history that were then tested through an examination of similar phenomena in other areas works well for many of the studies written before the late 1960s.[19] As Tyrrell himself notes, his critique of American historians' approaches to comparative history owes much to Raymond Grew, who several years earlier argued that critical topics in United States history were usually the starting point for forays into cross-cultural analysis, including those focusing on slave systems, frontiers, and race relations. Grew observed that issues arising in the study of the history of other societies had rarely shaped investigations of comparable phenomena in America, and he argued that even scholars who have made significant use of case evidence drawn from elsewhere in the Americas, Africa, or Eurasia rarely sustained a serious research commitment to these areas.[20]

The fine comparative studies by such scholars as George Fredrickson, Philip Curtin, Jack Greene, Samuel Baily, and Ian Steele render the categorical assessments of Tyrrell and Grew dubious at best.[21] But they are even more troubling in view of the unintended and ironic American-centrism that Tyrrell and Grew themselves exhibit. Neither takes into account the very substantial corpus of comparative historical work produced by American scholars that does not feature US case examples or American interaction with other societies.[22] On topics ranging

[19] Ian Tyrrell, 'American Exceptionalism in an Age of International History', *American Historical Review*, 96/4 (1991), 1032–9.

[20] Grew, 'Comparative Weakness', 99.

[21] See e.g. George M. Fredrickson, *White Supremacy: A Comparative Study in American and South African History* (Oxford, 1981) and *Black Liberation: A Comparative History of Black Ideologies in the United States and South Africa* (Oxford, 1995); Philip D. Curtin, *The Atlantic Slave Trade: A Census* (Madison, Wis., 1969); Jack P. Greene, *Peripheries and Center: Constitutional Development in the Extended Polities of the British Empire and the United States, 1607–1788* (Athens, Ga., 1986); Samuel L. Baily, *Immigrants in the Lands of Promise: Italians in Buenos Aires and New York City, 1870 to 1914* (Ithaca, 1999); and Ian K. Steele, *The English Atlantic, 1675–1740: An Exploration of Communications and Community* (New York, 1986).

[22] This oversight is shared by leading comparativists, such as Carl Degler and George Fredrickson, whose periodic reflections on the state of the comparative subfield make little mention of work that does not make significant use of US, or at the very least European, case examples. See Degler, 'Comparative History', and 'In Pursuit of American History', *American Historical Review*, 92/1 (1987), 1–12; and Fredrickson, 'Comparative History', in Michael Kammen (ed.), *The Past Before Us: Contemporary*

from colonialism and peasant protest to international immigration and environmental transformations, this scholarship has in fact contributed substantially to the development of the comparative and global subfields in terms of theory and methodology, in the identification of critical issues for study and debate, and not least in enhancing our understanding of the history of other peoples and regions, especially those in the 'non-Western' world, who had been long neglected or ignored by American historians. Grew may well be correct in concluding that because of the excessively inward-looking nature of much of American historical scholarship, it has not had an international impact commensurate with the high quality and innovativeness characteristic of much of a prodigious quantity of research and writing.[23] But if the major contributions American scholars have made to both comparative and global history beyond that centred on issues rooted in US historiography are taken fully into account, in these subfields of research and writing, at least, their influence proves a good deal more considerable than Grew allows.[24]

The need for the full integration of US history into comparative and global frameworks has perhaps been most convincingly demonstrated by the important ways in which cross-cultural studies have shaped the research agenda for a diverse range of subfields dealing with processes that have been central to the American experience. In core fields of research ranging from slave systems and racial ideologies to frontier expansion, industrialization and struggles for civil rights, comparative studies

Historical Writing in the United States (Ithaca, 1980), 457–73, and 'From Exceptionalism to Variability: Recent Developments in Cross-National Comparative History', *Journal of American History*, 82/2 (1995), 587–604.

[23] Grew, 'Comparative Weakness', 87.

[24] Among the more influential of this very substantial body of works are Jerry H. Bentley, *Old World Encounters* (Oxford, 1993); Marshall G. S. Hodgson, *Rethinking World History*, ed. Edmund Burke III (New York, 1993), and *The Venture of Islam*, 3 vols. (Chicago, 1974); Janet Abu-Lughod, *Before European Hegemony: The World System A.D. 1250–1350* (New York, 1989); William H. McNeill, *The Pursuit of Power* (Chicago, 1982); Philip D. Curtin, *Cross-Cultural Trade in World History* (Cambridge, 1984); Alfred W. Crosby, *Ecological Imperialism: The Biological Expansion of Europe, 900–1900* (New York, 1986); Peter N. Stearns, *European Society in Upheaval* (London, 1967); Louise A. Tilly and Joan W. Scott, *Women, Work and Family* (New York, 1978); Eric R. Wolf, *Peasant Wars of the Twentieth Century* (New York, 1969) and *Europe and the People Without History* (Berkeley, 1982); Benedict Anderson, *Imagined Communities* (rev. edn.; London, 1991); Robert Wohl, *The Generation of 1914* (Cambridge, Mass., 1979); Theda Skocpol, *States and Social Revolutions* (London, 1979); and most recently Kenneth Pomeranz, *The Great Divergence: China, Europe, and the Making of the Modern World Economy* (Princeton, 2000).

have since the 1960s proved critical to the development of US historiography. They have identified questions that need to be pursued, established issues worthy of serious debate, and plotted broader historical patterns that had earlier tended to be obscured by a surfeit of primary source materials and a privileging of specialized research.[25] All of these tasks were, of course, precisely those for which Marc Bloch argued many decades ago that comparative analysis was indispensable.[26] And though Americanists have applied comparative techniques to case examples far more separated in time and space, and thus more disparate in cultural and historical origins and trajectories than Bloch deemed prudent,[27] their work has proved as potent an antidote to assumptions of national exceptionalism as his seminal studies on medieval Europe.

In conceiving US history comparatively and thus integrating it meaningfully into a larger global context, it is essential to distinguish between exceptionalism and difference. Exceptionalist perspectives have by no means been confined to historians, social commentators, and politicians in the USA. Like their counterparts in earlier societies and in contemporary nations, American exceptionalists have almost invariably presumed the superiority of their own culture and, from the late eighteenth century, of the national character that culture had nurtured. But arguments for the uniqueness of the USA have been both more foundational and enduring, and they have tended to emphasize sources of superiority and trajectories of dominance that distinguish the

[25] Even a partial survey of the works in each of these subfields would require an extensive essay in itself. But to gain a sense of the influence of comparative studies on US historiography, one might reflect on the impact in the post-war decades of the seminal, if highly controversial, writings of Frank Tannenbaum and Stanley Elkins, and try to imagine the state of such critical fields as slavery, racism, and frontier settlement without the comparative contributions of Carl Degler, David Brion Davis, Eugene Genovese, George Fredrickson, John Cell, Philip Curtin, Sidney Mintz, Orlando Patterson, Jack Greene, Herbert Klein, John Thornton, Philip Morgan, Peter Kolchin, and Richard White.

[26] Marc Bloch's case 'Pour une histoire comparée des sociétés européennes' was first made in 1928 in Oslo, as a paper at the Sixth International Congress of Historical Sciences. My citations are from the English translation by J. E. Anderson, entitled 'A Contribution towards a Comparative History of European Societies', in Marc Bloch, *Land and Work in Medieval Europe: Selected Papers by Marc Bloch* (New York, 1969), 44–81.

[27] For an insightful critique of the limitations of Bloch's comparative vision that is centred on these issues, see William H. Sewell, Jr., 'Marc Bloch and the Logic of Comparative History', *History and Theory*, 6/2 (1967), 208–18.

history of the republic in fundamental ways from that of the rest of humankind. From the first decades of European settlement in North America, exceptionalists have almost invariably stressed unprecedented and qualitatively (and very often quantitatively) distinctive patterns of societal, and later national, development that transcend the environmental and social obstacles that are alleged to have prevented earlier civilizations or present-day rivals from attaining similar levels of individual and collective fulfilment. American exceptionalists tend to see the rise of the USA to global power as part of a larger teleological progression towards—depending on the observer and time frame in question—human virtue, utopian sublimity, civilization, development, or modernity. And, as I have argued above, in apparent contradiction to most of the foregoing assumptions, they have premissed their prescriptions for interaction with foreign peoples and cultures on assimilationist imperatives that exceed those of even their most expansive and chauvinistic rivals past or present.

I think it fair to argue that the findings of most comparativists who make extensive use of case evidence drawn from US history underscore the importance of difference as opposed to the exceptional nature of the American experience.[28] Though exceptionalist claims have only rarely been based on well-grounded comparisons,[29] that is, of course, the only way they can be empirically verified or disproved. But, as most of the cross-cultural analyses of key patterns in American history written in recent decades amply demonstrate, serious comparison is better suited to determining the extent to which, and why, developments in the USA paralleled or diverged from those in other societies. The fact that much of the comparative work done thus far has stressed difference rather than similarity has been troubling for a number of prominent advocates of internationalist history, such as Ian Tyrrell and Akira Iriye. They have urged

[28] A distinction that Allen Dawley insisted upon well over a decade ago. See 'Farewell to "American Exceptionalism"', in Jean Heffer and Jeanine Rovet (eds.), *Why Is There No Socialism in the United States* (Paris, 1988), 311–15. For a more recent stress on the importance of these semantic distinctions for American historiography more broadly, see Kammen, 'Problem of American Exceptionalism', esp. 15, 24, and 32.

[29] Here the works of Seymour Martin Lipset provide perhaps the most notable counter-example. But despite a proclivity for rhetorical flourishes, he, too, has stressed the differences that comparison can reveal. See e.g. his recent essay 'American Exceptionalism Reaffirmed', in Byron E. Shafer (ed.), *Is America Different? A New Look at American Exceptionalism* (Oxford, 1991), 1–45.

that we can best counter American exceptionalism by deploying international and transregional (encompassing, for example, the Atlantic basin or the Pacific rim) approaches that play down national differences and foreground cross-cultural similarities, which Iriye suggests are ultimately products of the unity of the human condition.[30] But both recurring and divergent historical patterns are proper subjects for comparative and international history. And both similarities and differences challenge American exceptionalism by placing US history in broader global frames of reference that allow us to identify and explore underlying commonalities in major patterns of societal development across time and space. *All* societies exhibit variations on these shared themes; and each has experienced transcultural processes of historical transformation, such as agrarian expansion, industrialization, or conquest, in distinctive ways.

Akira Iriye's realization, as a student in post-war Japan, that his national history 'could best be understood when it was examined from without as well as from within',[31] provides a compelling point of departure for historians of the USA who have argued, in a variety of ways, that comparative or international approaches can provide more inclusive, nuanced, and complex understandings of the American experience than those adhering to a constricted master narrative that has been informed by exceptionalist thinking since the seventeenth century. At the most basic level, comparative analyses and global perspectives have contributed significantly to the disaggregation of the unified visions that have long dominated the writing of US history. They demonstrate that national units, taken as a whole or conceived as autonomous entities, are difficult, if not impossible, to compare meaningfully. Comparative and world perspectives expose concepts of national purpose and character as the same sort of essentialisms associated with now discredited approaches to history that were grounded in racial, religious, or civilizational typologies. And they illustrate the ways in which isolated, national frames of reference can obscure or skew our understandings of cross-cultural interactions or transnational phenomena.

[30] Tyrrell, 'American Exceptionalism', 1034–8; and Akira Iriye, 'The Internationalization of History', *American Historical Review*, 94/1 (1989), 3–5.

[31] Iriye, 'The Internationalization of History', 9.

Rather than whole civilizations (a term that is problematic in and of itself) or unified national narratives, serious comparison and manageable world history compel us to focus on clearly delineated processes and particular types of institutions, social movements, or discourses. Somewhat paradoxically, this narrowing of the breadth of occurrences and issues to be studied requires comparativists and globalists to concentrate on the history of specific sub-regions, or even locales, that are then compared in depth to areas in other societies that evince the same types of transformations, institutional development, or socio-intellectual upheavals. This approach to historical analysis inevitably forces us beyond élite- and male-centric narratives that until recent decades have dominated the historiography of both the USA and the areas to which it has been compared.[32] In this way comparative and international perspectives have prompted or reinforced broader efforts by historians and other social scientists to give agency and voice to a diverse range of ethnic, gender, and class groups that had long been neglected, or altogether ignored.[33] Close attention to the ways in which global transformations and cross-cultural movements of peoples, ideas, and things have shaped and complicated diversity throughout American history would appear to be essential for a society that, viewed from the long-term vantage point of the history of humankind, is perhaps the most remarkable for its ever more complex pluralism and its intensely creative, multicultural synergy.

Beyond the identification in the history of the USA, as well as the societies to which it has been compared, of questions worth asking and underlying patterns deserving exploration, a broader contextualization of the American experience in world history is indispensable to understanding the nation's rise to global power. Whether one is concerned with frontier expansion, industrialization, overseas colonization, or America's critical roles in the spread of the capitalist world system, global perspectives on

[32] Several decades ago, Laurence Veysey perceptively drew attention to the correspondence between exceptionalist generalizations concerning national character and a unified narrative of American history that was all but monopolized by white males. See 'Autonomy of American History', 457–8.

[33] A trend that was emphasized by Joyce Appleby in her presidential address to the Organization of American Historians. See 'Recovering America's Historic Diversity', esp. 426–31.

these multifaceted processes are essential to any attempt to understand the motives, responses, and actions of those who actually participated in them. Intercontinental migrations supplied the manpower; North American frontier regions and overseas areas contributed much of the resource base (including investment capital until the last half of the nineteenth century); and foreign rivals—political, military, commercial, and ecclesiastical—often provided the impetus for the ever-increasing importance of cross-cultural exchanges in the history of the USA.

By the last half of the twentieth century, transnational exchanges had become so routinized and pervasive that they impinged on virtually all aspects of American life, hence literally globalizing contemporary US history. As early as the oil crisis of 1973, it was clear to all who were willing to see that what had been long been presumed to be *American* corporations had in fact metamorphosed into international conglomerates with bottom line priorities that often had little to do with the national interest. New waves of immigration—more likely in post-1960s decades to flow from Latin America, the Caribbean, and Asia rather than Europe—have complicated and increased the ethnic and cultural diversity of the USA to the point where the majority status of peoples of European descent is challenged, or has already been eclipsed, in the fastest growing and most dynamic areas of the country. The resources this polyglot population consumes, the products it produces, and the environmental consequences of both are now calibrated in terms of international capital flows and market exchanges as well as ecological agendas that are premissed on visions of the earth as a single entity.

Except at times of major international crises, it is unlikely that most Americans give much thought to world events in their day-to-day lives, even though those lives are permeated with consumer products, from basketball shoes to DVD players, manufactured in once 'exotic' regions like the Pacific rim or Central America. But from the Gulf War through a series of costly overseas interventions like those in Somalia, Bosnia, and Kosovo, international conflicts, which the press now routinely proclaim vital to the national interest, have more and more preoccupied a populace apparently resigned to paying the considerable costs—in taxes if not casualties—of America's self-appointed role as policeman of yet another new world order. And from the late 1930s, the executive guardians of more contested global dispensations devoted significantly higher portions of their personal energies and political capital to foreign affairs. During the Second World War and the Cold War decades, this shift in leadership priorities was more obvious than it was after the collapse of Soviet command communism. But it is striking that world events both made and undid the first post-Cold War president, George Bush, who engineered a Pyrrhic victory in the Persian Gulf only to be defeated in large part because he came to be perceived as a leader who had neglected domestic affairs. And overseas crises and foreign relations increasingly became the preoccupation of the last president of the twentieth century, Bill Clinton, whose major success in enacting domestic programmes was largely confined to those inextricably bound up in broader projects to advance globalization, such as NAFTA and GATT.

In view of the relatively isolated and peripheral position of the USA until at least the last decades of the eighteenth century, and arguably then again for much of the nineteenth, world historians might well be justified in minimizing the importance of colonial America and the young republic in terms of global developments in the early modern era and the first decades of the industrial age. And in fact many have. Other than to lament the myopia and provincialism of their American audience, prominent post-Second World War scholars, such as William H. McNeill, Marshall Hodgson, J. H. Parry, and Eric Wolf, whose pioneering cross-cultural writings and prescriptions for the study of world history revitalized a moribund field, made little use of US case examples and only rarely commented on American variations on larger global themes. Foreign area specialists—who abounded in the early decades of the Cold War when government, university, and foundation funding made possible the proliferation of language programmes and multidisciplinary centres—were even more determined than the pioneers of the new world history to promote the study of other peoples' societies and cultures. In pursuit of these new perspectives, they often quite consciously neglected related developments in the USA or American influences on their areas of expertise. In many instances they did so out of the conviction that the

American impact had already been excessively studied and its importance consistently overstated. Similar reasoning also helps to account for the scant coverage given to American case examples in college history courses with comparative and global dimensions in this formative period.

In the 1960s and 1970s, the growing influence within the historical profession of comparative approaches that very often included major US case examples, prompted many world historians and area specialists to reassess their often deliberate marginalization of America's impact on the broader historical experience of humankind. It was soon apparent that distinctive, but by no means exceptional, American versions of transcultural and intercontinental historical processes, such as settler colonialism, frontier expansion, slavery, racism, segregation, immigration, industrialization, and imperialism, were simply too integral to world history to be neglected or ignored. US variants on common global themes were also too important in terms of their scale, complexity, and international impact to be left out of broader cross-cultural narratives. Meaningfully integrating American history into global narratives and comparative analyses also countered the tendency for the writings and courses of area specialists and world historians to be ghettoized, confined in their appeal to relatively small numbers of readers and students. But above all, the traumatic descent in the 1960s into the Vietnam quagmire underscored the deficiencies and dangers of conceiving the world history of the early modern and modern eras without a meaningful US component. It also led to the realization that without serious enquiry into the history of the societies in the areas into which the Americans increasingly intruded and the larger global systems in which they came to play dominant roles, we cannot begin to understand the political, military, economic, and cultural impact on the rest of the world of America's emergence in the twentieth century to the precarious status of global hegemon.

6
The Idea and Practice of World Historiography in France: The *Annales* Legacy

LUTZ RAPHAEL

There are many French historians and they look back to a glorious past of world historiography before the days of the Enlightenment. A comprehensive view of this branch of French historiography, even just for the twentieth century,[1] would require more space than is available here. This essay therefore has a more modest aim. It will concentrate on one movement, *Annales* historiography, and mainly on two people, Henri Berr and Fernand Braudel, and their attempts to write global history.

From my point of view, this reduction in scope is justified because this legacy is more than pure tradition and memory; its idea and practice may be interesting for the writing of global history today. French world historiography received a new impetus from the reformers who criticized the somewhat narrow historical practice, centred on politics, biography, and political institutions, which French historians had established since the 1880s. Among the reformers was the philosopher Henri Berr (1863–1954).[2] In 1900 he began his career as an influential broker of ideas among French intellectuals, and particularly among scholars in the humanities. He criticized the fragmentation of

[1] It should be noted that during the 20th century at least nine Universal History collections were published in France: *Clio: Introduction aux études historiques*, 13 vols. (Paris 1934–52); *Nouvelle clio: L'histoire et ses problèmes*, 45 vols. (Paris, 1963–); Fernand Braudel (ed.), *Destins du Monde*, 9 vols. (Paris, 1957–); Henri Berr (ed.), *L'évolution de l'humanité*, 61 vols. planned or published under Berr's direction by 1961 (Paris, 1920–); E. Cavaignac (ed.), *Histoire du monde*, 13 vols. (Paris, 1922–48); Maurice Crouzet (ed.), *Histoire générale des civilisations*, 7 vols. (Paris, 1953–7); Gustave Glotz (ed.), *Histoire générale*, 13 vols. (Paris, 1925–47); R. Grousset and E. Léonard (eds.), *Histoire universelle*, 3 vols. (Paris, 1956–8); Louis Halphen (ed.), *Peuples et civilisations: Histoire générale* (Paris, 1926–69).

[2] Agnès Biard, Dominique Bourel, and Eric Brian (eds.), *Henri Berr et la culture du XXe siècle* (Paris, 1997).

historical studies in the name of positivist specialization and proposed what he called a new 'historical synthesis'.[3] In essence, this meant a new arrangement of accumulated knowledge about the past but also a new historical approach including the study of civilization, society, and the economy. It differed from earlier versions of a 'civilization' approach in that it started from a more solid scientific basis. Berr underpinned his approach with an eclectic philosophy of history that integrated the ideas of Bergson, Durkheim, and the contemporary neo-Kantians.[4] But it was less the content of his programme that made Berr famous and influential than the fact that his programme could serve as a kind of platform to bring together the new currents emerging and diverging in the French humanities during the first three decades of the twentieth century. Durkheim and his students, the founders of the new *Annales* school in history, Abel Rey and Alexandre Koyré and their students in the field of the history of science and technology, and many specialists in non-European cultures and histories were all living and working in Paris, and they all met Henri Berr. In different ways they participated in his intellectual enterprises that included a review,[5] a scientific foundation,[6] an annual conference,[7] and his great editorial programme of a world history in one hundred volumes.[8]

[3] Henri Berr, *La synthèse en histoire: Essai critique et théorique* (Paris, 1911). His interest in the theoretical and methodological problems of historiography dates back to his *thèse d'Etat*: *L'avenir de l'histoire: Esquisse d'une synthèse des connaissances fondée sur l'histoire* (Paris, 1899).

[4] Enrico Castelli Gattinara, 'L'idée de synthèse: Henri Berr et les crises du savoir dans la première moitié du XXe siècle', in Biard, Bourel, and Brian (eds.), *Henri Berr*, 21–38.

[5] Martin Siegel, 'Henri Berr et la Revue de synthèse historique', in Charles-Olivier Carbonell and Georges Livet (eds.), *Au berceau des Annales: Le milieu strasbourgeois, l'histoire en France au début du XXe siècle* (Toulouse, 1983), 205–18; Martin Fugler, 'Fondateurs et collaborateurs, les débuts de la Revue de synthèse historique (1900–1910)', in Biard, Bourel, and Brian (eds.), *Henri Berr*, 173–88.

[6] The foundation 'pour la science', created in 1925, financed the 'Centre international de synthèse', which since 1927 has been located in the Hôtel de Nevers in the 2nd Arrondissement of Paris. Cf. Giuliana Gemelli, 'Communauté intellectuelle et stratégies institutionelles: Henri Berr et la fondation du Centre International de Synthèse', *Revue de Synthèse*, 108/4 (1987), 225–59.

[7] Marina Neri, 'Vers une histoire psychologique: Henri Berr et les Semaines internationale de synthèse (1929-1947)', in Biard, Bourel, and Brian (eds.), *Henri Berr*, 205–18; Bernadette Bensaude-Vincent, 'Présences scientifiques aux Semaines de synthèse (1929-1939)', ibid. 219–30.

[8] Jacqueline Pluet-Despatin, 'Henri Berr éditeur. Elaboration et production de "L'Évolution de l'humanité"', ibid. 241–68. In 1937 the editor Albin Michel took respon-

World historiography was one important pillar of Berr's enterprise. In 1913 he launched his editorial project of a series on the 'Evolution of Mankind'. At first glance, this project looked rather conventional. It imitated the many German universal histories that were contemporary bestsellers. It was equally conventional in its emphasis on intellectual independence from German models, on the 'Frenchness' of its own approach—whatever that meant. But within the French academic world dependence on German models was strongly resented, and the idea of emancipation became even more popular after the outbreak of the First World War.[9]

What made the project into more than just another of those conventional world historiographies that today gather dust in the corners of our libraries? There are probably at least three reasons. The first concerns the founding philosophy or the intellectual programme of the series. Berr's philosophy of history was a sophisticated version of evolutionism. For him, 'Mankind' was the emerging result of converging developments in religion, society, art, and science. This evolution can be observed in the different histories of civilizations and human groups across the globe, but it culminates in the making of Western civilization. This eclectic blend of contemporary Western ideas on progress and its causes encompassed ideas of vitalistic philosophy, classical idealism, and materialistic approaches. At its centre we find the idea of the growing unity of world history, interpreted as a process of integration in the making. Berr stressed the part that 'collective rational enterprises' (Toulmin) such as science and art on the one hand, and the emancipation of the individual on the other, played and continue to play in this process. He therefore insisted on the inner evolutionary dynamics of 'reason' or 'esprit', which turned this 'idealistic' argument against purely sociological models of development. Thus Berr wrote: 'Our ambition . . . will be to understand and explain by its causes and to follow the movement of progress—that is not cumulative

sibility for continuing the publication of Berr's series after the death of the founder in 1954. Since the 1960s, many volumes in the original series have been reissued in paperback. The collection itself still continues, but it has given up the systematical approach of the original programme. Non-European history plays only a marginal role in it.

[9] Claude Digeon, *La crise allemande de la pensée française (1870-1914)* (Paris, 1959); Christophe Charle, *La République des universitaires 1870-1940* (Paris, 1994), 21–60.

continuously and absolutely, but overall and from certain viewpoints—that gives a sense to the life of mankind.'[10]

To get an idea of the kind of 'evolutionism' that Berr's series was inventing we must take a closer look at the plan of 1913. It was divided into four large chronological sections.[11] An introduction dealt with proto-history and the preconditions of history. The second part was devoted to Antiquity, the origins of Christianity, and the Middle Ages, and the two sections on modern history and the contemporary period respectively had not yet been conceived in detail when the plan was published before the First World War.[12] This scheme was rather conventional; the new accents become visible when we look more closely at the main sections, where chronological order is completely abandoned. Instead, we find individual volumes devoted to an entire civilization—especially those outside the traditional European area—or to religion, law, political institutions, the economy, art, or science. The classical historiography of battles, conquests, treaties, and dynasties was drastically reduced in this world historiography. The whole series was a collection of monographs, and each book was to have a unity of its own. Each volume had only one author or one responsible editor who organized the collaboration of other specialists. Berr did everything to distinguish his undertaking from the usual practice of other world histories that were mere collections

[10] 'Cette ambition animera donc notre œuvre, de faire comprendre, par ses causes, et de suivre le mouvement progressif—non pas continûment et absolument, mais dans l'ensemble et à certains points de vue progressif—qui donne un sens à la vie de l'humanité.' Henri Berr, 'Introduction à une histoire universelle', *Revue de synthèse historique,* 30/88 (1920), 26.

[11] I. Introduction (Préhistoire, Protohistoire); Antiquité (6 vols.); II. Le monde antique—Les empires et les civilisations de l'Orient (3 vols.); III. Le monde antique—La Grèce et la civilisation héllénique (6 vols.); IV. Le monde antique—Rome et la civilisation romaine (7 vols.); V. Le monde antique—en marge de l'Empire romain (4 vols.); 2nd section: Origines du christianisme et Moyen Age: I. Les Origines du christianisme et la crise morale du monde antique (4 vols.); II. L'Effondrement de l'Empire et l'affaiblissement de l'idée monarchique (5 vols.); III. L'impérialisme religieux (4 vols.); IV. L'art du Moyen Age et la civilisation française (1 vol.); V. La reconstitution du pouvoir monarchique (3 vols.); VI. L'évolution économique et la bourgeoisie (2 vols.); VII. L'évolution intellectuelle (3 vols.); VIII. Le passage du Moyen Age aux temps modernes (3 vols.). Henri Berr, 'La "bibliothèque de synthèse historique"', *Revue de synthèse historique,* 28/83–4 (1914), 337–42.

[12] When these sections were planned after 1918 Berr gave up the detailed scheme he had proposed for the two other sections and merely listed 22 new titles for the period from 1500 to 1800. He gave priority to the history of science and ideas (7 vols.) but non-European history was dealt with only in the context of European expansion (2 vols.).

of independently conceived articles or chapters written by specialists.

The second reason for Berr's success was his idea to enlarge the circle of scholars and disciplines participating in the enterprise. In his view, the authors should have different horizons and integrate the different approaches relevant to their particular field of research. Alongside historians, we find sociologists, philosophers, Orientalists, linguists, and so forth. Volumes one to six, comprising the introductory section, in particular, were written by specialists not in history, but in neighbouring disciplines. Here the public was exposed to new approaches to history. Thirdly, Berr's programme was open to experimentation. He presented an integrative plan for the whole series. However, many titles in his list were merely programmes for new research. In contrast to other contemporary philosophers of history such as Spengler or Toynbee, he did not try to create a new system of his own, but conceived of his collection as an empirical testing ground for some of his main ideas. In his mind, the collection was a kind of work in progress in world history. Again and again he used his prefaces to redefine the whole programme and to integrate the new findings represented by the volume just published.[13] But, as often happens with this kind of collective intellectual enterprise, intention and reality diverged. In fact, Berr maintained the direction of the series throughout his long life, and when he died in 1954, 52 of the 100 volumes had been published, while seven more volumes were in the making. Nevertheless, the programme as an identifiable whole did not survive the interwar period.

The First World War had seriously undermined the beginning of the project. Authors and plans had to be revised in the 1920s and Berr had had to struggle hard against the conventionalism of the academic milieu.[14] The collection became more traditional and conventional than Berr had originally intended. European history largely dominated, while the common perspectives for an integrative synthesis of global history faded away. Typically, the collective memory of the learned world has retained individual outstanding books more than the grand plan

[13] His prefaces are reprinted in Henri Berr, *En marge de l'histoire universelle*, 2 vols. (Paris, 1934, 1953).

[14] Pluet-Despatin, 'Henri Berr éditeur', 252, 261.

and the original programme. This is the case, for instance, with such brilliant volumes as those by Marcel Granet on Chinese thought and society, Marc Bloch on feudal society, and Lucien Febvre's study of religion at the time of Rabelais.[15] They were all published in Berr's collection. In some respects, however, we must speak of failure, mostly because Berr had no academic power to organize a school and to impose his ideas, in a practical way, on a more or less reluctant academic community. During his life he remained marginal to the academic establishment of the Sorbonne that rejected his heterodox ideas and his interdisciplinary approach.

These difficulties may partly explain why there was no major engagement with universal historiography and its problems among the first generation of *Annales* historians. Lucien Febvre and, to a minor degree, Marc Bloch, the founders of the new review in 1929 and leading figures of its first generation, both took part in the collective enterprise of Henri Berr's review,[16] and his editorial project.[17] But both reformers in the field of historical practice were convinced that substantial changes within their discipline could not be achieved by engaging themselves in a field in which the risk of amateurish failure and vague generalization was disproportionaly high,[18] and which would not convince the orthodox majority of their colleagues. Both preferred to speak of new subjects and new methods in medieval and modern European history rather than of historical synthesis.[19] It was here

[15] Marcel Granet, *La civilisation chinoise* (Paris, 1929); *La pensée chinoise* (Paris, 1934); Lucien Febvre, *Le problème de l'incroyance au XVIe siècle: La religion de Rabelais* (Paris, 1942), English trans.: *The Problem of Unbelief in the Sixteenth Century: The Religion of Rabelais* (Cambridge, Mass., 1982); Marc Bloch, *La société féodale* (Paris 1939–40), English trans.: *Feudal Society* (London, 1961).

[16] Jean-Pierre Aguet and Bertrand Muller, '"Combats pour l'histoire" de Lucien Febvre dans la Revue de synthèse historique (1905–1939)', *Schweizerische Zeitschrift für Geschichte*, 35 (1985), 389–448.

[17] In addition to his study on Rabelais, Lucien Febvre wrote two other volumes in the series: *La terre et l'évolution humaine* (Paris, 1922), English trans.: *A Geographical Introduction to History* (London, 1925); and with Henri-Jean Martin, *L'apparition du livre* (Paris, 1958), English trans.: *The Coming of the Book* (London, 1976). Lucien Febvre was still working on a third book for Berr's collection when he died in 1956. Robert Mandrou completed it under the title *Introduction à la France moderne* (Paris, 1961), English trans.: *Introduction to Modern France* (London, 1975).

[18] Cf. Febvre's critique, 'De Toynbee à Spengler: Deux philosophies opportunistes de l'histoire', in id., *Combats pour l'histoire* (Paris, 1953), 119–46.

[19] Bertrand Muller, 'Lucien Febvre et Henri Berr: De la synthèse à l'histoire-problème', in Biard, Bourel, and Brian (eds.), *Henri Berr*, 39–60.

that Marc Bloch advocated the comparative method.[20] His own contribution to Berr's collection was a masterly integrative view of European medieval society. However, he did not engage in a systematic comparison with other societies and periods in which constellations similar to European feudalism could be found, merely dedicating some final remarks to the Japanese case.[21] In fact, neither Febvre nor Bloch, by temperament or specialization, were global historians. Febvre confronted the problems of world history as one of the academic organizers of the new French encyclopaedia in the 1930s and, after the Second World War, of the UNESCO history of mankind. In the last four years of his life he was co-editor of the newly created review *Cahiers d'histoire du Monde*. But in neither case did his activities have any direct impact on the practice of *Annales* historiography. Nor did they stimulate him to reflect on the problems of historical synthesis at this level. Febvre's enthusiasm for co-ordinated research programmes in history, which had been intense before the Second World War, was renewed when he became president of the newly founded 6th Section of the École Pratique des Hautes Études in 1949. We shall see that this commitment to collective research laid the foundations for future initiatives in global history at this new school for the social sciences.[22] The first era of *Annales* historiography between the wars represents an interlude, and, as far as the practice of world historiography is concerned, even a step back from the large horizons which Berr's *synthèse historique* had opened. None the less, it was fruitful in stimulating further developments. Bloch and Febvre with their collaborators introduced new methods and ideas into historical research in France. They pioneered an interdisciplinary approach that widened the horizons of historical practice in France.[23]

[20] Marc Bloch, 'Pour une histoire comparée des sociétés européennes', *Revue de synthèse*, 46 (1928), 15–50.

[21] But he was always strongly interested in comparative studies on the Mediterranean or East European area. For a critical appraisal of Bloch's comparative European approach see Lucette Valensi, 'Retour d'Orient: De quelques usages du comparatisme', in Hartmut Atsma and André Burguière (eds.), *Marc Bloch aujourd'hui: Histoire comparée et sciences sociales* (Paris, 1990), 307–16; Evelyne Patlagean, 'Europe, seigneurie, féodalité: Marc Bloch et les limites orientales d'un espace de comparaison', ibid. 279–98.

[22] Lucien Febvre, 'Pour une histoire dirigée: Les recherches collectives et l'avenir de l'histoire', in id., *Combats*, 55–60.

[23] Peter Schöttler, 'Eine spezifische Neugierde: Die frühen Annales als interdisziplinäres Projekt', *Comparativ*, 1/4 (1992), 112–26.

After the Second World War, while Fernand Braudel reigned as the intellectual leader and organizer of the *Annales* movement,[24] world historiography was established as an integral part of the *Annales* programme. Unlike the founders of the *Annales* movement, Fernand Braudel always had great sympathy for a global view of the subjects of his own research.[25] All his major contributions, especially his three books on the Mediterranean world, his study of the history of civilizations, and finally his work on capitalism and the economic history of the modern period, are partly or completely conceived as contributions to problems of world history. As in the case of Henri Berr, we may distinguish between intellectual programme and practice. Early in his career Braudel had developed a global vision of history, a view that had unfolded since the 1940s.

At the core of his global approach we find a geographical perspective on the past and great sensitivity for the importance of the spatial dimension of history. His own approach was clearly expressed for the first time in his study on the Mediterranean world during the reign of Philip II of Spain.[26] Braudel profited from the strong intellectual ties between the French school of human geography and the *Annales* movement, but he was also influenced by Ratzel and the German school of historical geography.[27] He strictly rejected the geo-political programme linked with the name of Ratzel and the generalizations put forward by his pupils. However, Braudel took some essential theoretical inspirations from both schools. Thus in all his books he underlined the impact of geographical forces such as topography or climate on the course of civilizations, politics, and economics throughout history. He did not hesitate to speak

[24] J. H. Hexter, 'Fernand Braudel and the Monde Braudellien', *Journal of Modern History*, 44 (1972), 480–539.

[25] This aspect of Braudel's work is emphazised by Carlos Antonio Aguirre Rojas, *Fernand Braudel und die modernen Sozialwissenschaften* (Leipzig, 1999), and Giuliana Gemelli, *Fernand Braudel e l'Europa universale* (Venice, 1990).

[26] Fernand Braudel, *La méditerranée et le monde méditerranéen à l'époque de Philippe II* (Paris, 1949; 2nd edn. 1966), English trans.: *The Mediterranean and the Mediterranean World in the Age of Philip II* (London, 1972–3); cf. Samuel Kinser, 'Annaliste Paradigm? The Geohistorical Structuralism of Fernand Braudel', *American Historical Review*, 86 (1981), 63–105.

[27] Peter Burke, *The French Historical Revolution: The Annales School 1929–89* (London, 1990), 37; a more detailed view is found in Jürgen Osterhammel, 'Raumerfassung und Universalgeschichte im 20. Jahrhundert', in Gangolf Hübinger, Jürgen Osterhammel, and Erich Pelzer (eds.), *Universalgeschichte und Nationalgeschichten* (Freiburg, 1994), 51–72.

of determining forces—without adopting any monocausal explanation of historical events in terms of geography. Jürgen Osterhammel identifies four points where the geographical perspective is palpable in Braudel's work: his sensitivity to historiographical representation of space; the search for geo-historical patterns in secular economic or cultural developments; attention to the basic facts of migration, including movements of animals, plants, and microbes; and, finally, an interest in phenomena linked to the frontier.[28] There are many traces of this geo-historical view in Braudel's later books but his sensitivity to the restrictions and possibilities which geography imposed on the course of human actions never became a closed system of geographical explanation.

A second feature of Braudel's view of global history is the attention he paid to cultural conflicts or transfers between civilizations. Aversions and affinities induced by secular habits, religious beliefs, and everyday practices are interpreted as vital forces shaping spatial borders and cultural transfers between neighbouring civilizations. In Braudel's view there is a long chain of hidden homologies from the material life directly influenced by climate, soil, and topography to the most sophisticated aspects of culture, religion, and philosophy, linking the geo-historical and cultural particularities of each civilization. In his *History of Civilizations*, written at the end of the 1950s and published in 1963, Braudel defined civilizations in terms of four dimensions: spaces, societies, economies, and collective mentalities.[29]

Thirdly, Braudel's view of global history was deeply influenced by his conviction that we cannot explain the facts of the past or the present without looking at the effects of what he called the *longue durée*, of those structures that we find present for long periods of time.[30] These effects become visible only when we separate ourselves from the normal temporality of political events, economic cycles, and cultural epochs. In this respect, Braudel never accepted the well established chronological divisions of

[28] Osterhammel, 'Raumerfassung', 70–2.

[29] Fernand Braudel, *La Grammaire des civilisations* (Paris, 1963, 1987), 40–54, English trans.: *A History of Civilizations* (London, 1994).

[30] Fernand Braudel, 'Histoire et sciences sociales: La longue durée', in id., *Écrits sur l'histoire* (Paris, 1969), 41–84; English trans.: *On History* (Chicago, 1980).

Western historiography. This distance enabled him to take a fresh look at different temporalities in all civilizations and histories he encountered during his investigations in global history.

The fourth point concerns chronology. His specialization as a historian of the long sixteenth century made Braudel a historiographer of the process of globalization of history under the impact of European capitalism and colonial expansion.[31] Here he was working in a well established field of historical and sociological research. In some respects he took up the question which the 'younger German historical school' of national economy had formulated at the end of the nineteenth century and which outstanding works such as those of Werner Sombart and Max Weber had tried to answer. Like his German colleagues fifty years previously, Braudel started from economic facts but finished with society, culture, and science. Thus his book on the rise of Western capitalism became a kind of total history of all aspects with any relevance for an economic world history between the fourteenth and the nineteenth century.[32]

In his *History of Civilizations* Braudel identified civilizations as those units in which the effects of *longue durée* are the most visible and those realities that most obviously, even today, cannot be explained without history. He underlined the impact of the cultural background of all the economic and political problems dealt with by contemporary modernization theory or development schemes. Thus, when turning back to the classical problems of economic history in the 1960s, Braudel adopted the strong traditions of world historiography centred on the analysis of civilizations. He did not accept the impressionistic or purely descriptive practice often linked to this cultural approach. He repeatedly suggested constructing concepts and models capable of explaining sequences and continuities in global history.[33]

[31] Fernand Braudel, *Civilisation matérielle, économie et capitalisme XVe–XVIIIe siècle,* 2nd revised edn., vol. 1: *Les structures du quotidien* (Paris, 1979), English trans.: *The Structure of Everyday Life* (London, 1981); vol. 2: *Les jeux de l'échange* (Paris, 1979), English trans.: *The Wheels of Commerce* (London, 1982); vol. 3: *Le temps du monde,* English trans.: *The Perspective of the World* (London, 1983).

[32] The unexpected architecture of his trilogy was widely discussed and is still commented on by historians: Samuel Kinser, 'Capitalism Enshrined: Braudel's Triptych of Modern Economic History', *Journal of Modern History,* 53 (1981), 673–82; Immanuel Wallerstein, 'Braudel on Capitalism, or Everything Upside Down', in id., *Unthinking Social Science* (London, 1991), 207–17.

[33] Fernand Braudel, *La dynamique du capitalisme* (Paris, 1985), English version: *Afterthoughts on Material Civilisation* (Baltimore, 1977).

Comparing different units in time and space, Braudel did not hesitate to go back to authors arguing from an evolutionary or Eurocentric point of view, but he always kept his distance from Eurocentric views.

The fifth point concerns the way in which Braudel dealt with these problems of world history. While for many other historians world history was a suitable subject for a lecture, a mere question of intellectual pleasure, for Braudel it was a serious research activity and a matter of organization. He insisted on the necessity for further historical investigations in African, Asian, and American studies in order to provide a more solid basis of comparative practice that could dispense sufficient data and attain comparable standards of knowledge. Braudel was a convinced empiricist as far as the creation of sound historical models was concerned. In his view, inductive historical concepts should not be replaced by grand social theory or models imported from other human sciences.

Thus there is a much stronger link between theory and practice, between historiography and historical research in the case of Braudel than in the case of Berr. We must bear in mind that behind the author Braudel we find a staff of collaborators engaged in the research necessary for his books.[34] Thus the second edition of *The Mediterranean and The Mediterranean World in the Age of Philip II* reflects the collective research programmes which the historical research centre at the 6th Section of the École Pratique des Hautes Études (EPHE) had developed since the early 1950s. In the case of the first volume of Braudel's book on capitalism, the journal itself, the *Annales* ESC, and the CRH were involved, providing essential research, for example, for the project of the world atlas of plants and domestic animals or on enquiries about nutrition.[35]

Braudel's engagement with global history is strongly linked to the institutional framework he tried to build up as president of the 6th Section of the EPHE (1956–72). When creating the new

[34] Lutz Raphael, *Le Centre de recherches historiques de 1949 à 1975*, Cahiers du Centre de Recherches Historiques, 10 (Paris, 1993).

[35] In 1961 the journal introduced a special section for these 'enquêtes ouvertes': *Vie matérielle et comportements biologiques, Bulletin* 1f., *Annales ESC* 1961, 545 ff., ibid. 1962, 75 ff., 477 ff., 818 ff., 885 ff., 1141 ff., ibid. 1963, 138 ff., 521 ff., 1133 ff., ibid. 1964, 467 f., 933 ff., ibid. 1966, 1026 ff.; *Histoire de la vie matérielle, Bulletin* 2f., ibid. 1961, 723 ff., *Pour un Atlas d'Histoire de la vie matérielle: Cartes historiques des cultures vivières*, ibid. 1966, 1012 ff.

departments of the 'aires culturelles', he voted for the establishment of a completely new section.[36] This adopted the US subject of area studies, but transformed it by increasing the number of disciplines involved. Between 1956 and 1960 the first four centres for area studies (Africa, India, China, and Russia/Eastern Europe) were created; in the next twenty years another twenty research units followed.[37] The whole range of the humanities was to be present in the newly created departments, and history played an important part as the federating discipline. Typically the experts of the Rockefeller Foundation responsible for the first grants given for the new discipline of area studies in Paris in 1954 were reluctant to spend their dollars, intended to defend the West in the Cold War, on modernizing the world of historical research on such remote topics as, for example, the Sung era in China.[38]

Of course, there is no automatic link between the introduction of area studies and a turn towards global history. Nor was this the case among *Annales* historians. But during Braudel's presidency of the 6th section of the EPHE, we can observe a growing interest in a comparative approach and in exchanging research results between the different disciplines and across the borders separating the different research units (namely, on Russia, Islam, Africa, East Asia, and India). Naturally, this practice was heavily centred on Braudel who, in this respect, ensured that his institutional tasks as the president of the EHESS coincided with his personal interests as a historian of global ambitions and curiosities.

The last point characterizing the particularities of Braudel's approach concerns his theoretical ambitions. For him, world history was more than rearranging empirical data according to the classifications of Weber's historical sociology or of the other classics of sociology. Braudel never accepted a simple adoption of modernization theory, not even of the models of Immanuel Wallerstein that were largely inspired by his own ideas. Instead he insisted on the necessity to approach the realities of the past

[36] Brigitte Mazon, *Aux origines de l'E.H.E.S.S., le rôle du mécénat américain* (Paris, 1988), 119–36.

[37] Denys Lombard, 'De la vertu des "aires culturelles"', in Jacques Revel and Nathan Wachtel (eds.), *Une école pour les sciences sociales: De la VI Section à l'École des Hautes Études en Sciences Sociales* (Paris, 1996), 115–25.

[38] Mazon, *Aux origines*, 123.

more closely in proposing historiography as the best way of integrating the somewhat unilateral views and explanations of the other social sciences. In this respect, world history was to be the level at which mature historical models could be tested. The ongoing work for his study of the rise of Western capitalism in the late 1960s and 1970s led Braudel himself to formulate some general models to serve as guides for further investigations in global history. At the same time he insisted on the need for social theories to be subjected to rigorous empirical testing by historical investigation. Thus his own contribution in this field is not easy to sum up or to reduce to an abstract model. First, he developed the model of *économie monde*, a French neologism created to distinguish the two meanings of the German term *Weltwirtschaft*—the first referring to the world economy in the sense of an economy encompassing the globe (*économie mondiale*), and the second referring to an economic system structuring production, consumption, and distribution in one part of the globe (continent or region). Before the globalization of Western capitalism, all economic systems encompassed only parts of the globe. Therefore exchange and transfer between them, across their borders, and on their margins were essential to explain the dynamics of economic world history. In Braudel's model, each regional system gained vitality and dynamics from strong internal hierarchizations between an organizing political, cultural, and economic centre whose economic and military power and cultural attraction penetrated the whole area covered by the system (until the creation of nation-states and national economies at the end of the eighteenth century, this centre was always a city), an intermediary zone of attraction, and a periphery where the negative consequences of an essentially unequal exchange of men, goods, and capital accumulated. Braudel's idea was systematically developed and articulated by Wallerstein, but, as has just been mentioned, the French historian remained sceptical about the more schematical sociological models, without denying his fundamental agreement.

Secondly, this model implies the coexistence of different modes of production and of different temporalities within each regional economic system. The unequal flow of capital between centre and periphery is based on the coexistence of technologically advanced forms of production with older, traditional, or even archaic forms. The idea of the coexistence of different temporalities, first expounded in Braudel's book of 1949, gives way to a model of different economic spheres. Once again, there is a triad of everyday routines of consumption and the production needed for them, the market economy, and grand capitalism, whose essence lies in its capacity to monopolize the economic opportunities which large distances and different spheres of consumption and production offer for capital accumulation.

Development within these world economies is mainly the result of a cyclical movement of centripetal and centrifugal flows of capital linked with political and cultural struggles for hegemony inside the regions included in the economic system. As Braudel showed in the third volume of his book on the rise of capitalism, spatial shifts in the centres of the European economy more or less followed the rhythm of long-term economic cycles. Phases of *conjonctural baisse* always exacerbated the struggle for domination between competing economic and military powers, and thus often prepared a shift in regional leadership.

The globalization of the Western world economy is seen by Braudel as a special case of expansion, and particularly of the successful penetration of other world economies by one economic system. He emphasized the importance of American resources for the success of European trade and colonial expansion in the Asian economies.[39] Braudel risked formulating general models in economic history, but he was much more reluctant when cultural and political dimensions were at stake. He generally refused to give credit to any variety of cultural explanation for the rise of Western civilization. At the same time, he underlined the impact of differences between civilizations for the spatial structuring of economic areas and the formation of political or economic borderlands and peripheries.[40] Braudel's models were not intended to form a comprehensive theory, but to sum up the results of historical research and to guide further studies. Braudel himself revisited his own ideas again and again, and confronted them with the views of economists and sociologists.[41]

[39] Cf. Fernand Braudel, 'L'expansion européenne et la longue durée', in id., *Les ambitions de l'histoire* (Paris, 1997), 468–83.

[40] This idea is strongly expressed in his books on the Mediterranean world and in his history of civilizations.

[41] This dialogue can now easily be followed in the collection of his articles and

If we compare what happened in Paris around Braudel during the 1960s and 1970s with projects and activities in the academic world outside France, we suddenly see an important feature of the French way or the Braudelian approach. He did not relinquish the problems of global history and the grammar of civilizations to the social sciences or the historical sociology that was taking shape during the same period in other Western countries. Braudel defended his own discipline. He was convinced that there was a need for a genuinely historical approach to the current problems of world politics and that therefore historians had to defend their own area of research against the 'imperialism' of other disciplines through an all-embracing integrationism.

It is fascinating to see that even Braudel, one of the great figures in the academic world of the French social sciences between 1956 and 1972, did not succeed in implementing a coherent practice of world historiography based on empirical research. This invites further reflection on the institutional and intellectual preconditions and perspectives of any other global history project. The French case provides some elements for a debate on this question. First, we observe that the Braudelian commitment to world historiography was shared with enthusiasm by foreign scholars who went to Paris and worked with him.[42] However, among French historians interest was much smaller. It was not Braudel's global history of civilizations and economies that attracted the new *Annales* historians, but the programme of Labrousse, his colleague at the Sorbonne. Although strongly influenced by Marx, Labrousse's approach was strictly national, not even European in scope and outlook.[43] Thus the great majority of the books and articles written by *Annales* historians dealt with France. One cannot but see this as

conferences: Fernand Braudel, *Écrits sur l'histoire*; *Les Dynamiques*; *Écrits sur l'histoire II* (Paris, 1990); and *Les ambitions*.

[42] One of the most famous historians in this international group is Ruggero Romano who represented a personal link between the research groups in Paris and the Geneva group around P. Bairoch, the other outstanding figure of Francophone world historiography in the 20th century. Jean-François Bergier *et al.* (eds.), *Ruggiero Romano aux pays de l'histoire et des sciences sociales*, *Revue européenne des sciences sociales* 31/64 (1983).

[43] Burke, *French Historical Revolution*, 53–7, 74 f.; for a more detailed analysis see my own study, Lutz Raphael, *Die Erben von Bloch und Febvre: 'Annales'-Historiographie und 'nouvelle histoire' in Frankreich 1945–1980* (Stuttgart, 1994), 137–47, 244–314.

the revenge of the *longue durée,* when looking at all the great historians of this school writing about classical themes of French national history. Nation-centred school curricula and examination schemes had an impact, but perhaps we should pay attention to traditional and new public demands for national historiography that editors cannot avoid satisfying.[44]

We should not forget another effect, visible in the field of the area studies that developed quickly in the cosmopolitan world of Parisian scholarship. Scholars in the newly created centres of area studies followed the classical strategy of any specialized field of research: they did not waste time on questions concerning world history. They were reluctant to draw comparisons and strongly defended their own field of research against intruders from Europe or elsewhere. Thus the EHESS is still a vital centre for African, Asian, and Islamic studies, but it is not a booming centre of world historiography. The *Annales* tradition and the French approach to world history during the twentieth century must be placed in a broader context. It is evident that the *Annales* practice—and to a minor degree even its programme—was centred on Europe and European history. This became clear in the case of Berr's 'Evolution of Mankind' series, in which the highest intellectual values, like reason and science, were at stake and the Greek miracle was presented. It was obvious even in the case of Braudel when he clearly put the particularities and singularity of Europe at the centre of his third volume.

The second point concerns the problem of the epistemological preconditions for these practices. Before the Second World War a universalistic interpretation of world history dominated. This rationalistic unitarian view of a single history of mankind in the making was strongly tied to an evolutionary vision of the past. After 1945 cultural relativism and a pluralistic view of civilizations predominated, but it was counterbalanced by an interest in universalistic categorization and comprehensive models at the level of historical explanation. Finally, the third point takes up a distinction made by the German scholar Ernst Schulin

[44] Lutz Raphael, 'Flexible Response? Strategies of Academic Historians Towards Larger Markets for National Historiographies and Increasing Scientific Standards', in Rolf Torstendahl (ed.), *An Assessment of Twentieth-Century Historiography* (Stockholm, 2000), 129–50.

when he categorized the different approaches to world historiography during the twentieth century. In 1974 he distinguished between an analytic-structural approach and a spatial-relational one centred on geography, migration, and cultural contact.[45] In my view the French *Annales* legacy participates in both traditions and, at its best, the French way succeeded in combining the advantages of both in a special form of *synthèse historique.*

[45] Ernst Schulin, 'Einleitung', in id. (ed.), *Universalgeschichte* (Cologne, 1974), 11–65, at 42–4.

7

The Singularities of British *Weltgeschichte*

MICHAEL BENTLEY

An Anglo-Saxon view of world history: the perspective feels implausible at the outset. Yet when Ernst Troeltsch used the phrase in 1922 he had in mind Wells's *Outline of History* rather than a general disposition.[1] To the extent that Wells displayed anything specifically British then Troeltsch could see little in it beyond smallness of vision—'the . . . rigidly limited horizon of the Anglo-Saxons'[2]—which hardly revealed a latent potential for world-historical speculation. Before the war the question could presumably not have arisen in a historical culture soaked in the specialized, forensic empiricism associated with the generation of Maitland or Oxford's famous 'Class of '74' which, for all the Stubbsian translation of Ranke, always looked more likely to produce an R. L. Poole than a Spengler. Both for contemporaries and later historiographers, it was the war that effected ontological change. An invitation to deliver the first Raleigh Lecture to the British Academy in October 1919 prompted James, Lord Bryce to speak on the subject of 'World History' and he located his decision in the events of the past five years:

the flame lit on the Danube and the Rhine spread till it blazed along the coasts of the Atlantic, the Indian, the Pacific, and the Arctic Oceans. There was fighting in China and New Guinea, on the heights of Armenia and in the valley of the Jordan, on the Steppes of Siberia and Turkistan. Bolivia broke off relations with Germany, though she had no means of getting at the enemy, and the King of the Tonga Islands thought it necessary to proclaim his neutrality. Many forces . . . had been drawing the nations together. But it was the outbreak of war that first made us realize how mankind had become virtually one

[1] Ernst Troeltsch, 'Eine angelsächsische Ansicht der Weltgeschichte', *Historische Zeitschrift*, 126 (1922), 271–9.

[2] Ibid. 271.

> community, all the members whereof were to be thereafter linked together . . . Thus have all men been forced to feel that the parts of the world have grown into one, for weal or woe: thus comes it that now for the first time the History of the World in the full sense of the word can begin to be written.[3]

He could not quite see how to do it, other than by, rather lamely, 'narrating the facts as they happen, endeavouring to connect those that belong to one country with those which were contemporaneously happening elsewhere'. And he conceded that anyone capable of doing it would probably decide not to do so precisely because they would be intelligent enough to understand the dimensions of the task.[4] A story had been set in train, all the same, that would turn world history as a genre into a twentieth-century phenomenon whose pre-history had to be pulled into a complementary curve. World history, the greatest of all metanarratives, had begun to build its own great story.

The story has a trans-European dimension that far outruns Wells's *jeu d'esprit* of 1920. One thinks at once of Delbrück, though one should not, since his particular style of *Weltgeschichte* had little to do with what later exponents of the art thought it meant; his version had formed a preoccupation in his mind and teaching since the 1890s.[5] Perhaps he is better regarded as the land division of Mahon's naval operation,[6] bringing the world to structured order beneath the impress of a first-rate military mind. Closer is the Frenchman Cavaignac, at least to the extent that he identified the war as his inspiration and believed, like Bryce, that 'la solidarité mondiale n'apparaisse, avec une netteté frappante, que dans la guerre qui vient de finir', even if he had

[3] Lord Bryce, 'World History', *Proceedings of the British Academy*, 9 (1919–20), 188.

[4] Ibid. 191. 'It is sometimes asked why no satisfactory History of the World has yet been written . . . The answer seems to be that there have been very few persons possessing both the requisite learning and the amplitude of vision and the delicacy of insight sufficient to qualify them even to contemplate so great an undertaking, and that those few have declined it because they realized its magnitude' (192).

[5] Hans Delbrück, *Weltgeschichte: Vorlesungen, gehalten an der Universität Berlin 1896/1920*, 5 vols. (Berlin, 1920–8).

[6] Cf. Alfred Thayer Mahon, *The Influence of Sea Power upon History, 1660–1783*, 2 vols. (London, 1890–7); *The Influence of Sea Power upon the French Revolution and Empire 1793–1812*, 2 vols. (London, 1892); *The Interest of America in Sea Power, Present and Future* (London, 1897); *The Life of Nelson, the Embodiment of the Sea Power of Great Britain*, 2 vols. (London, 1897). It would be pleasing to add Froude for British colour but, whatever his mind was, it was not military. Cf. James Anthony Froude, *Oceania, or England and her Colonies* (London, 1886).

actually started work, like Spengler, some years before 1914.[7] But Wells wanted a world safe for heroes after the war to end war; and he thought that science and technology simultaneously made it available and threatened its destruction. He was a laboratory Whig. Cavaignac had none of that: he talked about power, like Delbrück, and saw the crux of the war in a lesson about maritime and colonial supremacy that became his theme and message:

> Il y a à chaque époque une puissance qui peut remplacer à peu près ce qu'est la Papauté au moyen âge, et qui, par son rôle éminent, offre un centre d'où les grands faits se laissent dominer sans trop d'artifice. En effet, les peuples européens qui, successivement, ont été à la tête du mouvement maritime et colonial, se sont trouvés par là en mesure d'exercer une influence prépondérante sur l'histoire interne de l'Europe.[8]

The wider reach of Wells's idea one finds reflected in other French writing, however, especially in Iorga's celebrated view from Bucharest,[9] and the enormous series of discrete volumes commissioned and edited in Paris by Gustave Glotz under the rubric of his *Histoire générale* between 1925 and 1947.

This moment of *Weltgeschichte* encompassed Wells and his strange, highly individual project. The next absorbed Toynbee without making him less eccentric than he was. Unlike Wells, Toynbee had held a university chair and his Directorship at Chatham House[10] gave him an off-centre podium which nevertheless kept him in the main arena of academic life. His *Study of History*, the 'nonsense book' as he tellingly called it,[11] arose from his obsessions about the classical world rather than from an intention to produce what it eventually became, a nomothetic proposal about what had driven western civilizations over

[7] E. Cavaignac, *Histoire du monde*, 13 vols. (Paris, 1922–30). ('World solidarity only appeared, but then with a striking clarity, in the war that has just finished.')

[8] Ibid. i. 366. ('In any era there is a power that plays a role similar to the papacy in the Middle Ages and whose actions, through its privileged status, carry far-reaching significance. In reality the European peoples who put themselves at the head of first the maritime and then the colonial initiatives found themselves in a position also to exercise a direct influence over the internal history of Europe.')

[9] N. Iorga, *Essai de synthèse de l'histoire de l'humanité*, 4 vols. (Paris, 1926–8).

[10] 'Chatham House' is the term universally used in Britain to denote the Royal Institute of International Affairs which Toynbee directed for thirty years between 1925 and 1955.

[11] See William McNeill, *Arnold J. Toynbee: A Life* (Oxford, 1989), 160–1.

several millennia. Not only was the enquiry written in the shadow of Spengler's *Untergang des Abendlandes*,[12] but other writing of the 1930s and 1940s suggests that Toynbee's own thinking formed one facet of a multiple reflection. This was so in the USA in the style of Swain's *History of World Civilization* that appeared in 1938 but it gathered force with first the promise and then the reality of American entry into the Second World War.[13] It was the more so, for obvious reasons, in Europe—in Belgium, for example, out of which the great Pirenne's son, Jacques, had been driven into exile in Switzerland where he began his monumental study of the past's *Grands Courants* which showed, '[d]evant l'âbime de détresse dans lequel l'humanité est tombée', that history was quite as much law-governed as Wells and Toynbee had contended.[14] It was a mood that absorbed Europe as it fell into a different 'âbime' between the new superpowers and felt the weight of world pressure across continents, producing compendia, vast and *weltgeschichtlich*, from Berne to Munich to Paris.[15] But not to London. Revill's unremarked single-volume survey of 1953 squeaked against thunder.[16]

As these weary narratives trudged to their close, a third wave

[12] Oswald Spengler's *Untergang des Abendlandes* was famously placed in Toynbee's hands by Lewis Namier in the summer of 1920. 'As I read those pages, teeming with firefly flashes of historical insight, I wondered at first whether my whole enquiry had been disposed of by Spengler before even the questions, not to speak of the answers, had fully taken shape in my own mind.' Arnold Toynbee, 'My View of History', in id., *Civilization on Trial* (New York, 1948), 9.

[13] Cf. Ralph Turner, *The Great Cultural Tradition*, 2 vols. (New York, 1941); Henry S. Lucas, *A Short History of Civilization* (New York, 1943); Erich Kahler, *Man the Measure: A New Approach to History* (New York, 1943).

[14] Jacques Pirenne, *Les Grands Courants de l'histoire universelle*, 7 vols. (Neuchâtel, 1945–56) ('in face of the abyss of despair into which humanity has fallen'). 'L'étude de l'histoire universelle établit, sans aucun doute possible', he wrote in the preface to the first volume in 1943, 'que l'évolution des sociétés, comme celle des individus, obéit à des lois en vertu desquelles une certain forme sociale accompagne un certain type économique, ou qui fixent des rapports constants entre les transformations du droit public et du droit privé . . . Il y a donc des réactions sociales comme il y a des réactions chimiques' (i, pp. xvi–xvii) ('The study of world history shows beyond any conceivable doubt that the evolution of societies, like that of individuals, obeys laws according to which a certain social configuration relates to a particular economic one or governs consistent relationships between public and private law. There are thus social reactions just as much as chemical reactions'). He signed his preface, appropriately, 'Clos Voltaire, Genève'.

[15] *Historia Mundi*, 10 vols. (Berne, 1952–61); *Weltgeschichte in Einzeldarstellungen*, 6 vols. (Munich, n.d. [1951–2]); M. Crouzet (ed.), *Histoire générale des civilisations*, 7 vols. (Paris, 1953–7).

[16] J. C. Revill, *World History* (London, 1953; 2-vol. edn. 1962).

of globophilia reached the shores of both Europe and the USA. The years 1962 and 1963 turned out to be key dates in the shift. In 1962 John Bowle's reworking of Wells's project formed a strand of the story and, more significantly, a widely read polemical essay by Geoffrey Barraclough extolled in the same year the necessity for a new world history.[17] In 1963 the inauguration of the UNESCO initiative to reconstruct all of human history contributed to a European mood of *Blutsbrüderschaft*, on the one hand, and, on the other, the appearance of William H. McNeill's *Rise of the West* altered not merely the compass of the subject but its essential nature.[18] Barraclough did not stand at a tangent to these developments, as had Wells and Toynbee. As a front-rank professional historian his reconceptualization of world history and willingness to press it on a sceptical Anglo-Saxon community acquired particular force. He fastened *avant la lettre* onto the idea of burgeoning globalization—'the present age of global politics and global civilization needs a global view of history'—and argued that such a history would not produce merely a wider range of comparative facts, as Bryce had believed: it would cut into reality, as he wrote in an elegant metaphor, at a different angle and thus expose new planes of analysis.[19] He tried his best for a number of years to make this case in British academic circles before, conscious of failure, moving to America. There is a lesson both in his achievement and in his depression. A torch had been lit which Roberts and later Patrick O'Brien and R. I. Moore would in their different ways take forward.[20] Barraclough's decision to relinquish it, conversely, argued the presence in Britain of an invisible, unclimbable mountain.

These three moments and three individuals must form part of any description of British world history in the twentieth century. But we have to distinguish historical writing from historiography.

[17] John Bowle, *A New Outline of World History* (London, 1962); Geoffrey Barraclough, 'World History', in H. P. R. Finberg (ed.), *Approaches to History: A Symposium* (London, 1962).

[18] *History of Mankind*, 6 vols. (1963–6); William H. McNeill, *The Rise of the West: A History of the Human Community* (Chicago, 1963).

[19] Barraclough in Finberg, *Approaches to History*, 88, 108.

[20] See in particular the later writings of J. M. Roberts: *The Pelican History of the World* (Harmondsworth, 1980); *The Triumph of the West* (London, 1985); *Shorter Illustrated History of the World* (Oxford, 1993); *The Penguin History of Europe* (1997); *Twentieth Century: A History of the World, 1901 to the Present* (London, 1999).

It is easy to find random individuals who at various times have chosen to write about the history of the world. The task of historiography lies in explaining why they did so—often using concepts and perspectives of which the practitioners were completely oblivious—and in asking questions about why the patterning of their incidence has taken the form and shape that it has. This is no simple matter. Historiographical insight does not hover above libraries as a sort of cloud formation waiting for historiographers to describe it. The pattern is invented in human minds and is made in a particular location from within a specific epistemological environment which means—it is an uncomfortable thought—that a history of historiography is no less the victim of its provenance than any other kind of history. Now it has been part of the British academic mind, excepting Acton and Butterfield, to regard the study of historiography as an example of Continental excess. This attitude brings great dangers as well as a certain emotional satisfaction. It means that, not having a historiography of your own, you have to borrow someone else's and make your history fit into it. In the case of world history this predicament may have been responsible for disguising the fact that the British story of *Weltgeschichte* has been made to look very like the German story for the excellent and sufficient reason that it was written in Berlin.

I

Foundational in the German story is Eduard Fueter. Someone, indeed, ought to write a book about the historical world that Fueter made.[21] Not that he may or should be slighted: the *Geschichte der neueren Historiographie* has rightly retained its status as a classic of historiographical enquiry since its publication in 1911, a book that 'swarms with apposite, often amusing, and frequently wounding judgements'.[22] So far as the present enquiry is concerned, however, it suffers from three constraints and one misfortune. The first constraint Fueter could do nothing about. He wrote during the lowest ebb of world-historical interest—a

[21] There is a helpful account of Fueter's life and the content of his books in Hans Conrad Peyer, *Der Historiker Eduard Fueter, 1876-1928: Leben und Werk* (Zurich, 1982); but the questions intended in the present essay are not those asked by Peyer.

[22] Ibid. 28.

moment of historical development when the Great Powers vied for supremacy in Europe and when the lecture halls of the University of Berlin still echoed to the recent nationalistic message of Treitschke and Sybel. Though he later wrote a *Weltgeschichte* of a kind, part of the post-war fashion that we have already noted, it concentrated on recent history and made Europe its centre.[23] Secondly, he wrote on a foaming wave of scientism which the historical method of the Rankeans and the excitements of the new economic history had built up to tidal proportions. Fueter deprecated the rubbishing of Lamprecht's cultural history and proclaimed some sort of identity with Voltaire by delivering his inaugural lecture on 'Voltaire as Historian'; but he never concealed his fundamental sympathy with the neo-Rankeans and wound up an enemy of unconventional method. Thirdly, he took a decision to exclude living historians from his discussion. This had the catastrophic result of excising Eduard Meyer, surely the most fertile universal historian of his day and in many ways the realistic starting-point (half a century before the usual narrative gets under way) for the European impulse towards world history.[24] The misfortune, finally, was neither his nor Germany's but Britain's. His book appeared just in time for George Peabody Gooch to make it scripture in the only serious piece of British historiography before Butterfield, Gooch's *History and Historians in the Nineteenth Century* (1913). These four contexts produced between them the intellectual space for *Weltgeschichte* with which national peculiarity had to arrange itself.

The story itself is familiar, by definition, and has been told most insistently in modern German historiography by Ernst Schulin and Jürgen Osterhammel. In the beginning was the Enlightenment. The Age of Reason produced a historiography which prided itself on its universalism—a style of history which dominated French thinking through the *philosophes*, German historiography through the important collection of historians at Göttingen, and which gave rise to significant British examples in the vast *Universal History* of the mid-eighteenth century and (in German eyes), Adam Ferguson's *Essay on the History of Civil Society*

[23] Eduard Fueter, *Weltgeschichte der letzten hundert Jahre, 1815-1920* (Zurich, 1921).

[24] For Fueter's self-denial over 'die Leistungen lebender Historiker' ('the achievements of living historians'), see *Geschichte der neueren Historiographie* (Munich and Berlin, 1911), 600–1.

of 1767.[25] This framework of explanation saw its subject as nothing smaller than the history of *l'esprit humain* and made some attempt to bring within the pale of historical writing an account of parts of the world beyond Europe and America. For its vision it had Voltaire, for its theory Condorcet, and for philosophical sustenance it could turn to the cosmopolitan perspectives of Kant and the later necessities of Hegel in whose hands 'the universal bec[ame] the master and the particular the mastered'.[26] Then came collapse. The German search for national roots and the development of Ranke's *wissenschaftlich* stipulations for the study of history brought a new and rising curve: *Die Entstehung des Historismus*.[27] For the generalities of historical *Stufentheorie* (theory of stages), the historians of the nineteenth century substituted a dissecting particularism which not only avoided but actively opposed nomothetic models. True, Ranke remained interested in and eventually began to write a version of universal history; but, '[m]aking a virtue out of necessity', he did so 'from the angle of individual nations' and produced only 'indirectly, and through its universal integrants' something resembling *Weltgeschichte*.[28] In Britain, meanwhile, the same curve seemed visible. For Osterhammel, one could see only traces of the old universalism by the time of Heeren in Germany and Macaulay in England:

Macaulay was the last British historian of the nineteenth century to see Britain's national history against the background of the development of European and universal civilization, although the aspect of civilization played a much smaller part for him than it had for the classic writers of the Enlightenment: Hume, Smith, and Gibbon.[29]

[25] *The Universal History from the Earliest Account of Time to the Present Compiled from the Original Sources*, 38 vols. (London, 1736–65); and for Ferguson see Benedikt Stuchtey and Peter Wende, 'Introduction: Towards a Comparative History of Anglo-German Historiographical Traditions and Transfers', in eid. (eds.), *British and German Historiography 1750–1950: Traditions, Perceptions, and Transfers*, Studies of the German Historical Institute London (Oxford, 2000), 1–24, at 7.

[26] 'The Spirit of Christianity', in Terry Pinkard, *Hegel: A Biography* (Cambridge, 2000), 139–44.

[27] Meinecke's formidable account has, of course, played no small part in confirming the global story: Friedrich Meinecke, *Die Entstehung des Historismus*, 2 vols. (Munich and Berlin, 1936).

[28] Ernst Schulin, 'Universal History and National History: Mainly in the Lectures of Leopold von Ranke', in G. G. Iggers and James Y. Powell (eds.), *Leopold von Ranke and the Shaping of the Historical Discipline* (Syracuse, NY, 1990), 76.

[29] J. Osterhammel, 'Nation und Zivilisation in der britischen Historiographie von Hume bis Macaulay', *Historische Zeitschrift*, 254 (1992), 338. Cf., on the British side, Peter

It was part of a 'closure of discourse and discipline in Germany' which Macaulay helped embody on the English side and which strengthened with the departure of Henry Thomas Buckle from English historical writing.[30] Candidates for closure vary; the story is the same. It was 'the end of an epoch'.[31] Particularism had squashed universalism and from that triumph 'a straight path led from the historicist theory of history to "national historiography"'.[32]

From 1870 the nationalist tendencies of Germany and Britain diverged as a Prussian model of *Staatsgeschichte* took control in Berlin and Anglophilia turned to jealous antagonism: a complex cultural shift that derived its nature from elements far beyond the academic.[33] But *historiographically* the undertow of illiberal nationalist history was expanded by Fueter, whose period of personal knowledge this was, into a general movement which could 'gradually also be seen in the Anglo-Saxon countries'.[34] Certainly he foresaw a 'transition to world politics', but one that would never mark a return to the universal histories with their 'polemical tendencies'.[35] The new world history, to the extent that it appeared at all, would rather reflect that Copernican revolution that historical science had still fully to complete.[36]

Ghosh's caustic reworking of Macaulay which emphasizes his distance from the Enlightenment heritage. Though 'undoubtedly a legatee of the Enlightenment', Macaulay failed to match its vision in abandoning a commitment to the coherence of non-political elements in the writing of history and in failing to integrate different structural levels into his analysis. His own legacy, for Ghosh, 'contributed to the descent of English historiography into a narrowing political stream epitomized by the work of Stubbs and Seeley, and by university syllabi after 1870'. 'Macaulay and the Heritage of the Enlightenment', *English Historical Review*, 112 (1997), 358–95, esp. 359–60.

30 Jürgen Osterhammel, '"Peoples Without History" in British and German Historical Thought', in Stuchtey and Wende (eds.), *British and German Historiography*, 274.

31 Ibid. 267.

32 Ulrich Muhlack, 'Universal History and National History: Eighteenth- and Nineteenth-Century German Historians and the Scholarly Community', in Stuchtey and Wende (eds.), *British and German Historiography*, 26.

33 See Charles E. McClelland, *The German Historians and England: A Study in Nineteenth-Century Views* (Cambridge, 1971); Paul M. Kennedy, *The Rise of the Anglo-German Antagonism, 1860–1914* (London, 1980).

34 *Geschichte der neueren Historiographie*, 601.

35 Ibid. 602.

36 'Was die Astronomie schon längst vollzogen, als sie die Erde aus dem Mittelpunkt des Sonnensystems rückte, was die Zoologie vollführte, als sie die Tierwelt nicht mehr nach dem Menschen als dem schlechthin vollkommenen Wesen orientierte, das muß nun in ähnlicher Weise auch die Geschichtschreibung [*sic*] tun' ('What astronomy long since accomplished when it shifted the earth away from the centre of the solar system,

World-historical writing could never return to Voltairean manifestos. ('It no longer needs to combat a Bossuet.') And in the short term it would become what Schulin later reported it to be, 'world histories more or less restricted to the point of view of power politics'.[37] The scene was thus set for the apotheosis of national power in the events of 1914–18 with the diastole and systole that we have already seen in its aftermath.

From 1913 this frame had its British emulator in Gooch. His declaration in the preface to the first edition that his methods and purposes had a quite different character from the 'admirable' Fueter's brooks no denial; but when he turned, towards the end of his volume, to what he called the 'History of Civilization', German persuasion and example gripped his text and his footnotes.[38] Others, following the pioneer, gripped the tails of Gooch's coat and, when they did not, they ran after his masters. So when Barraclough wrote his impressive essay of 1962, he may have espoused an original radicalism in calling for 'a history that looks beyond Europe and the west to humanity in all lands and ages', but his historiographical sensibility rested on Fueter, Reinhard Wittram, and Troeltsch; and his chronological curve followed theirs: Bossuet, Voltaire, *Universal History*, Göttingen School, followed by 'eclipse' of the universal sun.[39] Even in the far more sophisticated account by Patrick O'Brien, which opened the Major Themes of the International Congress of Historical Sciences at Oslo in 2000, the broad shape beginning with Voltaire finds an echo, though the British have their usual mention 'in the climate of pessimism and breakdown in the liberal consensus that followed the Great War when Spengler, Toynbee, Sorokin, Wells, Mumford and Dawson and

what zoology achieved when it stopped orientating the animal kingdom by humans as simply the most perfect being, must now also be done in a similar way by historiography'), ibid. 602.

[37] Ernst Schulin, 'Universalgeschichtsschreibung im zwanzigsten Jahrhundert', in id., *Traditionskritik und Rekonstruktionsversuch: Studien zur Entwicklung von Geschichtswissenschaft und historischem Denken* (Göttingen, 1979), 183.

[38] G. P. Gooch, *History and Historians in the Nineteenth Century* (London, 1913, 1920), pp. v., 573 ff.

[39] Barraclough in Findberg, *Approaches to History*, 84–5 and *passim*; R. I. Moore gets round the problem of making such a chronology by not making one and jumping from Voltaire to the twentieth century: 'World History', in Michael Bentley (ed.), *Companion to Historiography* (London, 1997), 944.

others wrote universal histories to help Europeans comprehend the decline and barbarism of the West'.[40]

What is one to make of this repeated, modulated prehistory? Within the most accomplished and theoretically astute historiographical culture in Europe—the German—this story gives little cause for concern since it largely amounts to a remodelling of indigenous experience: it implies a story of German intellectual leadership under the imprint of which European historical writing altered its paradigms. Even here, however, we encounter complexity which is only now receiving its due. As late as 1999 Georg Iggers thought it necessary to remind his countrymen that German culture had enjoyed a continuum of *Weltgeschichte* during the period when the discourse has often been deemed closed. He reminded non-German scholars, *pari passu*, that ethnocentrism had by no means been restricted to Germany in the nineteenth century.[41] Instead of placing national tiles on the map we should perhaps envisage a marbled mosaic. From a British point of view Iggers's point has some force because if Germany was not the unique focus of a predominant historical style, then the assumption that British *Weltgeschichte* fell victim to its blandishments looks weaker. There might be adduced, second, the diffficulty that an increase in scientism by no means predicts a decrease in world history: on the contrary that development can prove a major stimulant. German historians have noticed as clearly as their British colleagues that Wells reached his moment of *Weltgeschichte* out of exactly this imperative, of 'the tradition of evolutionism', as Schulin puts it, 'believing in progress in the brotherhood of peoples'.[42] In the German case the determination to refine their national historiography into a 'German School', one which eschewed world history for Fueterian reasons, has pushed its greatest nineteenth-century exponent, Eduard Meyer, into an obscurity (away from his well-known scholarship on the ancient world) which only an important recent collection of studies has served to dispel.[43]

[40] 'Is Universal History Possible?', in *Proceedings of the 19th Congress of Historical Sciences* (Oslo, 2000), 6-8.

[41] G. G. Iggers, 'Nationalism and Historiography 1789-1996', in Stefan Berger *et al.* (eds.), *Writing National Histories: Western Europe since 1800* (London, 1999), 17.

[42] Schulin, 'Universalgeschichtsschreibung', 175.

[43] William M. Calder III and Alexander Demandt (eds.), *Eduard Meyer: Leben und Leistung eines Universalhistorikers* (Leiden, 1990).

Much the most impressive attempt to reverse the traditional spin of this trajectory in regard to British *Weltgeschichte* is John Burrow's paper delivered to an Anglo-German conference in 1996 and published with the other contributions in 2000.[44] Intelligent and suggestive as always, Burrow began a quiet revision of the familiar narrative but accomplished it with a certain sleight of hand. He tentatively proposed, not that British *Weltgeschichte* had flowered after its sun was supposedly eclipsed, but rather that its spores had carried on the wind into neighbouring territory and gone unremarked as a result. Botanists were looking in the wrong place. The British impetus toward universalism in its historiography did not appear in conventional histories at all. Rather, it became part of a deep Victorian tradition of evolutionary social theory which owed much to French models from Lamarck to Guizot in the early part of the century and then, as conventional history turned 'German' in the second half, it found a life of its own. 'The outcome,' he writes, 'exemplified above all in Spencer, was a universal, conjectural history of mankind, from animal or at least "savage" origins shaped by concepts borrowed from biology. Here at last German intellectual tutelage seems largely to have been left behind, though perhaps to some extent replaced, for the earlier part of the century, by that of the French.'[45] Now naturally there is a good deal in this. We certainly see a genre of social theory that presents a view less of men than of Man, arranged in stages of development and pointing someone like Herbert Spencer in new directions. 'The narratives of political history . . . were for him irrelevant; what mattered was the discrimination, at the most abstract level, of the social typologies which could be converted into a kind of hypothetical universal history, if seen as the outcome of general laws of social evolution.'[46]

No less clearly, the reservations that one might want to enter about calling this 'conversion' world history lie embedded in the language that justifies it. Social theory produced its stages 'at the most abstract level'; but when a world historian like Jacques Pirenne spoke of 'des stades qui se suivent nécessairement',[47] he conceived his stages on a far from abstract plane and as the

[44] John Burrow, 'Historicism and Social Evolution', in Stuchtey and Wende (eds.), *British and German Historiography*, 251–64. [45] Ibid. 260. [46] Ibid. 252.

[47] *Les Grands Courants*, i, pp. xvi–xvii.

outcome of a mixing with the world: a blend of structure and agency of the kind that historians (and not just the Germans) always insist upon as their quarry. Burrow had removed the hook as soon as he bit on it by declaring at the beginning of his paper that he 'propose[d] largely to leave aside the question of the penetration of versions of universal history by historicist ideas'.[48] Yet one has a lingering suspicion that an ability to be so penetrated represents a defining characteristic of a plausible *Weltgeschichte* or, if it does not, then many voices should not have been raised in anger to defend world history, as did William McNeill in a significant paper, as an intellectual form that does not differ from history *tout court*.[49] It remains important that British evolutionary theory helped generate a comparative method of approaching historical questions and attaching its own style of metanarrative in constructing accounts of how man had reached his current stage of development. It helps us to see, for example, that Wells was more than an invisible man in the historiography: he had forebears and called on a tradition of genuinely indigenous British thought. But it does not explain the silences, the refusals to convert and modulate. It does not tell us why Buckle chose to investigate civilization in so unpromising and restricted a field as the history of England. It leaves us unclear why Carlyle, a born *Welthistoriker* if ever one breathed, decided to talk about the French Revolution and Frederick the Great instead. It shows who put soap on the slipways of British *Weltgeschichte* but leaves out of account the wedges that would leave even the smallest ship high and dry.

II

Suppose that one begins, not with a description of the histories, but with a model of what *Weltgeschichte* requires by its intrinsic nature from any national style of historiography. The preconditions for generating effective world history I take minimally to be five. (1) Cultural sustenance for an inclusive global metanarrative. (2) Receptivity to the spatial dimension of historical

[48] Burrow, 'Historicism and Social Evolution', 251.

[49] McNeill, 'A Defence of World History', *Transactions of the Royal Historical Society*, 5 (1982), 75–89.

explanation. (3) Commitment to an epistemology (and therefore method) that validates a global field. (4) A scholarly infrastructure that positively valorizes global conceptualization of historical problems. (5) Weak or absent counter-presuppositions that could render 1–4 inoperable. It may sharpen analysis of the British situation if we place the latter alongside such a typology and ask comparative questions about its functioning since the Enlightenment.

The most comprehensive metanarrative available historically in the West has been that offered by the Roman Catholic Church. Bossuet's *Universal History* of 1681 presented the past of the Church and the past of the world as asymptotic: one approximated to the other over time. By the second half of the eighteenth century, however, that very proclamation had helped produce in France an anti-clerical backlash of fearsome force of which Voltaire's *Essai sur les mœurs* notoriously hit hardest by wielding the known world, or parts of it, explicitly to discomfit Bossuet's followers. Catholic Italy avoided the *dix-huitième* aggression found in Paris. It produced its own vision of world history in the enormous and best-selling *Storia Universale* of Cesare Cantù, which had the distinction of provoking a Protestant counter-version in the 1870s.[50] Britain, on the other hand, lost its Catholic culture in the sixteenth century yet never acquired an anti-clerical ideology to rival that of the *philosophes*. Avoiding either of these outcomes might have helped foment an imagined past on a global scale. True, it produced its own *Universal History* of which Cantù made some use; but the Göttingen historian, Gatterer, complained at the time that the compilation never reached beyond individual national narratives. In fact the vaunted objective of England's *Universal History* went little further than synthetic abridgement: 'the principal end of the work . . . was, to save our readers all that vast expense of time and books which they must otherwise be at, to obtain a competent knowledge of the histories of the respective nations.'[51] It was a historio-

[50] On Italian world history see briefly the introduction. Padua, a Habsburg university until 1866, played a particularly important role in the teaching of world history.

[51] *An Universal History, from the Earliest Account of Time to the Present: Compiled from Original Authors; and Illustrated with Maps, Cuts, Notes, Chronological and other Tables*, 7 vols. (London, 1736, with later additions). The first volumes were dedicated to the Duke of Marlborough in memory of his grandfather, 'the Darling of this happy Nation', which hardly promised resistance to European triumphalism.

graphical *Reader's Digest.* The respective nations turned out little different from Bossuet's, moreover, apart from a lunge at Egypt and Armenia in volume three and an Orientalist diversion in the direction of Turks, Tartars, Moghuls, and Chinese in the Addition of 1750—just the moment when Voltaire was planning his own lunge in the same direction. This is unsurprising when the authors shared Bossuet's problematic if not his Church. 'Our general aera's [*sic*] are, the *Creation*, the *Flood*, and the Years *before or after Christ*.'[52] True again, British culture later produced a Catholic world historian in Christopher Dawson and a semi-Buddhist one in the younger Toynbee;[53] but two and a half swallows do not make a summer and the counter-propositions of Anglicanism played an immeasurably stronger role in British historiography. One has only to think of the 'Liberal Anglican' school associated with the elder Arnold and Henry Hart Milman,[54] to feel the distance from Catholic universalism, even if their devotion to Vico might have stirred in them the vision of *corsi e ricorsi*. That this religious sensibility exercised a vital sway over British historians until at least 1914 forms part of their distinctiveness seen in a European frame.[55] But the effect of Anglican religion did not lie in encouraging a world view. It pressed the mind in the direction of British exceptionalism and the need to defend a special heritage. One can object relevantly that Ranke was a Lutheran and yet retained a commitment to *Weltgeschichte*. His Lutheranism, however, ran into a mood of Hegelian universalism which he believed himself to despise yet frequently implied in his own writings.[56]

Hegel is worth a pause in this connection. He did not export

[52] Ibid., p. xxxi.

[53] For Dawson, see Stratford Caldecott and John Morrill (eds.), *Eternity in Time: Christopher Dawson and the Catholic Idea of History* (Eden, 1997), which does not include a study of his universalism, and Dawson, *The Dynamics of World History*, ed. John J. Mulloy (London, 1957). Toynbee's later marital involvement with Catholicism and his Buddhist vocabulary are discussed in McNeill, *Arnold J. Toynbee*, esp. 267–8.

[54] For the Liberal Anglicans, see Duncan Forbes, *The Liberal Anglican Idea of History* (Cambridge, 1952).

[55] Owen Chadwick, *The Secularization of the European Mind in the Nineteenth Century* (Cambridge, 1975) explains the frame. For a critique from a British point of view, see Michael Bentley, 'Victorian Historians and the Larger Hope', in id. (ed.), *Public and Private Doctrine: Essays in British History Presented to Maurice Cowling* (Cambridge, 1993), 127–48.

[56] See Leonard Krieger, *Ranke: The Meaning of History* (Chicago, 1977), esp. 246–8, 320–43.

satisfactorily to Britain, most certainly not through the opaque vehicle of Sterling's *Secret of Hegel*, which, as the wag said, clung on to its secret to the end.[57] It has been alleged that the consequence of Hegelian teaching was to emphasize the place of Europe and to detract from a world-frame for historical thinking.[58] The consequences were in fact double-edged. Though Hegel came to understand the state as the great outcome of the historical process, he was the first thinker to see history in processual terms at all, and with process came some of the presuppositions for a sustained metanarrative of the kind in which world history, in its nineteenth-century incarnations, was wont to engage. One could reverse the argument, therefore, and contend that the *lack* of a Hegelian understanding in Britain—indeed a positive antipathy to it—played a constraining role in the ability to conceptualize historical change.[59] Assuredly, the presence of that understanding would not have guaranteed the emergence of a wider frame of reference, but its absence may have increased resistance to it.

As it was, the single grand narrative produced in Britain through its period of professionalization, the so-called Whig conception of history, located the centre of attention in Britain, indeed in England, itself and produced two or three generations of historians for whom European civilization was somehow cross-threaded and irrelevant both to the issues that most preoccupied them (freedom, constitutionalism, progress, independence) and to their chronological logging-points: 1215, 1588, 1642, and 1689. Treitschke saw clearly enough that Macaulay had wanted all Europeans to be Whigs.[60] He could have added Acton. Freeman did his best to transcend the boundaries of England but wound up, as John Burrow astutely remarks, merely trying forlornly to be a Whig on a European

[57] John Hutchison Sterling, *The Secret of Hegel: Being the Hegelian System in Origin, Principle, Form and Matter*, 2 vols. (London, 1865).

[58] Jerry H. Bentley, 'Cultural Encounters between the Continents over the Centuries', *Proceedings of the 19th Congress of Historical Sciences* (Oslo, 2000), 30–1.

[59] Christopher Parker has attempted to see Idealism at the centre of British historical thought—see his *The English Idea of History from Coleridge to Collingwood* (Aldershot, 2000)—but the argument ignores considerable hurdles placed in the way of it within the British intelligentsia generally. Cf. Kirk Willis, 'The Introduction and Critical Reception of Hegelian Thought in Britain, 1830-1900', *Victorian Studies*, 32 (1988), 85–111.

[60] Muhlack, 'Universal History and National History', in Stuchtey and Wende (eds.), *British and German Historiography*, 145.

scale.[61] Britain's stories concerned great men who had made England's constitutional arrangements a site of effortless superiority and unchallenged permanence; they gave thanks for the achievement. These were *cheerful* stories. The grand narrative did not countenance cultural collapse or the possibility of state-generated evil. And it had a linear thrust: from worse to better. There was no cyclical portent of the kind identified by a Vico or Spengler until the mud and gas of Flanders darkened the future and by so doing questioned the past.

If temporal shaping imposed itself on the historical frame of reference in Britain, so did a certain conception of relevant space. Britain formed only an element in it but the rest took a largely imperial form. The fact of empire cannot be overstressed in offering a description of British susceptibilities about space. These survived despite an overwhelming volume of travel literature from every corner of the globe. Glancing though reviews in the *Quarterly Review* in the 1830s and 1840s, we find, for example, Southey on expeditions up the Amazon, Croker on a journey through Arabia, and Milman reviewing Lord Elphinstone's history of India and Prescott's history of the conquest of Mexico.[62] Enough here, one would have thought, to get the mind turning about the 'encounters' on which modern world historians dwell. Perhaps William Robertson might count as a respondent *avant la lettre* for he wrote not only about Spanish America but also his *Historical Disquisition Concerning the Knowledge which the Ancients had of India* (1791), a study 'exhilarating in the breadth of its concerns', in the view of a recent analyst.[63] Once afflicted by romanticism, however, these perceptions sheered off, like evolutionary theory, into other domains and formed the beginnings of an armchair anthropology of the kind that would make Sir James Frazer famous.[64] India was different, all the same: it was always different. An imperial historiography had focused on that country since at least the history of British India

[61] John Burrow, *A Liberal Descent: Victorian Historians and the English Past* (Cambridge, 1981), 182 ff.

[62] *Quarterly Review*, 57 (Sept. 1836), 1–29; 59 (July 1837), 87–133; 68 (Sept. 1841), 377–413; 73 (Dec. 1843), 187–235.

[63] See Geoffrey Carnall, 'Robertson and Contemporary Images of India', in Stewart J. Brown (ed.), *William Robertson and the Expansion of Empire* (Cambridge, 1997), 210–30, esp. 210–11.

[64] Sir James Frazer, *The Golden Bough: A Study in Comparative Religion*, 2 vols. (London, 1890); 3 vols. (London, 1900); 12 vols. (1907-15).

by James Mill;[65] and the idea of an inspiring imperial story became important to the later Victorians seeking to join up their own tales of derring-do with the historical spectacle of Raleigh, Drake, and Gloriana.[66]

These histories propagated another feature of professionalizing British history, moreover, that has not attracted sufficient attention and which greatly curtailed current conceptions of relevant space. They were conceived, written, and published in the English language whose status as a prescriptive cultural form produced a curious distortion in what was studied by English historians. The point is not one about Anglo-Saxon inadequacy in the face of learning French and German: all serious scholars knew both and many had Italian as well. More significant may have proved a certain cultural expectation that the speaking of English elevated the status of particular places and the human potential of those living there. This expectation could be the reverse of reactionary. Conservative writers would certainly deprecate any accommodation with the languages of savages: how would natives ever know anything better if civilized nations pandered to their gobbledegook? But one finds the same result for different reasons among radicals concerned to raise the status of peoples deprived of English. Those scholars who wanted to see greater teaching of extra-European languages such as Sanskrit found themselves confronted with the formidable argument that encouragement of 'minor' languages would propagate error: only English had the power to liberate the native mind from the tyranny of superstition.[67] The cosmopolitan language thus became all too literally a governing discourse within which the quaintness of travellers' tales and stories of 'the

[65] James Mill, *History of British India* (London, 1817). William Thomas has an important discussion of Mill in *The Quarrel of Macaulay and Croker: Politics and History in the Age of Reform* (Oxford, 2000), at 149–50, 231–2.

[66] Among many examples see James Anthony Froude, *History of England from the Fall of Wolsey to the Death of Elizabeth*, 12 vols. (London, 1856–70); James Anthony Froude, *English Seamen in the Sixteenth Century* (1895); John Robert Seeley, *The Growth of British Policy: An Historical Essay*, 2 vols. (Cambridge, 1895); S. H. Burke, *Historical Portraits of the Tudor Dynasty and the Reformation Period*, 4 vols. (London, 1879–83); J. S. Corbett, *Drake and the Tudor Navy: With the History of the Rise of Britain as a Maritime Power*, 2 vols. (1898–9); A. D. Innes, *Ten Tudor Statesmen* (London, 1906); Sir C. R. Markham, *Richard Hakluyt: His Life and Work* (London, 1896).

[67] See William Thomas's discussion of Macaulay and George Otto Trevelyan in *The Quarrel of Macaulay and Croker*, 150–5.

Orient' had to find the space and timbre allowed to them. When, in 1907, the American philologist E. H. Babbitt estimated that by the year 2000 there would be over a billion speakers of the English language, he articulated an assumption that lay behind a particular provincialism in the British psyche and which gave rise to that strange topos, the history of the English-speaking peoples, a singular form of exclusion that runs from Sir Charles Dilke to Sir Winston Churchill.[68] The view that imperial peoples had to be domesticated into metropolitan narratives and that all other sensible people ought to speak English whether they were imperial or not did nothing to sensitize British historians to the realities of global space.

But then—a deeper point—they knew very little about the globe apart from its geology and the travelogues of the reviews. One of the key stimulants in Germany to an appreciation of world history came in the form of a sophisticated understanding of human geography, especially through the evangelism of Friedrich Ratzel (1844–1904), whose thinking pointed in the direction of what Osterhammel evocatively terms 'a perspective based on spatial awareness and the history of relationships between things'.[69] How much more so did this geographical perspective condition the French cultural milieu. It has been claimed that virtually everything that became *Annales* originated in the work of Vidal de la Blache.[70] In universal history, too, he threw long shadows. Cavaignac may have been singular in dedicating his first volume in 1922 'à la mémoire de mon ancien

[68] Sir Charles Dilke, *Greater Britain: A Record of Travel in English-Speaking Countries during 1866 and 1867*, 2 vols. (London, 1868); Winston S. Churchill, *A History of the English-Speaking Peoples*, 4 vols. (London, 1956–8). Other examples may repay attention, such as R. B. Mowat and P. W. Slosson, *History of the English-Speaking Peoples* (New York, 1943) and the more spectacular study by Vaughan Wilkins, *Endless Prelude: A Survey of High Events, Great Adventure, Bloody Tragedy, Noble Romance, Queer Happenings, and Strange Scandal. Telling, in Part, the History of the English-Speaking Peoples* (1937).

[69] Jürgen Osterhammel 'Raumerfassung und Universalgeschichte im 20. Jahrhundert', in id., Gangolf Hübinger, and Erich Pelzer (eds.), *Universalgeschichte und Nationalgeschichten* (Freiburg im Breisgau, 1994), 51. 'In Friedrich Ratzels Schriften wurden viele der Zusammenhänge zwischen menschlichen Gesellschaften und ihren natürlichen Umwelten vorweggenommen, die in neueren universalhistorischen Studien wiederentdeckt und zum Teil ausgearbeitet worden sind' ('Friedrich Ratzel's writings anticipate many of the connections between human societies and their natural environments which have been rediscovered and sometimes taken further in more recent works of universal history'), 69.

[70] See my essay on 'Approaches to Modernity' in Bentley (ed.), *Companion to Historiography*, 466–8.

maître P. VIDAL DE LA BLACHE', but the dedication remains implicit in a French system of education that placed geography beside history in a permanent dual degree curriculum rather than as an alternative to it as so often in the English system. The point is obvious but demands emphatic statement none the less. Britain, perhaps especially England, has denied geography the intellectual status and curricular provision that it has enjoyed historically on the Continent.[71] The *Universal History* had advised upon the foolishness of such neglect, to be sure: 'GEOGRAPHY is an essential Part of History. Every historian that neglects it, must of necessity be confused in his relations.'[72] But its authors had intended nothing more than that authors must know the whereabouts of mountains and rivers. The only light at a critical moment around the turn of century emanated from Sir Halford Mackinder with his importation of the Swedish concept of 'geopolitics'. He energized students at the London School of Economics—the future Lewis Namier among them—with his vision, but his ideas never won integration into the academic structures of his day for all his radical redisposition of the globe's significant spaces around a new 'pivot' in Russia. 'He was . . . appreciated in America', a biographer writes of him, 'but it cannot be said that he was accorded the same recognition in his own country. The British political and academic establishments and the communications media, possibly because of the low status of geography in education, but mainly because of an island history insulated from the realities of conflict, proved incapable of giving serious consideration to geostrategic and geopolitical ideas.'[73] It was no way to inseminate a Braudel.

Rejecting geography bore a relation to rejecting the idea that history had a discernible 'field' at all. It all depended what one's questions were. This was a strength, understood at one level. It meant that British historiography could produce, if not a Braudel, then at least a Collingwood or Oakeshott: thinkers who had the discernment and philosophical weight of a Croce or Dilthey and who dismissed *ab initio* the idea that history could be subsumed under the rubric of science or import the language of

[71] There are still colleges in the English ancient universities today which refuse to elect Fellows in Geography on the ground that it is not an academic discipline.

[72] *An Universal History*, i, p. xxxi.

[73] W. H. Parker, *Mackinder: Geography as an Aid to Statecraft* (Oxford, 1982), 54.

a natural science. Neither, however, did they wish to see it reduced to an Idealist chimera. Yet one of these two approaches—the Idealist or the scientistic—seems necessary for the generation of universal history. Either one has to believe in the presence of an immanent process of becoming which ties together all the civilizations of the world along the lines that Toynbee would later follow. Or one has to commit oneself to a view of history as a form of positivistic, comparative science with a defined field. The *method* for prosecuting the latter commitment became available through the German economic history of the late nineteenth century and in Britain through the evolutionists discussed by Burrow. But the heuristic universe which such a method had been designed to serve did not exist among British historians. They abstracted the method when it suited them but they did not conceive the purpose of history to be that which Wells or Cavaignac later discerned. World history needed (and needs) the modernist perception (or delusion) that 'incommensurability' between spaces, cultures, and peoples can be overcome, that a proliferation of 'monographs' about different parts of the world has made available a new kind of study.[74] This has occurred only comparatively recently against the corrosions of relativism and postmodernism. A serious theoretical problem remains and the British are likely to see it first. If world historians are question-led, then so are the people who wrote its sources and their questions, when they are intelligible at all, do not replicate those of any given enquiry. One cannot pile up 'monographs' from all over the globe and treat them as though they were scientific reports responding to an agreed agenda, or value-free building blocks for some transcendent metanarrative.

The view that aspiring world historians were either unhinged speculators who had never been in an archive or naïve realists who had never read Collingwood has placed many obstacles in the way of the subject in Britain. One area in which British historians most certainly followed their German and American colleagues lay in the area of professionalization with its harsh understanding of what constituted historical training, its emphasis on the Rankean special subject, its Toutian undergraduate dissertation from primary sources, and the Germano-American Ph.D. which became *de rigueur* for those entering at faculty level.

[74] See O'Brien, 'Is Universal History Possible?', 14–16.

None of these exercises encouraged a broad view. The curriculum followed by British schoolchildren before they enter the university and their syllabus as undergraduates have not reflected the width of a liberal arts curriculum in the USA and would not normally contain even a World Civilizations component or an exposure to the historiography of *Weltgeschichte*. It is a plausible conjecture that, even today, fewer than 1 per cent of undergraduates in History emerging from a British university at the age of 21 or 22 will have read a single example of world history. At faculty level, meanwhile, central criteria for gaining promotion and prominence in the profession still enshrine a conception of 'research' (an absurd term culled from the wrong universe of discourse which misunderstands most of what can be misunderstood about the nature of historical work and the status of its conclusions): a situation that devalues comparative analysis of secondary literatures and places weight on the writing of close-textured monographs gleaned from primary, frequently unprinted, sources. Only when an accomplished professional historian of the calibre of John Roberts took his career-turn towards world history in the 1970s did attitudes of this kind come under scrutiny. They were far from suppressed at the millennium.

By running British experience through a model of requirements for a robust *Weltgeschichte* we see plainly enough that elements within the culture would always have placed resistances in the way of such a development. Explaining why something does *not* happen in history demands that one go a little further, however. Perhaps there were historical enterprises and preoccupations that did arise in Britain and which actively occluded or demoted the study of world history? Two preoccupations come at once to mind. First, British historians in the first half of the nineteenth century—the period when they stand most patently accused of ignoring the wider world—entered into a persistent focus on *France*: its history, its revolution, and its spectre.[75] No one can leaf through the periodicals of the period

[75] For the background see Hedva Ben-Israel, *English Historians on the French Revolution* (Cambridge, 1968). The notion of France as Other played a considerable role, of course, in Linda Colley's examination of eighteenth-century British identity: 'A powerful and persistently threatening France became the haunting embodiment of that Catholic Other which Britons had been taught to fear since the reformation', Linda Colley, *Britons: Forging the Nation 1707–1837* (New Haven, 1992), 368.

and its major historical works without forming the judgement that when British historians were not writing about their own country they were addressing the French problem. In the second half of the century, gathering force after 1870, came their understandable anxieties over Bismarckian Germany. Perhaps the dissolution of the Great Power system after 1914 has to be seen, therefore, as a crucial determinant of *Weltgeschichte*'s reassertion throughout Europe. It is undoubtedly the case that urgent concerns over two Continental threats throughout the long nineteenth century went some way towards retarding universalism in Britain. And behind those responsibilities stood the Empire in its most heated phase of development after 1865. It helped the 'world' to contract into those parts of it colonized by the British and deserving a narrative that revealed British qualities of valour and racial superiority. An even-handed commitment to the history of societies and civilizations across the globe would not begin from there.

III

It feels glib, all the same, to end there. Other cultures in Europe reflected some of these forms of resistance while still maintaining a thread of world history. Germany's domination by *Staatsgeschichte* never occurred in Britain; yet that culture could produce a Meyer when Britain could find no one with a broader historical mind than Freeman. Indeed, the British intelligentsia enjoyed the blessings of a universalizing liberalism for much of the nineteenth century. Uday Singh Mehta points out in his recent book connecting liberalism and imperialism that the liberals' need to universalize was not random but implicit in the nature of liberal ideology.[76] So why did they not universalize their history? It will not do, as we have seen, to blame the Germans: their versions of historicism only impinged on the British case after mid-century. With the English and Scottish Enlightenments at their back and the successful *Universal History* a model for other nations to follow, why did the British shrink into historiographical insularity? Why did the most powerful

[76] Uday Singh Mehta, *Liberalism and Empire: A Study in Nineteenth-Century British Liberal Thought* (Chicago, 1999), *passim.*

nation on earth lose interest in the earth apart from the bits that it happened to own? Reaching for clichés about the narrowness of the English mind merely confirms consequences rather than elicits causes. Pointing simply to structural obstructions in the nature of the profession has a certain potency but does not explain why a free-ranging, non-professional author like Buckle could not project his mind beyond Dover beach. The argument presented here has approached the issue from just two directions. It has challenged the widespread assumption that the historiography of British *Weltgeschichte* can be modelled on the German experience; and it has suggested the utility of a seismic model of world-historical potential in the face of which the British come out low on the Richter scale. Neither of these views dispatches the difficulty. 'The waste remains and kills.' Suspicion lingers that many arresting avenues remain to be identified and explored in the transformations of British historiography between 1750 and 1914, a period that should become the auditorium for a better understanding of Britain's singular silences.

8

Writing World History in Tsarist Russia and in the Soviet Union

THOMAS M. BOHN

Nowadays, the writing of world history in the successor states of the Soviet Union is not as popular as it seems to be elsewhere. For countries such as Ukraine or Belarus the reason is obvious. For now, their historians must create a new and unique national history. In Russia, the situation is more complicated. With the breakdown of the Soviet Union the country has lost not only its empire, but also its identity. Therefore, professional historians do not think much about the world outside Russia, leaving the task of defining Russia's role in the new international order to political journalists, who are mainly concerned with the constellation of geo-political power and the clash of civilizations. In general, however, 'class struggle' as the leitmotiv of history has been replaced by the 'national question'. Symptomatic of the new situation is the fact that the 'history of the fatherland' (*otechestvennaia istoriia*) is no longer called 'Russian history' (*russkaia istoriia*), but rather, 'history of the Russian empire' (*rossiiskaia istoriia*).[1]

In analysing the interpretation of world history in Tsarist Russia and the Soviet Union, we are concerned with the history of an empire or a superpower. The state tried to play a leading role in world politics on the one hand, and on the other was forced to consolidate its own political system by defending the ruling ideology against alternative worldviews. Under these conditions, Russian historians never enjoyed the German ideal of 'Freiheit der Lehre und der Forschung' (freedom of teaching

[1] See Jutta Scherrer, 'Das postsowjetische Rußland: Erinnerungskultur oder Vergangenheitspolitik?', in *Geschichtsdiskurs*, vol. v: *Globale Konflikte, Erinnerungsarbeit und Neuorientierungen seit 1945*, ed. Wolfgang Küttler, Jörn Rüsen, and Ernst Schulin (Frankfurt am Main, 1999), 46–72.

and research). Despite this, it is remarkable that the main determinants of the historical thought of pre-Revolutionary Russia remained stable throughout the Soviet period. Although the Academy of Sciences was founded in St Petersburg in 1725 and the first university was opened in 1755 in Moscow, one should keep in mind that the professionalization of the historical sciences in Russia dates back only to the 'era of the forties' in the nineteenth century (that is, 1836–48). This was a decade in which Westernizers and Slavophiles debated the relationship between 'Russia and Europe', their fatherland's place in world history, and the course of its further development.[2]

From the beginning, Russian historians had assumed that Russia was backward compared with the Western European countries. The main topics of eighteenth-century historiography had been the significance of the Varagians (Vikings) as founders of the first Russian dynasty in the middle of the tenth century, and the question of the origins of the Russian state. The historiography of the nineteenth century had focused on the reforms of Peter the Great in the first quarter of the eighteenth century, or on the modernization of state and society on Western European models. And the overall themes of the historiography of the twentieth century had been the Bolshevik seizure of power in the October Revolution, and the legitimization of the introduction of the socialist system in a former developing country.[3]

[2] See Alexander Vucinich, *Science in Russian Culture*, vol. i: *A History to 1860*; vol. ii: *1861–1917* (Stanford, 1963–70); id., *Empire of Knowledge: The Academy of Sciences of the USSR (1917–1970)* (Berkeley, 1984); Patrick L. Alston, *Education and the State in Tsarist Russia* (Stanford, 1969); J. L. Black, *Citizens for the Fatherland: Education, Educators, and Pedagogical Ideals in Eighteenth Century Russia* (Boulder, 1979); James C. McClelland, *Autocrats and Academics: Education, Culture, and Society in Tsarist Russia* (Chicago and London, 1979); Mervyn Matthews, *Education in the Soviet Union: Policies and Institutions since Stalin* (London, 1982); Samuel D. Kassow, *Students, Professors and the State in Tsarist Russia* (Berkeley, 1989); Larry E. Holmes, *The Kremlin and the Schoolhouse: Reforming Education in Soviet Russia, 1917–1931* (Bloomington, 1991); Trude Maurer, *Hochschullehrer im Zarenreich: Ein Beitrag zur russischen Sozial- und Bildungsgeschichte* (Cologne, 1998).

[3] See Anatole G. Mazour, *Modern Russian Historiography*, revised edn. (Westport, 1975); Joachim Hösler, *Die sowjetische Geschichtswissenschaft 1953 bis 1991: Studien zur Methodologie- und Organisationsgeschichte* (Munich, 1995); Thomas M. Bohn, 'Historische Soziologie im vorrevolutionären Rußland', *Historische Zeitschrift*, 265 (1997), 343–72; id., *Russische Geschichtswissenschaft von 1880 bis 1905: Pavel N. Miljukov und die Moskauer Schule* (Cologne, 1998); Thomas Sanders (ed.), *Historiography of Imperial Russia: The Profession and Writing of History in a Multinational State* (Armonk, NY and London, 1999); Rainer Lindner, *Historiker und Herrschaft: Nationsbildung und Geschichtspolitik in Weißrußland im 19. und 20. Jahrhundert* (Munich, 1999); Edward Thaden, *The Rise of Historicism in Russia* (New York, 1999).

The category of 'backwardness' indicates the Eurocentric worldview of Russian historians. For them, other parts of the world were of interest only as far as the borders of the Russian empire were concerned. Without doubt, the geographical extent of the Tsarist empire (and the Soviet Union) meant that it represented a continent of its own. Scholars who since the last third of the nineteenth century had been researching the development of the settlement of the Russian people had reasons to believe that 'Russian history is the history of a country which is colonizing itself' (*Istoriia Rossii est' istoriia strany, kotoraia kolonizuetsia*).[4] The concept of 'colonization' had a meaning different from that of the 'frontier' in American history. As the main proponent of the theory, Vasilii O. Kliuchevskii, pointed out, the problem was as follows: 'The state continued to swell, but the people pined away' (*Gosudarstvo puchlo, a narod chirel*).[5]

Given that during the eighteenth and nineteenth centuries the Academy of Sciences had to concentrate its resources on the internal problems of the Russian Empire, research on world history was pursued only in the universities. The introduction of different chairs for 'Russian history' (*russkaia istoriia*) and 'general history' or 'world history' (*vseobshchaia istoriia*) by the University Statute of 1835 could be regarded as a starting-point. After the October Revolution the Soviet government tried to reorganize the academic institutions along Marxist lines. History as a university subject, for instance, was integrated into the Faculty of Social Sciences from 1919 on. Meanwhile, the above-mentioned chairs had been abandoned. But with the conservative turnabout of Soviet patriotism in 1934, the traditional institutions were rehabilitated, and in addition, world history was now one of the subjects which came under the Academy of Sciences. And in 1969 the Historical Institute of the Academy of Sciences was finally divided into the 'Institute for the History of the USSR' (*Institut istorii SSSR*) and the 'Institute for General History' (*Institut vseobshchei istorii*). In regard to the history of the world as a whole, it should be mentioned that in Russia (and to a greater extent in the Soviet Union), a special interest in the Balkans, the Middle East, and the Far East had led to the introduction of such

[4] V. O. Kliuchevskii, *Kurs russkoi istorii* (Course of Russian history), vol. i (Moscow, 1987), 50.

[5] Ibid., vol. iii (Moscow, 1988), 12.

subjects as 'Byzantine studies' (*vizantinovedenie*), 'Slavic studies' (*slavianovedenie*), and 'Eastern Studies' (*vostokovedenie*). Since the nineteenth century the terms World History (*vsemirnaia istoriia*) and General History (*vseobshchaia istoriia*) have often been used synonymously. These terms were used to refer to the organization of academic and educational institutions, or in the titles of textbooks. Indeed, General History referred to all countries except Tsarist Russia and the Soviet Union. World History, on the other hand, still implies an international historical process presented in terms of gradual progress, or of the Marxist–Leninist social formation theory. Post-Soviet historiography has yet to develop a new concept.[6]

The founder of the Russian tradition of writing world history was Timofei N. Granovskii. Until the First World War, most Russian specialists in world history called him the forefather of their own work. In fact, Granovskii did not publish very much. His reputation was based on the famous lectures on the Western European Middle Ages which he gave as a professor at Moscow University, starting in 1839. It was not his factual analysis that inspired his successors, but his ability to present Western ideas and interpretations of history in a scholarly way, despite the official ideology. While in 1834 the Minister of Education, Sergei S. Uvarov, had advised schoolteachers and university professors in the Russian Empire to train the younger generation in the spirit of orthodoxy (*pravoslavie*), autocracy (*samoderzhavie*), and patriotism (*narodnost'*), Granovskii idealized the historical role of Catholicism and established Hegelianism as a principle of Russian historicism. His inaugural lecture of 1839, which was published posthumously (not before 1895), represented a programme for the writing of world history in Tsarist Russia.

[6] See. V. P. Buzeskul, *Vseobshchaia istoriia i ee predstaviteli v Rossii v XIX i nachale XX veka* (General history and its proponents in Russia in the 19th and at the beginning of the 20th century), pts. 1–2 (Leningrad, 1929–31); B. G. Mogil'nickii, *Politicheskie i metodologicheskie idei russkoi liberal'noi medievistiki serediny 70-ch godov XIX v.–nachala 900-ch godov* (Political and methodological ideas of liberal Russian medievalists from the middle of the 1870s to the early years of the 20th century) (Tomsk, 1969); V. A. Dunaevskii, *Sovetskaia istoriografiia novoi istorii stran Zapada, 1917–1941 gg* (Soviet historiography of the modern history of Western countries, 1917–41) (Moscow, 1974); Hans Hecker, *Russische Universalgeschichtsschreibung: Von den 'Vierziger Jahren' des 19. Jahrhunderts bis zur sowjetischen 'Weltgeschichte' (1955–1965)* (Munich, 1983); E. V. Gutnova, *Istoriografiia istorii srednich vekov* (Historiography of the Middle Ages) (Moscow, 1985); A. N. Nechukhrin, *Smena paradigm v russkoi istoriografii vseobshchei istorii. 90-ye gg. XIX v.–1917 g.* (Paradigm shifts in the Russian historiography of General History: From the 1890s to 1917) (Grodno, 1992).

Inspired by Hegel, Granovskii was convinced that the history of mankind is marked by a gradual development of the spirit, realized in successive epochs or social orders. His main interest was in historical change, especially the transition from Antiquity to the Middle Ages. Granovskii avoided predicting the future. But his audience understood that within his historical concept progress was evident, even for Russia. In effect, Granovskii defined 'World History' as Western European studies from a liberal point of view.[7]

Politically, Granovskii was opposed by a group of educated men from the nobility united under the banner of a 'conservative utopia'. The Slavophile credo was published in 1852 by Ivan V. Kireevskii, an essay entitled 'The Character of the Enlightenment in Europe and its Relation to the Enlightenment in Russia' (*O kharaktere prosveshcheniia Evropy i o ego otnoshenii k prosveshcheniiu Rossii*). For the Slavophiles, 'Europe' historically represented force and aggression, as well as rationalization and revolution. Therefore they sought salvation in the principles of the Russian people, which they defined as piety and community. They were ultimately convinced that there must be alternatives to the historical paths taken by the West. But they did not present their own conception of world history. Their spiritual ideals were unity, morality, and wholeness. And their publications were mainly on historical or religious philosophy.[8]

Indeed, professional historians in the second half of the nineteenth century aspired to Granovskii's goal of intellectual independence and progress modelled on Western European patterns.

[7] Lekcii T. N. Granovskogo po istorii srednevkov'ia. (Avtorskii konspekt i zapisi slushatelei) (T. N. Granovskii's lectures on the history of the Middle Ages). *Predislovie, podgotovka teksta i primechaniia S. A. Asinovskoi* (Moscow, 1961); Lekcii T. N. Granovskogo po istorii pozdnego srednevekov'ia. (Zapiski slushatelei s avtorskoi pravkoi) (T. N. Granovskii's lectures on the history of the late Middle Ages). *Predislovie, podgotovka teksta S. A. Asinovskoi. Primechaniia S. A. Asinovskoi i L. A. Nikitinoi* (Moscow, 1971). See Hans Hecker, 'Die Anfänge der modernen Universalgeschichte in Rußland: T. N. Granovskij und seine universalhistorische Konzeption von 1839', *Saeculum*, 31 (1980), 44–65; Priscilla R. Roosevelt, 'Granovskii at the Lecture: A Conservative Liberal's View of History', *Forschungen zur osteuropäischen Geschichte*, 29 (1981), 61–192; ead., *Apostle of Russian Liberalism: Timofei Granovsky* (Newtonville, Mass., 1986).

[8] See Nicholas V. Riasanovsky, *Russia and the West in the Teaching of the Slavophiles: A Study of Romantic Ideology* (Cambridge, Mass., 1952); Peter K. Christoff, *An Introduction to Nineteenth-Century Russian Slavophilism: A Study in Ideas*, vol. ii: *I. V. Kireevskij* (The Hague, 1972); Abbott Gleason, *European and Muscovite: Ivan Kireevsky and the Origins of Slavophilism* (Cambridge, Mass., 1972); Andrzej Walicki, *The Slavophile Controversy: History of a Conservative Utopia in Nineteenth-Century Russia* (Oxford, 1975).

Socially most of them belonged to the *raznochincy* ('people of different ranks'), a professional group which existed in addition to the official estates of the gentry, clergy, townspeople, and peasantry. Their family background could be described as lower middle class. The son of a priest, for example, who had been educated at a university or academy, was a typical member of this group. The famous Russian *intelligentsiia* recruited itself from the *raznochincy*. Since the 1860s, the *intelligentsiia* purported to represent public opinion in Tsarist Russia and consequently formed the opposition to autocracy. The credo of the *intelligentsiia* was no longer constituted by the dualism of Russia and Europe, but the antagonism of state and society. In the 1880s the progressive forces at the universities received a new impetus from the activities of the lecturers (*privatdocenty*) whose function was to replace those assistant professors (*docenty*) who had enjoyed the privilege of financial and functional integration into the official educational system. As members of a 'scientific proletariat', the lecturers used their energy for cultural work under the monopoly of the state. In regard to the university department of general history, another aspect was also important. For postgraduates preparing themselves for a chair, two years studying abroad was obligatory. As a result, the writing of world history in Tsarist Russia was always closely connected with that in Western Europe.[9]

The influence of German historicism, for instance, is most obvious in the works of Vladimir I. Ger′e. Ger′e, who was appointed to the chair of general history in Moscow in 1868, introduced the teaching of the modern age as a university course to Russia. He was an exception among his colleagues as he believed that ideas were the main moving forces of history.[10] In the 1830s specialists in Russian history had already been interested in the regularities of the historical process. They looked for historical laws and had been resistant to the idealistic doctrine of

[9] See Richard Pipes (ed.), *The Russian Intelligentsia* (New York, 1961); Philipp Pomper, *The Russian Revolutionary Intelligentsia* (New York, 1970); Otto Wilhelm Müller, *Intelligencija: Untersuchungen zur Geschichte eines politischen Schlagwortes* (Frankfurt, 1971); Christopher Read, *Culture and Power in Revolutionary Russia: The Intelligentsia and the Transition from Tsarism to Communism* (Basingstoke, 1990); Edith W. Clowes, Samuel D. Kassow, and James L. West (eds.), *Between Tsar and People: Educated Society and the Quest for Public Identity in Late Imperial Russia* (Princeton, 1991).

[10] See Hecker, *Russische Universalgeschichtsschreibung*, 117–23.

German historicism. In particular, the State School (*gosudarstvennaia shkola*) around the Moscow historian Sergei M. Solov′ev had been inspired by the determinism of Hegel's philosophy and by his juridical terminology.[11] Nevertheless in Russia it was Ger′e who first studied the history of the French Revolution, thus preparing the way for the *école russe.*

The term *école russe* covered more than a dozen general and legal historians who, under the theoretical and ideological influence of French and English positivism, studied the social and economic history of France in the last decades of the eighteenth century. Nikolai I. Kareev, Maxim M. Kovalevskii, and Evgenii V. Tarle, to mention only a few names, are among the better known. All of them received their education in the period between the emancipation of the peasants from serfdom in 1861 and the first Russian revolution in 1905. They were inspired by the era of the Great Reforms of the 1860s under Alexander II but had to present the fruits of their academic work in the reactionary era of the 1880s and 1890s under Alexander III and Nicholas II. The *école russe*'s first major publication was Kareev's dissertation 'The Peasants and the Peasant Question in France in the Last Quarter of the Eighteenth Century' (*Krest′iane i krest′ianskii vopros vo Francii v poslednei chetverti XVIII v.*), which was published in Moscow in 1879. The work demonstrates that the peasant emancipation of 1861 opened the eyes of Russian historians to social questions. It drew upon archival material which French historians had not used, and it was based on new statistical methods. Following this example, the other members of the *école russe* participated in introducing historical sociology to Russian historiography as a new scientific paradigm. Given that Russian studies of the French Revolution were fundamental works, many of them had been translated into French. No wonder that in the first quarter of the twentieth century the term *école russe* was used in Russian historical literature to point up the international recognition of the achievements of Russia's general historians.[12]

[11] See Klaus-Detlev Grothusen, *Die Historische Rechtsschule Rußlands: Ein Beitrag zur russischen Geistesgeschichte in der zweiten Hälfte des 19. Jahrhunderts* (Gießen, 1962).

[12] See N. I. Kareev, *Istoriki frantsuzskoi revoliutsii*, vol. iii: *Izuchenie frantsuzskoi revoliutsii vne Francii* (Historians of the French Revolution, vol. iii: Research on the French Revolution outside Russia) (Leningrad, 1925); Dmitry Shlapentokh, *The French Revolution in Russian Intellectual Life, 1865–1905* (Westport, 1996).

While the professionalization of Russian historiography led to a specialization of historical research, political writers offered popular syntheses and generalizations. A new concept of world history was presented by the statistician and botanist Nikolai Ia. Danilevskii. After its publication in 1871, his book *Russia and Europe (Rossiia i Evropa)*, became famous as the Bible of the Panslavists, whose aim was the unification of all Slavic peoples under the guidance of the Russian Tsar, and the liberation of the Orthodox capital, Constantinople, from the Ottomans. Danilevskii rejected the traditional divisions of world history into Antiquity, Middle Ages, and modern times. In his view this applied only to the development of Western European history. More importantly, he went so far as to limit the idea of Europe to the Germanic and Latin nations. His argument was that countries or nations, like living organisms, go through the special stages of childhood, youth, adulthood, and old age. But he denied that the development of human civilization was a general process. He therefore divided the world into particular civilizations or 'cultural historical types' and asserted that they all go through similar stages, but at different times. According to Danilevskii, a cultural historical type is defined by the following factors: a common language, political independence, a unique culture, a federal system, and a relatively short period of ascendancy. In this sense Danilevskii described a sequence of cultural historical types: (1) the Egyptian, (2) the Chinese, (3) the Assyrian–Babylonian Phoenician, Chaldean, Old Semite, (4) the Hindustani, (5) the Iranian, (6) the Hebrew, (7) the Greek, (8) the Roman, (9) the New Semite or Arabian, and (10) the Germanic–Latin. Danilevskii's aim, of course, was to predict the downfall of the Germanic–Latin and the rise of the Slavic cultural historical type.[13]

After the October Revolution, most scholars survived in one form or another within the new Soviet academic and educa-

[13] N. Ia. Danilevskii, *Rossiia i Evropa: Vzgliad na kul'turnye i politicheskie otnosheniia Slavianskogo mira k Germano–Romanskomu* (Russia and Europe: A View of Cultural and Political Relations between the Slavic and the Germanic–Latin World) (St Petersburg, 1995), 77–95, 398–431. See Konrad Pfalzgraf, 'Die Politisierung und Radikalisierung des Problems Rußland und Europa bei N. Ja. Danilevskij', *Forschungen zur osteuropäischen Geschichte*, 1 (1954), 55–209; Michael B. Petrovich, *The Emergence of Russian Panslavism, 1856–1870* (2nd edn.; New York, 1958); Hans Kohn, *Pan-Slavism: Its History and Ideology* (2nd rev. edn.; New York, 1960).

tional institutions. Those who had left the universities after the 1905 revolution to participate in the new parliamentary system, and especially those who had supported the White armies in the civil war, were forced to emigrate. Another group of around 200 scholars was expelled by the Soviet government in 1922. From then on the Moscow historian Michail N. Pokrovskii dominated the scene as Deputy People's Commissar of Education. He tried to change of the dominant scientific paradigm by translating the historical sociology of his predecessors into Marxist terminology. But the campaign against the so-called bourgeois historians began in earnest only in 1928. The first victim was Dmitrii M. Petrushevskii, whose book *Outlines of the Economic History of the European Middle Ages* (*Ocherki ekonomicheskoi istorii srednevekovoi Evropy*) was criticized by Pokrovskii's Society of Marxist Historians. Petrushevskii referred in his book to the 'ideal type' of Max Weber and the Neo-Kantianism of Heinrich Rickert, and to the thesis of the Vienna historian Alfons Dopsch, who described a continuity between Antiquity and the Middle Ages with the exception of revolutionary upheavals. In terms of economic laws and the theory of social formation, it was therefore easy to impute to Petrushevskii a lack of Marxism. The polemic against Petrushevskii was only the beginning of an attack which posed a physical threat to the so-called bourgeois historians. After the arrest and exile to the eastern parts of the Soviet Union of more than one hundred historians between 1929 and 1931, it seemed that the young Marxist historians had triumphed over their teachers. But only a few years later, many of the outlawed historians had been rehabilitated. The most prominent example was Evgenii V. Tarle, already mentioned above. At the end of the 1920s, he had been criticized for underestimating the class struggle and the inner contradictions of the capitalist West in the book *Europe in the Age of Imperialism* (*Evropa v epochu imperializma*). In the second half of the 1930s, he was heaped with honours for a more or less conventional biography of Napoleon. An explanation is easy to find. In response to the new patriotism, the Soviet Government condemned the Pokrovskii School for its sociological schematism and formalism. In a resolution of 1934, the Central Committee of the Communist Party advised educational institutions to teach more lively history with 'events' and 'heroes'. The government was not only interested in a more patriotic view of the history of Russia, it was also more active in foreign policy. Once again, the old experts in Russian and world history were needed.[14]

In this climate and against the background of the Great Purges and the Second World War, the Academy of Sciences tried to develop the concept of a Marxist version of World History in over thirty volumes. Nikolai M. Lukin was responsible for the preparation. In 1937 he had published an article on 'The Main Problems of Conceptualizing a World History' (*Osnovnye problemy postroeniia vsemirnoi istorii*). At the beginning Lukin criticized Hegel and the idealistic approach to world history. He argued that a common historical process had only become possible with the triumph of industrial capitalism at the end of the eighteenth century and with the crossing over national boundaries of the international division of labour. He therefore suggested a parallel periodization to the traditional divisions of Antiquity, Middle Ages, and modern times, and to the socio-economic formations of primeval society, slave-holder society, feudalism, capitalism, and socialism. His views were to a certain extent Eurocentric as he identified the Middle Ages with feudalism and interpreted modern times as the pre-history of the October Revolution. He denied the idealistic differentiation of peoples into historical and non-historical. In conformity with Soviet patriotism he declared that from the beginning of the twentieth century on, world history was under the sign of socialism. Lukin had no chance to take part in the realization of this project. For reasons unknown, he was imprisoned in 1938. He died two years later in the gulag.[15]

Five volumes of the Soviet World History had been prepared by the Second World War, but only the volume on the French Revolution had been published. After the war, the Academy of Sciences reduced its ambitious project from over 30 to 10

[14] See Edgar Hösch, *Evgenij Viktorovič Tarle (1875–1955) und seine Stellung in der sowjetischen Geschichtswissenschaft* (Wiesbaden, 1964); George M. Enteen, *The Soviet Scholar-Bureaucrat: M. N. Pokrovskii and the Society of Marxist Historians* (Pennsylvania, 1978); John Barber, *Soviet Historians in Crisis, 1928–1932* (London, 1981); Manfred Zimmermann, 'Das Ende der Zusammenarbeit auf dem Gebiet der Geschichte: Der Fall Dmitrij M. Petruševskij', *Jahrbücher für Geschichte Osteuropas*, NS 40 (1992), 501–13.

[15] N. Lukin, 'Osnovnye problemy postroeniia vsemirnoi istorii' (Main problems of conceptualizing a World History), *Istorik-marksist*, 3 (1937), 3–23. Reprinted in id., *Izbrannye trudy*, iii (Moscow, 1963), 431–53. See Hecker, *Russische Universalgeschichtsschreibung*, 190–6.

volumes, and these appeared under the guidance of the Japanologist Evgenii M. Zhukov from 1955 to 1965.[16] This project was directed against the 'spirit of colonialism', that is, the Eurocentric interpretation of bourgeois historiography, and against '"vulgar" economic materialism', that is, the Pokrovskii School. The history of mankind, according to the introduction of the first volume, should not be the history of 'world empires' or 'world civilizations', but the history of the masses. The editors emphasized that not only the economic base, but also the social, political, and cultural superstructure played an active role in the movement of the historical process. Although the editors played up the value of actions and events, they were nevertheless convinced that the history of mankind could be described as a process defined by economic laws and social contradictions. The main thesis implied that all societies, peoples, and nations have to go through the same process, but not simultaneously. In parts, the introduction may be read as a repetition of Lukin's statement of 1937. First, there is the assertion that the concept of a common world history is acceptable only in connection with the development of a world market and the international division of labour. Second, there is the decision to combine the traditional periodization defined by epochs with socio-economic formations defined by laws. In addition, the editors admit that in the periodization of history special events function as borderlines, and that a concentration of the story on the most progressive countries is unavoidable.[17] Conceptionally, primeval society was connected with prehistory, slave-holder society with the history of Egypt and the Middle East, feudalism with the history of China, some other Asian countries, and the Mediterranean area, capitalism with the history of Western Europe and North America, and socialism with the history of Russia.

The structure of the published World History is organized as follows: volumes one and two refer to primeval society and Antiquity up to the fourth or fifth centuries; volumes three and four to the Middle Ages from the fifth to the middle of the seventeenth centuries; volumes five to seven to modern times from the English Revolution to the October Revolution; and

[16] *Vsemirnaia istoriia v desjati tomach* (World History in ten volumes), i–x (Moscow, 1955–65).

[17] 'Ot glavnoi redakcii' (From the editors-in-chief), ibid. i, pp. v–xxxiii.

volumes eight to ten to contemporary history from 1917 to 1945. In the period 1977 to 1983 a supplement appeared in three volumes, which referred to developments from the Second World War to 1970.[18] In effect the Soviet World History represents a compilation of national histories. Class struggle and revolutions or 'events' and not socio-economic formations or 'laws' constitute the leitmotiv. Behind the enhancement of the status of Russia's place in the history of the world a tendency towards messianism is visible. Critics in the socialist countries have claimed that the interpretation of the neolithic, bronze, and iron ages does not reflect the most recent findings of modern archaeology, and that for the Middle and Far East, the category 'Oriental despotism' (Marx) is more appropriate than 'slave-holder society' (Lenin). In Western commentaries, the work has been characterized as a 'world history of Europe'. Not only the periodization, but also the terminology is based on Western categories. Indeed, in the story, slave-holder society equals Antiquity, feudalism stands for the Middle Ages, and capitalism for modern times.[19]

The quintessence of Soviet historiography was scientism, materialism, and determinism, while the traditional popular culture was based on paganism and spiritualism. It seems that in Soviet society there was a special popular need for myths, especially at times of crisis. Perhaps this is why the ideas of the Eurasians became popular in nationalist circles during the era of *perestroika*. Inspired by the symbolism of the Russian 'silver age' before the First World War and by cultural pessimism after the Bolshevik seizure of power, in the 1920s a small but active group of Russian emigrants denied the universal significance of European civilization. The discussion was launched by the linguist Nikolai S. Trubeckoi, who in 1920 published a brochure on 'Europe and Mankind' (*Evropa i chelovechestvo*). In a spirit of anti-colonialism Trubeckoi exposed European cosmopolitanism as Germanic–Latin chauvinism. On this basis he interpreted the

[18] *Vsemirnaia istoriia* (World History), xi–xiii (Moscow, 1977–83).

[19] See Georg Stadtmüller, 'Die neue sowjetische Weltgeschichte', *Saeculum*, 11 (1960), 295–384; Helmut Neubauer, 'Sowjetische Weltgeschichte', *Osteuropa*, 11 (1961), 109–12; id., 'Zum sowjetischen Verständnis der Weltgeschichte', *Saeculum*, 14 (1963), 53–7; Ernst Schulin, 'Universalgeschichtsschreibung im 20. Jahrhundert', in id., *Traditionskritik und Rekonstruktionsversuch: Studien zur Entwicklung von Geschichtswissenschaft und historischem Denken* (Göttingen, 1979), 163–202, at 179–83.

terms 'Europe' and 'Mankind' as an antithesis. Instead, Trubeckoi pleaded for the equality and diversity of all national cultures to be accepted. His argument was adopted by the geographer Petr N. Savickii (1895–1968), who declared in various writings in the first half of the 1920s that Russia belonged neither to Europe nor to Asia, but represented a continent of its own, 'Eurasia'. As the main ideologue of the Eurasians, Savickii influenced the young Russian historian George Vernadsky, who in the second half of the 1920s tried to enlarge the Eurocentric view of Russian historiography. In his eyes, his predecessors had been too concerned with the problems of European Russia. He therefore first presented a positive valuation of the Mongol rule over the Russian people in the Middle Ages. In addition, he described the expansion into Asia as one of the main factors of Russian history. After his emigration from Prague to the USA in the 1930s Vernadsky no longer defended the theses of his early writings. Nevertheless, his ideas had an unexpected revival in the Soviet Union in the 1980s. The main proponent of Eurasianism in recent times had been the ethnologist Lev N. Gumilev, who used *glasnost'* and *perestroika* to publish books on subjects such as *Ethnogenesis and the Biosphere of Earth* (*Etnogenezis i biosfera zemli*) or *Old Russia and the Great Steppe* (*Drevniaia Rus' i velikaia step*). In his writings, Gumilev discusses irrational phenomena in a scientific way and suggests a symbiosis of Russian and Mongol culture. The fact that his collected works are bestsellers indicates that many Russians today are looking for their own world.[20]

In conclusion, it should be noted that in Tsarist Russia and in the Soviet Union professional historians were always Westernizers who had followed European models. The writing of world history in Tsarist Russia was introduced as Western European studies. General historians were active members of the international scientific community. Although they published

[20] See Otto Böss, *Die Lehre der Eurasier: Ein Beitrag zur russischen Ideengeschichte des 20. Jahrhunderts* (Wiesbaden, 1961); Charles J. Halperin, 'Russia and the Steppe: George Vernadsky and Eurasianism', *Forschungen zur osteuropäischen Geschichte*, 36 (1985), 55–194; Leonid Luks, 'Die Ideologie der Eurasier im zeitgeschichtlichen Zusammenhang', *Jahrbücher für Geschichte Osteuropas*, NS 34 (1986), 374–95; Bruno Naarden, '"I'm a genius, but no more than that." Lev Gumilev (1912–1992), Ethnogenesis, the Russian Past and World History', *Jahrbücher für Geschichte Osteuropas*, NS 44 (1996), 54–82; Ryszard Paradowski, 'The Eurasian Idea and Leo Gumilev's Scientific Ideology', *Canadian Slavonic Papers*, 41 (1999), 19–32.

important studies on the Renaissance, the Reformation, the Glorious Revolution, and the French Revolution, they never published a synthesis worth mentioning. The task of presenting their own conception of world history was taken over by Slavophile amateurs, who were looking for a Russian *Sonderweg* (special path) to the future. Only during the Soviet era, when professional historians were isolated from the scientific community, had an official World History been prepared. The result was a repetition of the pre-Revolutionary concept of gradual progress, enlarged by the addition of Marxist terminology and the categories of Russian imperialism. As long as the old generation of Soviet historians keeps the key positions in the academic apparatus, and as long as the material situation of post-Soviet academia remains in such a sorry state, no innovations are to be expected. Indeed, apart from the rewriting of school textbooks, nothing really new has happened in the writing of world history since the breakdown of the Soviet Union.

From 1993 to 1996 a discussion about the periodization of European history in modern times took place in the journal *New and Newest History* (*Novaia i noveishaia istoriia*), edited by the Institute for General History of the Academy of Sciences in Moscow. The historians B. D. Kozenko and S. M. Sadova tried to modify a paradigm established by a group of textbook advisers around Stalin in 1934. Since then Soviet historians have had to accept the French Revolution, the Paris Commune, and the October Revolution as major events and milestones in modern history. Kozenko and Sadova therefore attempted to create a more differentiated picture of the historical process. Without abandoning the foundation of the social formation theory, they suggested a tripartite division of modern history. They located the development of capitalist economy and civil society between the English Revolution and the French Revolution. The time between the Napoleonic Wars and the First World War they identified as the age of industrial capitalism and imperialism. And from the Russian Civil War onwards they saw world history as a competition between capitalism and socialism. Responding to their critics, Kozenko and Sadova finally presented a simplified scheme, divided into early modern history (sixteenth or seventeenth century to the eighteenth century), modern history (nineteenth century), and contemporary history (twentieth century). Thus they have accepted the terms and patterns of Western European historiography.[21]

The presentation of a new concept is as problematic as periodization for post-Soviet historians. Indeed, the World History published in Minsk in 1996–8 in twenty-four volumes is no more than a revised version of the Soviet World History.[22] The preface to the first volume of the Minsk edition claims to offer a non-ideological narrative. But it refers to economic laws and the class concept as well as to the base–superstructure model and the theory of social formation. Under this premiss, the narrative remains Marxist. The fact that the editor refers only to the research on world history outside Russia before the Second World War is significant. It seems that for the authors of the Minsk edition the 'world' is only accessible through translations of concepts which are not even up to date.[23] For lack of alternatives a Moscow publishing house decided in 1999 to take part in the preparation of a popular and a luxury edition of the Minsk World History.[24] In the meantime, really new explanations of the world are given by outsiders.[25]

[21] B. D. Kozenko and G. M. Sadova, 'O periodizacii novoi i noveishei istorii v svete sovremennych traktovok' (The periodization of modern and contemporary history in the light of current treatises), *Novaia i noveishaia istoriia*, 4 (1993), 87–96; eid., 'K diskussii o periodizacii istorii stran Evropy i Ameriki' (On the discussion about the periodization of the history of European countries and America), *Novaia i noveishaia istoriia*, 1 (1996), 88–91.

[22] *Vsemirnaia istoriia v 24 tomach* (World History in 24 volumes), i–xxiv (Minsk, 1996–8; reprinted 2000–1).

[23] 'Ot redakcii' (From the editors), *Vsemirnaia istoriia v 24 tomach* (Minsk, 1997), i. 5–23.

[24] *Vsemirnaia istoriia*, i: *U istokov tsivilizacii: Bronzovyi vek* (World history. i: The sources of civilization: The bronze age); ii: *Vek zheleza: Drevneishie tsivilizacii Vostoka* (The iron age: The oldest civilizations of the East); iii: *Ellinisticheskii i rimskii periody* (The Hellenistic and the Roman period); iv: *Zakat Rimskoi imperii. Rannee srednevekov'e* (The breakdown of the Roman Empire. The early Middle Ages); v: *Krestovye podchody. U istokov Renessanca* (The Crusades. On the Sources of the Renaissance); vi: *Epocha prosveshcheniia. Severnaia voina* (The epoch of Enlightenment. The Northern War); vii: *Nachalo Kolonialinych imperii. Period angliiskoi revoliucii* (The beginning of the colonial empires. The period of the English Revolution); viii: *Velikaia Francuzskaia revoliuciia* (The French Revolution); ix: *Napoleonskie voiny. Grazhdanskaia voina u SShA* (The Napoleonic Wars. The American Civil War); x: *Pervaia mirovaia voina. Obrazovanie SSSR* (The First World War. The foundation of the USSR); xi: *Cholodnaia voina. Raspad SSSR. Sovremennyi mir* (The Cold War. The breakdown of the USSR. The modern world) (Moscow, 1999–2002).

[25] In the 1990s the Moscow physicist Anatolii T. Fomenko began to rewrite the history of Russia and the world in a pseudo-scientific manner. With the help of his so-called mathematical method he tries to demonstrate that the history of mankind is based on a falsification of sources. His alternative is a scientific fiction inspired by some ideas of the Eurasians. As the reactions of the main historical journals show, professional

historians took a defensive position. A. T. Fomenko, *Metody matematisticheskogo analiza istoricheskich tekstov. Prilozhenie k khronologii* (The methods of mathematical analysis as applied to historical texts. Supplement to chronology) (Moscow, 1996); G. V. Nosovskii and A. T. Fomenko, *Rekonstrukciia vseobshchei istorii. Novaia khronologiia* (Reconstruction of general history. New chronology) (Moscow, 1999). See 'Mify "novoi khronology" akademika A. T. Fomenko' (A. T. Fomenko's myth of a 'new chronology'), *Novaia i noveishaia istoriia*, 3 (2000), 6–57; 'Istoriia ne terpit diletantizma. (O "matematicheskom metode oplodotvoreniia istorii" A. T. Fomenko)' (History does not accept dilettantism. About A. T. Fomenko's 'mathematical method for the enrichment of history'), *Otechestvennaia istoriia*, 4 (2000), 3–9.

9

World Power and World History: Writing the British Empire, 1885–1945

BENEDIKT STUCHTEY

In his reflections on the impact of the First World War on the personal lives and professional work of British, German, French, and Belgian historians, Fritz Stern asks whether this *Urkatastrophe* of the twentieth century changed hitherto acknowledged views of the nature of mankind and the understanding of historical processes, or whether these remained unchallenged.[1] How did historians experience the war? Did their work take a new direction after it, and how was this reflected in the different national cultures? Thucydides had provided an excellent example when writing on the Peloponnesian War, in which he fought as a general on the side of Athens. Its defeat by the Spartan league prompted the historian to think generally about war as a teacher of evil, revealing man's inherent characteristic features and especially promoting the negative ones. Indeed, too many historians have taken on board the belief in progressive history in general, most famously represented by the 'Whig interpretation' in particular. However, military defeat offered a unique opportunity not to side with the winners in history, but to profit from the philosophical and historical findings that could be drawn from humiliation, destruction, and death. The losers in history, as Reinhart Koselleck says, are more interesting to the historian who wants to learn from the past rather than just to perpetuate it. The past, in the short term, was made by the winners; but history, in the long term, should be understood by empathizing with the losers.[2]

[1] Fritz Stern, 'Historians and the Great War: Private Experience and Public Explication', *Yale Review*, 82/1 (1994), 34–54 (originally given as Sir Isaiah Berlin Lecture, Oxford, 3 Dec. 1992).

[2] Reinhart Koselleck, 'Erfahrungswandel und Methodenwechsel. Eine historisch-anthropologische Skizze', in Christian Meier and Jörn Rüsen (eds.), *Historische Methode*, Theorie der Geschichte: Beiträge zur Historik, 5 (Munich, 1988), 13–61, at 51 ff.

Yet, while winning has only one clear result, losing suggests several. If we look at the generation of German scholars who worked before and after the First World War, their case does not seem to fit into Koselleck's model. Although Germany had lost the war, its historians were not prepared to accept this result for the benefit of historical insight. They did not make use of the great opportunities inherent in the 'culture of defeat'.[3] This comes as no great surprise considering their worldview before the war. A pacifist such as the historian Ludwig Quidde was an exception. Since the late nineteenth century the rule for German academia had become ardent nationalism and closing ranks with its governments' policies. The liberal-conservative *Bildungsbürgertum* (educated middle classes) championed racialist, social-Darwinist, and militarist views in close sympathy with what Houston Stewart Chamberlain embodied in Britain. Hitherto Anglophile German historians then actively joined in a war of pamphlets against Britain in which intellectual viewpoints were replaced by ideological and nationalist ones. In October 1914 almost all German university professors signed a declaration justifying Germany's war aims.[4] Few if any had the courage to withstand the intellectual and moral sell-out, as their Western colleagues commented disapprovingly four years later.[5]

In recent years the historical experience of the Weimar Republic has been given increasing attention as an example of a state whose failure was certainly partly the result of its citizens' lack of trust in parliamentary democracy. After 1918 many intellectuals remained prejudiced. They persisted in an anachronistic way of thinking, derived from the Kaiserreich, determined by conventional notions of the relationship between state and society, and of the nation-state. Instead of learning from the political, moral, and intellectual crisis of the war and establishing a strong democracy after it, they gave way to nostalgia for traditional power politics and the supposed glory of imperial

[3] Wolfgang Schivelbusch, *Die Kultur der Niederlage: Der amerikanische Süden 1865, Frankreich 1871, Deutschland 1918* (Berlin, 2001), 227–343.

[4] 'Erklärung der Hochschullehrer des Deutschen Reiches', reprinted in Bernhard vom Brooke, 'Wissenschaft und Militarismus: Der Aufruf der 93 "An die Kulturwelt!" und der Zusammenbruch der internationalen Gelehrtenrepublik im Ersten Weltkrieg', in William Calder, Hellmut Flashar, and Theodor Lindken (eds.), *Wilamowitz nach fünzig Jahren* (Darmstadt, 1985), 649–719, at 717.

[5] Matthew Stibbe, *Anglophobia and the Great War, 1914–1918* (Cambridge, 2001).

expansion. This resisted modern concepts of a democratic renunciation of national sovereignty for the benefit of international security. One of the major problems of the Republic of Weimar was the widespread hostility of the educated classes who saw the new democracy as an outcome of defeat. If that defeat was to be successfully reversed, Germany needed to fulfil its historic mission of creating a God-given Greater German empire.[6] The collapse of the Austro-Hungarian Empire and the international isolation of Bolshevik Russia gave Germany a unique opportunity to regain an *Imperium* that both Protestants and Catholics could identify with, that possessed a religious dimension, and that expressed the romantic, if not mythical, idea of the Reich, which had medieval origins.[7] Thus after Versailles German historiography did not open its gates but intellectually retreated back to its Germanic roots. The price of this isolation was high, as the following years were to show. Names such as Marc Bloch and Lucien Febvre in France, Henri Pirenne in Belgium, and Johan Huizinga in the Netherlands, who furthered a transnational historiography with a comparative perspective in the 1920s, are difficult to find in Germany.

This essay is concerned with this social and intellectual group, not the politically and economically weak, or the socially subjugated, who in any case would not have been given the chance to influence the historical process of which they were part. It looks instead at those members of society who, not least through their profession, possessed the knowledge to participate in political change that became historical change. Tragically and often pathetically they had the capacity to influence the course of events, but they failed to do so although they should have known the rules by which history was made. And history proved not to follow linear patterns or cyclical revolutions, or to produce predictable circumstances or dominant themes that repeated themselves over generations. Rather, history presented itself as a contingency of turning-points. Let us return to Fritz Stern's concern. Historians, then, were deeply responsible for change. Marc Bloch and the Englishman, Richard Tawney,

[6] Major work on this has been done by Klaus Hildebrand, *Vom Reich zum Weltreich: Hitler, NSDAP und koloniale Frage 1919–1945* (Munich, 1969).

[7] This thesis is developed by Heinrich August Winkler, *Der lange Weg nach Westen*, 2 vols. (Munich, 2000), i: *Deutsche Geschichte vom Ende des Alten Reiches bis zum Untergang der Weimarer Republik*.

certainly shared this sentiment; the German Gerhard Ritter was still too young and not yet influential enough to be grouped with these historians, and after the war he would soon devote himself to a biography of Luther (published in 1925) in order to demonstrate that Germany was not a Western country.[8] The German historians were, strictly speaking, reactionaries in their reluctance to acknowledge historical change. After 1918 they continued with what they had begun before 1914. Reflecting on his own work and the institutional situation of historical writing after the war in general, a leading exponent such as Georg von Below would not accept a revision of the 'old ideals' of the romantic tradition.[9] On the other hand, one of the sharpest contemporary critics of this state of affairs, Eckart Kehr, objected to his colleagues' lack of methodological innovations, and was one of the very few to advocate the 'primacy of domestic politics' on a Social Democratic basis in contrast to the prevailing conservative histories of diplomacy and foreign politics.[10] Naturally, however, Kehr remained an outsider.

Thus in Germany, the Great War did not cause a great historiographical revision. This is still an accepted interpretation today.[11] The strong tradition of German historical idealism remained intact, and the paradigm of the nation-state informing the course and aims of German history was not replaced, in part, certainly, because there was no new paradigm at hand. Despite fears of impending problems for professional historical writing,[12] historicism had been strikingly resilient in the face of

[8] Carole Fink, *Marc Bloch: A Life in History* (Cambridge, 1991), 111 ff.; Ulrich Raulff, *Ein Historiker im 20. Jahrhundert: Marc Bloch* (Frankfurt am Main, 1995), 79 f.; J. M. Winter, 'Tawney the Historian', in id. (ed.), *History and Society: Essays by Richard Henry Tawney* (London, 1978), 1–40; Christoph Cornelißen, *Gerhard Ritter: Geschichtswissenschaft und Politik im 20. Jahrhundert* (Düsseldorf, 2001).

[9] Georg von Below, *Die deutsche Geschichtsschreibung von den Befreiungskriegen bis zu unseren Tagen* (Munich, 1924); cf. Gideon Reuveni, 'Geschichtsdiskurs und Krisenbewußtsein: Deutsche Historiographie nach dem Ersten Weltkrieg', *Tel Aviver Jahrbuch für deutsche Geschichte*, 25 (1996), 155–86; Yehoshua Arieli, 'Deutsche Geschichtsschreibung und die liberale Tradition', in Rudolf von Thadden (ed.), *Die Krise des Liberalismus zwischen den Weltkriegen* (Göttingen, 1978), 69–95.

[10] Kehr's collected essays were edited by Hans-Ulrich Wehler as *Der Primat der Innenpolitik* (Berlin, 1965).

[11] For a very interesting generational approach see Ernst Schulin, 'Weltkriegserfahrung und Historikerreaktion', in Wolfgang Küttler, Jörn Rüsen, and Ernst Schulin (eds.), *Geschichtsdiskurs*, 5 vols., iv: *Krisenbewußtsein, Katastrophenerfahrungen und Innovationen 1880–1945* (Frankfurt am Main, 1997), 165–88.

[12] Ernst Troeltsch, *Der Historismus und seine Probleme* (Tübingen, 1922).

modern trends. Methodological orthodoxy withstood any intellectual moves that could threaten the conformity and continuity of the historical convictions of generations of scholars. If the state was the guarantor of the stability of political life, as the majority of German historians in the first half of the twentieth century believed, this nation-state 'continued to provide the central agenda for German historical writing during both the Weimar Republic and the Third Reich'.[13]

Historical writing as an established institution in German academia flourished after the First World War with the foundation of new institutions such as the Reichsarchiv, the Historische Reichskommission, and the official publication of *Die große Politik der europäischen Kabinette 1871–1914* (1919–27) sponsored by the German Foreign Office. However, this did not entail methodological modernization, but only the introduction of contemporary history into curricula. The immediate past of the war, its causes, the rivalry of European powers in the Age of Imperialism, the Kaiserreich, the problem of *großdeutsch* versus *kleindeutsch*, the question of the congruence of nation and state, the relationship between the establishment of the Reich in 1871 and liberalism or democracy, the foreign policy of the Wilhelmine state and Bismarck's policy of alliances: these and many others were the topics historians were mainly concerned with when debating the reasons for the decline and fall of Germany in 1918. To be sure, it was mainly the trend-setting and influential representatives of the profession who were occupied with these questions.[14] World-historical questions that had traditionally been so prominent in Germany since the eighteenth century did not lose their attraction and were also discussed in the context of their historiographical tradition.[15]

[13] Peter Lambert, 'Generations of German Historians: Patronage, Censorship and the Containment of Generation Conflict, 1918–1945', in Mark Roseman (ed.), *Generations in Conflict: Youth Revolt and Generation Formation in Germany 1770–1968* (Cambridge, 1995), 164–83, at 164; see also Bernd Faulenbach, *Ideologie des deutschen Weges: Die deutsche Geschichte in der Historiographie zwischen Kaiserreich und Nationalsozialismus* (Munich, 1980), 16–25, 181–8.

[14] See Bernd Faulenbach, 'Nach der Niederlage: Zeitgeschichtliche Fragen und apologetische Tendenzen in der Historiographie der Weimarer Zeit', in Peter Schöttler (ed.), *Geschichtsschreibung als Legitimationswissenschaft 1918–1945* (Frankfurt am Main, 1997), 31–51.

[15] Cf. Gerhard Masur, *Rankes Begriff der Weltgeschichte* (Munich, 1926); J. Kaerst, 'Studien zur Entwicklung und Bedeutung der universalgeschichtlichen Anschauung', *Historische Zeitschrift*, 106 (1911), 473–534, and 111 (1913), 253–320.

In 1911 one author could claim that no other Western country had attracted so many diverse judgements from its European observers, in particular from the Germans, as England. In both countries, the relationship between Germany and England had moved to the centre of public interest and private discussion alike.[16] Of course, countless studies were published of England, its history, politics, society, and much more. Here only a small selection concentrating on Empire and imperial expansion can be considered. The historical works analysed in this essay do not represent the well-studied heights of their profession, but avoided the great political challenges of their time. None the less, by addressing the history of the British Empire they at least did not shrink from a great historiographical challenge. Few, however, distinguished between the colonial Empire, the Commonwealth, and the special status of India and Ireland. Practical *Weltpolitik* was not questioned, nor was its theoretical assessment taboo despite widespread yet cautious agreement with Bismarck's famous statement that Germany could realistically acquire an empire only with Britain's consent. It was commonly agreed that, for Germany's position in Europe as the 'belated nation' in the concert of the imperial powers, it was vital to acquire a place in world politics. But as Max Lenz, for example, pointed out, German *Weltpolitik* was still too dominated by economic and industrial interests and did not possess the political–imperial character which was seen as typical of the British Empire and as an essential requirement for its successful expansion.[17] Its lack of engagement with international power-political constellations and the domestic political preconditions for imperial engagement was regarded as a major obstacle to its aims. In this respect none other than Britain could serve as an example for German imperial aspirations. Moreover, Adolf Rein, professor at the University of Hamburg and John Robert Seeley's first biographer, considered the historical emergence of great powers as the real subject of world history. The great powers 'carry within themselves "the world idea" as something they have renounced. They aspire to the aim of achieving universal rule, and of forming the peoples into a "historical

[16] Heinrich Spies, *Das moderne England: Einführung in das Studium seiner Kultur. Mit besonderem Hinblick auf einen Aufenthalt im Lande* (Strassburg, 1911), 17.

[17] Max Lenz, *Deutschland im Kreis der Großmächte 1871–1914* (Berlin, 1925).

humanity" (Ranke).'[18] Again, only the British Empire could fulfil this task and, in Rein's opinion, spread the 'world idea'. Essentially, then, the major purpose of the writing of world history was 'to describe the individual and repeated acts of establishing an empire, and its expansion, each of which aspire to fulfil the imagined destiny of the inhabitants of the earth'.[19] That the emergence of the Empire was much more chaotic and much less systematic than seen by the German authors has recently been shown by Linda Colley in her new book.[20]

The British Empire had reached its maximum extent during the inter-war period. It symbolized the archetype of modern colonial empires with its capacity to encompass an unparalleled ethnic and cultural diversity. Of course, German writers in the early twentieth century were well aware of the gradual decline of British imperial power and its unstoppable fall in the medium-term future. Against the background of the widely read bestseller, *Untergang des Abendlandes*: *Umrisse einer Morphologie der Weltgeschichte* (1918–22; *The Decline of the West*) by Oswald Spengler, one could expect a fascination with a philosophy of civilizations going through natural cycles of growth and decay. The metaphor of decline, however, suggests not a drama which will break out at a particular point in history, but a constantly changing backdrop to cultural history. Thus heyday and end almost fade into each other, and the feeling of coming to an end is less a symptom of decadence than of historical consequence—the theme of Johan Huizinga's still popular classic, *The Waning of the Middle Ages*, which was published in Dutch just one year after the First World War. Conceived before the war, Spengler's philosophy of universal history, which he called a 'morphology of world history', was probably the most influential since Hegel's, although it did not stimulate a new historical methodology.[21] Spengler was strongly influenced by the cultural pessimism, biologism, and social Darwinism of popular ideologies such as those of Chamberlain and Nietzsche. His ideas thus contrast with the much more optimistic view of, for example, Toynbee. His comparative study of

[18] Adolf Rein, *Die europäische Ausbreitung über die Erde* (Potsdam, 1931), 2–3; id., *John Robert Seeley: Eine Studie über den Historiker* (Langensalza, 1912)

[19] Rein, *Europäische Ausbreitung*, 4.

[20] Linda Colley, *Captives: Britain, Empire and the World 1600–1850* (London, 2002).

[21] John Farrenkopf, *Prophet of Decline: Spengler on World History and Politics* (Louisiana, 2000).

cultures 'substituted for the traditional linear view of history a cyclical theory that had been elaborated in the early eighteenth century by Giambattista Vico, according to whom each culture, like a plant, goes through an appointed course of youth, maturity, and decline'.[22] While disappointed by German *Weltpolitik*, Spengler was fascinated by the British Empire.[23]

An investigation of the world-historical perspective from which a substantial number of German historians studied the Empire can shed light on their understanding of its unique expansion and exceptional impact on the course of world history as a central part of world history itself rather than merely of British history. Also, a comparison with former and contemporary empires was not to be neglected.[24] The Empire's rise and decline meant the extension and contraction of the West, its civilization, and values. It is therefore interesting, according to the respected historian Dietrich Gerhard in his inaugural lecture of 1934, to ask why 'since the eighteenth century British history has expanded into world history',[25] an opinion that has indeed been constantly repeated to the present day.[26] In this view the Empire formed its own realm within the borders of the wider world. This is strongly reminiscent of what the later co-editor of the *Cambridge History of the British Empire*, J. Holland Rose, with A. P. Newton and other supporters of Seeley's imperial project, would suggest. While this theory only partly corresponded to the imperial reality, many English historians around 1900 drew on this vision rather than scholarly research, and German authors later also based their arguments on it.[27] Thus the idea of England as the 'workshop of the world' often could not be separated from its caricature and, towards the end of the 1930s, from

[22] Klemens von Klemperer, *German Incertitudes, 1914–1945: The Stones and the Cathedral* (Westport, 2001), 33.

[23] Ernst Schulin (ed.), *Universalgeschichte* (Cologne, 1974), 29 f., 36 ff.; Alexander Demandt (ed.), *Der Fall Spengler: Eine kritische Bilanz* (Cologne, 1994).

[24] Cf. Horst Dippel, 'Die Auflösung des Britischen Empire oder die Suche nach einem Rechtsersatz für formale Herrschaft', in Richard Lorenz (ed.), *Das Verdämmern der Macht: Vom Untergang großer Reiche* (Frankfurt am Main, 2000), 236–55.

[25] Dietrich Gerhard, 'Hauptprobleme einer Geschichte des britischen Empire', *Historische Zeitschrift*, 149 (1934), 57–74, at 57.

[26] Cf. Edward Ingram, *The British Empire as a World Power* (London, 2001).

[27] Benedikt Stuchtey, ' "Westward the course of empire takes its way": Imperialism and the Frontier in British and German Historical Writing around 1900', in id. and Peter Wende (eds.), *British and German Historiography, 1750–1950: Traditions, Perceptions, and Transfers* (Oxford, 2000), 289–334.

an even more distorted image. While Anglo-German relations in past centuries and the antagonism between the two countries in the age of imperialism have been studied quite intensively,[28] the contemporary reception of imperial matters has not. This essay will analyse some of the major issues concerning the British Empire and imperial expansion that were discussed by German writers between the end of the nineteenth century and the Second World War.[29] Gerwin Strobl sees the British Empire as a paradigm for Nazi expansion, and, as he points out, admiration for the colonial world principally derived from admiration for power and control over it: 'the focus of interest lay in the power that had created and now sustained the Empire.'[30] Whether as historians or *Anglisten*, journalists or simply propagandists (who naturally form a substantial number at times of war, in pre-war and post-war periods, and increasingly from the 1930s), these German writers addressed a number of issues.

1. As a number of recently published studies suggest, around 1900 all major imperial powers regarded acquiring and defending world power status as a *conditio sine qua non* for their political and economic survival.[31] But the right of conquest needed justification. Thus the doctrines of imperialism became doctrines of spreading civilization to 'barbarian peoples', planting *Kultur* in hitherto 'uncivilized' territories, and Westernizing 'backward', non-European cultures. The British civilizing mission, the French *mission civilisatrice*, and the German cultural mission all concurred in legitimizing the acquisition of sovereignty over 'primitive' parts of the world and thereby 'provided conceptual support for empire as a political form'.[32] As the regular guest

[28] Virtually countless studies have appeared since the later 19th century. Most concentrate on the fleet and the missed opportunity of an Anglo-German *rapprochement* in 1898. Famous examples are the study by Gerhard Ritter, *Die Legende von der verschmähten englischen Freundschaft 1898/1901* (Freiburg, 1929) and the influential study by Hermann Kantorowicz, *Der Geist der englischen Politik und das Gespenst der Einkreisung Deutschlands* (Berlin, 1929).

[29] For a general methodological investigation of England as model for Germany see Thomas Kleinknecht, 'England als Modell: Nachahmung—Kritik—Ablehnung', *Westfälische Forschungen*, 44 (1994), 1–23; for a discussion of recent literature on Anglo-German relations and the antagonism around 1900 cf. Stuchtey, 'Imperialism', *passim*.

[30] Gerwin Strobl, *The Germanic Isle: Nazi Perceptions of Britain* (Cambridge, 2000), 66.

[31] Sönke Neitzel, *Weltmacht oder Untergang: Die Weltreichslehre im Zeitalter des Imperialismus* (Paderborn, 2000).

[32] Sharon Korman, *The Right of Conquest: The Acquisition of Territory by Force in International Law and Practice* (Oxford, 1996), 62.

writer to the journal *Die Neue Zeit*, John Bertram Askew, wrote in a special issue devoted to British imperialism, since its early beginnings the Empire had generally been seen with much sympathy as a 'world-spanning democracy of the British people, which should be regarded as a model for the rest of humanity'.[33] According to this writer the British Empire developed as a world power whose parts grew organically into a greater whole representing unity in diversity. Yet despite the very Britishness of the Empire, he saw the German influence as particularly strong in fields such as education, philosophy, and historiography. Seeley's *Expansion of England* (1883) and *The Growth of British Policy* (1895) profited largely from the ideas of the (Protestant) imperial state which the German historians Treitschke and Sybel had formulated, as is generally known.[34]

To what extent did German observers understand the British Empire as a political entity which, as a world power, considerably shaped world history? In an age of national success, imperial expansion, industrialization, social modernization, wealth, and political stability, the history of the nation was perceived as an essential part of the history of the world. Gladstone's biographer John Morley once even reversed the priorities. In his essay 'On Popular Culture' he wrote that 'the history of the world ought to go before the history of England. This is no paradox, but the deliberate opinion of many of those who have thought most deeply about the far-reaching chain of human progress.'[35] Did German historians reflect on this opinion and did they have a similar understanding of English national history? How far did German authors also participate in the debate on the decline of empire, follow the arguments concerning the reasons for it, and confirm Askew's later criticism that democracy and imperialism were incompatible with each other and that the colonial world needed to achieve independence for the sake of international peace?[36]

[33] John Bertram Askew, 'Der britische Imperialismus', Special Issue of *Die Neue Zeit*, no. 19 (Stuttgart, 1913/14), 5.

[34] Ibid. 16; cf. Benedikt Stuchtey, 'Literature, Liberty, and Life of the Nation: British Historiography from Macaulay to Trevelyan', in Stefan Berger *et al.* (eds.), *Writing National Histories: Western Europe since 1800* (London, 1999), 30–46, at 36–7.

[35] John Morley, 'On Popular Culture', in id., *Critical Miscellanies*, 3 vols. (London, 1909), iii. 1–36, at 10.

[36] Askew, 'Imperialismus', 42–4.

2. 'Britain's colonial activities are a matter that concern the whole nation. They have the greatest imaginable influence on the conditions under which Britain exists, and at the same time they are a reality that reaches out beyond the British nation and equally affects the conditions under which the other peoples of the earth exist. There is no way of getting around the question of what would become of Britain without its empire, or, for that matter, of the world without the British Empire.'[37] When the French cultural historian Albert Demangeon wrote these words, soon translated into German, on the colonial geography of the Empire, he could be sure that his way of understanding the close connection between British centre and colonial periphery was shared by many German commentators. If they did not profit directly from his modern approach and innovative methodology of combining historical with geographical questions, they certainly accepted the view that world history provided no other example of an empire that could call so many aspects of the world its own—political, economic, and cultural.[38]

As early as the middle of the First World War, Felix Salomon, Professor of History at the University of Leipzig and author of a two-volume standard biography of William Pitt,[39] published a study on the *longue durée* of the development of the imperial idea in Britain. Clearly influenced by wartime impressions and the hostilities, he dedicated his book to his 'colleagues in the field'. However, as a strong admirer of the mechanism of British imperial expansion, he tried to be as objective as possible. Salomon argued that to understand the history of the rise and the decline of the British Empire it needed to be put into two contexts: universal history on the one hand, and British national history on the other. Moreover, to conceive of the growth and development of imperialism as a process that was deeply embedded in the history of the nation meant to understand it as an organic correlation between centre and periphery. The past and the present of the Empire mirrored Britain's past and present: 'the emergence and growth of the empire should be derived from the events and destinies of British history, and should be explained

[37] Albert Demangeon, *Das Britische Weltreich: Eine kolonialgeographische Studie* (Berlin, 1926), 3.

[38] Also in a more literary than scholarly overview such as Reinhold Schneider, *Das Inselreich: Gesetz und Größe der britischen Macht* (Leipzig, 1936), 497–552.

[39] Felix Salomon, *William Pitt*, 2 vols. (Leipzig, 1901 and 1906).

in connection with them.'[40] In the same years, as well as in the years before and after the First World War, a similar argument was developed by his contemporaries Brie, Deckert, Meyer, Konow, and others.[41]

Salomon described the crisis of the imperial system manifested in the First World War as not only a British phenomenom, but as a crisis of the Western world, if not of the world as a whole. Quoting a saying of Feuerbach's dating from 1814, Salomon claimed that world domination signified the grave of mankind. One hundred years later, he said, Britain had reached the stage of digging its own grave.[42] Modern imperialism had brought about the catastrophe of war because it could not tolerate the coexistence of equal empires. The future of the British Empire depended on whether it was capable of coping with worldwide competition. Britain and its empire had created world history, but they were increasingly losing control over it.[43] How far, then, were universal history, imperial history, and national history connected with each other for the outside observer trying to make sense of world power in the light of world history? How did German historians define the British 'idea of empire'?[44]

3. Impressed by Mahan's massive study of Britain's maritime expansion,[45] the majority of contemporary observers identified the strength of the British Empire with its sea power: Britain was a world power primarily because Britannia ruled the waves. More than on territorial possessions and control over them,

[40] Felix Salomon, *Der britische Imperialismus: Ein geschichtlicher Überblick über den Werdegang des britischen Reiches vom Mittelalter bis zur Gegenwart* (Leipzig, 1916), p. vi.

[41] Friedrich Brie, *Imperialistische Strömungen in der englischen Literatur* (Halle, 1916); Emil Deckert, *Das Britische Weltreich: Ein politisch- und wirtschaftsgeographisches Charakterbild* (Vienna, 1916); Eduard Meyer, *Das britische Weltreich* (Berlin, 1918); Sten Konow, *Indien unter der englischen Herrschaft* (Tübingen, 1915); W. Langenbeck, *Englands Weltmacht in ihrer Entwicklung vom 17. Jahrhundert bis auf unsere Tage* (Leipzig, 1907); Alexander von Peez and Paul Dehn, *Englands Vorherrschaft: Aus der Zeit der Kontinentalsperre* (Leipzig, 1912); Heinrich Siemer, *England und das Britische Weltreich: Wandlungen und Zustände* (Berlin, 1933); Erich Alport, *Nation und Reich in der politischen Willensbildung des britischen Weltreiches* (Berlin, 1933); Anton Mayer, *Aufstieg zur Weltmacht: Entstehung, Entwicklung, Vollendung des britischen Weltreiches* (Berlin, 1936).

[42] Salomon, *Der britische Imperialismus*, 220.

[43] Ibid. 223.

[44] Cf. Hermann Lufft, 'Zur Geschichte des Empire und des Empiregedankens', in id., *Das Britische Weltreich* (Leipzig, 1930), 574–93; id., *Das Empire in Verteidigung und Angriff* (Reichenau, 1936).

[45] A. T. Mahan, *The Influence of Seapower upon History*, 2 vols. (London, 1890–97).

Britain's power was based on its economic network, the language, British laws and customs, and the Protestant religion and culture, all characteristics which had been made known to the world via the sea.[46] Adolf Rein was convinced that it was essentially maritime colonial expansion which had brought about an 'international connection' between all nations and cultures: 'The unity of the surface of the earth has been achieved in a historical sense. In the narrower meaning of the word, Europeans, and among these, primarily the seafarers, first created world history. They have brought the peoples of the earth together in a mutually dependent existence.'[47] Although in geo-political terms the Empire did not possess the USA's advantage of territorial unity, its ubiquity combined with the fragmentation of its dependencies meant that the Indian Ocean, for example, had become a British inland sea. This geo-historical view of Johannes Stoye's may not have been shared by those of his colleagues who saw the imperial connection declining, but the author's argument developed from the conviction that even the loosening of imperial ties did not weaken British central control as long as Britain saw itself as an island independent of the European continent and gradually moving into a close partnership with the USA.[48] From this it followed that Stoye and a considerable number of other writers argued that in the early twentieth century England was facing the same condition it had faced in 1776. Yet the eventual loss of its colonies was material rather than spiritual, taking the imperial connection as 'unique in the constitutional law history of mankind'.[49] From what perspective did German authors study the Empire as a sea-power, apart from the most obvious, its naval policy and the rivalry between Britain and Germany?[50] To what principal features did they ascribe the Empire's capacity to survive, if not institutionally, then at least in spirit?

4. Finally, few other historiographical traditions possess as strong a practice of writing biographies as the English. The

[46] Alfred Hettner, *Englands Weltherrschaft* (4th edn.; Leipzig, 1928), 202 ff.

[47] Rein, *Europäische Ausbreitung*, 5.

[48] Johannes Stoye, *Das Britische Weltreich: Sein Gefüge und seine Probleme* (Munich, 1935), 326; cf. Walter Bargatzky, *Der Sinn der englischen Festlandspolitik* (Munich, 1939), 5 ff.

[49] Stoye, *Das Britische Weltreich*, 343.

[50] Angela von Schönberg, *Um den Twopowerstandard: Englische Flottenpolitik 1880–1895* (Stuttgart, 1933).

nation was mirrored in the great picture-gallery of collected biographies, the *Dictionary of National Biography* (1885–), companion to the National Portrait Gallery founded in 1856. When Leslie Stephen had the nation's history painted in the portraits of many of its leading exponents, he enormously popularized a general comprehension of English history and a common pride in it. Through the élitism of the *Dictionary* he also addressed the idea of the nation's superiority, its commitment to rule, its power, and admiration for imperial government. Seeley's attempt to replace *liberty* by *empire* as the new pattern of English history was echoed by Carlyle, Stephen, and other English historians who believed that the imperial philosophy, political authoritarianism, and national coherence embodied by some of its representatives was the most suitable remedy for the decline of the Western world-system as reflected in capitalism and democracy.[51] The German counterpart to Stephen, Rudolf Kircher, portrayed Lord Curzon, for example, in such a way that the Empire seemed to rest on the shoulders of a few giants: 'he felt the greatness of the British Empire, of British thinking in the world, and he did everything to be a worthy representative of it. . . . England never had a more worthy herald of its world claims than Lord Curzon.'[52] Did many German observers of the British Empire take this model as an example for their own biographies of 'Influential Englishmen', as Pückler termed his well-known sketches?[53] Were they convinced that in order to understand and judge British politics it was more important to get an impression of outstanding individuals than of political programmes or philosophies? 'Successful statesmen embody the political vices and virtues, the convictions and the doubts of the British people. By studying them and trying to understand the mystery of their success or failure, one gets to know the British people', said Pückler in his introduction.[54]

Kircher's *Wie's die Engländer machen* (How the English do things) was a popular book by a popular writer, well-written and not too long, but with a hidden right-wing agenda. When it was

[51] Stuchtey, 'Literature', 40.

[52] Rudolf Kircher, *Engländer* (Frankfurt am Main, 1926), 41.

[53] Carl-Erdmann Pückler, *Einflußreiche Engländer. Porträtskizzen englischer Politiker* (Berlin, 1938).

[54] Ibid. 13; see also Emil Daniels, *Englische Staatsmänner von Pitt bis Asquith und Grey* (Berlin, 1925).

published in 1929, he could expect a wide readership in Germany, keen to learn more about the politics, society, and culture of a country in which he had lived for almost ten years. The idea behind this book was that Weimar Germany should take Britain as an example and work for a better understanding between the two countries. Germany could also, it suggested, profit from the literature and philosophy, the political culture and the thinking of some of the exponents of British life. *Wie's die Engländer machen* explains British democracy, the workings of parliament and the monarchy, the meaning of Social Evolution, and the consequences of capitalism. In short, it deals with aspects of Western civilization that were regarded as particularly British. Yet there was one phenomenon that required more observation than the others, the most obvious symbol of British power and influence in the world: the Empire. Kircher's chapter on the idea of the British Empire could well be seen as the centrepiece of his book. It is framed by questions about the role of the USA in world politics, the mechanics of internationalism, and the chances and limits of the League of Nations caught between war and peace—the Empire as global player.

The oldest power structure in world history was also the most flexible. It was in constant flux, developing and changing its character and spirit from age to age. Thus the British Empire existed according to its own unwritten laws and without the need for a fixed recipe for its persistence.[55] It was a world power that made world history. Its history was the history of most of the world. Moreover, colonial expansion took place without any masterplan, as Seeley once famously said about the British Empire and Theodor Mommsen about the Roman Empire. Foreign territories were acquired in a state of absence of mind.[56] In this view colonial history and the history of the nation belonged closely together. The periphery of Australia and South Africa were as close to the metropolis of London as were the highlands of Scotland and the coast of Cornwall. Expansionism was at the nation's heart: colonization and decolonization of the

[55] Rudolf Kircher, *Wie's die Engländer machen: Politik, Gesellschaft und Literatur im demokratisierten England* (Frankfurt am Main, 1929), 102.

[56] J. R. Seeley, *The Expansion of England* (London, 1883), 1; see Julius Karl Hatschek, *Britisches und Römisches Weltreich* (Munich, 1921); Benedikt Stuchtey, 'The International of Critics: German and British Scholars during the South African War (1899-1902)', *South African Historical Journal*, 41 (1999), 149–71, at 153.

world amounted to the Empire's systole and the diastole, following the rhythm of its cardiac muscle, the English mother country. While British imperial politics were made in Westminster, Whitehall, and the City, they were successful only because of the interaction between centre and periphery. Compared with the French or German cases, the British nation was an imperial nation *sui generis*. One of Germany's most popular figures to beat the drum for imperialism, Carl Peters, maintained that to try to understand the British Empire from the European perspective without first considering its centre would result in many misconceptions. Rather, the English nation and the Empire belonged together: 'Thus this empire, however international it may be in composition and especially in its assumptions, is English through and through.'[57] From Charles Dilke and James Anthony Froude in the later nineteenth century to modern historical research of the late 1990s, this concept of a 'Greater Britain' has attracted much attention. Kircher's study, one of many in his time, was indeed apprehensive of contemporary British imperial thinking.[58]

What, then, did British imperialism mean in the context of world history, if it was so central to the national history of its country? The narrative of German studies of the British Empire had discussed this problem quite intensively ever since British colonial power had been perceived as the greatest in world history since that of Rome. Before the First World War and in the inter-war period in particular, many German works were published that were concerned with the world-historical phenomenon of the Empire, its development into the Commonwealth, and the connection between metropolis and the colonial world. Kircher called the British Empire 'a link between nation and world'.[59] By contrast, French imperialism was often regarded as providing a mere substitute for the loss of territory to Germany after 1871 and as the only way for France to regain its reputation and glory as a great power. If French

[57] Carl Peters, *England und Engländer* (Berlin, 1905), 277.

[58] Charles Dilke, *Greater Britain: A Record of Travel in English-Speaking Countries during 1866 and 1867*, 2 vols. (London, 1868); id., *Problems of Greater Britain*, 2 vols. (London, 1890); James Anthony Froude, *Oceana, or England and her Colonies* (London, 1886); on contemporary research on this question see Benedikt Stuchtey, 'Nation und Expansion: Das britische Empire in der neuesten Forschung', *Historische Zeitschrift*, 274/1 (2002), 87–118.

[59] Kircher, *Engländer*, 108–9.

and Russian imperialism wanted to conquer the world in order to possess and exploit it (*Eroberungsimperialismus*), a characteristic feature which one author depicted as having its roots in the High Middle Ages, British imperialism had the civilizing mission of bringing Western values to the non-Western world.[60] For example, Lord Cromer's policies in Egypt, reinforced by his later publications *Modern Egypt* (1908) and *Ancient and Modern Imperialism* (1910), were regarded as exemplary. Any colonial administrator could learn from them to pursue a vigorous yet harmonious government seeking to reconcile the nationalist movement with the imperial system.[61]

Among the above-mentioned values one stands out: the abolition of slavery. According to one author the abolitionists gave the citizens of the Empire a new mentality by encouraging them to regard themselves as brothers and sisters in the same world. As such, the imperial idea was no longer compatible with slavery, and the Empire identified itself with abolitionism, not only intellectually and culturally, but primarily on political grounds. This culminated in the victory of the North over the South in the American Civil War in 1865. Britain sided with neither party but morally supported the North.[62] As William Gladstone would later argue, England's mission was to defend the values and rights once gained at home and to take them to the colonial world.[63] Thus to German historians it seemed no coincidence that on the same day as the news of the defeat of the Southern states arrived in London (8 May 1865), the first debate on the extension of the franchise and the right to be elected took place in Westminster. This debate eventually led to the Reform Act of 1867. National and imperial politics were closely intertwined, displaying the 'imperial spirit of a people which feels it is justified in dominating the world because it

[60] Cf. Fritz Kern, *Die Anfänge der französischen Ausdehnungspolitik bis zum Jahre 1308* (Tübingen, 1910); Fritz Roepke, 'Erscheinungsformen des französischen Imperialismus vor dem Weltkriege', *Vierteljahrschrift für Sozial- und Wirtschaftsgeschichte*, 25/2 (1932), 130–40.

[61] Karl Vollers, 'Lord Cromer und sein Egypten', *Historische Zeitschrift*, 102 (1909), 57–86; Theodor Rothstein, 'Die Engländer in Ägypten', Special Issue of *Die Neue Zeit*, no. 10 (Stuttgart, 1910/11); id., 'Die Engländer in Ägypten', *Die Neue Zeit*, 26/1 (1907/08), 117–25.

[62] Max Silberschmidt, 'Das Britische Reich und die Abolition des Sklavenhandels', *Archiv für Kulturgeschichte*, 24 (1934), 90–109, at 105–7.

[63] W. E. Gladstone, 'England's Mission', *The Nineteenth Century*, 4 (Sept. 1878), 560–84.

believes it is fulfilling a world mission'.[64] Even the Labour Party, hitherto known for its critical distance to imperial policy, which it identified with economic exploitation, developed a new vision of what it called 'socialist imperialism' in order to spread the achievements of socialist policy from the home country to the periphery.[65] The German socialist paper *Die Gesellschaft*, edited by the pacifist and SPD politician Rudolf Hilferding, invited the Labour MP L. Haden Guest to inform its German readers about Labour's views on empire. His article made it clear what sort of mission he had in mind: the application of the socialist ideology at home as well as abroad, which, of course, meant that the Empire needed to continue to exist. Any loss of Empire would also mean a significant weakening of the socialist movement and its fields of operation.[66]

The weekly *Die Neue Zeit*, official organ of the German Social Democratic Party, regularly published on issues concerning the British Empire, employing a similar argument. Max Beer, for example, the London correspondent of *Die Neue Zeit*, addressed the relationship between world history and British imperial history in one of the newspaper's earliest articles on 'modern' forms of imperialism. Comparing the empires of the past in a global perspective, Beer came to the conclusion that the British Empire was peculiar in that it not only cultivated the singular, outstanding personality—probably most obviously Rhodes and Chamberlain at his time—but also had substantive motives based on political, economic, military, and humanitarian grounds. After all, in Beer's terms the empire embodied a great dream, the political and economic unification of the world. No other European state could achieve this to represent 'the final phase of the middle-class world'.[67] That this final phase was not only the climax, but could also signal the beginning of cultural decline if imperial overstretch put the mother country under too much strain, was the conviction of the author of a contemporary

[64] Silberschmidt, 'Das Britische Reich und die Abolition', 109.

[65] Egon Wertheimer, *Das Antlitz der britischen Arbeiterpartei: Mit einer historischen Einleitung von G.D.H. Cole* (Berlin, 1929), 85 ff.

[66] L. Haden Guest, 'Die britische Labour Party und das Imperium', *Die Gesellschaft: Internationale Revue für Sozialismus und Politik*, 3 (1926), 17–28, at 25; see also Franz Linden, *Sozialismus und Religion: Konfessionssoziologische Untersuchung der Labour Party 1929–1931* (Leipzig, 1932).

[67] Max Beer, 'Der moderne englische Imperialismus', *Die Neue Zeit*, 16/1 (1897/98), 300–6, at 306.

study which enjoyed wide circulation. Like Beer, Steffen argued that modern Britain had a high potential, but faced the danger that as 'Greater Britain' it could not maintain those qualities for which the other powers envied it so much.[68] This idea was to become a major issue in the coming years, especially during and after the South African War, and as a result of it.[69] Indeed, *Die Neue Zeit* did not shun this discussion.[70] After 1902 and towards the First World War, however, the paper concentrated almost exclusively on problems of the German Empire. It devoted a few articles to French and Russian imperialism, taking these as examples of belated expansionist attempts rather than the real thing, as in British imperialism.

Its sheer power and the unparalleled size of its expansion made the British Empire the symbol of a success story because to gain it and hold it together must have required more effective means than just the imperial flags of soldiers and tradesmen. The secret lay in what was regarded as the English worldview and a special English predisposition towards designing world history. At times of political, social, and economic insecurity in Germany before and between the wars, many authors naturally turned to investigate the past and present of the world's largest empire so far, and the cultural and philosophical determinants of the mother-country.[71] What was the philosophy of life of this empire and what gave it its peculiar strength? Fascination for it and the desire to learn from it led German scholars and popular writers alike to publish studies on the British Empire. The quality of these works certainly differed and they provide relatively few historical insights that are still of value today. In reviewing a major publication by Gerhard von Schulze-Gaevernitz, the Austrian politician and Social Democrat Otto Bauer expressed his views on current German works on imperialism. He believed that the less information they provided on their subject, the more valuable they would be for the historian

[68] Gustaf F. Steffen, *England als Weltmacht und Kulturstaat: Studien über politische, intellektuelle und ästhetische Erscheinungen im britischen Reiche* (Stuttgart, 1899).

[69] Cf. Stuchtey, 'The International of Critics', *passim.*

[70] Max Beer, 'Betrachtungen über den Niedergang Englands', *Die Neue Zeit*, 19/1 (1900/01), 804–11; Theodor Rothstein, 'Der südafrikanische Krieg und der Niedergang des englischen Liberalismus', ibid., 19/2 (1900/01), 452–7.

[71] See e.g. Paul Meissner (ed.), *Grundformen der englischen Geistesgeschichte* (Stuttgart, 1941), pp. vii–xx for a general assessment of England as 'Vormacht der bürgerlichen Welt'.

'who one day will portray the history of the cultural movements in German middle-class society at the beginning of the twentieth century'.[72]

Few German colonial enthusiasts at the turn of the century were as well placed to write on imperial politics as the author of *England und die Engländer* (1905), Carl Peters. Because of his political and social attitudes Peters is today rightly regarded as the exponent of an aggressive German colonialism who had little respect for its national and international consequences and no respect for the indigenous population of the future colonies. At his time, however, he was admired as the founder of the Society for German Colonization which sponsored the settlement of German East Africa.[73] On its 50th anniversary, the monthly paper of the Reichskolonialbund, the *Deutsche Kolonialzeitung* published a comparison between Peters and Cecil Rhodes, suggesting to its readers that Britain was an example of a nation with great courage and a strong will for global dominance. Having lived in England for several years in the early 1880s, Peters, the German equivalent to Rhodes, could learn from daily experience that 'colonial policies were the concentrated result of the awareness of national power'.[74] Peters had actually gone to England to develop plans for Germany's colonial expansion along the lines of the British example, although his motives were less economic considerations than land settlement policies. As well as a colonial pioneer abroad, to build and defend an empire required the support of the people at home. While Britain possessed both, Germany lacked the latter and consequently lost its status as a colonial power once its status as a nation could no longer be guaranteed. This was the case in 1918. In sum, for the *Deutsche Kolonialzeitung* Peters was the right man in the wrong country. 'The official mind' of Germany did very little to encourage its people to acquire a taste for imperialism.

Peters himself had complained about this state in the same paper many years earlier when he had described Germany's

[72] Otto Bauer, 'Über britischen Imperialismus', *Die Neue Zeit*, 25/1 (1906/07), 535–40, at 535; the book under review was Gerhard von Schulze-Gaevernitz, *Britischer Imperialismus und englischer Freihandel zu Beginn des zwanzigsten Jahrhunderts* (Leipzig, 1906).

[73] See e.g. Heinrich Schnee (ed.), *Deutsches Koloniallexikon*, 3 vols. (Leipzig, 1920), iii. 40.

[74] Alfred Funke, 'Cecil Rhodes und Carl Peters', *Deutsche Kolonialzeitung*, 50/10 (1938), 334–6, at 336; cf. Bernhard Voigt, *Fürs größere Vaterland: Der Lebenstraum des Rhodes* (Hamburg, 1933).

colonial policies from the English viewpoint. 'Rule Britannia', he said, was no empty talk. The Empire, greater than any previous empire in world history, was only the expression of British patriotism. The freeborn Englishman could travel almost anywhere in the world and find the same values and customs, language and traditions to which he was accustomed at home; he was respected and feared by the colonized peoples, which led to pride in his nation and empire. The freedom of British citizenship contrasted sharply with the many restrictions faced by Germans: 'The English polity resembles a tree, which has air and light enough for its branches and twigs to grow freely and profusely. The German polity resembles an even nobler tree, but one which has grown in a ravine in a rugged mountain range, which now prevents it from giving its prodigious power for growth free rein in all directions.'[75] Moreover, Peters concurred with what Seeley, quoted above, thought about the absentmindedness of the coming about of the British Empire. Unlike the expansion of the Roman Empire, which was directed by the state and resulted from war, the British Empire was essentially the work of individuals and economic interests without an explicit will for military conquest. Trade came before the flag, if the latter was necessary at all. Driven by the mission of a colonial policy to unify the world and confer on it the achievements of the English (trading) culture, the British Empire, more than the Roman Empire and any other before and since, could claim to have embodied the 'most brilliant manifestation of the genius for state-building'.[76]

The philosophy of German idealism was seen as important background to the political thinking of leading British colonial pioneers, statesmen, and writers such as Raleigh, Clive, Drake, Hastings, Pitt, Nelson, Disraeli, Asquith, Haldane, Grey, Milner, Rhodes, Amery, Lothian, Halifax, Curzon, and Macdonald.[77] With Carlyle's notion of the 'hero and heroship' in the intellectual

[75] Carl Peters, 'Deutsche Kolonialpolitik aus englischer Perspektive', *Deutsche Kolonialzeitung*, 1/7 (1884), 129–32, at 131.

[76] Peters, *England*, 258 ff., quotation at 278.

[77] To give but a few examples: Wolfgang Hoffmann-Harnisch, *Lord Clive: Abenteuer eines Lebens* (Berlin, 1936); Dagobert von Mikusch, *Cecil Rhodes: Der Traum einer Weltherrschaft* (Berlin, 1936); Hermann Proebst, *William Pitt: Begründer der britischen Macht* (Berlin, 1938); Wolfgang Greiser, *Raleigh* (Bremen, 1935); Hans Rühl, *Disraelis Imperialismus und die Kolonialpolitik seiner Zeit* (Leipzig, 1935).

rucksack, it was easier to march down the road emphasizing the heroism of British imperial history.[78] The widely read *Heralds of British Imperialism* had not even been translated before it appeared on the list of a popular Leipzig publisher.[79] If Germany did not conquer the world, at least Britain's plans for a world empire substantially profited from the impact of German idealism.[80] As modern research has repeatedly pointed out, the nineteenth-century German colonial movement, which came into being long before 1884–5, found an outlet for its energies in the British Empire. Whether as natural scientists, explorers, or missionaries, Germans were looking for occupations in British colonies.[81] The fact that before the short-lived German Empire came into being German imperial activities helped to strengthen Britain's position in the world was not only a thorn in the flesh of the *Deutsche Kolonialzeitung* but also a constant topic of discussion among writers from the later nineteenth century. They argued that only those nations which actively made world politics themselves deserved a chapter in the books on the history of the world. Accordingly, Peters entitled his collected political essays *Zur Weltpolitik* (Towards an interpretation of world politics).

When Carl Peters's book on world politics came out two years before the outbreak of the First World War, world history was written only by the power in whose capital, London, Peters was living. That, at least, was his opinion. Peters was forced to leave Germany for England in the late 1890s for a second time (only returning to Germany in 1914) after he had become the subject of fierce criticism in the Reichstag because of his political behaviour in East Africa and the misconduct of the German colonial administration there. While he devoted much space in his book to German colonial politics, the relationships between Germany,

[78] H. Rosenberg, *Die Entwicklung der modernen imperialistischen Doktrin in England von Carlyle bis zur Gegenwart* (Leipzig, 1922); H. Ahmels, *Studien über die Ideologie und die politischen Methoden des liberalen Imperialismus in England* (Heidelberg, 1921); Friedrich Brie, *Der Einfluß der Lehren Darwins auf den britischen Imperialismus* (Freiburg, 1927).

[79] Max Spatzier (ed.), *Heralds of British Imperialism* (Leipzig, 1935).

[80] This is the thesis of Klaus Dockhorn, *Die englische Reichsidee der Gegenwart* (Bochum, 1939).

[81] Imperialism before empire is currently a popular topic, cf. Frank Lorenz Müller, 'Imperialist Ambitions in *Vormärz* and Revolutionary Germany: The Agitation for German Settlement Colonies Overseas, 1840-1849', *German History*, 17/3 (1999), 346–68; Ulrike Kirchberger, *Aspekte deutsch-britischer Expansion: Die Überseeinteressen der deutschen Migranten in Großbritannien in der Mitte des 19. Jahrhunderts* (Stuttgart, 1999).

Britain, and France, the issue of colonial scandals and rebellions, and the role of socialism and international conflicts over colonial territories, the main question he wanted to answer concerned the significance of British world politics.[82] Peters started by arguing that Britain ruled the world thanks to what he called the unity of British society and its reputation reaching from Australia to Canada and from South Africa to Scotland. The Imperial Conferences, held for the first time in 1887 (until 1911 they were named colonial conferences) and thereafter until 1937, perfectly symbolized the unity of the citizens of the Empire as citizens of the world. Therefore the Empire was first of all an organization with a common spirit, language, and values, whose members had common commitments and profited from economic confederation. Above all, both centre and periphery wanted a uniform and central decision-making process on, for example, military and defence questions. Peters saw the 'imperial ideal', as he termed this state of things, as the reason for Britain's strong position as compared with its European competitors.[83] But despite its undisputed strengths, the Empire required reform. Its tax system needed to be unified. What Germany had achieved in 1871, namely the unity of the state, would finally consolidate the imperial connection of this 'unique and most genuine empire that has ever existed'.[84]

Peters's ideas were expressed in strong words, but they were certainly not unparalleled. The English 'philosophy of the world and of life', as one author called it, based on the ideas of evolutionism, utilitarianism, individualism, materialism, and the conviction of the superiority of Western civilization, paved the way for the acquisition of an empire precisely because that was seen as the moral right of the nation. It could also become a strong legal argument.[85] As the historian Erich Marcks, an influential neo-Rankean intellectual around 1900 who advocated that Germany should enter world politics, put it, English national

[82] Carl Peters, *Zur Weltpolitik* (Berlin, 1912), 182–241.

[83] Ibid. 186; on the same question for the interwar period see Benedikt Stuchtey, '"Not by law but by sentiment": Great Britain and Imperial Defense, 1918–1939', in Roger Chickering and Stig Förster (eds.), *The Shadows of Total War* (Cambridge, 2003), 255–70.

[84] Peters, *Weltpolitik*, 191.

[85] Heinrich Gade, 'Die englische Welt- und Lebensanschauung: Ihr Wesen und Werden', *Preußische Jahrbücher*, 183 (1921), 370–91.

history and English imperial history complemented each other so perfectly because of the will of the English people to play a formative part in the world. And Felix Salomon, who wrote for the influential *Zeitschrift für Politik*, was convinced that English imperial history was primarily shaped by one leitmotiv which had not changed since at least the sixteenth century. It also, in his view, formed the basis for the 'splendid agreement' of the present: the concern for political security, whether national or imperial.[86] Imperialism as such was just the expression of the desire of European nations to shape the world according to their cultural ideals. It was thus a modern phenomenon, yet rooted in old colonial traditions from early modern times. If Germany's limits were becoming so painfully obvious in contrast to England's this could be explained by reference to Germany's lack of experience of colonialism. By comparison, the British Empire in its world-dominating shape was merely a continuation of the prevailing national historical development.[87] Like many of his generation, Marcks orientated himself closely with the political values and the historical thinking of the Kaiserreich, although he claimed an intellectual return to Ranke's universal concepts of history. He interpreted Germany's defeat in 1918 as a deep humiliation which plunged him and his contemporaries into an intellectual crisis that made them even more susceptible to National Socialism. Marcks's notion of the 'great men in history' and the crucial role they played in the rise and decline of nations, the heroic individual and, in connection with this, the aestheticism of history, reflected the insecurity of German historical writing of his time. No other publications document Marcks's sense of Germany's national decline as well as his speeches, and no other publications document his admiration for Britain's imperial status as clearly as his posthumously edited collected papers on 'England's Power Politics'.[88]

Consequently Marcks, an admirer of Bismarck and a powerful state, approved of the long periods of time that successfully and teleologically led to a historical goal. English foreign policy

[86] Felix Salomon, *Die Grundzüge der auswärtigen Politik Englands vom 16. Jahrhundert bis zur Gegenwart* (Berlin, 1910), 70; also published in *Zeitschrift für Politik*, 3 (1910).

[87] Erich Marcks, 'Die imperialistische Idee in der Gegenwart', in id., *Männer und Zeiten: Aufsätze und Reden zur neueren Geschichte*, 2 vols. (Leipzig, 1911), ii. 265–91, at 289.

[88] Erich Marcks, *Englands Machtpolitik: Vorträge und Studien*, ed. and introduced by Willy Andreas (Stuttgart, 1940).

from Elizabeth I, Cromwell, the Stuarts, and the eighteenth-century aristocracy to the victory over Napoleon and the establishment of the English middle classes; from Shakespeare, Milton, and Newton to Scott, Byron, and Shaw; from the Reformation to industrialization: in Marcks's interpretation this was a history of exceptional success. In his view it was driven by the power of singular men in whose influence on the course of history Marcks deeply believed, and almost equalled world history, in particular, in the nineteenth century. Individual men shaped their times—hence the title *Männer und Zeiten*—and individual states shaped the history of the world. That was the creed of Leopold von Ranke's *Die großen Mächte* of 1833, one of the key texts of nineteenth-century German historiography. Marcks followed closely in these universal footsteps when he argued that England 'is among these great individual states, each of which has its own face, its own special position, its particular structure, its special geographical and political situation, its natural, racial, religious, constitutional, and cultural givens, and thus also its special traditions and natural historical aspirations which always somehow renew themselves in every change: in each one, Britain as much as France, Prussia, Austria, Russia, and so forth. These national traditions are nowhere more unified, clearer, or, if you will, more coarsely developed than in Britain.'[89]

Or was this perhaps a German translation of the Whig interpretation of English history rather than neo-Rankean historicism? Indeed, Macaulay, the personification of this philosophy of the freedom and progress of the nation, impressed more German intellectuals than did, for example, the highly Germanophile nineteenth-century British historian Thomas Carlyle (who, admittedly, received more popular praise for his biography of Frederick the Great). Macaulay, biographer of Hastings and Clive and author of the best-selling *History of England,* had perceived modern England as the result of all that was found by all generations of Englishmen to be wise, noble, and in accordance with God's truth.[90] These words by the author of a comparison between Macaulay and Carlyle were

[89] Erich Marcks, 'Die Einheitlichkeit der englischen Auslandspolitik von 1500 bis zur Gegenwart', in id., *Männer und Zeiten,* ii. 233–63, at 261.

[90] Otto Krauske, 'Macaulay und Carlyle', *Historische Zeitschrift,* 102 (1909), 31–56, at 55.

based on a conviction of Macaulay's unsurpassed position as *the* historian of the nation who had worked in the colonial administration of India. According to this view, historical writing and colonial political activities were closely intertwined. The progress of the history of civilization guaranteed the success of the history of the nation. In fact, for Macaulay, English history was at the centre of the history of Western civilization, from which it followed that the history of the English nation and its empire equalled world history. For contemporay writers, most of all for Anglophile authors such as Marcks and his generation, the result of this observation was that Britain did not need sophisticated concepts of world history. Macaulay, it was suggested, was not even fully aware of universal ideas that were above parties and peoples, and that gave world history its extent and set its aims.[91] Nor was there any need to separate national from imperial history. Rather, it was a challenge for the historian to try to understand both in their connection with world politics.

In the introduction to a collection of essays on the British Empire originally given as public lectures at the University of Berlin in winter 1920, Erich Marcks explained this by reference to the emergence of the colonial idea in England from 1500. This idea grew out from the core of the nation to the peripheries of the world, and centuries later received back the repercussions of this development. In Marcks's words it had a significant impact on the history of the world, and provided an outstanding example for any national history, particularly German history, which still needed to define its place within the countries of the world, both in opposition to and profiting from the experiences of the British Empire.[92] A generation later, after the Second World War and in the light of its causes, historians at last gave up this fatal notion that the Empire was representative of Germany, and returned to a more balanced picture. Describing the historical conditions of British imperialism since the Tudors and the emergence of colonial nationalism since the later nineteenth century, Fritz Wagner, for example, characterized the Empire as a transnational partnership whose system of aban-

[91] Ibid. 43.

[92] Erich Marcks, 'Vorbemerkung', in *Lebensfragen des Britischen Weltreiches* (Berlin, 1921), p. vii.

doning total sovereignty could reverberate throughout the European balance of power. According to this author England had been the first to conquer the world and to determine its order, but it had also been the first to modernize it: 'The Western spirit, which has always in its way filled the English people, first stepped up to the loom of bloody and acquisitive times in order to insert the weft of peaceful, truly creative ideas into the warp of discord.'[93]

Marcks diverged quite substantially from this viewpoint. For him the history of the Empire had begun in 1588. England's victory against Spain had been a victory over Catholic Europe and a decisive step away from the Continent towards the Atlantic world. According to Marcks, the battle against the Armada had been fought when England realized the great advantage of its insular position. The country could prepare itself for more autonomy while loosening European ties when the fleet opened the 'gates to world history'.[94] The consolidation of the nation went along with the expansion of England. Economic ambition, moral rigour, political vigour, and the Puritan faith were becoming the characteristic features of the 'English world mission'. From the perspective of Protestant German historians, Puritanism in particular played a most important part.[95] For example, biographies of Oliver Cromwell, the embodiment of the struggle against Catholicism, whom Samuel Rawson Gardiner once provocatively called the greatest because most typical Englishman,[96] multiplied in the 1920s and 1930s.[97] Cromwell's time represented 'a first imperialism with a religious motivation and a fiery passion',[98] as Marcks put it. Comparing developments in Germany and England at the time of the great European crises since the Reformation, he maintained that Protestantism could develop much better in a country that had been spared the Thirty Years War and the

[93] Fritz Wagner, *England und das Europäische Gleichgewicht 1500–1914* (Munich, 1947), 60.

[94] Erich Marcks, 'Entwicklung und Hauptziele der britischen Reichspolitik', in *Lebensfragen*, 1–48, quotation at 4.

[95] See Karl Arns, *Der religiöse britische Imperialismus* (Bochum, 1919); Otto Baumgarten, *Religiöses und kirchliches Leben in England* (Leipzig, 1922).

[96] Samuel Rawson Gardiner, *Cromwell's Place in History* (London, 1899), 116.

[97] For example: Hermann Oncken, *Cromwell: Vier Essays über die Führung einer Nation* (2nd edn.; Berlin, 1935); Michael Freund, *Oliver Cromwell* (Lübeck, 1933); Mirko Jelusich, *Oliver Cromwell* (Vienna, 1933).

[98] Erich Marcks, 'Entwicklung', 6.

consequent political, social, economic, cultural, and religious devastation. Instead, Oliver Cromwell led his country on to the *Sonderweg* (in Marcks's terminology *Sonderleben*) which cut it off from the European continent. At the same time, he 'embarked on a Protestant world policy which did not, however, lack an English national realism'.[99]

Other aspects of world-historical relevance, such as the struggle against the Dutch and the French for mastery of the colonial world, the invention of the policy of the balance of power in Europe, the economic system of mercantilism, and even the great military victories of Marlborough, Clive, Rodney, and Nelson, could largely be regarded as the outcome of what many German observers called the pillar of Britain's imperial success: the Puritan worldview. It is striking that books published from the 1940s onwards, a large number of them clearly Nazi publications, especially stressed this point.[100] And in the early twentieth century Schulze-Gaevernitz's highly praised study of the impact of free trade on the imperial idea had already concentrated on this question, if only to prove that, as he termed it, English religious life had lost its vigour and its capacity to focus the economic, political, and social energies of the nation.[101] Ferdinand Tönnies, an expert on Hobbes's writings ever since his first visit to England in 1878, author of the classic *Community and Civil Society* (first published in 1887), and subsequently professor of political science at the University of Kiel, had also confirmed this more critical view of the Empire when he based his argument mainly on critical English sources. He wanted to show that British world politics was gradually losing its moral legitimation as it lost touch with its religious basis.[102] In any case, however, the disciplinary quality of Protestantism, whether in decline or not, was seen as an essential prerequisite for the success of the nation.

With religious peace came national stability, which was

[99] Erich Marcks, 'Deutschland und England in den großen europäischen Krisen seit der Reformation', in id., *Englands Machtpolitik*, 29–62, at 38.

[100] Cf. Martin Dibelius, *Britisches Christentum und britische Weltmacht* (Berlin, 1940); Paul Ritter, 'Die geistigen Voraussetzungen der englischen Empirepolitik', in id., *Lebensgrundlagen britischer Weltherrschaft* (Munich, 1941), 7–18, here 10–14; Hans Stolze, *Englische Politik: Form und Methode* (Berlin, 1943), 89–93.

[101] Von Schulze-Gaevernitz, *Britischer Imperialismus*, 333 ff., 376–404.

[102] Ferdinand Tönnies, *Englische Weltpolitik in englischer Beleuchtung* (Berlin, 1915).

followed by the desire for imperial expansion. This, at least, was the view of the Göttingen historian Arnold Oskar Meyer, one of the most prominent conservative historians in the Weimar Republic, who expressed nationalist convictions in a massive biography of Bismarck. He concealed his disappointment with the Germans as a 'people without space' under his fascination for the English as a 'people with the biggest living space that a nation has ever gained, since history began'.[103] The two nations dovetailed, for better or for worse, but the Germans, who had not been unified in religious or national terms for most of their history, would be well advised to take this 'first of the international peoples' as an example: 'In the seventeenth century England had conquered itself; in the eighteenth century it set about conquering the world.'[104] Here Meyer profited substantially from Salomon who, in his own words, had elaborated the spiritual conditions under which England's colonial expansion took place.[105] According to Meyer, England was the only nation qualified for imperialism on a grand scale because since 1688 it had identified its national mission with its world mission: 'the striving for world domination was not only England's right—it was a duty. But the world could only gain if England became its master.'[106]

Meyer turned out to be a good disciple of Erich Marcks and Dietrich Schäfer. The latter, himself a student of Treitschke, built up a profile as an expert on the academic literature of colonial Britain by establishing a monopoly on reviewing it, in particular in the *Historische Zeitschrift*. When Schäfer published a survey of colonial history in 1903 (*Kolonialgeschichte*), he did so for theoretical as well as practical reasons. First, he was convinced that the academic study of imperial history in Germany was still in its very early beginnings and therefore needed a comprehensive treatment,[107] and secondly, he thought German politicians should actually learn from the British, 'our teachers in matters

[103] Arnold Oskar Meyer, 'England und das Britische Weltreich', in id., *Deutsche und Engländer: Wesen und Werden in großer Geschichte* (Munich, 1937), 263–305, at 305.

[104] Ibid., both quotations at 273.

[105] Meyer in his review of Salomon's *Englische Geschichte von den Anfängen bis zur Gegenwart* (Leipzig, 1923), in *Historische Zeitschrift*, 131 (1925), 114–20, at 115.

[106] Meyer, 'England', 276.

[107] Dietrich Schäfer in his review of Alfred Zimmermann's book, *Die Kolonialpolitik Großbritanniens*, in *Historische Zeitschrift*, 84, NS 48 (1900), 141-3, at 141.

concerning imperialism'.[108] In the later 1920s Schäfer turned to a revisionist historiography, preparing the ideology of '*Lebensraum* (living space) in the east'. He saw his public role as to provide a service for German expansion into eastern Europe, and increasingly regarded Britain as Germany's chief rival in international conflicts. The British Empire's success story was a 'teacher' especially as far as colonial exploitation and naval power were concerned, partly also on the question of emigration to the colonies.[109] With few exceptions, such as Gustav Schmoller, Lujo Brentano, and Otto Hintze, who as contemporaries of Schäfer were more concerned with the academic problems of imperial rivalry and the consequences of the tensions between imperialism and trade for world politics,[110] the majority of German authors, national-conservative in their outlook, agreed with Schäfer's popularizing attempt to integrate colonial studies into the field of political historiography. As a result, the history of imperialism was seen in a comparative perspective showing that it was a 'natural' European phenomenon which was common to all major European states: colonialism as the moral duty and the 'white man's burden', and, above all, as the civilizing mission of the Western, Christian cultures. Schäfer's close affinity with the histories of the Empire by Froude and Seeley and their intellectual disciples Hugh Edward Egerton and Charles Prestwood Lucas became all the more evident in his many reviews of their works for the *Historische Zeitschrift*.[111]

While no other nation was so clearly destined for imperial expansion as Britain, and no other national history demonstrated as well as England's that the Empire was not an artificial construct but a living organism within a greater design, this did not mean that the late-comers in the international concert had

[108] According to Schäfer's reviewer, Theodor Kükelhaus, *Historische Zeitschrift*, 94, NS 58 (1905), 322.

[109] As elaborated by Arnold Seifert, *Britische Jugendauswanderung: Geschichte der planmäßigen Auswanderung von Kindern und Jugendlichen aus Großbritannien und Irland nach überseeischen Reichsteilen. Von den Anfängen bis zum Weltkrieg* (Leipzig, 1932).

[110] Gustav Schmoller, 'Die künftige englische Handelspolitik, Chamberlain und der Imperialismus', *Schmollers Jahrbuch*, 28 (1904), 829–52; Lujo Brentano, *Eine Geschichte der wirtschaftlichen Entwicklung Englands*, 3 vols. (Jena, 1929), esp. vol. iii, pt. 2 on the British Empire, 1929; Otto Hintze, 'Der britische Imperialismus und seine Probleme', *Zeitschrift für Politik*, 1 (1908), 297–345; id., 'Imperialismus und Weltpolitik' (1907), in id., *Historische und politische Aufsätze*, 4 vols. (Berlin, 1908–9), iv. 144–59.

[111] For a more detailed analysis see Stuchtey, 'Imperialism', 319–29.

fewer rights and smaller chances to acquire their place.[112] Hermann Oncken, a defender of the primacy of foreign policy whose work mainly concentrated on the tension between power politics and the morality of power, suggested the following explanation: 'The British Empire is the plumpest and ripest fruit produced by the power struggle of the European energy centre. Although this power structure, extraordinary in the history of the earth, does not approach the Roman Empire in terms of uniformity, it surpasses all its predecessors in the internal richness of its system of rule, which it spreads over the earth. The history of British foreign policy uniquely combines internal consistency with the freest movement. It, like British life in general, is carried by a strong tradition, but it draws nourishment equally from the reality of life as seen in the horizon of the world.'[113] In sum, *Weltpolitik* was an aim to which all states should aspire. It would be followed by the struggle for *Weltstellung*, a position in the world, and, finally, admission into the canon of world history.

This is not surprising given the strong tradition of Protestant historiography in Germany, which in the nineteenth century and large parts of the twentieth century understood itself as a discipline offering political and cultural orientation. Given the close affinity of German Protestant historical writing with the power of the nation-state, the justification for the *kleindeutsche* solution, and the belief in a Prussian mission to achieve national unity, it is understandable that these intellectuals favoured a victorious perspective on history. Thus the *Preußische Jahrbücher*, for example, published articles on the strength of the imperial connection whose future lay not only in close economic ties but also in the 'agreement between Britain and its daughter nations on power politics'.[114] The author, speculating on the future of the Empire, believed that the twentieth-century separatist movements were not strong enough to destroy its unique combination of authority and freedom which revealed it to be the only empire appropriate

[112] Dietrich Schäfer, 'Weltlage und Kolonialpolitik', in id., *Aufsätze, Reden und Vorträge*, 2 vols. (Jena, 1913), ii. 242–9.

[113] Hermann Oncken, *Die Sicherheit Indiens: Ein Jahrhundert englischer Weltpolitik* (Berlin, 1937), 7.

[114] Emil Daniels, 'Die Zukunft des englischen Imperiums', *Preußische Jahrbücher*, 202 (1925), 47–57, quotation at 48–9; Fritz Hesse, 'Zur Politik der britischen Imperialisten', *Preußische Jahrbücher*, 203 (1926), 277–91.

to the modern world system.[115] Wilhelm Dibelius, master narrator of Weimar Germany and a sensitive authority on England, referred to the intensity of the religious creed that gave the English people the conviction of being God's chosen people destined to guide the world in 'religious idealism'.[116] First published four years after the Great War, Dibelius's book on England could not free itself of the shadows of the war. However, he tried to minimize the political argument in his description of England and its empire as a model for the solution of present-day problems and for political reform in Germany. The danger that praise for English achievements could too easily be interpreted by his contemporaries simply as blame for German grievances was anticipated and accepted by Dibelius.[117]

Erich Marcks's preventive measure against this danger was a methodological one. He wisely divided his concept of empire between two chapters: one on the period of mercantilism and liberalism (1500–1880), and the other on the age of high imperialism (1870–1920). As 'model and workshop of the world',[118] internationally unchallenged since 1815, and internally and politically stabilized in 1832, England could allow itself economic liberalism and the freedom of colonial administration. Only where state power was at risk would it intervene. Otherwise the Empire before the age of imperialism was the expression of a liberal connection whose members had shared economic interests and were averse to any aggressive conquest. This Empire 'was part of the nation's daily life and most elevated existence'.[119] Indeed, the nation was politically so much occupied with itself that the colonial 'periphery' was part of daily business, and vice versa.[120]

In the age of high imperialism the British Empire had to learn to share its 'planetary' existence and give up the privilege of filling the pages of world history books on its own. The Berlin historian Ludwig Riess thought that the 'periphery' instinctively saw England as the 'mother country', the 'old native country', but that it would also gradually start to compare its ability to guarantee the security of the Empire, whether formal or informal, with that of other powers.[121] Marcks identified the turn of

[115] Daniels, 'Zukunft', 53.

[116] Wilhelm Dibelius, *England*, 2 vols. (4th edn.; Stuttgart, 1925), ii. 74 f.

[117] Ibid., vol. i, preface p. xii. [118] Marcks, 'Entwicklung', 15. [119] Ibid. 16.

[120] Ibid. 19.

[121] Ludwig Riess, *Englische Geschichte, hauptsächlich in neuester Zeit* (Berlin, 1926), 346 f.

the nineteenth to the twentieth century as both a crisis and a test. He believed it was particularly a test for the English mind. Edmund Burke, Thomas Carlyle, Charles Dilke, and John Robert Seeley had cultivated the idea of a powerful empire with a mission to impose cultural unity on the world. As such, English history should not reflect primarily the constitutional past of the British Isles but imperial history. Dilke's *Greater Britain* and Seeley's *Expansion of England* made a great impression on their contemporaries precisely because both expressed the idea of a close relationship between nation and empire. Here the qualities of a strong state became obvious, said Marcks the student of Treitschke's belief in the past as a guide to the present, and here lay the heart of history and the future, wrote Marcks the admirer of Seeley's concept of imperial history.[122] The result was 'universal imperialism in its highest form'.[123] As if he wanted to top the British historians' concept of nation and imperial expansion, Felix Salomon's *Englische Geschichte* of 1923, one of the first total histories of England in the German language, emphasized the *longue durée* of this British colonial tradition: 'There had long been imperial interests in English history—one could speak of imperialism permeating English history from the late Middle Ages on. It was a feature of modern imperialism that imperial interests affected the whole of national existence right down to its roots.'[124] Like Seeley and Dilke, Salomon was convinced that what he called the spirit of the Empire had survived down the centuries because of its organic expansion.[125]

Universal imperialism or imperialism reflecting nationalism as the two driving forces of modern times? Not all contemporaries would concur with Marcks in his optimistic assessment of the British Empire. Either its political, economic, and cultural future was seen as unstable and England's social development as especially unpredictable because of what one author called the rise of Bolshevism,[126] or it was compared with other imperial powers such as the USA, Russia, Japan, Italy, and France. Thereby its

[122] Felix Liebermann on Marcks in his review of *Lebensfragen des britischen Weltreiches*, 'Seeley fühlt er sich kongenial', in *Historische Zeitschrift*, 131 (1925), 109–14, at 110.

[123] Marcks, 'Entwicklung', 22, 37.

[124] Felix Salomon, *Englische Geschichte von den Anfängen bis zur Gegenwart* (Leipzig, 1923),259.

[125] Ibid. 277 ff., 306 ff.

[126] Daniels, 'Zukunft', *passim*.

ability to survive was relativized, in particular as regards the unparalleled strengths of colonial nationalism in the British Empire, that is, the national movements against the colonial power.[127] The former colonial governor and Reichstag deputy, Heinrich Schnee, was strongly influenced by his work in the German overseas civil service, as was his writing. Nostalgia for the irretrievable loss of the German colonies was mixed with great respect for British nationalism as the basis for successful imperialism. At the same time, Schnee suggested that the Empire merely profited from Germany's defeat in 1918 instead of being interested in helping to build up a new world order based on peace and prosperity: England 'is not only trying to organize the British Empire in such a way as to ensure that its component parts stay together, but, with an insatiable imperial appetite is trying to incorporate even more areas into the British Empire that already covers one quarter of the earth and includes one quarter of the world's population by seeking to annex the German colonies which were entrusted to it as mandates in good faith'.[128]

Something similar can be said of Wilhelm Solf, former under-secretary of state in the German colonial office, in which position he travelled extensively, not only in the German colonies of South-West Africa, East Africa, Togo, and Cameroon, but also in the neighbouring British colonial possessions. Solf, who had studied Orientalism and Indology in Berlin, London, and Calcutta, had hoped for a negotiated peace in 1918 and had gone so far as to start an informal resistance group against Hitler in 1933, could not get over the loss of the German Empire. After the war he did not give up hope of regaining some of Germany's former colonies from Britain. His understanding of colonial rule was as a Western duty to civilize what he called the 'minor races of the world'. Thus Germany had to accomplish this pioneering duty—under the condition that Britain, returning to the moral standards of an imperial nation (in Solf's view something it had lost during the war), accepted Germany as an equal partner in the international community of 'white sister-nations'.[129]

Whereas Schnee and Solf had a professional background in

[127] Heinrich Schnee, *Nationalismus und Imperialismus* (Berlin, 1928), 68–159.

[128] Ibid. 337.

[129] Wilhelm Solf, *Kolonialpolitik: Mein politisches Vermächtnis* (Berlin, 1919), quotations on pp. vi and 62; using the same argument and the attempt to regain the German colonies in Africa: Rudolf Karlowa, *Englische Mandatsverwaltung in Afrika* (Berlin, 1940).

the colonial service, many German authors either relied on English sources and English literature when describing the Empire, or reflected on their personal experiences of visits to Britain. Otto Koellreutter, for example, a good popular writer rather than an academic, used journalism in his descriptions of Britain's status as a world power. Drawing on Oswald Spengler's image of Britain's insular identity, he interpreted the 'Anglo-Saxon feeling for the world' as the expression of a maritime empire that, in contrast to continental empires such as that of Russia, defined itself by opening up rather than closing its frontiers.[130] Since the Imperial Conference of 1926, however, one could no longer speak of a unified Empire. The dominions had gone their own ways in, for example, economic and migration policy, and Ireland, Egypt, and India had taken the most obvious step away from the colonial connection. England, in the perception of its German observers, was therefore well advised to look for a new role of its own within the British Empire, given that the centrifugal powers made a new definition of imperial policy necessary.[131] Salomon, for example, maintained that at least since the age of high imperialism England had given up its identity as an island: 'We must get used to thinking in terms of continents from now on when we are dealing with England, its interests and the conditions prevailing there.'[132] A world power could write world history as long as it avoided provincialization.

Analogous thoughts were expressed in all political camps, but especially in the liberal-conservative to far right camp.[133] Severe political and economic setbacks, and military and strategic problems were predicted as the consequence of imperial overstretch. England's world supremacy was endangered by three factors: first, by the rise of the other European powers, the USA, and Japan as colonial powers;[134] secondly, by colonial nationalism and separatist movements;[135] and thirdly by the growing criticism

[130] Otto Koellreutter, *Der englische Staat der Gegenwart und das britische Weltreich* (Breslau, 1930), 9.

[131] Ibid. 115 ff.

[132] Salomon, *Englische Geschichte*, 331.

[133] Karl-Heinz Pfeffer, *England: Vormacht der bürgerlichen Welt* (Hamburg, 1940), 165–74.

[134] Kurt von Stutterheim, 'Quo vadis Britannia?', in id., *England: Heute und morgen* (Berlin, 1937), 259–316.

[135] A. L. Carthill, *Verlorene Herrschaft: Wie England Indien aufgab* (Berlin, 1924), esp. 272–93; Karl Bartz, *Englands Weg nach Indien: Schicksalsstunden des britischen Weltreiches* (Berlin, 1936), 294–306 on Gandhi.

of imperialism in England itself, whether in Parliament or socialist debating clubs.[136] Probably the last point was of specific relevance in so far as critics of Empire had had a voice in England since Adam Smith, and were also heard in Germany. As Joseph Roth had shown in his short tale *Die Büste des Kaisers*, the Austro-Hungarian Empire had declined not as a result of the arguments of intellectual critics and those who wanted to destroy the imperial idea, but through the growing disbelief of previous supporters, that is, among others, the colonial officials at home and abroad who were supposed to believe in the Empire's sustaining world power, but who became increasingly disillusioned with its 'civilizing mission'.

A book on the 'troubles of the British Empire' by the head of the department of world economics at the University of Leipzig, published in the month of the outbreak of the Second World War, addressed exactly this problem when pointing to what the author termed the 'moral decline' of Britain.[137] Schultze was not known by his contemporaries as particularly Anglophile. The author of books such as *England als Seeräuberstaat* (1915) and *Die Blutspur Englands: Geschichte der englischen Kriegsgrausamkeiten* (1940), he explained world crises and the outbreak of world wars in terms of the gradual dissolution of the Empire, which, in turn, caused the instability of the international political system. This recurrent topic of the tension between strong British power politics on the one hand and the unavoidable break-up of the imperial system on the other had already famously been taken up by Erich Marcks in 1915 in a volume that became a classic and served several generations of scholars in their assessment of international relations and imperial politics.[138] While this volume had been edited by such distinguished historians as Otto Hintze and Friedrich Meinecke, who collected notable authors

[136] Arnold Hillen Ziegfeld, 'Das Ende des Kolonialgedankens', in id., *England in der Entscheidung: Eine freimütige Deutung der englischen Wirklichkeit* (Leipzig, 1938), 113–31.

[137] Ernst Schultze, *Sorgen des Britischen Weltreichs* (Leipzig, 1939), 335–7. For similar arguments see also Reinald Hoops, *Die Zukunft des britischen Weltreichs* (Berlin, 1937); *Probleme britischer Reichs- und Außenpolitik*, ed. by the Hochschule für Politik (Berlin, 1939); Erich Obst, *England, Europa und die Welt: Eine geopolitisch-weltwirtschaftliche Studie* (Berlin, 1927); Friedrich Wilhelm Fernau, *Der Orient im Britischen Weltreich* (Hamburg, 1937); similarly, about 30 years earlier in Deckert, *Das britische Weltreich, passim.*

[138] Erich Marcks, 'Die Machtpolitik Englands', in Otto Hintze, Friedrich Meinecke, Hermann Oncken, and Hermann Schumacher (eds.), *Deutschland und der Weltkrieg* (Leipzig, 1915), 297–322.

including Carl Becker, Hans Delbrück, Gustav von Schmoller, and Ernst Troeltsch, thus claiming academic respect and aiming for political objectivity despite the war, Schultze's book certainly aimed at the reverse. And although *Deutschland und der Weltkrieg* can surely not be called indifferent in apportioning blame for the outbreak of war in 1914, it at least tried not to be part of the common warmongering. But that is precisely what Schultze intended in September 1939. He did not refer to Marcks, but based his findings on revisionist literature. He argued that once they had reached the peak of their might, all empires from that of Alexander the Great to that of the Romans, the Spanish, and the Portuguese, were destined to lose their influence when confronted by other rising nations. The British Empire, he went on, had made the same mistake, passing the zenith of its power at the moment when it underestimated the importance of international agreement.[139]

Marcks, by contrast, had paid respect to Seeley, Froude, and Dilke, and argued along the same lines. The British Empire, he suggested, could best be understood as a universal empire, together with the rising world power, the USA, both forming the core of the spheres of interest of the English-speaking countries. Under threat, however, Britain would call for the defence not only of its Empire, but also of the security, stability, and freedom of the world. Identifying the Empire with the world both in meaning and concept meant equating the decline and fall of Western civilization in Spengler's terms with the decline of British imperialism in the light of the new world order of the twentieth century.[140] According to Marcks, the British imperial past, present, and future had its glorious and less glorious sides. After all, the time had now come to see that Britain could no longer justly claim universal prestige: while world history had further developed and was heading in new directions, the former world power too plainly revealed the discrepancy between its pretence of representing mankind's interests and British national interests: 'The history of Britain's past, to which it clings and which it tries to carry over into the present is—and this is the sum of these observations—a history of wars of conquest, of wars of aggression whose purpose was to conceal its penetration of the world, and to destroy every European rival; it

[139] Schultze, *Sorgen*, 16. [140] Marcks, 'Machtpolitik', 308, 320.

is a history of wars, of aggressive policies, of aggressive world policy, always and everywhere. Some find this magnificent, and this world people still has grand connections today, in terms of population and land possession, culture and power. But only hypocrisy or the stupefaction of others, whom it tries to deceive, allows English self-confidence and cant to identify it with the interests of mankind. It is fighting for itself and for an old-fashioned world domination, whose claims must destroy the national life of today and tomorrow; it is fighting for a universal validity which, in truth, is the most particular and self-confident thing known to the world today.'[141]

This opinion, partly resulting from the bitter post-war disillusionment of previously Anglophile German authors, and partly fed by popular nationalist sentiment, was echoed by numerous studies published in the late 1930s and later.[142] Few would continue to subscribe to positive, or at least objective, descriptions of the British Empire in the tone used twenty years earlier. Many, indeed, addressed the gradual break-up of the Empire, and speculated about its most likely successor, the USA. For A. Sanders it was an indisputable fact that the USA would control the majority of British possessions either militarily, politically, or economically, once Britain faced a united European continent in war. What this would involve for the future of Europe was more difficult to predict than for the future of the world. In any case, a world power in decline needed to be reincorporated into European history, a challenge posed to European unity at times of universal diversity.[143] Only as long as there was peace internationally was Britain capable of holding its imperial ties together. The *Deutsche Kolonialzeitung* commented on the 'crisis of the Empire', saying that it was no longer a federation of common interests with agreed values and beliefs, but that it consisted merely of a group of loosely connected states gradually becoming estranged from one another.[144]

One could either accept that these things would develop as

[141] Ibid. 322.

[142] Cf. G. T. Waddington, 'Haßgegner: German Views of Great Britain in the later 1930s', *History*, 81 (1996), 22–39, with particular reference to Hitler and the NSDAP.

[143] A. Sanders, *Um das Erbe Großbritanniens: Zur Wandlung der politischen Struktur der Übersee* (Munich, 1941), 86.

[144] Erich Student, 'Das Empire in der Krise', *Deutsche Kolonialzeitung*, 51/2 (Berlin, 1939), 35–6, at 36.

they did, or look at exemplary British statesmen who, in the opinion of their German admirers, combined the national with the imperial idea and were able to find a political solution at difficult times. Biographical studies, whether of Chamberlain more recently,[145] or more historically Pitt the Elder, were consulted by aesthetic historians convinced that history was a *magistra vitae*. Karl Alexander von Müller, originally a conservative Weimar historian who had rejected the Versailles peace treaty, soon moved to a *völkisch* nationalist position that brought him into close contact with the Nazis. He had earlier worked with Erich Marcks, and together they had edited the three-volume *Meister der Politik* (1922–3), for which he wrote the essay on Pitt.[146] As editor of *Knaurs Weltgeschichte* (1934) and the *Historische Zeitschrift* (1935–45) von Müller held a key position in German historiography, and he had also edited an early German version of Seeley's *Expansion of England* (1928). Von Müller was a typical representative of German middle-class historical writing in the Weimar Republic that did not believe that it could learn from the defeat of 1918. It aimed for a continuity between the Kaiserreich and a powerful new Germany. Dedicating his book to Oriel College, Oxford, where he was the first German Rhodes Scholar, von Müller admired in Pitt what he regarded as the roots of the successful working of the British Empire: 'a strong will, pride, and a lofty imagination that send this whole people overseas and make it capable of ruling the whole world'.[147] And what was true for the earlier eighteenth century continued to hold good for his time. Despite his bitterness, the historian of the conflict between England and Germany saw himself forced to acknowledge the qualities of the enemy whose strength lay in the unique relationship between home and colonial periphery: von Müller interpreted British colonial expansion as Seeley had done, in terms of an 'England abroad'. No other empire could identify with world history so closely as the British, no other national history was twinned with imperial history so obviously as the English.[148]

This is reminiscent, in tone and attitude, of what the

[145] Vladimir Halperin, *Joseph Chamberlain: Der Mann und sein Werk* (Zurich, 1942).

[146] Reprinted as Karl Alexander von Müller, *Der Ältere Pitt* (Munich, 1937).

[147] Ibid. 27.

[148] Karl Alexander von Müller, *Deutschland und England: Ein weltgeschichtliches Bild* (Berlin, 1939), 27–9 and *passim*.

Kolonialzeitung had written about fifty years earlier, in the year of its first publication. Introducing its readers to the history of British imperialism from its beginnings, its significance for the British state and economy, and the status of the Empire in the contemporary world system, the paper was full of admiration for the success of a truly imperial nation 'which extends over the whole earth, and whose trade significantly surpasses that of every other country'. As such, the British Empire was unique; Germany would never be able to acquire the same position. And given that the two countries were so unlike each other, it was not advisable 'to sanction any mere imitation of British aspirations in the field of colonial policy'.[149] In the same year, the *Deutsche Kolonialzeitung* quoted from a report that had been published by the London *Chamber of Commerce Journal* on competition to British imperial trade from US and Russian expansion. Admiration for British achievements was already mixed with the expectation of decline because 'England no longer feels capable of world domination; it thinks it can rest on the laurels it has already acquired'.[150] This was the danger faced by all imperial powers, whether territorial or sea-based, and of which English colonial élites were certainly aware: imperial overstretch resulting in imperial surfeit. In 1884 few could see the writing on the wall, though clear indications were given by crises from Egypt to South Africa. By the later 1930s, however, the intellectual debate had long since entered the parliamentary stage. A German observer could be convinced that Britain no longer had a special role in world history, which it had once dominated so overwhelmingly.[151] It was no great step from academic publications to political pamphlets, pre-war and wartime Nazi publications condemning Britain and the Empire, and pointing to the many dangers they faced throughout the world.[152] Spengler's language and his philosophy of decline were too powerful for many authors to resist.[153]

[149] A. Bayerdörffer, 'England und sein Kolonialbesitz', *Deutsche Kolonialzeitung*, 1/1 (Berlin, 1884), 223–6, quotations at 223 and 226.

[150] Ewald Paul, 'Britische Kolonialpolitik', *Deutsche Kolonialzeitung*, 1 (Berlin, 1884), 336–7, at 336.

[151] Hans Reepen, 'Kolonialdebatte im englischen Parlament', *Deutsche Kolonialzeitung*, 48/5 (Berlin, 1936), 109–10.

[152] Wolf von Dewall, *Gefahrenzonen britischer Weltpolitik* (Berlin, n.d.); Rudolf Kapp, *Die nationalreligiöse Ideologie Englands im gegenwärtigen Kriege* (Stuttgart, 1940); Anton Zischka, *Englands Bündnisse: Sechs Jahrhunderte britischer Kriege mit fremden Waffen* (Leipzig, 1940).

[153] See e.g. Carl Brinkmann, *Der englische Wirtschaftsimperialismus* (Berlin, 1940), 27–38;

Conversely, a highly acknowledged authority on classical history, the Berlin historian Eduard Meyer, strongly influenced Spengler. Meyer's œuvre on Greece, Rome, and particularly the Orient rightly claimed to formulate a universal history that tried to find a place for classical history in the course of the history of humanity. When Meyer published two slim and angry polemical studies directed against England during the First World War, he referred to a question similar to the one addressed by Fritz Stern and mentioned at the beginning of this essay. How were the winners and losers in world history, their roles, and the consequences for historiography to be defined? This was less a question of period—whether the Great War or any other period in world history—than one of particular constellations that resembled each other in past and present. This was a question that losers of the war, like the Germans, needed to reflect upon, as also did a still supposedly unrivalled power like the British Empire: 'And anyone who surveys the course of world history in context, senses, behind all these problems, the uneasy question of whether the analogy with the Punic Wars does not go much further, of whether, with the outbreak of war, modern cultural development has not also passed its peak and is heading for decline. Indeed, wherever one looks, the symptoms of this are openly on display.'[154] The historian of the decline and fall of the classic civilizations was well placed to understand the decline of the modern Western cultures that had brought them into the war. And Britain fought this war only to defend its Empire.[155] Twenty years later, Otto Graf wrote an equally polemical literary essay in which he speculated on the loss of the 'adaptability, flexibility and power' which had given Britain its empire. In the end, history's lesson was always the same. No empire lasted forever, and to reflect on defeat and decline in the universal context of world history could be very fruitful for its historiography: 'This is what the Babylonians, the Assyrians, Alexander, the Romans, Arabs, and Spanish all found out.'[156]

Wolf von Dewall, *England: Triumph der Inkonsequenz. Ein Überblick* (Freiburg, 1948), 20–47; William Joyce, *Dämmerung über England* (Berlin, 1940), 157–77; Hans Grimm, *Englische Rede: Wie ich den Engländer sehe* (Gütersloh, 1938), 15 ff.

154 Eduard Meyer, *England: Seine staatliche und politische Entwicklung und der Krieg gegen Deutschland* (Stuttgart, 1916), 206.

155 According to Felix Liebermann's review of Meyer's *Das britische Weltreich* (Berlin, 1916), in *Historische Zeitschrift*, 120 (1919), 336–40, at 337.

156 Otto Graf, *Imperium Britannicum: Vom Inselstaat zum Weltreich* (Leipzig, 1937), both quotations at 302.

10

Fitting Africa into World History: A Historiographical Exploration

ANDREAS ECKERT

'Africa is at once one of the most romantic and the most tragic of continents . . . There are those, nevertheless, who would write universal history and leave out Africa.'[1] When W. E. B. Du Bois, one of the fathers of Pan-Africanism, lodged this complaint in 1915, Africa was widely regarded as a continent without history. Things have changed considerably since then, but to the present day, the majority of 'mainstream' historians probably still hold the view that all in all Africa had little relevance for world history.[2] On the other hand, 'world history' is not a major preoccupation for historians in sub-Saharan Africa, and, in fact, only very few Africanist historians outside the continent, notably Philip D. Curtin, promote this branch of historiography or are part of the 'world history movement'.[3] Not surprisingly, Africa is rarely mentioned in the *Journal of World History*. However, Steven Feierman draws our attention to the fact that the emergence of

[1] W. E. B. Du Bois, *The Negro* (New York, 2002; 1st edn. 1915), 23 f.

[2] Even the great Eric Hobsbawm stated some years ago that 'the dynamics of the greater part of the world's history in the Short Twentieth Century are derived, not original. They consist essentially in the attempts by the elites of non-bourgeois societies to imitate the model pioneered in the West.' Cf. Eric Hobsbawm, *Age of Extremes* (London, 1994), 200. According to Hobsbawm, in Africa particularly, the imitations have descended into both farce and tragedy. Cf. Terence Ranger, 'Africa in the Age of Extremes: The Irrelevance of African History', in Simon McGrath *et al.* (eds.), *Rethinking African History* (Edinburgh, 1997), 269–91, esp. 283–5. In the early 1990s, the 17th-century specialist John Kenyon noted with satisfaction that in 'history departments hastily cobbled-up courses on Indochina or West Africa faded away as soon as these areas ceased to be of immediate current concern'. Quoted in Richard J. Evans, *In Defence of History* (London, 1997), 178.

[3] See e.g. Philip D. Curtin, *Cross-Cultural Trade in World History* (Cambridge, 1984); id., *The World and the West: The European Challenge and the Overseas Response in the Age of Empire* (Cambridge, 2000); id., 'Location in History: Argentina and South Africa in the Nineteenth Century', *Journal of World History*, 10 (1999), 41–92; id., 'Graduate Teaching in World History', *Journal of World History*, 2 (1991), 81–9.

African history 'has changed our understanding of general history, and of Europe's place in the world, in profound ways'. And he adds: 'It is no longer possible to defend the position that historical processes among non-European peoples can be seen as the consequence of all-encompassing influences emerging from a dominant European center.'[4] According to this view, Africans seen as living in coherent but not isolated 'worlds of their own' were in productive tension with broader currents of world history.[5] Yet the eternal problem of linking a careful analysis of complex local practices in Africa with macro-historical processes remains. Taking the example of public healing on the northern frontier of Rwanda, Steven Feierman has shown that these healing mediums did not fit into Western narrative conventions. It can no longer be assumed that there is a clear national or regional scale that must be used in every study. However, to focus exclusively on the micro level does not solve the problem either. It may simply leave untouched all the usual macro accounts of the sweeping success of colonial conquest and capitalist expansion.[6]

For a long time, world history was conceptualized as 'the rise of the West'.[7] The claim to be writing world history often only concealed an extremely ethnocentric approach. Moreover, most professional historians denied that there was any African history worth knowing. This view was expressed most explicitly by the Oxford don Hugh Trevor-Roper who, in the early 1960s, wrote that the African past only involved 'unrewarding gyrations of

[4] Steven Feierman, 'African Histories and the Dissolution of World History', in Robert H. Bates *et al.* (eds.) *Africa and the Disciplines: The Contributions of Research in Africa to the Social Sciences and Humanities* (Chicago, 1993), 182. Maghan Keita follows the same line in 'Africa and the Construction of a Grand Narrative in World History', in Eckhardt Fuchs and Benedikt Stuchtey (eds.), *Across Cultural Borders: Historiography in Global Perspective* (Lanham, 2002), 285–308. On the general challenges of decentring 'world history', see Michael Geyer and Charles Bright, 'World History in a Global Age', *American Historical Review*, 100 (1995), 1034–60.

[5] Joseph C. Miller, 'History and Africa/Africa and History', *American Historical Review*, 104 (1999), 29.

[6] Cf. Steven Feierman, 'Colonizers, Scholars, and the Creation of Invisible Histories', in Victoria E. Bonnell and Lynn Hunt (eds.), *Beyond the Cultural Turn: New Directions in the Study of Society and Culture* (Berkeley, 1999), 182–216. On this problem see also, for instance, Michael Adas, 'Bringing Ideas and Agency Back In: Representation and the Comparative Approach to World History', in Philip Pomper *et al.* (eds.), *World History: Ideologies, Structures, and Identities* (Oxford, 1998), 81–104.

[7] William H. McNeill, *The Rise of the West: A History of the Human Community* (Chicago, 1963).

barbarous tribes in picturesque but irrelevant corners of the world'.[8] Thus from the outset the relationship between academic African history, which gained wider recognition only some forty years ago, and any concept of universal and world history was ambivalent.[9] Especially within the nationalist–modernization ethos of the 1960s and early 1970s, numerous Africanist historians concentrated on state formation or on 'trade and politics' and tried to show that at least the African societies they were investigating could be understood in the same terms as Western history.[10] Because this generation of historians was pleading for the respectability of African history, much argument was dominated by analogies with other histories. There was an obvious danger inherent in this approach. As Richard Rathbone put it: 'It was heroic to fight against a perception of Africans as exotic, but in the war against exceptionalism, some lost the continent's historical particularity.'[11] On the other hand, numerous Africanist historians continued to underline the 'otherness' of Africa's past, now seen, however, in

[8] Hugh Trevor-Roper, *The Rise of Christian Europe* (London, 1965), 9. With Hegel's statement (Georg Wilhelm Friedrich Hegel, *The Philosophy of History*, trans. J. Sibree, reprint New York, 1956; German orig. 1837, 99: 'What we properly understand by Africa, is the Unhistorical, Underdeveloped Spirit, still involved in the conditions of mere nature, and which has to be presented here as the threshold of the World's History') Trevor-Roper's infamous remark is still often quoted as an example of Eurocentric arrogance.

[9] Cf. Adam Jones, 'Africa in World History', *Storia della Storiografia*, 35 (1999), 76. The emergence of African history as a field of academic study has been the subject of countless articles and books. See, e.g., Bogumil Jewsiewicki and David Newbury (eds.), *African Historiographies: What History for Which Africa?* (Beverly Hills, Calif., 1986); Toyin Falola (ed.), *African Historiography: Essays in Honour of Jacob Ade Ajayi* (Burnt Mills, Harlow, 1993); Andreas Eckert, 'Dekolonisierung der Geschichte? Die Institutionalisierung der Geschichtswissenschaft in Afrika nach dem Zweiten Weltkrieg', in Matthias Middell *et al.* (eds.), *Historische Institute im internationalen Vergleich* (Leipzig, 2001), 451–76; Miller, 'History and Africa/Africa and History'. Two pioneers of academic African history have published their autobiographies: Jan Vansina, *Living with Africa* (Madison, 1994); Roland Oliver, *In the Realms of Gold: Pioneering in African History* (Madison, 1997).

[10] Jones, 'Africa in World History', 77; Ralph A. Austen, 'Africanist Historiography and its Critics: Can there be an Autonomous African History?', in Falola (ed.), *African Historiography*, 203–17, esp. 206 f. A good example of such an effort, mentioned by Jones, is Ivor Wilks's voluminous monograph *Asante in the Nineteenth Century: The Structure and Evolution of a Political Order* (Cambridge, 1975), in which the author attempts to describe the development of formal-rational bureaucracy in an important pre-colonial kingdom of what is today Ghana. Here Wilks evokes Max Weber's work in postulating the existence of a historic Asante 'bureaucracy'. For a fierce critique of this attempt see T. C. McCaskie, *State and Society in Pre-Colonial Asante* (Cambridge, 1995), ch. 1.

[11] Richard Rathbone, 'The Africans', *Economy and Society*, 25 (1996), 562.

positive terms, claiming, for example, that Africa was culturally distinctive because of Africans' supposedly communitarian, holistic vision of life.[12]

This essay attempts to demonstrate how during the second half of the twentieth century historians *of* Africa (in most cases non-Africans) have tried to fit African history more closely into world history without necessarily labelling their efforts 'a contribution to world history'. Three wider historiographical fields will serve as examples: first, the Afrocentric movement, which, although it had far older roots, basically started with the work of the Senegalese scholar Cheikh Anta Diop (1923–86). Diop argued that Ancient Egypt, which he considered part of 'Black Africa', was the mother of and model for Western civilization. By now, Afrocentrism has largely degenerated into a counter mythology, proclaiming the innate superiority of African-descended people. Secondly, the debates about (often forced) migrations and diasporas, which highlighted the fact that since the days of the Atlantic slave trade Africans have established numerous global networks, which now embrace continents, worlds, and cultures. Thirdly, the many books and articles dealing with the role of Africa in the capitalist world, initially mainly linked with the world system and dependency schools, which basically argued that Africa was poor because world capitalism required it to be poor. This approach has now been replaced by more subtle interpretations which suggest, for instance, that Africa is marginalized both economically and culturally because it has always been difficult to exploit the continent. Needless to say that in this essay it will not be possible either to mention all relevant positions and approaches (let alone to do justice to all of them), or to come up with a definitive statement about Africa's role in world history.

As already mentioned, for centuries, racist and Eurocentric bias has blocked or distorted knowledge of Africans, their histories and cultures. The redressing of Hegel's view that Africa 'is no historical part of the World'[13] has been one the most important intellectual transformations of the second half of the twentieth century. Cheikh Anta Diop's works played an early and

[12] One of the strengths of John Iliffe, *The Africans: The History of a Continent* (Cambridge, 1995) is that the author maintains the particularity of Africa without exoticizing it.

[13] Hegel, *The Philosophy of History*, 93.

important part in challenging Eurocentric attitudes by heavily criticizing European colonial arrogance and its latter-day legacies. Diop is by far the most important single figure in the development of what is now called Afrocentric thought. As Stephen Howe emphasizes: 'Indeed, one might even say that every significant idea or claim put forward by Afrocentrists today was earlier expressed by him.'[14] In essence, Diop and his Afrocentric heirs offer a reinterpretation of the history of Western civilization by arguing that it derives from Africa, or, to be more precise, from Ancient Egypt, which they characterize as a 'black civilization'. Especially in the 1950s, when Diop published his first books, such a claim was a huge provocation. This approach can be seen as an attempt to put Africa on the map of world history, while its main deficiency is that the Eurocentric model is simply turned upside down.[15] Moreover, as Adam Jones rightly criticizes, 'by emphasising the allegedly positive achievements of the Egyptians—writing, a complex hierarchy, specialised craftsmen, monumental architecture—the Afrocentrists unintentionally denigrate the achievements of all African cultures that did *not* have such things—i.e. of the overwhelming majority'.[16]

The claim that Ancient Egypt was a genuine African culture can already be found in the writings of pre-Civil War African-American intellectuals.[17] This idea later played an important

[14] Stephen Howe, *Afrocentrism: Mythical Pasts and Imagined Homes* (London, 1998), 163. Howe's book is by far the most comprehensive study of this movement. An excellent overview of Afrocentrism is also provided by Katja Füllberg-Stolberg, 'Afrozentrismus: Afrika aus dem Blickwinkel der Diaspora', in Jan-Georg Deutsch and Albert Wirz (eds.), *Geschichte in Afrika: Einführung in Probleme und Debatten* (Berlin, 1997), 261–81; Clarence E. Walker, *We Can't Go Home Again: An Argument About Afrocentrism* (Oxford, 2000). On Diop see also, among others, Chris Gray, *Conceptions of History: Cheikh Anta Diop and Théophile Obenga* (London, 1989); François-Xavier Fauvelle, *L'Afrique de Cheikh Anta Diop* (Paris, 1996).

[15] For a related critique on Diop, see Wyatt MacGaffey, 'Who Owns Ancient Egypt?', *Journal of African History*, 20 (1993), 515–19; Isidore Okpewho, 'Cheikh Anta Diop: The Search for a Philosophy of African Culture', *Cahiers d'études africaines*, 21 (1980), 559 f.; Alain Froment, 'Origine et évolution de l'homme dans la pensée de Cheikh Anta Diop: Une analyse critique', *Cahiers d'études africaines*, 31 (1991), 29–64; Augustin Holl, 'African History: Past, Present and Future. The Unending Quest for Alternatives', in Peter R. Schmidt and Thomas C. Petterson (eds.), *Making Alternative Histories: The Practice of Archaeology and History in Non-Western Settings* (Santa Fe, 1995), 183–211, esp. 197–208.

[16] Jones, 'Africa in World History', 79 (original emphasis). See also François-Xavier Fauvelle-Aymar, 'Naissance d'une nation noire: Multimédia, mondialisation et nouvelles solidarités', *L'Homme: Revue française d'anthropologie*, 161 (2002), 77.

[17] See e.g. Frederick Douglass, *The Claim of the Negro: Ethnologically Considered. An Address* (Rochester, NY, 1854), 17, 25.

role in the Pan-African movement.[18] In the 1930s, the representatives of *Négritude* also drew new self-assurance from their belief in the grandeur of 'African' Pharaonic Egypt. As Léopold Sédar Senghor noted: 'Dans les heures de graves difficultés, dans les heures de découragement et de doute, il nous suffit de penser à l'Egypte des Pharaons pour nous convaincre que l'Afrique a joué dans l'élaboration de la civilisation un rôle primordial.'[19] From the 1950s Diop vigorously developed this thesis in numerous articles and books.[20] But while Senghor did not see the ancient Egyptians as 'black', but as a mixed population, and associated this perception with his general positive view of hybridity, Diop employed a far stricter view of race.[21] According to him, Africa was the location of the biological origin of humanity and the emergence of civilization,[22] and he insisted that Egypt was specifically a black civilization, representing the fullest flowering of a cultural system unifying the whole African continent. He argued that most important aspects of human social and intellectual development originated there. Moreover, it was distinct from Eurasian societies in its matriarchal, spiritual, peaceable, and humanistic character. Ancient Greece—and hence all European civilization—had taken almost everything of value usually claimed to be theirs from this antecedent African–Egyptian culture. Diop concluded that Africa must recover the glories of its ancient past, rejecting the

[18] For details see Imanuel Geiss, *The Pan-African Movement* (London, 1974; German orig. 1968).

[19] Quoted ibid. 426 (in German original). ('At times of great difficulty, at times of discouragement and of doubt, it was sufficient for us to think of the Egypt of the Pharaohs in order to convince us that Africa did play a fundamental role in the elaboration of civilization.')

[20] Diop's main books include *Nations nègres et cultures* (Paris, 1955); *The Cultural Unity of Black Africa* (Chicago, 1989; French orig. 1960); *Precolonial Black Africa* (New York, 1987; French orig. 1960); *Black Africa: The Economic and Cultural Basis of a Federal State* (Westport, 1984; French orig. 1960); *Antériorité des civilisations nègres* (Paris, 1967); *Parenté génétique de l'égyptien pharaonique et des langues négro-africaines* (Paris, 1987); *Civilization or Barbarism: An Authentic Anthropology* (New York, 1991; French orig. 1981). A number of his articles have been published in the posthumous collection *Alerte sous les Tropiques: Articles 1946–1960. Culture et développement en Afrique noire* (Paris, 1990).

[21] See e.g. Léopold Sédar Senghor, *La Poésie de l'action: Conversation de l'action avec Mohamed Aziza* (Paris, 1980). On the differences between Senghor and Diop see Gray, *Conceptions of History*, 43 ff.; Howe, *Afrocentrism*, 170. See also Jacques Louis Hymans, *Léopold Sédar Senghor: An Intellectual Biography* (Edinburgh, 1971): Janet G. Vaillant, *Black, French, and African: A Life of Léopold Sédar Senghor* (Cambridge, Mass., 1990) for Senghor's general ideas about Africa's place in world history.

[22] My summary of Diop's central theses follows that in Howe, *Afrocentrism*, 165 f.

racist, Eurocentric mystifications which had obscured those glories, and progress to the future by drawing on the lessons of the old Nile Valley philosophies. This recovery of a glorious past should lead to the construction of a single, federal African state, which, taking confidence from the unique greatness of past African achievements, would stand equal with Europe and the rest of the world. Thus for Diop 'history is nothing but a means to serve the realization of a political plan'.[23] By replacing the classical theme 'all that is European is civilized; all that is African is barbarous' by 'all that is African is civilized and beautiful', Diop's publications in many ways represented an early and radical manifestation of African nationalist historical writing.[24]

Diop, who alongside his academic work pursued an intense but decreasingly successful political career, was never accepted, and mostly ignored, by the historiographical mainstream. He had to pay a price for his provocative, uncompromising, often polemical style and for explicitly combining scholarship with political projects.[25] Moreover, one of his main strengths proved to be one of his main weaknesses. He combined so many academic subjects, sources, and methods that it was easy for specialists—especially linguists and archaeologists—to dismiss his controversial hypotheses as amateurish.[26] Apart from the

[23] Mamadou Diouf and Mohamad Mbodj, 'The Shadow of Cheikh Anta Diop', in Valentin Y. Mudimbe (ed.), *The Surreptitious Speech: Présence Africaine and the Politics of Otherness 1947–1987* (Chicago, 1992), 120.

[24] See Valentin Y. Mudimbe, *The Invention of Africa: Gnosis, Philosophy, and the Order of Knowledge* (London, 1988), 169.

[25] Diouf and Mbodj, 'Shadow', 129, write: 'In fact, Cheikh Anta Diop has been victimized by the reduction of his theses to ideology, which consequently excluded them from any serious scientific analysis: "one believes or one does not!" For those "who believed," Cheikh Anta Diop became the object of an adulation that was more symbolic than instrumental. Put on this pedestal, a series of rather trivial formulas was all that was noticed from his work: "The Blacks were the first people to be civilized," "The political unity of Africa is the key to its emancipation," "There is only one nation in Black Africa," "Precolonial Black Africa knew a political, social, and economic harmony that the West came to destroy," and so on.' Bogumil Jewsiewicki, 'Introduction: One Historiography or Several? A Requiem for Africanism', in id. and Newbury (eds.), *African Historiographies*, 10, adds: 'Many Western historians who would be prepared to argue the questions relating to pharonic negritude, were the debate to be carried out in its own terms, do not do so because they do not want to offend the sensitivities of their African colleagues. Diop's discourse divides African historians into unconditional supporters or opponents . . . but full debate is never engaged in by either group.'

[26] See e.g. Thurstan Shaw, 'The Prehistory of West Africa', in J. F. Ade Ajayi and Michael Crowder (eds.), *History of West Africa* (3rd edn.; Burnt Mill, Harlow, 1985), i. 176 f.

Congolese scholar Théophile Obenga, Diop has had few productive disciples among African historians.[27] Even worse, American Afrocentrists who referred to his work proved to be the worst enemies of his wider reputation. Molefi Kete Asante, currently Head of the African-American Studies Department at Temple University, Philadelphia, is regarded as the most influential Afrocentric writer today. His mission is 'to uncover and use codes, paradigms, symbols, motifs, myths and circles of discussion that reinforce the centrality of African ideas and values as a valid frame of reference for acquiring and examining data'.[28] Asante's central manifestos[29] provide only a poor imitation of Cheikh Anta Diop's theses, culminating in the claim that African-Americans are a nation—or, more properly, part of the unitary African nation—with its own civilization, values, belief system, social practices, and even language. These are superior to those of other groups, he argues, and especially to those of European-descended peoples. Like so many Afrocentric writers, he insists on the centrality of race to all questions of human society and is convinced 'that the denial of the reality of race is merely a Eurocentric obfuscation designed to undermine African pride'.[30] Other authors worked even harder to discredit the Afrocentric project by oversimplifications, for example Leonard Jeffries, professor at New York's City College. Jeffries became notorious for his infamous belief that whites are biologically inferior, greedy, and extremely materialistic because of their relative lack of melanin and their genes malformed by the Ice Age, as compared with the innate superiority of black 'Sun People', and for his claim that Jews bore the main responsibility for the Atlantic slave trade.[31]

[27] A critical assessment of Obenga's work is provided by Jean-Pierre Chrétien, 'Les Bantu: Des Indo-Européens noirs?', in François-Xavier Fauvelle-Aymar *et al.* (eds.), *Afrocentrisme: L'histoire des Africains entre Égypte et Amérique* (Paris, 2000), 271–93. See also Howe, *Afrocentrism*, 180 f.

[28] Molefi Kete Asante, *Kemet, Afrocentricity, and Knowledge* (Trenton, NJ, 1990), 6. On Asante, the 'godfather of Afrocentrism', see esp. Howe, *Afrocentrism*, ch. 17 and Clarence E. Walker, 'Les a posteriori de Molefi K. Asante', in Fauvelle-Aymar *et al.* (eds.), *Afrocentrismes*, 65–77.

[29] Asante, *Kemet*; id., *Afrocentricity* (Trenton, NJ, 1987).

[30] Howe, *Afrocentrism*, 275.

[31] Ibid. 221 f. Jeffries's irresponsible and demagogic insistence on the particular guilt of the Jews for the slave trade provoked detailed criticism from some of the main specialists in the field. See Seymour Drescher, 'The Role of Jews in the Transatlantic Slave Trade', *Immigrants and Minorities*, 12 (1993), 113–25; David Brion Davis, 'The Slave Trade

While it is easy to dismiss the writings of Asante and especially of the representatives of 'wild Afrocentricity' (Howe) like Jeffries as full-blown racism which usually lacks scholarly elements, the work of Martin Bernal, though full of contradictions and also extremely vulnerable to attack, must be taken more seriously. In his truly multi-disciplinary two-volume study entitled *Black Athena*, Bernal, a British specialist on China and Vietnam teaching at Cornell University, argues (very much like Diop) that Greek civilization was heavily indebted to African and Asian influences, primarily to the Egyptians and the Phoenicians.[32] But, unlike Diop and others, and contrary to the expectations suggested by the title *Black Athena*, Bernal focuses mainly on the claim that ancient Greece was an ungrateful, derivative legatee of Egypt's achievements, while he is not so much concerned with the question of whether ancient Egypt was a *black* African civilization. In fact, he treats this question as well as the problematic meanings of 'blackness' and 'race' in rather incoherent ways.[33] Moreover, his archaeological, linguistic, and other evidence, as well as the historiographical framework of his study, have been challenged by different camps.[34] Probably the most serious charge against *Black Athena* and the whole issue of 'Black African Ancient Egypt' was voiced by Kwame Anthony Appiah:

> Yet it seems to me that Diop—whose work is clearly among the best in this tradition—offers little evidence that Egyptian philosophy is more than a systematized but fairly uncritical folk philosophy, makes no

and the Jews', *New York Review of Books*, 22 Dec. 1994, 14–16, reprinted in David Brion Davis, *In the Image of God: Religion, Moral Values, and Our Heritage of Slavery* (New Haven, 2001), 63–72.

[32] Cf. Martin Bernal, *Black Athena: The Afroasiatic Roots of Classical Civilization*, vol. i: *The Fabrication of Ancient Greece* (London, 1987), and vol. ii: *The Archaeological and Documentary Evidence* (London, 1991). Two further volumes have long been promised, but have not yet appeared. Instead the following volume was recently published: Martin Bernal and David Chioni Moore (eds.), *Black Athena Writes Back* (Durham, NC, 2001).

[33] See Howe, *Afrocentrism*, 197 ff.; Robert Young, 'Egypt in America; Black Athena, Racism and Colonial Discourse', in Ali Rattansi and Sallie Westwood (eds.), *Racism, Modernity and Identity: On the Western Front* (Cambridge, 1994), 150–69; Bogumil Jewsiewicki, 'Le primitivisme, le postcolonialisme, les antiquités "nègres" et la question nationale', *Cahiers d'études africaines*, 31 (1991), 191–213.

[34] For a related critique of Bernal see Mary Lefkovitz, *Not out of Africa: How Afrocentrism Became an Excuse to Teach Myth as History* (New York, 1994) and esp. Lefkovitz and Guy MacLean Rogers (eds.), *Black Athena Revisited* (Chapel Hill, 1996); Jacques Berlinerblau, *Heresy in the University: The Black Athena Controversy and the Responsibilities of American Intellectuals* (New Brunswick, 1999). A balanced treatment of Bernal's arguments is provided by Howe, *Afrocentrism*, 193–211.

argument that the Egyptian problematic is that of the contemporary Africa, and allows for a hovering, if inexplicit, suggestion that the Egyptians are important because the originators of the Pharaonic dynasties were black . . . it is absurd to argue that because a thought is African, and the prehistory of thought lies in Africa, that thought will help us to understand Western thought.[35]

All in all, Howe is right to argue that the Afrocentric movement is guilty of reproducing all the central features of the outmoded Euro-racist scholarship, and that it is a symptom of, rather than a cure for, desperate political and economic problems.[36] It obscures rather than emphasizes Africa's role in world history. However, at least in its milder form it reminds us that for more than 150 years 'scientific objectivity' has served to legitimize cultural thefts and historical fictions directly damaging to Africans, and denying the relevance of Africa and Africans for world history.[37]

It would be wrong to reduce the debate about African history and world history to intellectual history. The requirements of global capitalism have pulled Africans into a global labour market for the last five centuries: from the slave plantations in the New World to the transitory black labourers who built railways and worked on other infrastructural projects in the Americas in the second half of the nineteenth century; to the African soldiers who fought (and died) in both world wars and to those Africans who worked in factories in France after 1945; to the current brain drain of African professionals and academics to the West.[38] A fresh look at African diasporas led to a new assessment of the role

[35] Kwame Anthony Appiah, *In My Father's House: Africa in the Philosophy of Culture* (Oxford, 1992), 101.

[36] See Howe, *Afrocentrism*, esp. 1–16.

[37] See MacGaffey, 'Who Owns Ancient Egypt?', 518.

[38] Emmanuel Akyeampong, 'Africans in the Diaspora: The Diaspora and Africa', *African Affairs*, 99 (2000), 186; Joseph Harris, 'Introduction', in id. (ed.), *Global Dimensions of the African Diaspora* (2nd edn.; Washington, DC, 1993), 8 f., distinguishes four phases of the African dispersion: 'The primary stage is the original dispersion out of Africa; the secondary stage occurs with migrations from the initial settlement abroad to a second area abroad; the tertiary stage is movement to a third area abroad; and the circulatory stage involves movements among the several areas abroad and may include Africa.' See generally Darlene Clark Hine and Jacqueline McLeod (eds.), *Crossing Boundaries: Comparative History of Black People in Diaspora* (Bloomington, 1999). More recently, the frequency of migration processes and the easy availability of long-distance means of communication have added a strong dimension of 'translocality' to many local communities in Africa. The rapidly expanding genre of local histories, written and published by non-academic historians, attempts to make sense of these changes. See Axel Harneit-

of Africans in broad inter-regional and inter-continental networks. For instance, recent contributions to the debates concerning the Atlantic slave trade have attacked Eurocentric conceptions of Atlantic history and have emphasized that Africans made a major impact upon certain aspects of culture in the Western hemisphere.[39] Related studies contribute to an understanding of the roles, functions, and influences of Africans in relation to what we recognize as the modern world.[40] John Thornton established the simple but easily forgotten fact that more Africans than Europeans reached the Americas until sometime early in the nineteenth century, and then powerfully stressed the role played by Africans in the construction of the Atlantic economy and the new colonial societies in the Americas.[41] According to Thornton, Africans (or at least African rulers) were creative participants, not passive and helpless victims, in these historical processes. 'We must accept', Thornton writes, 'that African participation in the slave trade was voluntary and under the control of African decision makers. This was not just at the surface level of daily exchange but even at deeper levels.

Sievers (ed.), *A Place in the World: New Local Historiographies from Africa and South Asia* (Leiden, 2002).

[39] For studies which focus on the north Atlantic to the virtual exclusion of the 'black Atlantic' see Bernard Bailyn, 'The Idea of Atlantic History', *Itinerario*, 20 (1996), 19–44; David Hancock, *Citizens of the World: London Merchants and the Integration of the British Atlantic Community, 1735–1785* (Cambridge, 1999). For a more coherent view see Horst Pietschmann, *Geschichte des atlantischen Systems, 1580–1830* (Göttingen, 1998).

[40] The principal revisionist attack on the Eurocentric conception of Atlantic history is Paul Gilroy, *The Black Atlantic: Modernity and Double Consciousness* (London, 1993). However, he approaches this issue from the perspective of the African (intellectual) diaspora; thus Africa figures in his treatment as an object of retrospective discovery, rather than as an active agent. For the development of a more 'Africancentric' perspective see Robin Law and Paul Lovejoy, 'The Changing Dimensions of African History: Reappropriating the Diaspora', in McGrath *et al.* (eds.), *Rethinking African History*, 181–200; Paul Lovejoy, 'Identifying Enslaved Africans in the African Diaspora', in id. (ed.), *Identity in the Shadow of Slavery* (London, 2000), 1–29. However momentous and powerful the experience of the Atlantic diaspora, it is important not to overlook the commencement of Africa's experience of a slave trade and forced migration connected with the Transsaharan slave trade. John Hunwick, 'African Slaves in the Mediterranean World: A Neglected Aspect of the African Diaspora', in *Global Dimensions of the African Diaspora*, 289, writes: 'Beginning some eight centuries before the transatlantic slave trade, and not ending until several decades after the latter was halted, the movement of slaves across the Sahara, up the Nile Valley, and the Red Sea, and across the Indian Ocean to the Persian Gulf and India, probably accounted for the uprooting of as many Africans from their societies as did the transatlantic trade.' See also Robin Cohen, *Global Disaporas: An Introduction* (London, 1997), 34.

[41] John Thornton, *Africa and Africans in the Making of the Atlantic World, 1400–1800* (2nd edn.; Cambridge, 1998).

Europeans possessed no means, either economic or military, to compel African leaders to sell slaves.'[42] The critical role played by African agency in the operation of the Atlantic slave trade is now widely accepted.[43] As regards the enslaved population in the diaspora, Thornton insists upon a high degree of continuity of traditions (such as language, music, dance, and religion) from Africa to the New World.[44] Others have demonstrated the continuous involvement of members of West African coastal communities in trans-oceanic networks. Parts of the area that Europeans called the Slave Coast (the coast of what is today Togo, Benin, and south-western Nigeria) were integrated into the Atlantic world not only by business links, but also by resultant cultural and social ties, on such a scale and intensity that the commercial and ruling élites might be considered to be participating in what may be reasonably termed an 'Atlantic community'.[45]

The twentieth century saw new and complex modes of migration from, to, and within Africa. One interesting case is that of the Soninke, who constituted the majority of the migrants from sub-Saharan Africa to France. François Manchuelle's pioneering study on Soninke labour migration points to the internal dynamics of migration processes.[46] He shows that these migrations

[42] Ibid. 125.

[43] See e.g. Herbert Klein, *The Atlantic Slave Trade* (Cambridge, 1999); David Eltis, *The Rise of African Slavery in the Americas* (Cambridge, 2000); David Eltis and David Richardson (eds.), *Routes to Slavery: Direction, Ethnicity and Mortality in the Atlantic Slave Trade* (London, 1997). See also the articles in *William and Mary Quarterly*, 3rd ser. 58 (2001).

[44] Thornton challenges in particular Sidney W. Mintz and Richard Price, *An Anthropological Approach to the Afro-American Past: A Caribbean Perspective* (Philadelphia, 1976), who have emphasized the culturally deracinating effects of enslavement, transportation, and plantation life. For arguments along Thornton's lines see Law and Lovejoy, 'The Changing Dimensions of African History', 189 ff.; Michael A. Gomez, *Exchanging our Country Marks: The Transformation of African Identities in the Colonial and Antebellum South* (Chapel Hill, 1998); Gwendolyn Midlo Hall, *Africans in Colonial Louisiana: The Development of Afro-Creole Culture in the Eighteenth Century* (Baton Rouge, 1992); Linda Heywood (ed.), *Central Africans and Cultural Transformations in the American Diaspora* (Cambridge, 2002).

[45] Robin Law and Kristin Mann, 'West Africa in the Atlantic Community: The Case of the Slave Coast', *William and Mary Quarterly*, 46 (1999), 307–44. For an intriguing example of some of the dynamics of reconnection between Africa and Africans in the diaspora during the 19th century see J. Lorand Matory, 'The English Professors of Brazil: On the Diasporic Roots of the Yoruba Nation', *Comparative Studies in Society and History*, 41 (1999), 72–103. Another insightful study in this context, mainly dealing with the 20th century, is Philip S. Zachernuk, *Colonial Subjects: An African Intelligentsia and Atlantic Ideas* (Charlottesville, 2000).

[46] François Manchuelle, *Willing Migrants: Soninke Labor Diasporas, 1848–1960* (London, 1997). See also Akyeampong, 'Africans in the Diaspora', 198 f.

were not so much forced by the colonial state through coercive violence and taxation as driven by a search for improved economic options and by the aim of maintaining élite status back at home. In the post-colonial period, numerous African traders, often operating on the margins of the law, developed a truly global network of ethnicity, kinship, religion, and friendship.[47]

Africa's communities have long been open to the world and, as John Lonsdale emphasizes, 'Africans are like the rest of us, shaped by both external and internal relations. They are not unusually disturbed by the threat of cultural cosmopolitanism, however much they suffer the inequalities of international trade.'[48] And as the French political scientist Jean-François Bayart recently reminded us, Africa 'is neither more nor less than part of the planet, and it is pointless to pretend that, to quote one French former colonial governor [Hubert Deschamps], it leads a "traditional existence shielded from the outside world, as though it were another planet", which passively absorbs the shock of having been made dependent on other parts of the world'.[49] The dependency paradigm has long been dominant in historical studies dealing with Africa's position in the world economy. However, it conceded Africans merely a passive role on the stage of world history. Immanuel Wallerstein, for instance, theorizes only the European side of structured, unequal exchange among the elements of what he calls the modern world system and therefore excludes Africa for much of its history as beyond the 'peripheries' of this system. 'What has become hardest to defend about dependency and related theories', Fred Cooper argues, 'is the contention that the poverty of the periphery can be explained by its functionality to the world system as a whole.'[50] The world system/dependency

[47] See Janet MacGaffey and Rémy Bazenguissa-Ganga, *Congo-Paris: Transnational Traders on the Margins of the Law* (Oxford, 2000).

[48] John Lonsdale, 'Globalization, Ethnicity and Democracy: A View from "the Hopeless Continent"', in A. G. Hopkins (ed.), *Globalization in World History* (London, 2002), 195; see also Frederick Cooper, 'What is the Concept of Globalization Good For? An African Historian's Perspective', *African Affairs*, 100 (2001), 189–213.

[49] Jean-François Bayart, 'Africa in the World: A History of Extraversion', *African Affairs*, 99 (2000), 217.

[50] Frederick Cooper, 'Africa and the World Economy', in F. Cooper *et al.*, *Confronting Historical Paradigms: Peasants, Labor, and the Capitalist World System in African and Latin America* (Madison, 1993), 192. Immanuel Wallerstein, *The Modern World System*, vol. i: *Capitalist Agriculture and the Origins of the European World Economy in the Sixteenth Century* (New York,

approach, according to which only structure matters, is increasingly being replaced by arguments like the one put forward by Bayart who, without denying the existence of a relationship of dependence between Africa and the rest of world, argues that 'Africans here have been active agents in the *mise en dépendence* of their societies, sometimes opposing it and at other times joining in it'.[51] Bayart even writes of 'dependence as a mode of action' and attempts to grasp the long and complex history of the relationship between Africa and the world with the term 'extraversion'.[52] In this connection he claims that dependence has often been created by Africans anxious to assert their control over others within their own societies, or, on the other hand, by people seeking to break the domination of those who enjoyed a monopoly of cultural or commercial relations with the external world to the benefit of specific sectors of the population. According to Bayart, 'numerous social groups in Africa have built their strategies on a situation of dependence, and the most successful among them have drawn handsome rents from it, in the form of financial and material benefits'.[53] Examples of attempts to turn external constraints into instruments of domestic political or economic control include, as Bayart points out, participation in different branches of the slave trade controlled by European or Muslim traders, collaboration with colonial powers, the diplomatic and military alliances of the Cold War, and the adoption of the rhetoric of democratization.

While Bayart's trenchant thesis certainly needs to be carefully differentiated historically, his overall argument about African agency in the history of economic relations meets with considerable approval. One example here is the high degree of autonomy of action on the part of African traders during the transition from the slave trade to so-called 'legitimate' commerce during the first

1974), vol. ii: *Mercantilism and the Consolidation of the European World Economy, 1600–1750* (New York, 1980), vol. iii: *The Second Era of Great Expansion of the Capitalist World Economy, 1730–1840s* (New York, 1989). For a critique see Miller, 'History and Africa/Africa and History', 19; Feierman, 'African Histories and the Dissolution of World History', 173.

[51] Jean-François Bayart, *The State in Africa: The Politics of the Belly* (Harlow, 1993; French orig., 1989), 21.

[52] Bayart, 'Africa in the World'.

[53] Jean-François Bayart, 'The Social Capital of the Felonious State or the Ruses of Political Intelligence', in J.-F. Bayart, Stephen Ellis, and Béatrice Hibou, *The Criminalization of the State in Africa* (Oxford, 1999), 43.

two-thirds of the nineteenth century.[54] Another approach, put forward in particular by Frederick Cooper, suggests that Africa's history is characterized, among other things, by the frustrations of would-be exploiters, local and overseas, with the difficulties of tapping the continent's labour power: 'As kings, colonialists, and multinational corporations have learned, Africa's spaces and Africa's social structures have offered powerful means of resistance to control over labour, and the external orientation of African economies is as much a consequence as a cause of the standoffs that repeatedly have taken place in the struggle over the control of work inside Africa.'[55] Elsewhere Cooper argues that 'much of what Africa is up against today—the narrowness of its economic prospects and the denigrating terms in which its future is debated—is not a consequence of "failure" so much as of the partial success of a large number of its people in staving off, appropriating, or deflecting efforts at economic domination'.[56] However, Africa pays a high price for successful resistance to capitalist advance. Part of the price has been its decreasing economic significance. As Ralph Austen pointed out in his seminal *African Economic History*, the continent has become more and more involved in and responsive to global economic trends while at the same time its labour and its products have become less important to the world economy.[57] The other part of the price is the way in which Africa is talked about, and the way in which the people it has given to the rest of the world are talked about: global markets and economic growth are presented by the opinion-makers of Europe and North America as if they were natural phenomena; Africa appears to be a peculiar exception, a continent connected with violence, crime, incompetent government, corruption, unproductive economies, and uncontrolled

[54] A recent case study is Martin Lynn, *Commerce and Economic Change in West Africa: The Palm Oil Trade in the Nineteenth Century* (Cambridge, 1997). For a historiographical overview see Robin Law, 'The Historiography of the Commercial Transition in Nineteenth-Century West Africa', in Falola (ed.), *African Historiography*, 91–115; id., 'Introduction' in R. Law (ed.), *From Slave Trade to 'Legitimate' Commerce: The Commercial Transition in Nineteenth-Century West Africa* (Cambridge, 1995), 1–31.

[55] Cooper, 'Africa and the World Economy', 192.

[56] Frederick Cooper, 'Africa in a Capitalist World', in Hine and McLeod (eds.), *Crossing Boundaries*, 396. Here Cooper takes issue with David Landes, 'Why Are We So Rich and They So Poor?', *American Economic Review*, 80 (1990), 1–13; id., *The Wealth and Poverty of Nations: Why Some Are So Rich and Some So Poor* (New York, 1998).

[57] Ralph A. Austen, *African Economic History: Internal Development and External Dependency* (London, 1987).

population growth. The popular press and some areas of academic social science write Africa off, seeing it as marginal to the future progress of mankind.[58]

Historians attempting today to fit Africa into world history thus have to challenge the widespread thinking which sees Africa as peculiar and other places as normal. While it is useless to counter this essentialist view by claiming the innate superiority of Africans and African-descended peoples, it should be stressed that for a long time, Africans and people for whom Africa is a crucial point of reference have been actors on a world scene. Fred Cooper is, I think, right in claiming that 'Africa's engagement with the rest of the world has been painful and tragic, but the struggles of Africans for one or another form of liberation have, among other things, vitally affected what it means to be "free". Africans have not had an equal voice in determining what "universal" values are, but theirs has been a vital voice nonetheless.'[59]

[58] See Cooper, 'Africa in a Capitalist World', 392–4.

[59] Frederick Cooper, 'Africa's Pasts and Africa's Historians', *Canadian Journal of African Studies*, 34 (2000), 299; see also Lonsdale, 'Globalization, Ethnicity and Democracy'.

11

Provincializing the West: World History from the Perspective of Indian History

VINAY LAL

I. *The World in Indian Thought: Prolegomenon Towards a History*

It is a truism, nevertheless often contested, that for much the greater part of their history Indians, and especially Hindus, never had an interest in writing history or in thinking historically. To admit this is not to surrender to the Hegelian proposition that India had no history to speak of, that it was always outside the orbit of history, nor is it to accept the Orientalist dogma that, lacking a history, the Indians could not be considered a rational people and consequently were bound to be placed almost at the bottom, a notch or two above African savages, in the scale of civilization.[1] Even less should the view that Indians never bothered much with history be associated with those formulations that easily content themselves with a description of the Hindu worldview as rooted in indifference to the 'real' world and 'linear' notions of time. It has been one of the tragedies of recent interpretative work on India that the historian, unable to conceptualize the ahistorical features of the Indian sensibility as anything other than a 'lack', continues to

[1] I am adverting here to the writings of James Mill, Thomas Babington Macaulay, and others, and have discussed this question at much greater length in my paper, 'History and the Possibilities of Emancipation: Some Lessons from India', *Journal of the Indian Council of Philosophical Research*, Special Issue: Historiography of Civilizations (June 1996), 95–135. Macaulay's view might be taken as representative: writing in 1835, in a document which was intended to lay down the colonial government's educational policy, he thought it 'no exaggeration to say, that all the historical information which has been collected from the books written in the Sanscrit language is less valuable than that which may be found in the most paltry abridgments used at preparatory schools in England'. See his 'Minute on Education', reprinted in *Sources of Indian Tradition*, ed. William Theodore de Bary, 2 vols. (New York, 1958), ii. 46.

write the history of the ahistorical in India as a form of prehistory and primitivism.

Considering the supreme indifference of Indians to their own history, one scarcely expects that they would have bothered with the rest of the world or with the enterprise of 'world history'. Indeed, very little thought has been given to understanding what the 'world' may have meant to Indians in the period before the European powers began to make their presence felt in India. Secular Indian intellectuals note with considerable shame that a more or less precise chronology of Indian history begins with the aid of an exogenous source, namely the recording by Greek and Latin writers of Alexander's invasion, so-called, of India in or around 332 BC.[2] This mighty event appears to have made no impression upon Indians, considering that no mention of it is to be found in any Indian text until well into the Christian era; indeed, until the advent of modern historical scholarship, the accounts by the second-century AD historian Arrian continued to be the main source for Alexander's military campaigns in India. At most one might push the beginning of a verifiable chronology to the birth or death of Buddha, but this owes everything to the historical sensibility of the Buddhists rather than the Hindus.[3]

The Arab geographer Alberuni, who was a member of the court of Mahmud of Ghazni and accompanied the invader on at least one of his numerous predatory visits to Hindustan, around AD 1000, was inclined to attribute the poor state of historical and geographical knowledge among Indians to their arrogance, since they believed themselves to be possessed of superior knowledge in every respect.[4] One could even take the view, commonly encountered in the writings of Bernard Lewis, Paul Johnson, Elie Kedourie, David Landes, and other like-minded scholars, that whatever the faults and evils of the West, intellectual curiosity remains the defining characteristic of the European and his descendants.[5] As James Blaut has observed in a recent study of

[2] Harihar Das, 'The past is present. And absent', [Sunday] *Times of India* (11 July 1993), 17.

[3] This point is also made by E. Valentine Daniel, *Charred Lullabies: Chapters in an Anthropography of Violence* (Princeton, 1996), 218 n. 12.

[4] *Alberuni's India*, ed. and trans. Edward C. Sachau (London, 1888; reprinted Delhi, 2 vols. in 1), ii. 10–11.

[5] See e.g. Bernard Lewis, 'The Roots of Muslim Rage', *Atlantic Monthly* (Sept. 1990), 47–54.

prominent Eurocentric historians, there is a 'still widely held belief in the unique "rationality" of Europeans'.[6] Since it has become difficult to defend colonialism, not that the attempt has been altogether abandoned,[7] it is at least possible to say that no civilization ever displayed the insatiable curiosity about the rest of the world that is encountered among the Europeans. Among Hindus, according to the received view, the problem is compounded: curiosity about the rest of the world was positively discouraged, and those who dared to cross the *kala pani* or ocean faced the ostracism of their community. A great many Hindus born in the nineteenth century, none as eminent as Mohandas Gandhi, recorded the consequences of defying the apparent prohibition on overseas travel. Gandhi himself faced the disapprobation of his caste brethren when he insisted upon departing for England to become qualified in law, and was served a writ of excommunication by the caste council of his elders; upon his return to India a few years later, he had to undergo acts of expiation, and even then a segment of his caste community refused to admit him into their midst.[8] In extreme circumstances, where the penalized person refused to display the appropriate signs of repentance and was without the capacity to maintain some degree of financial independence, such outcasting was calculated to jeopardize the purported offender's right to life and livelihood. If travelling was one of the principal modes by means of which knowledge of the world was acquired, then Indians seemed to have disavowed this mode of accessing world history. This representation of Indian social life and intellectual production sits well, of course, with the view that Indian village life had remained largely unaltered over two millennia or more, and that historically Indians never moved very far from their village roots. Vegetating in the teeth of time, as Marx put it, these idyllic village communities would in all likelihood have

[6] J. M. Blaut, *Eight Eurocentric Historians*, vol. 2 of *The Colonizer's Model of the World* (New York, 2000), 16. Andre Gunder Frank, in *ReORIENT: Global Economy in the Asian Age* (Berkeley, 1998), similarly argues that 'Europe did not pull itself up by its own economic bootstraps, and certainly not thanks to any kind of European "exceptionalism" of rationality, institutions, entrepreneurship, technology, geniality, in a word—of race' (p. 4).

[7] David Landes, *The Wealth and Poverty of Nations: Why Some Are So Rich and Some So Poor* (New York, 1998).

[8] M. K. Gandhi, *Autobiography or The Story of My Experiments with Truth* (vol. 1, 1927; vol. 2, 1929; 2nd edn., 2 vols. in 1, Ahmedabad, 1940), 27–30, 65–6.

remained the 'solid foundation of Oriental despotism', restraining the 'human mind within the smallest possible compass', had not the evil genius of the English intervened to put Indian society on the road to history.[9]

It is not sufficient by way of a possible rejoinder to suggest that even in the West, world history finds its first incipient form in the writings of the French encyclopaedists of the late eighteenth century, and that its disciplinary origins can be traced no further back than Spengler and Toynbee. Gibbon never aspired to be a historian of the world; most of the famous British historians, from Hume to Trevelyan and Macaulay, confined their labours largely to British history. Nevertheless, a very substantial body of world travel literature began to emerge in Europe in the sixteenth century, and certainly nothing even remotely resembling it can be found in Indian literature, though Arab history and literature are not so barren in this respect.[10] The Indian merchants living in Moscow in the seventeenth and eighteenth centuries about whom Stephen Dale has written appear not to have penned their observations of Russian society.[11] Even Indian accounts of travels within India are few and far between, and one suspects that the travel narrative of Dean Mahomet, a subaltern officer in the army of the East India Company, derives most of its celebrity from its singular status as an Indian travel narrative of the eighteenth century.[12] Indian historians are indebted to visitors to the country from Central Asia and Europe,[13] and most particularly to Chinese travellers who from

[9] Karl Marx and Friedrich Engels, 'The British Rule in India', in *The First Indian War of Independence 1857–59* (Moscow, 1958), 20. In a subsequent piece, penned over a month later in July 1853, Marx and Engels wrote: 'Indian society has no history at all, at least no known history.' See 'The Future Results of the British Rule in India', ibid. 32.

[10] The Arab historian, al-Masudi, who was born between AD 893 and 898, was widely travelled and visited Spain, Russia, Ceylon, China, Syria, Egypt, and India among other places; five centuries later, Ibn Batuta (1304–1378 ?) would become the most famous traveller of the medieval period. Both left detailed accounts of their visits to India; they, alongside Alberuni, were among the more famous Muslim travellers to India. See Ahmad Shboul, *Al-Mas'udi and His World: A Muslim Humanist and his Interest in Non-Muslims* (London, 1979), and Franz Rosenthal, *A History of Muslim Historiography* (2nd edn.; Leiden, 1968).

[11] Stephen Dale, *Indian Merchants and Eurasian Trade, 1600–1750* (Cambridge, 1994).

[12] Michael H. Fisher (ed.), *The Travels of Dean Mahomet: An Eighteenth-Century Journey Through India*, introduction by the editor (Berkeley, 1997).

[13] There are dozens of well-known European travel narratives of India, but see also Richard Foltz, 'Two Seventeenth-Century Central Asian Travellers to Mughal India', *Journal of the Royal Asiatic Society*, 3rd Series (1996), 367–77.

time to time—most notably, Fa-hien in the fifth century and Hsuan-Tsang (Chwen Chuang) in the seventh century—furnished extensive narratives of their sojourns in India,[14] but I am not aware of any Indian travel narratives of China,[15] much less of any that the Chinese find indispensable for a study of their own history. The supposition that this must be on account of the prohibitions placed upon caste Hindus, to which I have already adverted, must be dispensed with at once. Since at least the thirteenth century, and possibly earlier, Indians were part of a vast trading network that has been described by Janet Abu-Lughod as a pre-European expansion world system.[16] The links between India, China, and South-East Asia went much further back, but, as recent scholarship has indubitably established, trading began to acquire distinct patterns by the eleventh century. 'Indian merchants from the Coromandel [or Tamil] Coast', writes Abu-Lughod, 'were actively journeying eastward in the tenth, eleventh, and twelfth centuries', and twelfth-century Chinese accounts mention pearls, coral, betelnuts, cardamoms, and cotton products among the items that were shipped from the ports which had fallen under Chola suzerainty.[17] The Coromandel ports had been important since almost the beginning of the Christian era. However, if Greek vessels called at these ports often and the Tamilians seldom ventured westwards, it has not much to do with the attribution by E. H. Warmington of a difference between 'western' and 'eastern' minds and energy,[18] but rather with the role of Tamil merchants in making their ports terminals where goods were gathered from afar and from where they were then transported by Greek vessels to the world outside.

With respect to the west coast of India, an even more

[14] Jawaharlal Nehru, in *The Discovery of India* (New Delhi, 1981; 1st edn. 1946), speaks of the 'two-way traffic between India and China', but the Indian monks who travelled took Buddhism to China, and do not appear to have left behind any record of their travels in China (pp. 192–7).

[15] Ibn Batuta spent several years in China in the mid-eighteenth century as the ambasssador of the Sultan of Delhi, but he was an Arab, not an Indian.

[16] Janet L. Abu-Lughod, *Before European Hegemony: The World System A.D. 1250-1350* (New York, 1989).

[17] Ibid. 269.

[18] E. H. Warmington, *Commerce Between the Roman Empire and India* (2nd rev. and enlarged edn.; New Delhi, 1974), 6, as cited by R. Champakalakshmi, *Trade, Ideology and Urbanization: South India 300 BC to AD 1300* (Delhi, 1996), 180.

dramatic story can be told of Indian merchants and their reach to the outside world. Amitav Ghosh has evoked the world of the west-coast merchant and his place in the Indian Ocean trading network with extraordinary subtlety in *In an Antique Land*,[19] which Ghosh was prompted to write after he chanced upon a letter written in AD 1139 by a merchant, Khalaf ibn Ishaq, then resident of Aden, to a fellow merchant by the name of Abraham Ben Yiju, who made his home in Mangalore, north of Calicut and Cochin. The twelfth-century documents with which Ghosh began to work furnish us with arresting traces of the hybridity of language and dialect, the written and the spoken word, Hebrew and Arabic, and Muslims, Hindus, and Jews: that world begins to look more cosmopolitan and fluid than the late twentieth century, yet another reminder that the postmodern may well have prefigured the modern. Ben Yiju's trading partners included Arabs, Persians, Tulus, Gujarati Banias, and Ismailis, and Ghosh states with prescience that 'in matters of business, Ben Yiju's networks appear to have been wholly indifferent to many of those boundaries that are today thought to mark social, religious and geographical divisions'. The world inhabited by the Indian Ocean traders was indeed very expansive.[20]

Remarkable as is the story narrated by Ghosh, it is well to remember that the locus of action there is the south-west or Malabar coast of India, and that further north, in the promontory bordered by the Gulf of Kutch and the Gulf of Cambay, Gujarati merchants had long since acquired those trading instincts, business acumen, and sailing skills which had carried them to the Middle East, the Mediterranean, and the east coast of Africa, and which are still in ample evidence today as one ponders over the contemporary spread of the Gujarati diaspora.[21] Classical sources suggest that Gujarati merchants may have been present in Egypt in remote antiquity, and their presence in the ports of the Persian Gulf and the Red Sea, along the Arabian littoral, and on the east coast of Africa, where there seems to be some evidence of Indian settlements from around

[19] Amitav Ghosh, *In an Antique Land* (New Delhi; London, 1992; New York, 1993).

[20] Compare K. N. Chaudhuri, *Asia before Europe: Economy and Civilisation of the Indian Ocean from the Rise of Islam to 1750* (Cambridge, 1990).

[21] For one contemporary popular account of the Patels among the Gujarati diaspora, see Steve Zwick, 'Who Are All These Patels?', *Reader* [Chicago] 29, no. 19 (11 Feb. 2000), 1, 28–31.

the tenth century, is well documented. By the late Middle Ages, they appear to have gained dominance in the trade with East Africa, and obtained control over the ports in the opposite part of India, that is along the Coromandel coast. Melaka [Malacca], which Sanjay Subrahmanyam describes as 'perhaps the most conspicuous port-city and state created in the fifteenth century', was dominated politically by the Gujaratis until the late fifteenth century, and he has no hesitation in terming Gujarat the 'linch-pin of the western Indian Ocean trade'.[22] One can reasonably conjecture that the Gujarati merchants, characterized as a 'forgotten thalassocracy', left their imprint upon large parts of the portion of the world that seemed to matter before Europeans became ascendant, and that they knew a great deal about this world. One does not hear of any caste prohibitions among Gujarati Hindus and Jains which constrained their travels, and the adverse consequences of violating caste norms by overseas travel seem to bear an inextricable relationship to the advent of European colonialism in India, rather than being grounded in what is presumed to be the intrinsic conservatism of the Hindus.

The Indian Ocean trade, and the long history of maritime, political, and cultural relations of India with south-east Asia, eastern Africa, the Persian Gulf, and the Mediterranean, suggest that India was admirably open to the 'world' before the arrival of Europeans. But Indian civilization clearly furnished other pretexts for arriving at some conception of the 'world'. Buddhism, let us recall, was already a 'world religion' before Christianity had been born, and it is emissaries from India who first took the teachings of Buddhism to China, Sri Lanka, and south-east Asia. It is no exaggeration to speak of a Buddhist network, of which India was a principal nodal point before the precipitous decline of Buddhism in the land of its birth in the latter part of the first millennium. An even more arresting conception of India's engagement with the 'world' is suggested by one Indologist's formulation of what he terms the 'Sanskrit Cosmopolis' from AD 300 to AD 1300. The immense temporal magnitude of this 'cultural formation in the premodern world' is

[22] Sanjay Subrahmanyam, 'Of Imarat and Tijarat: Asian Merchants and State Power in the Western Indian Ocean, 1400 to 1750', *Comparative Studies in Society and History* 37/4 (Oct. 1995), 757, 763.

matched by its transregional geographic reach: as Sheldon Pollock notes, in the greater part of the area from Gandhara in present-day Afghanistan to as far east as Annam (south Vietnam) and central Java, Sanskrit became the premier instrument of political and public expression. Though the imperial work performed by other cosmopolitan languages such as Latin, Arabic, Persian, and Chinese is well recognized, Sanskrit also created its own world, a 'new kind of vast zone of cultural interaction, what some might name an ecumene'.[23] Much like the Gujarati thalassocracy, the Sanskrit Cosmopolis remains an immensely complex and comparatively little known world cultural formation.

II. *Europe as the Lodestar of History: The Diminishing Horizons of 'World History' in Colonial India*

In so far as they do think about the 'world', even Indian intellectuals who pride themselves on their repudiation of provincialism have habituated themselves to the idea of a bi-polar world of India and the West. This is the condition of colonized people everywhere, and in recent years the idea of the 'West' itself has, among some segments of the population, become reduced to 'America'—or to what are commonly perceived as appendages of America, such as Australia and Canada. (Indeed, middle-class Indians view Australia and Canada as America without the infernal problems of America, but we need not be detained by these considerations.) Nor should one ascribe this view merely to the great unwashed, the aspiring middle classes in the underdeveloped world, and the intellectually uninitiated, since this tendency is commonly found among the overwhelming majority of those scholars who describe themselves as comparativists. The field of 'comparative history' means, in general, little more than contrasting India with Europe, or Latin America with Europe, or Africa with Europe, or China with Europe and America. Europe or the West is the constant reference point in such endeavours, and the scholar's nationality or geographic specialization, usually in a

[23] Sheldon Pollock, 'The Sanskrit Cosmopolis, 300–1300: Transculturation, Vernacularization, and the Question of Ideology', in Jan E. M. Houben (ed.), *Ideology and Status of Sanskrit: Contributions to the History of the Sanskrit Language* (Leiden, 1996), 199.

single country or small region, generally provides the other pole of study. The subaltern historians of India, who have acquired a reputation for their theoretical sophistication, the range of their intellectual interests, and their rigorous critique of the political and social structures of colonialism, predictably deploy the intellectual findings of Foucault, Barthes, Derrida, Gramsci, and others in their work; but even the monographs that are cited are almost invariably drawn from the field of European history.[24] Some comparative historians have, obviously, gone so far as to consider India in relation to Africa in 1900, or to contrast decolonization in India and Indonesia, but in such instances the frame is self-evidently furnished by European colonialism. It is not altogether surprising that the broadest comparative framework, outside the work of those immersed in world systems theory and the histories of the trading worlds of the Mediterranean and the Indian Ocean, is still entertained by scholars who work in the history of the British or French empires, as though the mandate of the now deceased empires had passed down to the scholarly caretakers of these empires.

There is nothing in the history of India before the period of European expansion which would enable us to understand how the Indian conception of the world gradually became so narrow as to exclude all but Europe. India had maritime relations with large parts of the world for several centuries before the Portuguese arrived on the west coast five hundred years ago, and I have not even made any reference so far to the extensive land relations with China, central Asia, and west Asia. Yet, as I have suggested, it is not Indians alone who are predisposed to thinking of their history as largely inconsequential and stagnant in the extended period that, following the model of European history, is referred to as 'medieval'. As one Japanese historian has written:

> the majority of Japanese even today believe that the politico-cultural universe of the Edo period was fundamentally determined by the closure of the country. They also think that the opening of Japan can be reduced to the development of exchanges with the West, following the birth of the Meiji regime. It is hard for them to imagine that Japan

[24] For greater elaboration of some of these points, see Vinay Lal, 'Subaltern Studies and Its Critics: Debates over Indian History', *History and Theory*, 40 (February 2001), 135–48.

developed in relation with other Asian countries, since they are hardly used to appreciating Asian cultures.[25]

The narratives which posit, as Sanjay Subrahmanyam says, 'a surprisingly static vision of Asia before the European impact' will become increasingly hard to sustain.[26] Consequently, it is necessary to revisit the proposition, which has nothing behind it but colossal ignorance, that whatever the evils of colonialism, it had the salutary effect of bringing India out of the morass of degradation and stagnation into which it had sunk and opening it to the energizing and uplifting winds of the West. Multiculturalists will make a virtue even of colonialism.

The integration of India into the orbit of world history and the Euro-American modern world system cannot be said to have begun on an auspicious note. In the late fifteenth century, the Arab and Indian hegemony over the Western Indian Ocean trade networks was effectively contested by the Portuguese. Had the Portuguese incursion into Indian territories merely signified the replacement of one set of hegemons by another hegemonic power, there might have been nothing to bemoan the arrival of the Europeans. Such was the cosmopolitanism of India's west-coast traders—Bohras, Ismailis, Jains, Parsis, Armenians, various Hindu castes, Moplahs, Arabs, among others—that the presence of a new element in the trading zones would have been scarcely noticed, but for the fact that the Portuguese, unlike all the other parties to the trading network, refused to abide by the tacit understanding that, notwithstanding the occasional acts of piracy that took place in the Indian Ocean, the various nations would not attack the ships of competing parties. On the other hand, in the Mediterranean, Abu-Lughod remarks, 'a perpetual state of naval warfare existed from the ninth century onward, and commercial ships, therefore, always traveled in military conveys'.[27] This is the world that the Portuguese inhabited; this is the world that they sought to bequeath to Indians, as enlightened Europe's first gift to the underdeveloped East. Purveyors of

[25] Yuko Tanaka, 'Le Monde comme représentation symbolique: Le Japan de l'époque d'Edo et l'univers du mitate', *Annales, Historie, Sciences Sociales,* 50/2 (1995), 281, cited by Sanjay Subrahmanyam, 'Connected Histories: Notes towards a Reconfiguration of Early Modern Eurasia', *Modern Asian Studies* 31/3 (July 1997), 735.

[26] Subrahmanyam, 'Connected Histories', 741.

[27] Abu-Lughod, *Before European Hegemony*, 275.

an impoverished worldview and morality, the Portuguese imagined that Indians were similarly bereft of civilized norms of behaviour. Not only did the Portuguese claim the sole right to navigate the seas, they interdicted the ships of the Zamorin or ruler of Calicut, shelled the coast with artillery fire, and took hostages to ensure their safe passage. In the severe but not unreasonable judgement of the notable historian K. M. Pannikar, 'the Portuguese [in India] recognized no principle save that of strength', and their singular contribution to Indian society appears to have been to introduce a new threshold of cruelty and barbarous conduct. They certainly had no goods to offer to the Indians. 'The Portuguese of the 16th and the 17th centuries', Pannikar states boldly, 'had nothing to teach the people of India except improved methods of killing people in war and the narrow feeling of bigotry in religion.'[28]

Though the British assiduously and with considerable success sought to cultivate the view that an exceptional divide obtained between them and the Portuguese, in the history of the Indian encounter with the Portuguese lies the template, admittedly with some modifications, for all histories of European expansion in India. If the Portuguese assumed the Indian Ocean trade was subject to the same forms of terror and lawlessness that prevailed in the Mediterranean, so the British, accustomed to endemic religious warfare in Europe, presumed that relations between Muslims and Hindus were unfailingly characterized by unremitting hostility and violence. They even inferred a corporate 'Hindu' identity when one scarcely existed. Doubtless, there were instances of Hindu–Muslim animosity, and the Portuguese must have deemed themselves fortunate to find in the king of Vijayanagar a ruler who shared their disdain and hatred for Muslims;[29] but this is not the same as averring that Hindus and Muslims had been set on a path of mutual destruction since Islam established itself in India. However, from the standpoint of ascertaining how it is that the Indian conception of the world was so radically diminished, it is the British triumph of arms in the mid-eighteenth century which bears the closest resemblance

[28] K. M. Panikkar, *Malabar and the Portuguese, Being a History of the Relations of the Portuguese with Malabar from 1500 to 1663* (Bombay, 1929), 170–1, 212. Ch. 1 of the author's better-known *Asia and Western Dominance* (London, 1953), 21–54, appears to be a highly condensed but revised version of the earlier book.

[29] Panikkar, *Asia and Western Dominance*, 31.

to the Portuguese ascendancy in the Malabar coast. It is comforting for Indian nationalists to suppose that the Indians had no answer to the naval guns of the Portuguese or to the firepower that the East India Company could command in the mid-eighteenth century, and that the technological prowess of the Europeans in each instance assured their victory. Nehru was inclined to attribute European triumphs to their superior administrative and bureaucratic skills;[30] others have pointed to the repeated inability of Indians to present a united front of resistance against the encroachments of foreigners, and the presence of 'collaborators' among their ranks. Both the English and the Portuguese, as is commonly known, found Indian allies. Yet the accounts call for a radical revisionism, and both in Malabar and Bengal we are confronted with all the signs of the defeat of a pluralistic and syncretistic civilization by a nation-state that acted with the singular intent characteristic of all parochial political formations. No previous political power in India had the ambition to cast Indian society entirely into the mould of its own choosing; none presumed to act with the complete confidence that its own history was the only worthwhile history; and certainly none so systematically deployed social engineering, derived from a mechanistic conception of the world, permanently to 'fix' the nature of Indian society.

The details of British ascendancy and expansionism in India need not be rehearsed here, except to point to the consequences of the spread of British institutions and the ideology of imperialism for India's relations with the rest of the 'world'. There was not much of a 'world' to speak of, since British rule appears to have had the effect of erasing the consciousness of India's earlier, more democratic, and certainly more complex engagement with Asia. The most remarkable part of the story, namely the near excision from Indian memory of links to other parts of the globe, and the suspension of other civilizational dialogues, has seldom been told. The received view, to the contrary, is that as Indian élites in the nineteenth century begin to make their way to England, and on occasion to other parts of Europe, their conception of the world was immeasurably expanded. One cannot doubt that this brought them to an awareness of their

[30] See, in particular, the discussion in Jawaharlal Nehru, *The Discovery of India* (Delhi, 1946), 276-81.

own abhorrent social practices and the immense limitations of their social worlds, just as it opened them up to more vigorous and sustained traditions of learning and intellectual enquiry. By the late nineteenth century, the cream of the modern Indian intelligentsia in Bengal, where the British presence had been most dramatically and effectively institutionalized, was being educated in Britain, and it is to this period that the first substantive accounts of life in Britain by Indians can be dated.[31] But it is just as indubitably clear that educated Indians—and Bengalis in particular—resolutely refused to look beyond Britain and Europe, and their intellectual outlook appears to have been shorn of any reference to India's numerous civilizational pasts, including those pasts which had been dialoguing with Africans, Malays, Chinese, Persians, Afghans, Turks, and numerous others for several centuries. It is the crushing defeat inflicted upon Russia by Japan in 1905 that, for instance, seems to have first brought Japan into the orbit of Indian intellectual and political life. The 'extremists' among the Indian nationalists, as the British described them, imbibed from Japan's triumph the lesson that a nation-state that acted with determination and the force of arms could earn a place in world history. Indian nationalists are still acting out this scenario, as the resurgency of Hindu militancy and India's attempt to earn a place in the 'nuclear club' suggest, but that story cannot be told here.

This evacuation of the 'world' from world history was all the more complete because the mantle for the supposed reawakening of India fell upon the Bengalis. For nearly 150 years, before the British shifted their capital to Delhi in 1911, and before Gandhi subtly effected a change in the politics of the Indian National Congress that would have the effect of considerably mitigating the impact of Bengal upon nationalist politics, the

[31] There is a longer history of Indian visitors to Britain, first documented by Harihar Das, 'The Early Indian Visitors to England', *Calcutta Review*, 3rd Series, 13 (1924), 83–114; a more extended account is to be found in Rozima Visram, *Ayahs, Lascars and Princes: Indians in Britain 1700–1947* (London, 1986), and Shampa Lahiri, *Indians in Britain: Anglo-Indian Encounters, Race and Identity, 1880–1930* (London, 2000). For the twentieth century, one can turn to other (largely untapped) documents in an effort to understand what Europe and the wider 'world' may have meant to Indians. I have in mind, for instance, the thousands of letters written home by some of the million Indian soldiers who served in Europe, the Middle East, and elsewhere. For a selection of this correspondence, see David Omissi (ed.), *Indian Voices of the Great War: Soldiers' Letters, 1914–18* (Hampshire, NY, 1999).

political, social, and intellectual life of the country was largely centred upon Bengal. In the waning part of the nineteenth century, various centres of intellectual activity and political resistance began to emerge in present-day Maharashtra, but the hegemony of Bengal is not questioned by historians. Though Bengal had a syncretistic culture,[32] the Bengalis could not claim on behalf of themselves that history of inter-Asian relations, much less relations with Africa, that had so decisively shaped the cultures of India's west coast. Moreover, there was almost nothing to mediate the resounding and totalizing impact of British institutions and intellectual practices upon them. Bengal's encounter with Europe, in other words, produced anxieties from which the Gujaratis and other people of the west coast had been largely free. It is these anxieties that have determined the contours of Bengali modernity from the time of Rammohan Roy and Bankimchandra Chatterji in the nineteenth century down to Nirad Chaudhuri, who dedicated his autobiography to Pax Britannica with the observation that it had given Indians the only taste of political and intellectual freedom they had ever known,[33] and R. C. Majumdar, the doyen of the previous generation of Indian historians, who dedicated one of his works 'To the Memory of BENGAL THAT WAS by One who Has the Misfortune to Live in BENGAL THAT IS While the CROAKING AHOM [Assamese] FROGS Kicked with Impunity the DYING BENGAL ELEPHANT and the PEOPLE AND GOVERNMENT OF INDIA Merely Looked On'.[34] For at least six generations, Bengali modernizers have behaved as though the world revolved around Calcutta and England; and since the advent of mass air transportation, the tendency to bypass the rest of the world has received much encouragement. One suspects that often before the Bengali is even a Bengali he is an Anglophile.

In this respect as in many others, Gandhi, a figure of disdain among the great majority of Bengali intellectuals, may have been closer to the truth when he once remarked that

[32] Richard Eaton, *The Rise of Islam and the Bengal Frontier, 1204–1760* (Berkeley, 1993); Asim Roy, *The Islamic Syncretic Tradition in Bengal* (Princeton, 1983).

[33] Nirad Chaudhuri, *The Autobiography of an Unknown Indian* (Berkeley, 1957).

[34] R. C. Majumdar, *Glimpses of Bengal in the Nineteenth Century* (Calcutta, 1960), upper case in the original. I am grateful to Dipesh Chakrabarty for drawing my attention to this work.

Rammohan Roy was, in the long timespan of Indian history, something of a 'pygmy'.[35] His remark outraged most Bengalis, who have been accustomed to viewing Rammohan as the 'Father of Modern India', but the entire question of the Bengal Renaissance, as it is customarily described, must be revisited if we are to understand how Rammohan, while doubtless initiating the 'great awakening', led Indians into another kind of slumber. The present generation of scholars who have habituated themselves to the task of finding Orientalist traces in the writings of Indian nationalists have predictably found in Rammohan the makings of an Orientalist, but that is scarcely the most objectionable part of Rammohan's intellectual legacy. Even someone with Rammohan's intellectual perspicacity and sensitivity scarcely understood the encumbrances he had placed upon himself, and his followers and admirers, whether in Bengal or elsewhere, are scarcely inclined to renew India's conversations with cultures outside the West.

It is surely no accident that of the three Indians who in the previous one hundred years most inhabited an expansive conception of the world—Gandhi, Tagore, and Nehru—none embraced the course of what I have described as Bengali modernity. The Bengalis never let Gandhi forget that he was a Gujarati *bania*, but he had little use for their jejune enthusiasm for Britain and Europe. He alone was singularly unimpressed by the claims advanced on behalf of industrial civilization, and as for the much-vaunted lessons of history, he resolutely held on to the view that European history was wholly uninspiring for anyone who was dedicated to the principles of *ahimsa* (non-violence). In a characteristic moment, Gandhi had written: 'I believe that a nation is happy that has no history.'[36] The case for Nehru is perhaps less easily argued, when we consider that, with respect to the intellectual and material progress made by the West, he apparently believed that India would do well to industrialize rapidly, worship at the altar of science, and shape a society in accordance with rational principles of social organization. Yet Nehru had an extraordinarily ecumenical conception

[35] Gandhi in *Young India*, 13 Apr. 1921, in *The Collected Works of Mahatma Gandhi*, 100 vols. (New Delhi, 1958–94), xix. 477.

[36] M. K. Gandhi, 'My Jail Experiences–XI', *Young India* (11 Sept. 1924), reprinted in *The Collected Works of Mahatma Gandhi*, xxv. 128.

of the world, one scarcely encountered among his peers in the West, or even among contemporary secular Indian intellectuals, much less the Hindutvavadis. His *Glimpses of World History*,[37] a rambling and labyrinthine account of the world written as a series of letters to his daughter Indira, roves over the entire world, and neither Europe nor even India is privileged in that narrative.[38] Nehru's foreign policy, likewise, was intended to steer India away from the Euro-American nexus, and his advocacy of non-alignment, which is conventionally seen purely as an expression of his desire that India should not be a party to the Cold War, must be viewed in relation to his ambition to resuscitate and strengthen those civilizational links that India had had in the past with Asia and Africa. Nehru also, let us remind ourselves, hailed from Kashmir—here India met with Afghanistan and central Asia; and here Sufism, Buddhism, Tantrism, and Shaivism together pointed to a pluralistic conception of the world long before that possibility had even been entertained in most other places. As for Tagore, his work offers a deep engagement with the folk, the non-modern, and the ahistorical; it manifests a deep encrusting in the Indian mythos. Though the Bengali middle classes hold Tagore in deep veneration, they have largely ignored his discourses on the profoundly violent course of Western civilization.[39]

III. *Incommensurability and the Future of World History*

The prospects for the writing of world history in India cannot be described as promising or healthy. There is clearly no precedent for such an enterprise, but that can be no reason for disowning the attempt. The difficulties, this essay endeavours to suggest, run much deeper and can be put forth baldly as a set of simple propositions. The Indian sensibility is largely ahistorical, and the greater number of Indians still do not converse in the language

[37] Jawaharlal Nehru, *Glimpses of World History: Being Further Letters to his Daughter, Written in Prison, and Containing a Rambling Account of History for Young People* (London, 1934; reprinted New Delhi, 1982).

[38] For a more detailed discussion of this point, see Vinay Lal, 'Nehru as a Writer', *Indian Literature*, no. 135 (Jan.–Feb. 1990), 20-46, esp. 23-31.

[39] The hagiography by Krishna Dutta and Andrew Robinson, *Rabindranath Tagore: The Myriad-Minded Man* (New York, 1996), misses all the contradictions and ambivalences.

of history; moreover, the recourse to historical records, and from thence to scientized history, may well be calculated, as the dispute over the Babri Masjid showed, to aggravate social and political tensions, particularly when historical discourse shows itself incapable of accommodating faith and religiosity. However, since historical thinking is clearly ascendant among the middle classes, some may see there an opening for world history. Considering that the interpretation of Indian history is at long last largely an Indian affair, dominated by schools in Delhi and Calcutta rather than by historians in Britain or the USA, Indian historians may well feel emboldened to widen their canvas. There is already, for example, a substantial body of Indian historians whose work focuses on French and Russian history. But does that take us any closer to world history?

The conception of the 'world' to which Indians subscribed narrowed after British dominion over India was established, and the process greatly accelerated under the modernizing tendencies associated at first with the Bengal Renaissance, and subsequently with the embrace of the paradigms of Western modernity, including the ideas of the nation-state, development, and big science, by most of the nationalist intelligentsia. Some might argue that a greater awareness in recent years of the far-flung Indian diaspora has at least the potential to widen the notion of the 'world' held by middle-class Indians, though it is telling that the Indian diaspora began to evoke the interest of Indian scholars mainly after Indians in the Anglo-American world began to acquire influence and the affluence of the Indian Americans became evident. Had the Indian diasporic population been confined to Fiji, Mauritius, Trinidad, and other largely 'inconsequential' places, it is doubtful whether the Indian diaspora would have become as large and respectable a field of study as it is now poised to become. There is nothing on the horizon to suggest, then, that a world history under Indian dispensation would not become, as it generally does everywhere, a history of the West energizing the rest of the world, with doubtless some appropriate digressions on the greatness of the Indian past.

My own wish is to advance the much stronger argument that, at least in the present circumstances, the enterprise of world history, from whatever angle it is attempted, must be disowned and repudiated. This is not for the reasons commonly advanced against the professional study of world history, extending from the unusual demands it makes upon its practitioners, such as fluency in a number of (preferably diverse) languages, to the superficial generalizations to which world histories are often prone. I have sufficiently interrogated, from the perspective of Indian civilization, the terms 'world' and 'history' to show the difficulties that lie ahead in the way of Indians who would wish to write world histories. There is, of course, a considerable body of literature, drawn from social history, anthropology, sociolinguistics, and folklore, to suggest why 'writing' is not merely an innocuous form of representation. Oral cultures still predominate in most of India, and, as A. K. Ramanujan's work suggests, Indian folklore displays evidently counter-hegemonic tendencies, rejecting and even mocking commonly accepted notions of caste hierarchy and the supposed learning of the Brahmins.[40] Indeed, it is no exaggeration to say that writing is as much associated with history as orality is with myth, though our understanding of this must be immensely complicated by the awareness that Indian myths are grounded in a body of written literature just as history has traditionally lacked a written corpus. Are those who write world history attentive to the hermeneutics of writing? Under what circumstances does history become a mode of forgetting? What do we begin to understand of history when we also view it as a mode of obliterating certain pasts and homogenizing the future? The most popular and still dominant models of world history, which take as their centrepiece the history of Europe and the history of Europe's impact upon the rest of the world, foreclose the various pasts of people, those pasts which are resistant to the designs of an encroaching modernity which claims a singular universality for itself. The lesser developed, let us recall, have not yet arrived at the year 2000; by the time they do so, those who are now part of the present wave of globalization will have moved on to yet loftier planes. As far as I am able to judge, 'world history' informs the greater part of the people in the world that the only history they have is to catch up to someone else's history, or else they themselves will become history. Such a history has every potential to be a form of

[40] Introduction by Stuart Blackburn and Alan Dundes to section on folklore in Vinay Dharwadker (ed.), *The Collected Essays of A. K. Ramanujan* (New Delhi, 1993), 349.

'cultural genocide', politically disempowering, and destructive of the ecological plurality of knowledges and lifestyles.

Clearly, we must ask who we write world histories for, and with what intent. Like a great many enterprises which are conceived with at least partly a noble impulse—and doubtless that is how many of its practitioners think of it, fired by the desire to expand the contours of historical knowledge, encourage multicultural education, understand the diverse modes through which culture is expressed, and so forth—world history presents itself as an endeavour to increase what in popular parlance is called 'cross-cultural understanding'. To be sure, one can use more elevated language to describe its ambitions, from the comprehension of history as a form of conflict resolution to an awareness of history as a celebration of diversity.[41] I have no doubt that world history will even begin to be used, if that day has not already dawned, as part of what in management circles is known as 'diversity training'. In the present state of affairs, keeping in mind the enormous inequities in the world system, the vastly different conditions under which research is conducted and produced in the North and the South, and the dominance of modern knowledge systems, there can be no more desirable outcome than to reduce the contact between cultures and reject certain kinds of conversations. In the totalizing conditions of modern knowledge, perhaps best encapsulated now in the primacy accorded to historical knowledge, the intellectual and political imperative—from the standpoint at least of a civilization such as that of India which on the ground has always been pluralistic—must remain one of increasing incommensurability. To deny the South this choice, to compel it to enter the stream of world history whose teleological centre is the Euro-American world, would be the clearest sign of a resurgent colonialism masquerading as ecumenism.

[41] One of the most eminent practitioners of world history, reflecting on his long engagement with world history, recently wrote of it: 'I commend it to you as a worthy and fascinating pursuit, apt for our age, and practically useful inasmuch as a clear and vivid sense of the whole human past can help to soften future conflicts by making clear what we all share.' See William H. McNeill, 'The Changing Shape of World History', in Philip Pomper, Richard H. Elphick, and Richard T. Vann (eds.), *World History: Ideologies, Structures, and Identities* (Oxford, 1998), 40.

12

The 'Middle Kingdom' Struggles to Survive: The Chinese Worldview in the Nineteenth Century

RICARDO K. S. MAK

I. *Introduction: Old Visions in a Changing World*

It is widely believed that the Chinese conception of the world order took shape at about the time of the Qin dynasty (221 BC–207 BC) when China, most of whose inhabitants were Han people, achieved political and cultural unity. According to this conception, the Chinese Emperor or *tianzi* (the Son of Heaven), who possessed superior moral and intellectual qualities, ruled not only the Chinese, but also the *tianxia* (universe). In fact, he administered the huge empire with help from a group of scholar-officials, while the royal family and its favourites occupied a number of fiefs. Externally, the universal overlord of China felt compelled to civilize the peripheral barbarians. Some of these peoples, who had earlier been conquered by the Chinese, gradually became China's internal vassals, while many seeking trade with China paid regular tribute to the Chinese Emperor, who in return gave them gifts and protection. Until the mid-nineteenth century, China saw this tributary system as universally valid. Even Europeans such as the Portuguese, who came to China in the sixteenth century for business purposes, were believed to be paying tribute to the Son of Heaven.[1] For this reason, in 1793 when Lord Macartney refused to kowtow in front of Emperor Qianlong, he was accused of not 'observing the appropriate procedures and ceremonies in their contact with the Son of Heaven'.[2] Geographically and culturally,

[1] John King Fairbank, 'A Preliminary Framework', in id. (ed.), *The Chinese World Order: Traditional China's Foreign Relations* (Cambridge, Mass., 1968), 4–11.

[2] Yen-ping Hao and Wang Er-min, 'Changing Chinese Views of Western Relations, 1840-1895', in *The Cambridge History of China,* vol. xi: *Late Ching,* ed. John King Fairbank and Liu Kwangching (Cambridge, 1980), 144.

China was closer to East and South-East Asian countries such as Korea and Vietnam. Inner Asian peoples were sometimes China's allies but sometimes its foes. The Mongolians, for instance, rode into China in 1234 and ruled the Han people in the next century. China and Europe, situated at the two ends of the Eurasian continent, had little direct contact in premodern times.[3]

Growing contact with the European nations since the late Ming dynasty (1368–1644) had forced the Chinese scholar-officials to adjust their worldview. Understanding the contemporary world, especially the European nations which were undergoing tremendous economic, intellectual, and technological changes, became an urgent task after the Opium War (1839–41), in order to revive the declining 'Middle Kingdom'. In fact, the changing cultural climate of the first quarter of the nineteenth century allowed them to look outside China from a new perspective. Leading Chinese thinkers of the nineteenth century, who were becoming impatient with the *hanxue* (Han learning) that had imprisoned Chinese literati in pedantic and apolitical philological studies since the early Qing dynasty (1644–1912), revived the *jingshi* (statecraft) developed by late Ming great scholars such as Gu Yanwu (1613–82) and Huang Zongsi (1610–95), but were silenced by the Manchu rulers. New generations of Chinese intellectuals who emphasized the uses of administrative competence endeavoured to rediscover the utilitarian side of Confucianism. They came to believe that the search for wealth and power, and the upholding of Confucian ethical principles, were the two most important elements of Confucian Orthodoxy.

It is true that 'blind xenophobia arose early and recurred sporadically over local issues, and a great deal of cultural pride continued to exist' in mid-nineteenth-century China.[4] Yet the new philosophical trend of the mid-nineteenth century that divided the Chinese tradition into a changeable and an unchangeable side left room for Chinese intellectuals to reconsider China's relations with the West.[5] For instance, the debate

[3] Frederick Wakeman, Jr., *The Fall of Imperial China* (New York, 1975), 112–13.

[4] Liu Kwangching, 'The Nineteenth Century', in Ho Ping-ti and Tang Tsou (eds.), *China in Crisis: China's Heritage in the Communist Political System*, 2 vols. (Chicago, 1968), i. 94.

[5] Philip Yuen-sang Leung, 'The Tragic Passage to a New World: The Changing Views and Attitudes of Chinese Intellectuals toward the West in the Nineteenth Century', in Philip Yuen-sang Leung and Edwin Pak-wah Leung (eds.), *Modern China in Transition: Studies in Honor of Immanuel C. Y. Hsu* (Claremont, Calif., 1995), 18–20.

over *ti* (substance) and *yong* (function), *ben* (ends) and *mo* (means), and *li* (metaphysical substance) and *qi* (physical substance) led to the conclusion that knowledge beyond the Chinese tradition, though still inferior in nature, could contribute to the revival of the Chinese civilization. Zhang Zhidong's (1837–1909) slogan 'Chinese learning as the *ti*, Western learning as the *yong*', was one of the best expressions of this new attitude.

The political and economic conditions and ideological foundations for China's modernization slowly emerged in the mid-nineteenth century. More liberal intellectuals opened their eyes to the outside world and tried to relocate China in the international context. Secure in the faith that knowledge derived from the outside world could rejuvenate the declining empire without disturbing the traditional order, they began to study regions and nations that their ancestors had overlooked or despised for centuries. The first group of Chinese intellectuals, represented by Lin Zexu (1785–1850) and Wei Yuan (1794–1856), adhered to the principle 'learning the techniques of the barbarians, in order to control the barbarians'. On the other hand Guo Songtao (1818–91) and Xue Fucheng (1838–94), who knew the European powers better, had to admit with a mixture of fear and joy about three decades later that the expansion of Western civilization was no longer resistible. At the turn of the twentieth century Wang Tao's (1828–90) and Yan Fu's (1854–1921) optimism turned into pessimism. They claimed, in a Darwinian tone, that nations on earth, advanced or backward, were now caught in a struggle for survival in which only the strongest could continue to exist.

II. *Fending off Western Penetration: Lin Zexu and Wei Yuan*

Lin Zexu, who led the Chinese army against the British in the Opium War, was one of the first members of the Chinese élite to become aware of China's dangerous situation. As early as the 1830s he realized that the opium problem and commercial disputes would eventually lead to large-scale Sino-British conflicts. His encounter with the British merchants and officials in Canton in 1838 awakened him to the need fully to understand China's potential enemies. In one of his letters to the Chinese

Emperor he wrote: 'Since a war with the barbarians is likely now, we should know them as thoroughly as possible. We cannot formulate a strategy against them without knowing their strengths and weaknesses.'[6] In 1839 he by chance received a set of maps, a book on geography, and a globe from an American doctor, and he quickly organized a group of scholars to translate these materials as *Sizhou Zhi* (*A Treatise of the Four Continents*), which laid the foundation of Wei Yuan's *Haiguo Tuzhi* (*Illustrated Treatise on the Sea Kingdom*, 1844). *Sizhou Zhi*, however, collected impressionistic information about different countries. All Africans, for instance, appeared in this work as poor, rude, and pitiful creatures,[7] while Egyptians were mostly villains who attempted to exploit other people.[8] Russia, though a European country, lagged far behind the Western European nations.[9] In contrast, the Dutch were endowed with industrial and artistic skills, and Prussia was a leading European agricultural nation.[10] France, according to *Sizhou Zhi*, was the most powerful nation on earth.[11] It is not an exaggeration to say that *Sizhou Zhi* reflected the European rather than Lin Zexu's conception of the world.

As a scholar-general, Lin Zexu was most concerned about the military strength of the Western powers and how to deal with them. Lin's later works included a summary of the British navy's strengths and weaknesses. Before 1840, Lin was convinced that British military force was superior to the Chinese in two ways. Firstly, its armoured ships were too strong for Chinese cannons to break. Secondly, the British navy had the advantage of the Chinese navy in offshore battles. However, he believed that the *yingyi* (British barbarians) were not invincible. Bulky British ships, for instance, lost their fighting capacity once they entered the inner rivers.[12] In addition, he thought that British sailors in full gear were unable to fight on land.[13] Nevertheless, knowing that China needed a real technological breakthrough to match the British, Lin wished that a total war involving civilians and

[6] Lin Zexu, *Lin Wenzhong Gung Chunshu* (*Collected Works of Lin Zexu*) (Taipei, 1978), 170.

[7] Lin Zexu, *Sizhou Zhi* (*A Treatise of the Four Continents*), chs. 9 and 10, in *Xiao Fanghu Zhai Yudi Congchao Zaibo Bian* (Geographical Works of the Xiao Fanghu Study, the newest revised edition), ix (Taipei, 1964).

[8] Ibid., ch. 8.

[9] Ibid., ch. 34.

[10] Ibid., chs. 19 and 23.

[11] Ibid., ch. 20.

[12] Lin Zexu, *Lin Wenzhong Gung Zougao* (*Lin Zexu's Memorial to the Throne*), 3 vols. (Taipei, n.d.), ii. 676.

[13] Ibid.

the modification of strategies could enable China to defeat its enemies. In his view, the British navy, without shelter and a continual supply of food and fresh water, could not afford a prolonged war. In contrast, China, fighting a battle on its own soil, could fully utilize its geographical advantage and continuous supply of war materials and manpower.[14] The fact that the British navy could not break through the line of defence in Hong Kong in the early phase of the Opium War taught Lin the importance of maritime defence combining coastal fortifications and a Chinese navy that could combat the Western enemies offshore. New naval leaders who could develop new naval strategies and inhabitants motivated to defend coastal China were essential.[15] Lin, with very little desire to integrate the Western barbarians into China's world order, was interested only in finding ways to shut Western enemies out of China. Humiliated by Western enemies on the battlefield and upset by Britain's economic penetration of China, he saw little reason to learn from the Western barbarians with whom he was not familiar.

Wei Yuan's *Haiguo Tuzhi* expressed a new attitude toward Western expansion into Asia. As Jane Leonard points out, Wei Yuan's work broke new ground by proposing an anti-Western alliance between China and its tributary states, with whom China had lost touch since the seventeenth century.[16] In the founding years of the Qing Dynasty the confrontation with the Ming loyalists, who occupied Formosa, compelled Emperor Kangxi (ruled 1661–1722), Emperor Yongzheng (ruled 1723–35), and Emperor Qianlong (ruled 1736–95) to prohibit maritime trade. In addition, in order to stop the Western missionaries from evangelizing coastal and southern interior provinces and to prevent foreign merchants from disturbing the social and economic order of China, Emperor Yongzheng placed bans on Catholics proselytizing in these areas, limited contacts between Chinese and foreign traders, and checked immigration. In 1754 Emperor Qianlong institutionalized the Sino-Western trade system which allowed Western traders to contact only the Canton Co-hong merchants.

[14] Ibid. 678.

[15] *Lin Zexu Shujian* (*Lin Zexu's Correspondence*), ed. Xie Guojin (Fujian, 1981), 197.

[16] Jane Kate Leonard, *Wei Yuan and China's Rediscovery of the Maritime World* (Cambridge, Mass., 1984), 65.

Wei Yuan's mission of clearing China's coastal waters of pirates and smugglers aroused his interest in the outside world, motivating him to focus upon maritime defence in his early work *Huangchao Jingshi Wenbian* (*Statecraft Writings of the Qing Period*). His encounter with a number of British captives during the Opium War enriched Wei Yuan's knowledge of Britain and Europe, which later became an important component of his *Haiguo Tuzhi*, whose first edition in 50 chapters was completed on 3 January 1843. He expanded it into a second edition of 60 chapters in 1847, and a final edition of 100 chapters in 1852. Based on traditional Chinese sources, contemporary works like Xie Qinggao's *Hailu* (*Records of the Seas*, 1820) and Wang Dahai's *Haidao Yizhi* (*A Treatise on the Islands of the Sea*, 1791), and Western sources like Charles Gützlaff's *World Geography*, *The Treatise of Commerce,* and the *East–West Monthly Magazine*, and, later, works by Robert Morrison, D. B. McCartee, Richard Quarterman, and Elijah Bridgman, Wei's work reconstructed the image of *Nanyang* (the South Pacific) and Sino-Nanyang relations since Ming, and vividly depicted contemporary conditions in those areas.[17]

In the 'Introduction', Wei Yuan made it clear that the aim of this work was 'to learn the superior technology of the barbarians in order to control them'.[18] In addition, he emphasized that in dealing with global changes, the Chinese should acquaint themselves with the outside world.[19] Considering the modernization of China's coastal defences an urgent issue, he used the first four chapters to discuss the best ways to strengthen them and to modernize its navy. To achieve the former aim, Wei Yuan suggested building fortified ports, combining the Green Standard Army and Local Militia, who were familiar with surrounding areas and ready to protect their homeland, developing new naval strategies, setting up a coastal patrol consisting of Chinese wooden ships and Western steamers, acquiring the modern technique of shipbuilding, and recruiting élite naval corps.[20] In the last twenty chapters he gave a fuller exposition of modern military and marine technology.

Wei Yuan indicated that European nations expanding in various directions would soon upset the traditional tributary

[17] Ibid. 114–17.
[18] Wei Yuan, *Haiguo Tuzhi*, 3 vols. (Changsha, 1998), i. 1.
[19] Ibid. i. 7.
[20] Ibid. 1–42.

system, posing threats to coastal China.[21] He was also clear that in a real fight with European powers, China needed allies. His *Haiguo Tuzhi* thus aimed not only to study in detail the cultures, national characters, institutions, and technology of European nations, but also to examine the history, the strengths, and the weaknesses of the *Nanyang* and Inner Asia peoples with whom China would one day fight shoulder to shoulder as allies. Wei Yuan paid relatively little attention to nations like those in the Middle East because they had hardly any direct relations with China.

In Wei Yuan's eyes, the inner ring of China's tributary system formed by Burma, Vietnam, and Thailand would be able to cushion a direct attack by the Western powers.[22] Wei Yuan found enough reasons to trust the East and South-East Asian nations. According to his descriptions, the regional kingdoms formed by these nations still showed great respect to China, while China sent them gifts and took punitive actions against rebellious forces when it was necessary for China to fulfil its duties as overlord.[23] The ancient trade linkage with these countries further drew them together to form a natural alliance. In the case of a war with the Western powers, Wei Yuan believed that Burma, Vietnam, and Thailand would provide valuable support. Historical experience proved that the Vietnamese had been able to beat the Dutch,[24] and that even the British had had difficulty taming the rich but warlike Burmese.[25] Both adjacent to Singapore, Burma and Vietnam could join forces to engage British Singapore, while Thailand, given its economic and military strengths, could contain any possible British attack. Surprisingly, Wei Yuan saw Russia, which was not on good terms with China, as an ally, because the Anglo-Russian rivalry over North India could weaken the British in the East.[26] Even states in central India were regarded by Wei Yuan as potential partners, because if they cut their economic links with Britain, Britain could hardly maintain its empire in the East.[27]

Lin Zexu and Wei Yuan were among the first modern Chinese intellectuals to explore the world. However, defence

[21] Ibid. ii. 1103.
[22] Ibid. i. 348.
[23] Leonard, *Wei Yuan and China's Rediscovery of the Maritime World*, 132.
[24] Wei Yuan, *Haiguo Tuzhi* i. 371.
[25] Ibid. 454.
[26] Ibid. 710.
[27] Ibid. 729.

and diplomatic considerations rather than a real interest in foreign cultures and history dominated their works. Striving to shut Western aggressors out of the orbit of Chinese civilization once and for all, neither had much reason to revise the Confucian world order. Although they began to appreciate the economic and military achievements of the Europeans, the Western barbarians, in their eyes, remained barbarians.

III. *Close Encounters with Western Civilization: Guo Songtao and Xue Fucheng*

The Second Anglo-Chinese War of 1860 and a number of resulting conflicts hastened the downfall of the Chinese Empire. As well as realizing the urgency of reform, many Chinese intellectuals were more eager than ever to find out how the European powers, which had been inferior to China, had been able to overtake China in almost every aspect in less than a century. They had a deep desire to find a solution to the problem of China from the historical experience of Western nations. Something similar to the discourse of modernization emerged in the works of Guo Songtao and Xue Fucheng, both of whom had visited the West. Although their bias and perceptions prevented them from fully comprehending developments outside China, their view reflected the *Weltanschauung* of the Chinese intellectuals in a period of transition.

Guo Songtao, born in 1818, was one of the most important Chinese diplomats in the nineteenth century. Sent by the Qing Court to Britain to apologize for a conflict between British officials and Chinese provincial officials in Yunnan, Guo Songtao upon arrival in London received an order to stay as the Chinese ambassador to Britain. Guo's diaries contain highly important descriptions of the Western world and the areas under Western influence. Guo had been exposed to Western cultures during his early life in Shanghai and Canton, two of the most Westernized Chinese seaports. Fighting in both the Opium War and the Taiping Rebellion (1850–66), he personally experienced the military and technological strengths of Britain. He was also one of the co-founders of the *Tongwen Guan* (Tongwen Academy), which was built in 1862 as a centre of Western learning. At this time he began to surmise that the rapid progress of Western countries was a result of the development of the empirical sciences. He suggested that to catch up with the Western powers, China should selectively adopt Western sciences, institutions, and technology.

Leaving China for London on 2 December 1876, he first came to Hong Kong, a city that the British had ruled for more than twenty years. The social order, the living conditions, the education system, and even the management of prisons in Hong Kong showed him how a rationalized society functioned.[28] His admiration for Britain's superior administration increased after his visits to Singapore and Ceylon, which were under British influence. He frequently used phrases such as 'well organized' and 'good order' to describe Westernized societies.[29] The closer he moved toward Europe, the more amazed he felt. He was surprised that even the small Mediterranean island of Malta was so well administered.[30] Summing up his account of the first part of his journey, Guo, although a traditional scholar-official, could not but appreciate the positive changes Western nations had brought to the non-Western countries. In his opinion, the most valuable elements of Western civilization were education that sought to attain the ultimate truths,[31] rationally organized society, civil liberties that included freedom of speech and economic freedom,[32] and codified but simple laws.[33]

Guo's visits to London and Paris enhanced his knowledge of Western culture and politics. The well-regulated British parliament convinced him that freedom produced order instead of chaos. Systematic civil and military services, a well-planned and well-controlled national budget, and an advanced education system all came together to illustrate that a rationally organized society founded on empirical science had helped to create Britain's prosperity. In his opinion, the French political system, although differing from the British, was far more advanced and effective than the Chinese one. Likewise he attributed the

[28] Guo Songtao, 'Shisi Zhicheng (Records of the Mission to the West)', in Zhu Weizheng (ed.), *Guo Songtao Shisi Riji Liuzhong* (Six Diaries of Guo Songtao and other Chinese Diplomats visiting Western Nations) (Hong Kong, 1998), 4–6.

[29] e.g., ibid. 10 and 24.

[30] Ibid. 59.

[31] Guo Songtao, 'Lundun Bali Riji (Diaries in London and Paris)', in *Guo Songtao Shisi Riji Liuzhong*, 102, 151, and 165.

[32] Ibid. 120.

[33] Ibid. 147.

revival of Turkey and Russia to Westernization. Guo emphasized that since Western institutions and learning had helped to revive a declining Turkey in less than a century,[34] China should not shun the path of Westernization, but use the achievements of the West in a way that fitted its needs.

Xue Fucheng was another prominent Chinese diplomat who represented China in Belgium, Britain, France, and Italy. More conservative than Guo Songtao, Xue was nevertheless an important figure in the Self-Strengthening Movement. Although he never succeeded in achieving higher academic degrees, his military and administrative talent won for him Tseng Guofan's patronage. Because of his outstanding performance, he was sent to Britain as a representative in 1889. Over the next four years, he visited Belgium, Britain, France, and Italy. His diary, describing what he saw during his stay in Europe, not only enriched contemporary China's knowledge of the outside world, but also revealed the feelings of a Chinese conservative thrown into a new world.

Compared with many Chinese conservatives, Xue Fucheng was honest enough to admit that the world had changed greatly since the time of Confucius. By saying that the telephone and steamers had become real things in his time, he admitted the limitations of the teachings of the past masters for modern times.[35] But at the same time, his faith in China's cultural superiority was so strong that he attributed many Western inventions to Chinese origins. For him, modern chemistry, physics, and many modern machines had their roots in ancient Chinese civilization,[36] and modern Western bureaucracies that practised divide-and-rule were similar to that in China's Tang Dynasty (618–907).[37] In his eyes, Britain, now the most advanced country in the West, began to create its civilization only in the middle of the eighteenth century.[38]

Xue Fucheng insightfully observed the interaction of Chinese and Western cultures in a global context. He postulated that in ancient times, each civilization had developed independently. However, independent development soon gave way to mutual

[34] Ibid. 104.

[35] Xue Fucheng, 'Chushi Yingfa Yibi Siguo Riji (Diaries in Britain, France, Italy and Belgium)', in *Guo Songtao Shisi Riji Liuzhong*, 274.

[36] Ibid. 326.

[37] Ibid. 293.

[38] Ibid. 327.

borrowing after international contacts had become frequent. Since Western peoples did not hesitate to adopt Chinese inventions in the prime of Chinese civilization, he saw no reason why Chinese civilization could not borrow from its Western counterpart at a period of Western domination. If Western nations could achieve progress by standing on the shoulders of China, China could stand up again with the help of Western institutions and technology.[39] Taking medicine as an example, Xue pointed out that Western doctors were good at surgery, while Chinese medical practitioners were capable of improving the health conditions of patients. Theoretically speaking, Chinese and Western medicine, instead of being mutually exclusive, could support one another.[40] Nevertheless, Xue Fucheng had reservations about Westernization. For instance, though discussing in his diary the bicameral parliament in Western Europe with admiration, he did not think that it would be appropriate to China's situation.[41]

Despite Xue Fucheng's faith in Chinese civilization, he wondered if China could catch up with the advanced Western nations. He could not deny that the productivity of Britain, France, and even Russia was growing in geometric progression, leaving China and other non-Western nations behind.[42] Since Chinese merchants and industrialists, unlike European ones, were slow to discover new resources, to develop advanced skills, to invent new products, and to facilitate the communications network,[43] he wished that the Chinese government would take the initiative to reform the economy and pass relevant legislation to protect its infant industries and to improve its administration. The growing international conflicts also worried him. Equating the contemporary situation with the Chinese *Chunqiu* (Spring and Autumn period, 722 BC–481 BC), when feudatories had struggled for mastery, he felt that growing competition might turn the civilized world back into a jungle.[44] For him, in a world where battles were the order of the day, even the sages of ancient China could not bring peace and order without resorting to violent means.[45] China's task was to strengthen its military and to reform its economy in order to survive in a world perceived as hostile.

39 Ibid. 277. 40 Ibid. 280-1. 41 Ibid. 310. 42 Ibid. 316.
43 Ibid. 298. 44 Ibid. 301. 45 Ibid. 292.

In the 1870s, China's world order was on the verge of collapse. Guo Songtao understood that Western inventions and institutions followed trade routes to the East. Even states which had century-long connections with China had been absorbed into the sphere of influence of Western civilization that was expanding incessantly. Western penetration tore down the archaic social structure in these areas, producing many changes. However, as Xue Fucheng observed, an international struggle in which only the strongest survived had become the order of the day.

IV. *The Struggle for Survival: Wang Tao and Yan Fu*

In the last quarter of the nineteenth century not only the progressive but also the conservative Chinese intellectuals had to admit that China was doomed to decline. The Taiping Rebellion that threw south and south-east China into turmoil drained the financial resources of the Chinese Empire and weakened its provincial administration. No nations regarded China as a military power after it was defeated in the Sino-French War over Annam (1883–4). Even Japan, which grew in strength thanks to the Meiji Reform, seized all opportunities to exploit economic advantages in China. In contrast to Guo Songtao and Xue Fucheng, the new generation of Chinese intellectuals began to question whether the expansion of Western civilization could benefit China. For Wang Tao and Yan Fu, all nations were now caught in a struggle for survival. Since traditional wisdom could not help China cope with this situation, China, paradoxically, had to learn from the outside world in order to resist external threats.

Wang Tao's view of the outside world underwent great changes after the 1860s. Western learning shook Wang's traditional mind in 1847 when he arrived in Shanghai, the meeting point of East and West. His work as a translator in the *Haimo Shuguan* (Haimo Academy) and his affiliation with a Christian Church soon turned him into a marginal figure whose world-view was incompatible with that of many of his compatriots. However, though Wang admired Western civilizations in many ways, he opposed the opening of China to the West on a number of grounds. First, the experience of India showed him that even an ancient civilization would be steamrollered mercilessly by a commercial nation such as Britain. Secondly, like many of his contemporaries, he insisted that not all Western technology was suitable for China. Thirdly, he maintained that Chinese learning was a set of eternal truths that Western learning could hardly replace.[46] Planting his feet in the Chinese tradition, Wang Tao believed that China should adopt Western inventions selectively. For instance, superior Western firearms and steamers that could protect China's coasts were what China needed most. Academies like *Tungwen Kuan* should be established in every seaport. Underlying his idea that a fine-tuning of the Chinese culture was enough to elevate China was a cyclical view of history that promised China's eventual revival.

Because of his suspected collaboration with the Taiping rebels, Wang Tao was forced to flee Shanghai, and settled down in Hong Kong in 1862. His five-year stay in this British colony led him to believe that, if adopted wisely, Western institutions and technology might help to modernize China. On 15 December 1867 Wang Tao set out from Hong Kong for Europe, where he spent the next 28 months travelling through England, Scotland, and France. Accompanied by James Legge, one of the earliest Scottish Sinologists, Wang Tao was able to observe various aspects of Western ways of life. Western national governments, which clearly defined people's rights and duties, impressed him. Wang Tao also began to appreciate international free trade, believing that given its rich resources and cheap labour, China would have little to lose and much to gain in the world market. If the Chinese government could take positive measures such as issuing new currency and setting up a national bank to encourage trade, China would soon rise up again as an economic giant.

A sense of *Realpolitik* emerged as a major component of his political thought during these years. Wang Tao equated contemporary Europe with the *Chunqiu* period in China when naked power prevailed over justice.[47] In his eyes, European

[46] Paul A. Cohen, *Between Tradition and Modernity: Wang Tao and Reform in Late Ching China* (Cambridge, Mass., 1974), 23–31.

[47] Wang Tao, 'Bianfa Zhiqiang', in Zhu Weizheng (ed.), *Taoyuan Wenlu Xinpin* (New Edition of the Essays of Taoyuan) (Hong Kong, 1998), 38.

nations divided by cultural, racial, and economic differences combated each other mercilessly once they found international laws did not function in the way they liked to see.[48] Technological and economic advancements, instead of civilizing people, enhance their will and ability to fight. Paul Cohen therefore emphasizes: 'From Wang Tao's understanding of contemporary interstate relations and his perceptions of individual countries, we can extrapolate the vision of a world in which justice counted for little and brute power was set at a premium.'[49]

What worried Wang Tao most was that a struggle for mastery like that in Europe would spread to the East.[50] Wang, like any of his contemporaries, was aware of the threats surrounding the Chinese Empire. Russia, for instance, which Wang described as a cannibal, greedily stared at China's north-west territories.[51] Though he recognized the cultural affinity between China and Japan and appreciated Japanese hospitality, Wang was upset by Japan's aggressive policy towards China. However, seeing Russia as the most dangerous enemy, he still regarded Britain and Japan as partners in a possible confrontation with Russia.[52]

Wang Tao's theory impressed the late Qing Social Darwinists by highlighting China's need to survive in a hostile world in which justice played a minor role. Though still rating virtue far above power, Wang Tao was also clear that China could not survive in a hostile world by *wangdao* only. This new attitude partly explained why he saw Prussia, which rose dramatically in the second half of the nineteenth century to become a military and industrial machine, as a successful nation. However, to become wealthy and powerful, China should wholeheartedly learn from the West. In his essay 'Bianfa Zhiqiang' (Reforms and Self-Strengthening), published around 1870, he criticized the advocates of the Self-Strengthening Movement for 'copying the superficialities of [their] method, adopting the terminology

[48] Wang Tao, 'Taishi liyiu bukezhi (Western Treaties are not Reliable)', ibid. 79–8.

[49] Cohen, *Between Tradition and Modernity*, 108.

[50] Timothy M. K. Wong, 'The Contemporary World in Wang Tao's Historical Work', in Kai-yin Lam and Timothy M. K. Wong (eds.), *Wang Tao and the Contemporary World* (in Chinese) (Hong Kong, 2000), 190.

[51] Wang Tao, 'Eren Zhizai Pinjian (The Russians Intend to Expand)', ibid. 71–2.

[52] Wang Tao, 'Zhongwai Heli Fange (China and the Foreign Countries' Joint Force to Resist Russia)', ibid. 75.

of Western civilization but little of its substance'.[53] Attributing the strengths of the West to commercialism, constitutionalism, an enlightened ruling élite, and efficient bureaucracy, he called for sweeping institutional reforms. The principle of 'learning from the barbarians in order to control the barbarians' secretly reappeared in Wang Tao's thought.

Yan Fu was commonly regarded as the father of Social Darwinism in China because he was the first Chinese intellectual systematically to introduce the theories of Herbert Spencer and Thomas Huxley. Although Yan Fu received a traditional education in his early years, he studied marine engineering after his father passed away leaving him without financial means. In 1876 Yan Fu was sent to Britain with a Chinese study group to learn Western technology. Spending almost three years in England, Yan Fu acquainted himself with the leading schools of intellectual thought in nineteenth-century England. Like other contemporary Chinese progressive intellectuals, he felt obliged to lead China out of poverty and to free it from foreign domination. However, without a recognized academic degree, he had to be content with the post of principal of the Naval School in Fujian. China's war with Japan in 1894 became a turning point in Yan Fu's life. Heartbroken by the quick collapse of the Chinese navy, Yan Fu translated Huxley's *Evolution and Ethics* into Chinese in an effort to highlight the urgent need for sweeping reform. In the decade that followed, he formulated his reformist thought by translating, among others, the major works of Adam Smith, Montesquieu, Spencer, and John Stuart Mill.

Taken together, the five articles Yan Fu published in 1895 and his *Tianyan Lun* (the Chinese version of *Evolution and Ethics*) formed his reform programme. In his 'Lun Shibian Jizhi' (On Changes), 'Yuanqiang' (On Strength), and 'Yuanqiang Xubian' (On Strength: Further Elaboration), he depicted the contemporary world as a jungle in which all races struggled for limited resources.[54] In order to survive in a hostile environment, China had to change. His Darwinian assertion was, however, followed by Adam Smith's solution. He saw freedom as the essence of

[53] 'Bianfa Zhiqiang (Reforms and Self-Strengthening)', ibid. 39; here quoted from Lee Chi-fang, *Wang Tao (1828–1897): His Life, Thought, Scholarship, and Literary Achievement*, Ph.D. Dissertation (University of Wisconsin, 1973), 183.

[54] *Yan Fu Ji* (Works of Yan Fu), ed. Wang Shi, 5 vols. (Beijing, 1986), i. 1, 5–6.

Western civilization. Western institutions that enabled people to pursue their own ends not only gave rise to power and wealth, but also an unintended social order founded on formal laws.[55] For Yan Fu, Chinese people enjoyed no real freedom. To maximize the strength of China, the Chinese should first be freed from ignorance and authority. In 'Pi Han' (In Refutation of Han Yü) and 'Jiuwang Juelun' (On Salvation), his next two articles, he attacked the old legal institutions and mentality that had created nothing but blind loyalty to the king, obsession with an outmoded examination system, and premodern laws that imprisoned the Chinese people in the long night of ignorance.[56] For this reason, China should be reformed from above and from below, lest it lose in the 'struggle for survival'. He did not believe that China should adopt all Western institutions and cultural values, but he added that China could not be strong without learning from the West because ancient customs and institutions that had been used in China for hundreds or thousands of years were no longer appropriate to its situation.[57] Yan Fu's *Tianyan Lun* reiterated the principles of 'survival of the fittest'. However, a core idea he adapted from Huxley was that at the higher stage of civilization, human wisdom replaced natural force as the determinant of evolution. In this sense, *Tianyan Lun* was a philosophical treatise that again emphasized China's need for reform.

After finishing the translation of *Tianyan Lun*, Yan Fu concentrated on the translation of Adam Smith's *The Wealth of Nations*, Mill's *On Liberty* and *A System of Logic*, Montesquieu's *The Spirit of the Laws*, Herbert Spencer's *The Study of Sociology*, and Edward Jenks's *A History of Politics*. All these works could be pieced together to produce a reform model. In his remarks on *The Wealth of Nations* (1897), Yan Fu attributed England's success to free trade and economic activities. For him, thanks to its free economic policy, Britain towered over nations like Germany which still adopted restrictive economic, social, and cultural policies.[58] Like Adam Smith, Yan Fu believed that in a quest for individual interests a new kind of morality would arise and replace the outdated dogmas that repressed men.[59] In the Chinese translation of Mill's *On Liberty* (1899), Yan Fu continued the discussion in 'On Strength', reiterating the importance of

[55] Ibid. 3. [56] Ibid. 34–5. [57] Ibid. 50. [58] Ibid. iv. 897. [59] Ibid. 1082.

freedom of speech and freedom of thought. He believed that it was the only way to grasp the truth and fully to develop the human mind.[60] Mill's *Logic* (1897) and Spencer's *The Study of Sociology* (1900–2) that followed continued to urge people to get rid of bias, prejudice, and superstition and to look at the growth of society from a scientific perspective. Agreeing with Smith and other liberals, Yan Fu believed that to ensure free competition, there should be formal laws protecting everybody's rights. Therefore, in his translation of Montesquieu's *The Spirit of the Laws* (1900–9) he attacked traditional Chinese laws that sought to safeguard the privileged classes and the existing social order.[61] For him, the lack of a rational and formal legal system accounted for China's weakness and a reform on the Western model was the only way to transform China's legal institutions.

It seems clear that Yan Fu, like most late Qing progressive intellectuals, saw the self-strengthening of China by imitating the political, social, and economic system of Western nations as the only way for it to escape from foreign penetration. Impressed by British liberalism and the unprecedented economic, political, and military achievements of Victorian England, he believed that free competition, tolerance, and the rule of law that had interacted to raise Britain to the apex of the world could also benefit China. Yan Fu saw the translation and spread of these ideas to China as a way of saving his country. Classical liberals' insistence that the free interplay of individual self-interests created social harmony and material well-being really won the heart of Yan Fu.

V. *Conclusion*

The Chinese intellectuals of the nineteenth century were slow to see that new global changes had shattered the traditional Chinese world order. Reluctantly they admitted that the economic, cultural, and political centre had moved slowly from East to West. Their desire to cope with this shift motivated them to study the new rising Western powers and to redefine China's position on earth. This practical interest, however, prevented

[60] Ibid. i. 134. [61] Ibid. iv. 938–9.

them from revising their conception of the world. For Lin Zexu, Wei Yuan, Xue Fucheng, and Wang Tao, no matter how advanced Western civilization was, Western nations would be China's enemies or competitors, but never its partners. Western civilization, in their eyes, was instrumental for the reform of China only. Even more liberal Chinese intellectuals such as Guo Songtao and Yan Fu, who had much greater exposure to Western values and institutions, also thought in this way. Moreover, Chinese intellectuals reserved only insignificant positions for nations which today form the Third World. Vietnam, Burma, and nations on the periphery of China were discussed in the works of Lin Zexu and Wai Yuan simply because the 'Middle Kingdom' needed their services in a possible large-scale confrontation with its Western enemies. The Westerners are always criticized for creating their own image of China instead of understanding China. The above discussion, however, shows that Chinese intellectuals in the nineteenth century also created their own image of the world instead of pursuing research into different cultures and nations.

13

High Anxiety: World History as Japanese Self-Discovery

JULIA ADENEY THOMAS

Most cultures expect to find awesome monsters and uncivilized barbarians at the boundaries of the known world. Herodotus had the Scythians; the Chinese mapped extraordinary semi-human oddities in the *Shang jing*; Renaissance mariners conjured huge sea creatures at the ocean's horizon; and the twentieth century projected power-hungry space aliens. For many, writing world history has been a matter of making the acquaintance of these monsters and barbarians, taming them, miniaturizing them, and ultimately wrapping them in familiar narratives and structures. In other words, writing world history in many places, perhaps most particularly in Western Europe and the USA, has been a process of unmasking the fearsome as comprehensible. By contrast, in Japan, the barbarian, the deformed, the unknown often seems to be within rather than without. In these circumstances, the project of writing world history is suffused with the quest for self-understanding.

This essay argues that the various modes of world history in Japan can best be understood *not* as attempts to comprehend the Other but as forms of self-exploration. Whether Chinese culture was magnificent or corrupt, whether 'the West' was properly ethical or not, these distant cosmopolitan civilizations were cast as intelligible, while Japan remained a mystery to itself. These other civilizations were seen to structure global interchange and thus world history, while Japan had to define and defend itself within these comprehensible but alien systems. Only during the Pacific War was the Japanese nation held to have become the active agent structuring world history, but even then most scholarly and bureaucratic historiography did not focus on explaining other places or on describing the structures governing the new world order. Instead, they focused on the mysterious nature of the Japanese nation itself as it led the world toward 'self-consciousness of spiritual totality'.[1] In short, in Japan, world history, from the early modern period to the post-war era, was fraught with high anxiety about national identity. Although it can be argued that all knowledge is partly self-reflexive, Japan's world historiography was governed to an unusual degree by the conceit that the Other required less explanation than the Self.

In this essay, five somewhat arbitrary stages in the Japanese understanding of world history from the Tokugawa era (1600–1868) to the post-war period will be presented, beginning with the Tokugawa acceptance of a China-centred universe and then turning to the Tokugawa attempt to create a Japan-centred universe instead. The essay argues that the same pattern was repeated after the overthrow of the Tokugawa bakufu in 1868 and the establishment of regular international diplomatic and trading relations, except that this time 'the West' was first accepted and then rejected as the civilization structuring world history. In the Meiji (1868–1912) and Taishō (1912–26) periods, the acceptance of Western models introduced three 'scientific' modes of understanding world history which caused Japanese scholars and bureaucrats to ponder the place of their nation (1) in the diplomatic exchanges of Rankean internationalism, (2) in terms of evolutionary progress, and (3) in the Marxist dialectic. The fourth stage of historiography emerged during the war years of the 1930s and 1940s as a revolt against these 'scientific' modes of temporal history. It relied on the conceit that, in essence, Japan was without history, preserved from the fractured, relentless temporality of modernity by the unbroken Imperial lineage even as it was destined to triumph over the world. After the defeat in 1945, a progressive model of world history and anxiety about Japan's place in the temporal trajectory of world history once again took centre stage. This fifth stage will be sketched by briefly examining the 1965 dialogue between the historians Matsumoto Sannosuke and Harry D. Harootunian.

[1] Nishitani Keiji, 'Sekai tenkanki to shite no gendai', ch. 2, section 1 of *Sekai to kokkakan* (World View and National View) (Tokyo, 1941), 67.

I. *Tokugawa*

During the long Tokugawa period from 1600 to 1868, the Japanese had virtually no contact with the outside world. Like other Asian countries (notably Tibet and Korea), the Japanese government severely limited diplomatic exchange and stringently controlled foreign trade. Nevertheless, despite little contact with its continental neighbours, Japan's sense of the world was largely dominated by Chinese ideas, most particularly the Neo-Confucian concept of a strictly hierarchical world order presided over by a Central Kingdom. Because these ideas had been articulated initially in China, China held pride of place as *the* political, cultural, ethical, and, on many maps, geographical centre of the world.[2] According to good Confucian common sense, this order was changeless, history-less in the conventional sense because it endured forever as the fundamental structure of the world. On this basis, world history, if such it can be called, was not a matter of diplomatic or economic relations, not a matter of emerging cultures or technologies, but an ancient and changeless order of precedence.

Many Japanese Neo-Confucianists revered China as *chūgoku* (Middle Kingdom) or *Chūka* (central efflorescence). China was considered the pinnacle of a universal empire that spread out slowly from the middle of the world toward its murky edges where barbarians dwelt. Japan, by this reckoning, was necessarily a barbarian kingdom. Many Tokugawa scholars, Kaibara Ekken among them, accepted the nomenclature of 'barbarian' applied to themselves, and thus constructed a sense of world order, if not of world history, in relation to the overwhelming power of this central kingdom.

There was, it is important to recognize, a magnanimity to the Neo-Confucian conception of Chinese centrality. Sharp dividing

[2] The long history of Chinese graphic accounts of the world is often dated from the 6th century BCE *Shujing* (Classic of History), particularly the chapter called 'Yugong' or 'The Tribute of Yu' which portrays the world as divided into 'five major concentric geographical zones emanating outward from the capital: royal domains, princely domains, a pacification zone, the zone of allied barbarians, and the zone of savagery'. Richard J. Smith, *Chinese Maps: Images of 'All under Heaven'* (Oxford, 1996), 23. See also the discussion of this work in John B. Henderson, 'Chinese Cosmographical Thought: The High Intellectual Tradition', in J. B. Harley and David Woodward (eds.), *Cartography in the Traditional East and Southeast Asian Societies,* ii, bk. 2 (Chicago, 1994).

lines did not exist in either physical or moral space between central virtue and immoral periphery. Knowledge of Confucian rectitude could travel toward barbarian edges. Conversely, barbarians on the rim of civilization were drawn to the Chinese emperor 'from the four quarters of the earth', as the *Zhongyong* (Doctrine of the Mean) puts it, and accepted under his sway. As T'ang scholar Chen Yan commented: 'Some people are born in barbarian lands but their actions are in harmony with rites and righteousness. In that case, they are barbarian in appearance but they have a Chinese heart and mind.'[3] Given the solubility of the border between *Chūka* and its circumference, Japanese scholars like Itō Jinsai (1627–1705) could insist that a Japanese person, barbarous though he admittedly was, might attain virtue by scrupulously following the Way. Echoing Chen Yan, Jinsai argues:

> No matter where under Heaven or where on earth [they may live], *all men are equally men.* Even a barbarian, if he but possesses ritual and righteousness, is part of the Middle Kingdom. Even a Chinese, should he lack ritual and righteousness, cannot escape being barbarian.[4]

In other words, the type of centrality ascribed to China did not exclude non-Chinese individuals from the role of historical subject, albeit in a minor key.

Not surprisingly, however, individual reclamation within the Central Kingdom was not enough for many Tokugawa political thinkers who anxiously hoped to realize a role for their country as a whole within this China-centred universe. Their method was to examine Japanese history in order to find a way to insert their own country in their conceptual universe that was so dominated by continental civilization. One approach was to equate the way of the Chinese Sages with the way of Japan's native Shintō deities. Historian Kate Nakai includes Neo-Confucian scholars Hayashi Razan (1583–1657), Kumazawa Banzan (1619–91), Yamaga Sokō (1622–85), Yamazaki Ansai (1618–82), and Ogyū Sorai (1666–1724) among those who drew this analogy.[5] These Neo-Confucianists contrasted China's history of

[3] Quoted in Smith, *Chinese Maps*, 8.

[4] Quoted in Bob Tadashi Wakabayashi, *Anti-Foreignism and Western Learning in Early-Modern Japan: The 'New Theses' of 1825* (Cambridge, Mass., 1986), 25.

[5] Kate Wildman Nakai, 'The Naturalization of Confucianism in Tokugawa Japan: The Problem of Sinocentrism', *Harvard Journal of Asian Studies*, 40 (1980), 159–60.

military defeats, civil wars, and dynastic overthrows with Japanese invincibility and the continuity of its imperial line, suggesting that these historical facts provided proof that centralness need not be inhabited geographically by a nation to be enacted morally. However, as Nakai points out, these exertions involved Neo-Confucianists in the 'contradictory interplay between efforts to universalize, or de-Sinify, Confucianism on the one hand, and to affirm the Sinitic essence of the way of the sages on the other'.[6]

Gradually, the connection between Central Kingdom virtues and China loosened as Japanese scholars became more insistent on their own national success and more sceptical of Chinese achievements. Bob Tadashi Wakabayashi argues that by the late eighteenth century, 'the Sinocentric Middle Kingdom world view had been so relativized, or compromised to Japanese values and socio-political realities, that it was untenable'.[7] During this period, Japanese scholars did not relinquish the idea of a natural, static political centre of world history; instead, scholars of Japanese or native learning, the *kokugakusha*, began to elevate Japan's imperial centre as pre-eminently blessed. Thus, in this second, reactionary nationalist stage of world historiography, Japan became the Central Kingdom.

Kamo no Mabuchi (1697–1769), foremost among the *kokugakusha*, laid the groundwork for asserting the superiority of Japan over China. For instance, in *Kokuikō* (1765), Mabuchi declares, with unbridled delight and energy, that there is nothing worthy of Japanese admiration in the history of the Sage Kings, Chinese medical theory, the Chinese writing system, Chinese incest taboos, or the Chinese insistence on honouring human beings above birds, beasts, and other living things. Indeed, the natural goodness of the human heart 'turns evil' when it comes into contact with Confucianism's unnatural obsession with doctrine.[8] 'In reality', Mabuchi argues, 'this land [of Japan] was ruled in conformity with the heart of heaven-and-earth' before the introduction of Confucianism from China, and it is to this gentle original state that he urges it to return. In other words, if the Japanese can come to know the cryptic self

[6] Ibid. 165.
[7] Wakabayashi, *Anti-Foreignism and Western Learning*, 51.
[8] Kamo no Mabuchi, *Kokuikō* [1765], in *Nihon shisō taikei* (Tokyo, 1972), xxxix. 382.

whom they have for so long neglected in the shadow of Chinese culture, they will instinctively embrace the proper world order.

Motoori Norinaga (1730–1801) not only accepted most of these ideas after meeting Mabuchi, but elaborated them through research into the *Kojiki* (Japan's earliest compendium of mythic history) and into the prose and the poetry of ancient times. Although the study of eighth-century documents might not appear to be the most direct way of reshaping world history, Norinaga claimed that his research demonstrated Japan's moral precedence as the land where the sun goddess Amaterasu was born and the land in which her descendants ruled ever after. These imperial descendants (the emperor or *sumera mikoto*) possessed a majesty that radiated throughout the world. Norinaga declares: 'So far as heaven and earth extend, so long as sun and moon dispense their light, and however many tens of thousands of generations have passed our great ruler remains immutable.'[9] Japan through the imperial line serves as the pivot of the universe.

Given the logic of a world system based on changeless hierarchy, to elevate Japan was to denigrate other nations. *Kokugaku* scholar Hirata Atsutane felt certain that Europeans were 'barbarians [who] spew forth such shallow falsehoods . . . because they were born in filthy, remote countries, far from the Divine Land' (despite his own reluctant respect for Western medicine, astronomy, and even Christianity).[10] The eclectic thinker Ōkuni Takamasa (1792–1871) insisted that Japan's mission was to aid other countries to 'conform to the original wishes of the Ruler in Heaven and the Creator, and have them regard Japan as the central nation, and revere the Emperor as the great center of the human world'.[11] According to Takamasa's book, *Bankoku kōhō* (The New True International Law), both the Chinese world system and the code of international law articulated by Hugo Grotius (1538–1645) were doomed before the majesty of Imperial Japan. Another scholar, Aizawa Seishisai (1782–1863), one of the Mito school's most famous and flamboyant disciples, orchestrated geographical description, metaphors of the body, and claims to moral superi-

[9] Motoori Norinaga, *Naobi no mitama* (The Spirit of Renovation), trans. Harry D. Harootunian, in *Readings in Tokugawa Thought: Selected Papers* (Chicago, 1994), ix. 123.

[10] Donald Keene, *The Japanese Discovery of Europe, 1720–1830* (Stanford, 1952), 159.

[11] Ōkuni Takamasa, *Bankoku kōhō*, trans. John Breen, in *Readings in Tokugawa Thought*, ix. 245.

ority to support the claims to Japanese pre-eminence. In the opening pages of *Shinron* (New Theses) published in 1825, he declares:

> All things exist as nature (*shizen*) dictates. Thus, our Divine Realm is at the top of the world. Though not a very large country, it reigns over the Four Quarters because its Imperial Line has never known dynastic change. The Western barbarians represent the thighs, legs, and feet of the universe. This is why they sail hither and yon, indifferent to the distances involved. Moreover, the country they call America is located at the rear end of the world, so its inhabitants are stupid and incompetent. All this is as nature (*shizen*) dictates.[12]

Although Seishisai's concept of history was more dynamic than the somnolent Neo-Confucian and *kokugaku* vision of an 'unchanging Heaven-and-Earth', the basic understanding the world as a strict hierarchy guaranteed by nature endured.

In the course of the Tokugawa period, Japan had been transformed from a barbarian satellite of Chinese civilization to the Divine Realm at the top of the world, not by understanding the world better, but, I would argue, by understanding its own glory more fully. It could well be said that this Tokugawa literature is hardly 'world history' as we know it, but the intellectual tropes developed in the Tokugawa period persisted, shaping more modern, analytical, research-based approaches to the subject. In particular, the impulse to position Japan either at the top or towards the bottom of world systems imagined elsewhere endured. The consequent focus on national history, on crafting stories of the mysterious Self against the background of a knowable Other, re-emerged after the old Tokugawa shogunate crumbled in 1868.

II. *Meiji to Wartime*

In 1869, one year after the new Meiji government came to power, an Imperial Edict declared that 'Historiography is forever an immortal state ritual'.[13] In 1872 the Meiji government estab-

[12] Aizawa Seishisai, *Shinron* (New Theses), in *Mitogaku taikei* (Tokyo, 1941), ii. 2-3. Translation from Wakabayashi, *Anti-Foreignism*, 149. I have also consulted the translation by J. Victor Koschmann in *Readings in Tokugawa Thought*, ix. 197–233.

[13] Margaret Mehl, *History and the State in Nineteenth-Century Japan* (New York, 1997), 1.

lished a Department of Historiography under the Council of State (dajōkan), the highest executive organ. However, world history was not its great concern. The purpose of this department was to gather documents and compile an official *national* history. Later, this treatment of Japanese history as separable from other histories would be institutionalized at Tokyo Imperial University where the first ever department of history in Japan was devoted solely to European history and called *shigakka*, the department of scientific history, and a separate department of Japanese history, established in 1889, concentrated on *kokushi* or national history.[14] As Hattori Shiso would comment seventy-five years later: 'Until very recent times Japanese looked out upon the world from the perspective of their own history only; rarely did they see Japan as part of world history.'[15] Only a few early Meiji histories, such as Fukuzawa Yukichi's *Bunmeiron no gairyaku* (Outline of a Theory of Civilization, 1875) and Taguchi Ukichi's *Nihon kaika shōshi* (A Short History of Enlightenment in Japan, 1877–82) attempted fully to integrate Japan's trajectory into the history of human progress. During this third stage in Japan's understanding of world history, the stage between 1868 and the violence of the 1930s, three major approaches emerged in Japanese universities and political discourse, all revolving around 'scientific' methods adapted from European schools of thought, and all concerned with the dynamic interaction over time among nations rather than one eternal hierarchy. Their shared emphasis on time marked a spectacular departure from the previous conception of a static world order.

The first of these Meiji approaches could claim a loose genealogical link with Leopold von Ranke (1795–1886). In 1887 one of von Ranke's students, Ludwig Reiss, was invited at the tender age of 26 to teach history at the new Tokyo Imperial University. Reiss's approach, incorporating a causal treatment of events within a chronological framework, impressed Japanese historians as more systematic and comprehensive than the traditional annalistic Chinese form of history-writing. Historian Shigeno Yasutsugu commented that 'unlike Japanese and Chinese histories, which confine themselves to factual statement,

[14] Ibid. 95.

[15] Hattori Shisō, 'Absolutism and Historiographical Interpretation', *Japan Interpreter*, 13/1 (Summer 1980), 15. Originally published in *Sekai* (Nov. 1947).

Western histories inquire into causes and consider effects, provide detailed accounts of their subjects and vivid pictures of conditions of the time with which they are concerned. There can be no doubt that their form and method embody many points of value to us.'[16] Applied to world history, this Rankean-inflected approach eschewed a progressive teleology. Instead, each nation-state was deemed to develop individually, particularly through foreign interchange. From this perspective, Japan's long Tokugawa seclusion from the world, the period of *sakoku* (closed country) as it came to be designated, appeared a great misfortune. In removing itself from diplomatic, intellectual, and commercial engagement with other nations, Japan had not come to know itself as it should, and it needed to catch up.[17]

The sense that Japan had not developed 'normally' according to the European chronometer was augmented by the even more tremendous influence of Herbert Spencer and social Darwinism in Japan, the second Western model of stage three. So overwhelming was the Spencerian influence that his name was reverentially evoked by advocates of democracy such as Baba Tatsui,[18] as well as by advocates of imperial oligarchy. Socialists too found inspiration in Spencer, as a respectful death notice in the 27 December 1903 issue of *Heimin shinbun* (The Commoners' Newspaper) demonstrates. Educational establishments from elementary schools to universities adopted the view that the world was governed by the struggle for survival. Indeed, historian of philosophy Gino Piovesana claims that 'the first years of Tokyo University were known as the time of *Daigaku Shinkaron* (lit. University Evolutionism), so much was this institution a centre of diffusion of ideas on evolution'.[19]

[16] Quoted in Leonard Blussé, 'Japanese Historiography and European Sources', in P. C. Emmer and H. L. Wesseling (eds.), *Reappraisals in Overseas History* (Leiden, 1979), 199–200.

[17] Watsuji Tetsurō would make this the central theme of *Sakoku–Nihon no higeki* (The Closed Country: Japan's Tragedy), first published in 1950.

[18] Baba Tatsui translated the first chapter of Spencer's *First Principles* as 'Supensaru shi tetsugaku ron' (On the philosophy of Spencer) in 1884 and advocated Spencerian ideas in 'Heikin ryoku no setsu' (An Explanation of the Force of Equilibrium) (1879) and 'Shinka bunri no niryoku' (The Dual Forces of Union and Disunion) (1879). Baba used Spencerian ideas in direct response to Katō Hiroyuki's attack on the people's rights movement in 'Homi Katō Hiroyuki kun *Jinken Shinsetsu*' (Reading Mr Katō Hiroyuki's *New Explanation of Human Rights*) and *Tenpu jinkenron* (A Discussion of Natural Rights).

[19] Gino Piovesana, *Recent Japanese Philosophical Thought, 1862–1996*, with a new Survey (1963–1996) by Naoshi Yamawaki (Richmond, Surrey, 1997) 25.

Certainly, Katō Hiroyuki, president of Tokyo Imperial University, was an influential proponent of social evolution, which he saw as a universal process in which Japan was a less than supremely fit organism.[20] Since, according to Katō, evolutionary forces lay outside human control and did not always work to human advantage, and since foreign countries already dominated in the struggle for survival, caution was essential to national progress. Moving slowly, Japanese society would eventually evolve democratic forms finally joining in 'a great universal community where all the countries of the world abide by a central institutional framework and uniform laws',[21] but this utopia would not be attained for several generations. In the meantime, Katō argued that skilled leaders like himself and his friends among the oligarchs must manage the struggle for survival in Japan from above, suppressing a premature, if naturally mandated, desire for democracy.

Katō's political opponents, including Baba Tatsui, were eager to point out that unless democracy, acknowledged as the highest social evolutionary state, was immediately adopted by Japan, Japan would perpetually trail the West. These opposition leaders insisted that Japan needed a representative and responsible government immediately unless it was to suffer all the stages of anguish and revolution that had accompanied the achievement of democratic forms in Europe, but these optimistic social Darwinists did not carry the day. More pessimistic followers of Social Darwinism thought it impossible for Japan to leapfrog over the intervening stages of evolution and catch up with the West. They accepted the idea that Japan was condemned to perpetual subordination. For instance, Inoue Tetsujirō (1855–1944) felt Japan's inferiority and vulnerability keenly. In particular, Inoue feared that allowing mixed residence throughout Japan would inevitably result in Westerners gaining control of all commerce and the government because of their superior intelligence, physique, and spirit of independence. Inoue urged a frank admission of 'our weak and inferior civilization' for the sake of national security on social Darwinistic grounds.[22] Such a world picture was bleak.

[20] Katō compares Japan unfavourably with Europe, which he describes as the most superior civilization. Katō Hiroyuki, *Jinken shinsetsu*, in Uete Michiari (ed.), *Nishi Amane, Katō Hiroyuki* (Tokyo, 1984) 449–50.

[21] Ibid. 451.

[22] Inoue Tetsujirō, 'Naichi zakkyo zokuron' [1889], in Yoshino Sakuzō (ed.), *Meiji bunka zenshō* (Tokyo, 1928), vi. 508.

By 1893, Tokutomi Sohō among others reacted with disgust against this threatening presumption of naturally determined Western hegemony over Japan and over world history. From his former acceptance of Spencer, particularly Spencer's view that developed industrial societies were necessarily pacifist, Tokutomi moved to embrace a militarily assertive Japan. The 1895 victory over China, he said, showed that Japanese, too, had a 'character suitable for great achievements in the world'.[23] A decade later, Japan's victory in the Russo-Japanese war dramatically overturned the international model of nations arrayed in strict order on the evolutionary ladder. In practice, it seemed that social evolution could not explain such contingent and unpredictable outcomes as Japan's victory over a European power. In ideological terms, social evolution created difficulties for the government seeking to define the Japanese polity in a way that would win it international power and recognition. While Japanese social Darwinism contrasted with Tokugawa ideas of history in introducing dynamism and strife into world history, it resonated with the earlier view in its keen sense of a global hierarchy.

The third historiographical approach of the pre-war decades, Marxist theory, did little to dispel the perception of a hierarchical world order in which Japan lagged behind. Here too the quest was not to understand the world order, which was deemed comprehensible, but to understand Japan's place in it. The strident debates in the 1920s between the Kōza-ha and the Rōnō-ha, for instance, attempted to define exactly where Japan stood in the teleological spectrum from feudalism to bourgeois democracy to proletarian revolution. The Kōza-ha suggested that Meiji Japan had attained bourgeois revolution, albeit incompletely, and could hope for a proletarian takeover shortly. The Rōnō-ha, on the other hand, argued that the late-Tokugawa economy had not been on a par with that of Western Europe, and that Japan still had to effect bourgeois revolution before advancing to the final stage. At stake in this debate were questions of contemporary strategy in organizing workers and farmers. Finally, the Comintern weighed in to settle the dispute. Just as Spencer had dismissed the 1889 Meiji Constitution (the first Constitution ever written by an Asian country) as a 'gross miscarriage of justice' in

[23] Quoted in W. G. Beasley, *Japanese Imperialism, 1894–1945* (Oxford, 1987), 31.

being too progressive, so too the Soviet leadership, fresh from their revolutionary victories in Russia and Mongolia, proclaimed Japan as yet far too undeveloped for full revolution. In the late nineteenth and early twentieth centuries, then, historians adapted several models of world history, but in all of them Japan was in the rear, lacking the dynamism developed through diplomacy, or lagging in evolutionary development toward democracy, or failing to have achieved a bourgeois revolution. Meiji and Taishō world history embraced change in the way that Tokugawa history had not, but it did not relinquish the model of world hierarchy.

III. *Wartime*

Disgusted with these patterns of world history giving precedence to 'the West', some Japanese intellectuals and bureaucrats asserted a new model of world history with Japan as its culmination. Borrowing from German idealism and dialectical analysis, this model elevated Japan to pre-eminence as the ultimate historical subject, awakened to its world-historical mission to unite all nations on a transcendent level. On a concrete level, this effort at unification had begun through Japan's various imperialist and colonial adventures including the victory over Russia in 1905, the formal annexation of Korea in 1910, and the attack on Manchuria. By 1938, on the first anniversary of the Marco Polo Bridge Incident that had precipitated war against China, Miki Kiyoshi, a member of the Shōwa Kenkyūkai, an advisory group to Prime Minister Konoe, argued that the China Incident had 'World Historical Significance' that could only be realized by greater penetration into the continent. Miki urged that Japanese and other Asian peoples cast aside 'the historical frame of reference that accepts a belief in the dominance of the European'.[24] Instead Miki suggests: 'If we consider Japan's historic mission in spatial terms, it means the unification of Asia; if we consider it temporally, this mission means the resolution of the contradictions of capitalist societies. Each of these tasks must be realized by the China incident.'[25]

[24] Quoted in James Crowley, 'Intellectuals as Visionaries of the New Asian Order', in James William Morley (ed.), *Dilemmas of Growth in Prewar Japan* (Princeton, 1971), 363.
[25] Quoted ibid. 366.

Not only was Asian unity in the Co-Prosperity Sphere at hand through Japan's acceptance of its world mission, but global unity as well. Indeed, philosopher and state ideologue Nishitani Keiji argued in 1941 that 'it was . . . precisely the ascendancy of the status of Japan as a great power that first caused world politics to become world-political'.[26] Global history had only become truly global when Japan emerged as a great power at the beginning of the twentieth century. With Japan in the lead, a new stage was at hand. In his 1944 essay, *Kokutairon* (On National Polity), Nishida Kitarō, another professor who supported the ultra-national state, concurred, suggesting that 'Japan's uniqueness . . . consists in its religiosity and sacredness as something that is historically world-formative'.[27]

This self-discovery of Japan at the culmination of world history, as the maestro of time, has an odd twist during these years. Despite the emphasis on the dialectic of history, almost all these writers were passionately concerned with the still, unchanging imperial presence at the heart of Japanese identity. This presence guaranteed Japanese national identity in that it had never been altered. Indeed, no historical transformation of any sort whether dialectical, progressive, revolutionary, or scientific could blemish the purity of the unbroken imperial line. Because of this lineage, there was at the core of Japanese history and thus at the core, even, of a world dialectic, an 'eternal now' (as many called it), a continual present that stretched all the way back to the age of the gods and all the way forward into eternity. Nishida, for all his concern for dialectical history and mutual transformation, argues that 'the Imperial Household, symbolizing the absolute present embracing past and future, is the beginning and end of our world'. As he explains in his 1943 essay, 'Sekai no shinchitsujo no genri' (Fundamental Principles of the New World Order), 'Our nation's Imperial Household is not merely the centre of one racial nation. For, in our nation's Imperial Way is included the fundamental principle of world-formation whereby, "the eight directions constitute one universe".'[28] This concept of an 'eternal

[26] Nishitani Keiji, 'Sekai tenkanki to shite no gendai', ch. 2, section 1, of *Sekai to kokkakan* (World View and National View) (Tokyo, 1941), 66.

[27] Nishida Kitarō, *Kokutairon* (1944) (Supplement to the Fourth Collection of Philosophical Essays), *Nishida Kitarō zenshu* (Tokyo, 1966), xii. 398-9.

[28] Nishida Kitarō, 'Sekai no shinchitsujo no genri' (1943), in *Nishida Kitarō zenshu*, xii. 434.

present' provided a bulwark against the ravages of modernity as well as a beacon to the world. Just as the nativist histories of the Tokugawa period (the second stage) had been a revolt against a China-centred world order, so too the national mission of the war years (this fourth stage) was a revolt against a Western-centred world. Once again, this change in perspective was prompted less by reconceptualizing the world than by reconceptualizing Japan itself.

IV. *Post-war*

The problem of where to place Japan in world history was not solved by the trauma of defeat. In 1951 Japan's leading twentieth-century political scientist Maruyama Masao lamented:

> Neither practicing politicians nor political scientists have yet clearly seen the pattern and direction of Japan's modern social and political development, a fact that suggests how difficult it is to assign Japan a place in world history. . . . The ideological diversity throughout Japan is a result of the confusion that still surrounds the country's position in world history. Ultimately, the complexity of Japanese nationalism originates in this confusion.[29]

Indeed, after the defeat, both Marxists and modernization theorists expressed the desire to amend national consciousness, so fraught and contradictory, so that it might accord with the seemingly regular, transparent patterns of the outside world.

For instance, in 1965 Matsumoto Sannosuke deplored the lack of true democracy in Japan, arguing that 'one of the most important causes of this tragedy [of Japanese militarism] was the superficiality of Japan's modernization. It had stopped at the level of outward forms, i.e. institutions and laws, and had failed to penetrate the inner realms of the individual's value consciousness and the interpersonal relationships that govern superficial modernization.'[30] Thus, Japan needed to catch up with world history, with the progress shown by countries like China where 'non-ideological nationalism', as Matsumoto called it, had

[29] Maruyama Masao, 'Nationalism in Japan: Its Theoretical Background and Prospects', in Ivan Morris (ed.), *Thought and Behaviour in Modern Japanese Politics* (Oxford, 1963), 135.

[30] Matsumoto Sannosuke, 'Introduction', *Journal of Social and Political Ideas in Japan*, 4/2 (1966), 5.

sparked a revolutionary move in 1949 toward true modernization. Once again, this sense of Japan's unique and problematic status, its persistent self-image of being out of step—usually dawdling in the rear but sometimes in the glorious vanguard—rested on a hierarchical paradigm of world history. Given the assumption that the global pattern of events was comprehensible, Japan was left to ponder first and foremost the oddity of itself.

In direct response to Matsumoto's argument, Harry D. Harootunian challenged the precept of an easily comprehensible world trajectory toward democracy and freedom. Urging Japanese intellectuals to realize that 'Japan is in fact a modern society and must confront the problems raised by modernity not modernization', Harootunian suggests that modernity itself, 'as we are beginning to learn, has nothing or very little to do with the achievement of democracy. . . . Modernity is showing, to the contrary, that its purpose is the establishment and spread of a rational and efficient "unfreedom".'[31] From Harootunian's perspective, Matsumoto and his colleagues, in claiming inferiority to Western modernization and democracy *and* to Communist Chinese nationalism, are avoiding the larger challenge of unfreedom that faces every mass society. The old Japanese paradigm of seeking to understand a problematic Self in relation to a comprehensible and unproblematic world order allowed scholars to evade their responsibility to grasp the true condition of the modern world.

V. *Conclusion*

It has recently been suggested by an American scholar that all non-Western cultures seek equality with or superiority to the West.[32] Although such a position may be instrumental in American debates over identity politics, as a statement of historical fact, it is incorrect.[33] Self-assertion is not the axiomatic,

[31] Harry D. Harootunian, 'Comment on Professor Matsumoto's "Introduction" ', *Journal of Social and Political Ideas in Japan*, 5/2–3 (1967), 320.

[32] Stefan Tanaka, *Japan's Orient: Rendering Pasts into History* (Berkeley, 1993), p. ix.

[33] For instance, the Canela of Brazil created a myth to justify their inferior status in relation to Brazilians of European descent, and they use this inferior status to claim benevolence and material goods from outsiders. See William H. Crocker and Jean Crocker, *The Canela: Bonding through Kinship, Ritual, and Sex* (New York, 1994), 22–4.

ahistorical mind-set of all peoples at all times. Oppression, colonialism, sexism, and racism take their toll by eroding the self-confidence of individuals and groups, worming their way into the very psyche of those they damage. Even in the best of circumstances, asserting equality or supremacy is often far less important to a culture than crafting and maintaining the complex conceptual structures that give experience meaning. The imperative of culture is to bestow meaning, not similarity of status or ascendancy. In a chaotic world, the creation of a system of comprehensibility, whatever its strategic consequences, provides a bulwark against the cold horror of a world without sense or pattern, without cause or effect, without necessity or freedom. Once created, systems of meaning, because of their crucial importance, are protected, re-encoded, even turned upside down, but they endure with remarkable tenacity. Furthermore, as we have seen in the case of Japan, that which is deemed most comprehensible may not even be the self, and therefore selfhood cannot always serve as the fulcrum for understanding the world.

Let me put this another way. If we begin with the assumption that every culture always seeks equality or superiority, then the references by Japanese intellectuals to themselves as 'barbarians' in relation to China, or as 'late-developers' or 'failed revolutionaries' in relation to 'the West' become signs of a psycho-social pathology. Only declarations of superiority can be classed as psychologically 'normal', and, tragically, such declarations in Japan during the 1930s and 1940s accompanied the most brutal forms of world history, written in the blood of Asia. If, however, we take the desire to graft systems of meaning on to the chaos of existence as our basic premiss about human cultures, we understand Japanese patterns of apprehending the world in a different way, one indebted to history rather than psychology. The historical relationship between China and Japan, a hierarchical model recast on to the relation between the West and Japan, becomes the perduring structure guiding Japan's understanding of the world and its anxious concern for self-definition within global structures.

One final point. Although the Japanese tendency to think of the countries arrayed in hierarchical order and to focus on discovering Japan's position through dichotomies of knowability and unknowability, transparency and mystery provides, to my mind, no positive model of how to approach world history, studying this phenomenon suggests two cautionary notes. First, Japanese scholars were right to recognize that writing world histories can never be an ideologically neutral activity. Whatever choices are made, they will always empower one narrative over another, one set of political possibilities over another set. Secondly, the oft-repeated trope of hierarchy and the search for self-understanding in Japanese writings reminds us of the potency of all structures of knowledge and how deeply enmeshed all peoples and languages, Japanese and non-Japanese, are in inherited codes of meaning. Even rebels consciously trying to overturn an inherited paradigm can find themselves, consciously or not, reproducing traditional structures, if in mirror form. These old patterns and also the reaction to them can blind observers to radically new problems as is demonstrated by Matsumoto's position in the post-war period. The systems of meaning to which we are currently wedded—the categories of the nation-state; ideas of class, race, and gender; the political strategies of liberals, socialists, and reactionaries—were forged in the nineteenth century when the modern world was structured. Now, on the far side of modernity, we need to be cognizant that a new round of research and a new round of fierce disagreements lie before us as we reconceptualize 'the world', constituted today through global population pressures, environmental limits, and cultural and economic exchange in ways never before experienced.

14

The Opened and the Closed Country: Conflicting Views of Japan's Position in the World

SEBASTIAN CONRAD

When the historian Ienaga Saburō published his 'New History of Japan' in 1947, he pointedly opened it with a coloured map of the world. Revealingly, on his map Japan was no longer represented at the centre but had been moved to the fringes of the globe. After defeat in 1945, the Japanese people, Ienaga was convinced, 'now knew about Japan's position in the world'. For him, this insight implied the need to interpret the Japanese past as an integral part of this larger framework.[1]

Such examples abound in early post-war Japan. Allusions to a world history (*sekaishi*) were inevitably found in any work that departed from the narrowly nationalistic views of the wartime period. The enthusiasm for universal history resulted in a number of handbooks and surveys delineating historical development around the globe. More common, however, was the use of the concept as a point of reference to interpret the Japanese past. Thus 'world history' was invoked in order to situate Japan *vis-à-vis* the other Asian nations or the 'West'. This preoccupation with a positioning of Japanese history has remained a constant concern in Japanese post-war historiography.

In coming to terms with Japan's relationship to the world, two concepts have been especially influential. The contradictory notions of 'opening the country' (*kaikoku*) and 'national seclusion' (*sakoku*) not only denote different periods in Japanese history, but have come to be used metaphorically to denote different ways of situating Japan within world history. In this essay, I shall use these concepts to illustrate conflicting perspectives on Japan's

[1] Ienaga Saburō, *Shin Nihonshi* (Tokyo, 1947), 130.

position in the world that emerged in the latter half of the twentieth century.

I. *'Kaikoku': Introducing Japan into World History*

1. *Laws, Stages, Europe*

Shortly after the end of the Second World War, when the eminent social scientist Maruyama Masao referred to Japan's position in the world, he called for a 'third opening of the country'.[2] This demand expressed the sentiment of many critical intellectuals at the time: beginning with its withdrawal from the League of Nations in 1931, Japan had in many respects isolated itself from the world, and (as Maruyama saw it) this retreat had proved to be utterly detrimental both for international peace and for Japanese society. The American occupation in 1945 signalled (and forced) another 'opening' (*kaikoku*) of Japan, reminiscent of earlier instances of intensified contact with the Western world. In the sixteenth century, Portuguese missionaries had started to spread Christianity and artefacts of European culture (most notably, guns) before being driven out by the Japanese Shogun in the early decades of the seventeenth century. The edict of expulsion in 1603 marked the beginning of some 250 years of national seclusion (*sakoku*), during which virtually all ties with other countries were cut; contact was subsequently restricted to one Dutch and one Chinese vessel a year allowed entry at Japanese ports. This phase of relative isolation lasted until 1853, when an American, Commodore Perry, landed in the bay of Uraga and forced the Shogunate to grant access to Japanese ports. This second 'opening' initiated a process of increasing exchange with the Western world—of goods, ideas, and institutions—culminating in the Meiji Restoration and the subsequent 'modernization' along Western lines after 1868.[3]

When the term *kaikoku* was now employed to describe the

[2] Maruyama Masao, 'Kaikoku', in id., *Shū* (Tokyo, 1996), viii. 45–86. Japanese names are rendered according to Japanese custom, with surnames first.

[3] The conventional rendering of the period of 'seclusion', that was influential in the early post-war years, has in recent times been challenged. See Katō Eiichi, 'Research Trends in the Study of the History of Japanese Foreign Relations at the Start of the Early Modern Period. On the Reexamination of "National Seclusion"—From the 1970s to 1990s', *Acta Asiatica*, 67 (1994), 1–29.

post-Second World War order, it alluded to these earlier initiatives to end national and cultural isolation. Maruyama's plea to 'open' Japan to the world again was typical of the intellectual atmosphere of the time. This new perspective, to be sure, was implemented in the first place by the American occupation authorities; their politics were echoed, among Japanese historians, by calls for a new interpretation of the Japanese past that situated it clearly within a global setting. The feeling was widespread that Japan should jettison claims to cultural peculiarity and embark on a path that was in accord with world history.[4]

This call for an international, world-historical perspective was particularly prevalent among the large numbers of Marxist historians. In the wake of military surrender, Marxism soon emerged as the dominant influence on the interpretation of Japanese history. During the war, Marxist thought had been suppressed and most of its representatives were banned from the academy. After 1945, the tide turned and Marxism now appeared as the only intellectual current that was not implicated in the nationalist propaganda of the war years.[5] For this reason, the American occupation army, too, co-operated readily with Marxist intellectuals. At least until 1948, the occupation officers treated the Marxist opposition as welcome allies against the fascist elements in Japanese society. The Japanese Communist Party, in turn, greeted the American forces as liberators from wartime oppression. The social reforms initiated by the American occupation were hailed by some Japanese Marxist historians as the moment of a bourgeois revolution in Japan. In these first years after the war, then, Japanese politics witnessed an unlikely coalition of American occupation politics and Marxist intellectual discourse. At the universities, this resulted in the relegation of the most ardent representatives of a nationalist historiography. In their stead, Marxist economists and historians were soon called back to the institutions that had relegated them

[4] For an account of the reactions of Japanese intellectuals in the early post-war years, see J. Victor Koschmann, *Revolution and Subjectivity in Postwar Japan* (Chicago, 1996); id., 'Maruyama Masao and the Incomplete Project of Modernity', in Masao Miyoshi and H. D. Harootunian (eds.), *Postmodernism and Japan* (Durham, NC, 1989), 123–42; and Tsurumi Shunsuke, *A Cultural History of Postwar Japan 1945–1980* (London, 1987).

[5] For an account of Marxist historiography in Japan, see Germaine Hoston, *Marxism and the Crisis of Development in Prewar Japan* (Princeton, 1986); Tōyama Shigeki, *Sengo no rekishigaku to rekishi ishiki* (Tokyo, 1968).

a decade before; within a few years, their interpretation of modern Japanese history was well established as the leading paradigm in Japanese historiography.[6]

A fundamental tenet of the Marxist approach was its strategy of inscribing the Japanese past into the framework of world history. As a consequence of this perspective, calls for a new world history (*sekaishi*) were almost ubiquitous in the early post-war years. The first 'World History' was published in 1949 by the newspaper *Mainichi shinbun*. Its seven volumes were edited by the geographer Izuka Kōji from Tokyo University, who was inspired by Vidal de la Blache and Lucien Febvre. The fourth volume of the series, written by three prominent Marxist historians, was dedicated to the history of Japan. The world-historical perspective of this volume consisted mainly in the mode of periodization, which adapted the Marxist point of view to the Japanese setting. Japanese history was depicted as the succession of a classless society, a slaveholder society, feudalism, and modern capitalism.[7] World history was assumed to evolve according to universal laws and within a set of given stages of development. From this perspective, understanding world history implied gaining knowledge of the fundamental historical tendencies that applied everywhere. Japanese history, accordingly, could then be narrated with reference to this universal process.

Although the concept of world history was most prominent among Marxist and other modernist historians,[8] in the early post-war years its significance was not limited to the proponents

[6] This coalition of American occupation politics and Japanese Marxist historiography did not, however, last very long. As a result of the so-called 'reverse course' in occupation policies in 1948, the *raison d'être* of virtually every programme of the occupation was the contribution it made to the struggle against communism inside and outside Japan. See Howard B. Schonberger, *Aftermath of War: Americans and the Remaking of Japan 1945–1952* (Kent, 1989); John Dower, *Embracing Defeat: Japan in the Wake of World War II* (New York, 1999).

[7] Tōyama Shigeki, Ishimoda Shō, and Takahashi Shinichi, *Nihon* (*Sekai no rekishi*, vol. iv) (Tokyo, 1949).

[8] The term 'modernists' (*kindaishugisha*) in contemporary parlance referred to a number of social scientists such as Maruyama Masao or Ōtsuka Hisao, who subscribed to a critical view of Japanese modernization but were influenced more by Max Weber than by Karl Marx. Despite many commonalities between the two groups, the 'modernists' were heavily attacked by Marxist historians in the early post-war years. See Tōyama, *Sengo no rekishigaku*, 53–5; Inumaru Giichi, 'Sengo Nihon Marukusushugi shigaku ni kansuru oboegaki', in Rekishigaku kenkyūkai and Nihonshi kenkyūkai (eds.), *Kōza Nihonshi 10: Gendai rekishigaku no tenbō* (Tokyo, 1971), 97–172.

of Historical Materialism. Even the highly conservative Ministry of Education (*Monbushō*) engaged in the developmental thinking that dominated Japanese intellectual debates after the war. Courses in World History were now established in the school curriculum; the instructions of the ministry on this occasion included the advice to 'have the students understand the necessary character of historical development'.[9] Across the spectrum of Japanese historiography, therefore, the belief in universal laws of world history was widespread.[10]

The most intense and ardent discussions about world history were nevertheless conducted among historians of a Marxist hue. In a sense, the bulk of discussions and controversies among different schools of Marxist historiography can be read as one major attempt to inscribe the Japanese past into the frame of world history. The general plot was thus treated as a pre-existing mould; controversy arose only over the correct inscription of particular (Japanese) events into the universal narrative. The annual meeting of the influential Marxist historians' organization (*Rekishigaku kenkyūkai*) in 1949 reflected this consciousness of the problem: the general theme for all sections was 'The fundamental laws of world history'.[11] These presumably regular patterns of historical development, however, could not be observed just anywhere. World history had not manifested itself to the same extent all over the globe. To arrive at the laws of world history directly and without contamination, the historian needed to turn to the European past.

Takahashi Kōhachirō, a historian of France at Tokyo University, explained this relationship in the preface to a volume on European economic history he edited in 1947. It was the aim of this collection of essays to analyse 'the emergence of the structure of the modern world in Western Europe', since these structures 'embodied the stages of development of world history (universal history) in their "pure and classical" form'. Research into

[9] See Naruse Osamu, *Sekaishi no ishiki to riron* (Tokyo, 1977), 71.

[10] In the 1950s, one can nevertheless differentiate between the Marxist paradigm of universal stages of world history and the more conservative approach, manifest in a number of world history textbooks, of constructing a 'world history' by simply conflating the older disciplines of Western history (*seiyōshi*) and Oriental history (*tōyōshi*). See Naruse, *Sekaishi*, 143–52.

[11] Rekishigaku kenkyūkai (ed.), *Sekaishi no kihon hōsoku: Rekishigaku kenkyūkai 1949 nendo taikai hōkoku* (Tokyo, 1949).

European history, accordingly, was not an end in itself; rather, it was a means to discover the fundamental laws of world history, which seemed to be accessible only in their European incarnation.[12] These laws could subsequently be applied to understand the Japanese past. 'Even if we deal with this problem only in a hypothetical way, it is possible to claim that from the perspective of the classical European stages of development we can deduct a new point of view for the analysis of Japanese society as well.'[13]

In these early post-war years, the renewed interest in world history was less an expression of a wider geographical scope than an attempt to understand the Japanese particulars through reference to a global process. The new paradigm of *sekaishi* thus implied not so much situating the Japanese past *within* world history, but rather interpreting Japan *as* world history. When a world-historical perspective was invoked, what was called for was not a study of more or less distant regions and their relation to Japan. The large bulk of historical writing in Japan, consequently, made only superficial reference to international relations, to the pressure of the major powers, or to influences from abroad. Instead, Japanese history seemed to evolve firmly within the boundaries of the Japanese nation-state; in these narratives, colonialism, the Second World War, or the Chinese Revolution—to name but a few events—had virtually no influence on the development of Japanese society. The world-historical character of these accounts hinged not on an insight into the inextricable entanglement of the histories of the world. Instead, *sekaishi* implied interpreting the past with reference to a universal standard.[14]

[12] For a more detailed analysis of this problem, see Sebastian Conrad, 'What Time is Japan? Problems of Comparative (Intercultural) Historiography', *History and Theory*, 38 (1999), 67–83.

[13] Takahashi Kōhachirō, *Kindai shakai seiritsu shiron* (Tokyo, 1947), 1, 16, and 17. See also Ōtsuka Hisao, *Shogen: Wareware wa hōkensei kara shihonshugi e no idō katei o dono yō ni mondai to suru ka*, in Ōtsuka Hisao, Takahashi Kōhachirō, and Matsuda Tomoo (eds.), *Seiyō keizaishi kōza: Hōkensei kara shihon shugi e no idō*, vol. i: *Hōkensei no keizaiteki kiso* (Tokyo, 1960), 1–44, at 3–4.

[14] The irony that a world-historical perspective increasingly led to the exclusion of all events outside Japan did not go unnoticed. Among Marxist historians, there were fierce debates over the issue of *ikkoku hatten dankai ron* (the history of Japan according to the theory of the stages of development). See Nagahara Keiji, *Rekishigaku josetsu* (Tokyo, 1978), 124–5. For a more sympathetic account of the world view of post-war Japanese social science, see Sugiyama Mitsunobu, 'The World Conception of Japanese Social Science: The Kōza Faction, the Ōtsuka School, and the Uno School of Economics', *Positions: East Asia Cultures Critique*, 6/1 (1998), 67–112.

2. *'Datsu-A': Dissociating Japan from Asia*

What was striking in these early post-war years was the complete neglect of all historical ties that Japan had established with its Asian neighbours. Within the unquestioned paradigm of the times, Japanese history was systematically 'de-Asianized'. World history was largely identified with the development of Western Europe, while Asia figured as a region of stagnation and backwardness. Within this framework, it seemed only logical to dissociate Japan from Asia. As in the late nineteenth century, when the philosopher Fukuzawa Yukichi had encouraged Japan to 'leave Asia' (*datsu-a*) in its quest for progress and modern civilization, in the early post-war period Japanese historians once again interpreted Japan within a non-Asian context. To borrow Karatani Kōjin's words, 'postwar "space" consists of a domain that has discarded Asia'.[15]

One of the rare critics of this perspective was Takeuchi Yoshimi, who explicitly argued against the dominant *datsu-a* ideology. In a critical essay published in 1948, Takeuchi denounced Japanese modernity as a mere copy of the West under capitalist auspices. In his view, Japan acted as Europe's model student (*yūtōsei*) and had long discarded all cultural autonomy. While China met the Western challenge with resistance, Japan had refused to resist and was therefore devoid of all subjectivity. For Takeuchi, Japan was neither part of Asia nor of the West, but 'nothing at all' (*nani mono demo nai*).[16]

Takeuchi's critique was directed primarily against the Marxists and Modernists who dominated intellectual debates in the 1950s. But the general perspective of 'de-Asianization' was not modified even when academic fashions changed. In the

[15] See Karatani Kōjin, 'The Discursive Space of Modern Japan', in Masao Miyoshi and Harry D. Harootunian (eds.), *Japan in the World* (Durham, NC, 1993), 288–315, at 296.

[16] Takeuchi Yoshimi, *Kindai no chōkoku* (Tokyo, 1983); see also Harry D. Harootunian, 'Visible Discourses/Invisible Ideologies', in Masao Miyoshi and Harry D. Harootunian (eds.), *Postmodernism and Japan* (Durham, NC, 1989), 63–92; Nagahara, *Rekishigaku*, 255. One of the few historians with a similar view of the relationship between Japan and Asia was the China specialist Niida Noboru; see also Naruse Osamu, *Sekaishi*, 96–8. In the 1960s orthodox Marxist historians also realized the need to incorporate Asia into their interpretations of Japanese history. See e.g. Ubukata Naokichi, Tōyama Shigeki, and Tanaka Masatoshi (eds.), *Rekishizō saikōsei no kadai: Rekishigaku no hōhō to Ajia* (Tokyo, 1966).

1960s modernization theory became increasingly popular among Japanese historians. Led by the prominent Harvard historian Edward O. Reischauer, who became ambassador to Japan in 1961, modernization theory was systematically introduced as the appropriate alternative to Marxist historiography. The new gospel soon gained a broad following and remains influential to the present day. The picture of Japanese history that modernization theory presented was explicitly directed against the prevailing Marxist view, and it was brightly coloured: the implicit *telos* of Japanese history was no longer fascism and the war, but rather post-war democracy and a flourishing economy. This point of view produced a new version of the Japanese past, in which the 'distortions' and 'feudal remnants', in Marxist parlance, were transformed into 'traditions' and a cultural reservoir for indigenous modernization.

Again (as in the case of Marxist historiography), modernization theory was perceived as an attempt to transcend narratives of national peculiarity and inscribe the respective pasts into a global framework. The path of modernization was believed to be open to anyone, and complying with the prescribed requirements promised successful development in accordance with the patterns of world history. However, the historical writings produced within this framework were concerned with the 'world' only in a very particular sense. Much as in the case of Historical Materialism, 'world history' was invoked largely to derive developmental patterns according to which a specific history could be interpreted. As a consequence, the past could safely be analysed within the confines of the Japanese archipelago. Modernization emerged out of native traditions, or it was not to be. Influences from without, interference, or intervention were not an important part of the terminology of this kind of historiography. The gaze of the modernization theorist rarely crossed the borders of the Japanese state.[17]

Also within this new paradigm a by now familiar worldview prevailed: world history was identified with the 'West', and Asia remained the repository of backwardness. The idea of the

[17] For an account of modernization theory in Japanese historiography, see Kinbara Samon, *'Nihon kindaika'ron no rekishizō. Sono hihanteki kentō e no shiten* (Tokyo, 1968); Wada Haruki, 'Kindaikaron', in Rekishigaku kenkyūkai and Nihonshi kenkyūkai (eds.), *Kōza Nihonshi 9: Nihon shigaku ronsō* (Tokyo, 1971), 255–82.

'West', vague and homogenizing as it was, nevertheless underwent significant transformations. During the early post-war years, it was largely identified with Western Europe (Germany, after ostensibly having failed at modernization, no longer being an integral part of the picture). In the course of the 1960s, however, the comparative perspective shifted to include, and, indeed, focus on the USA. With modernization theory arriving in Japan, the Harvard University image of the world emerged as the model of world history.[18]

Conflating world history with the 'West' not only produced a yardstick by which to measure the Japanese past objectively. At the same time, it implied that by catching up according to the unchanging laws of world history, Japan itself would eventually become part of the 'West'. This has become common knowledge in the social sciences, where, as Noam Chomsky has remarked, 'of course Europe now includes Japan, which we may regard as honorary European'.[19] In Japan as well, attempts were made to establish Japan as part of the 'West'. Since the late 1950s, when the American occupation had ended and economic recovery was becoming palpable, Japanese historians felt compelled to explain not only fascism and the loss of the war, but also the apparent success of the post-war system. The apparent time lag (*vis-à-vis* the 'West') that had characterized Japan's modernization until then seemed to have been almost overcome, and the changing situation seemed to call for a new perspective on world history as well.

An early example of this tendency is an article by the cultural anthropologist Umesao Tadao that was published in 1957 in the journal *Chūō kōron*. Umesao was clearly influenced by Arnold Toynbee's visit to Japan the previous year, and his argument can partly be understood as a reaction to Toynbee's theses. In his quest for Japan's 'exact coordinates' in the world, Umesao fervently rejected the common view that Japan was part of the Orient.[20] Instead, he stressed its commonalities with Western Europe. In his view of history, the 'old world' comprised Europe, Northern Africa, and Asia. Within these regions, only a

[18] See Harry D. Harootunian, 'America's Japan/Japan's Japan', in Miyoshi and Harootunian (eds.), *Japan in the World*, 196–221.

[19] Noam Chomsky, 'The New World Order', *Agenda*, 62 (1991), 13–15.

[20] For an incisive analysis of Japan's relationship to the 'Orient', see Stefan Tanaka, *Japan's Orient: Rendering Pasts into History* (Berkeley, 1993).

handful of countries could pride themselves on successful development—namely, the nations on the periphery of the Eurasian landmass. 'On a national scale, only Japan and—on the opposite fringe [of the continent]—the Western European countries have produced a highly civilized state. There is still a great difference from countries like China, Southeast Asia, India, Russia, the Islamic countries or Eastern Europe.'[21] From this perspective, which hinged on economic growth and national independence as the principal parameters of 'successful development', the edges of the Eurasian continent—that is, Japan and Western Europe—appeared to belong to the same cultural sphere. According to Umesao, these commonalities could not be understood, as might be surmised, as the result of a massive import from Europe after the Meiji Restoration in 1868. Instead, he held universal patterns of world history responsible for the striking similarities. 'The development of Japanese civilization since the Meiji period was nothing but a necessary process determined by the laws of world history and was not the result of a cultural conversion or Europeanization.'[22]

The common denominator that characterized both Japan and Western Europe was, for Umesao, the experience of feudalism. Only the social formation of feudalism, he argued, had made a bourgeois revolution possible, which, in turn, was a necessary prerequisite for capitalist development. This precondition he found lacking in other countries that had been ruled autocratically or had been colonized in the course of their history. By thus establishing feudalism as the pivot of historical development, Umesao felt it was legitimate to treat Japan and Western Europe as part of a connected (if not integrated) whole. According to the regularities of world history Europe was no longer the only model. For Umesao, Japan itself was part of the 'West'.

[21] Umesao Tadao, 'Bunmei no seitai shikan josetsu', *Chūō kōron* (Feb. 1957), 32–49, at 37.

[22] Ibid. 41.

II. '*Sakoku*': *National Isolation and Japanese Civilization*

1. *Japan against the West*

A model of world history that essentially drew on the experience of Western Europe and the USA was the dominant paradigm in the 1950s and 1960s. Both Marxism and modernization theory, while fierce opponents in the political sphere, shared a historicist version of global development as their common rationale. Even though this perspective (with all due revisions and adaptations) continues to be a powerful frame of interpretation to the present day, there have since been a number of attempts to wrest Japan from what was perceived as Western historiographical dominance. In fact, a universalizing outlook long hailed as 'progressive' by the majority of Japanese historians has now come under attack by some revisionists. The post-war orthodoxy is increasingly discredited as an American import and derogatorily termed the 'Tokyo War Crimes Trial interpretation of history' (*Tōkyō saiban shikan*).[23] Although always a minority among Japanese historians, revisionists have, since the 1960s, repeatedly tried to establish an alternative historiography that presented Japan not as catching up with, but rather pitted against, the West.[24]

An early example of this tendency is the thesis of the '100 years' war' by the writer and literary critic Hayashi Fusao. In his massive study published in 1964, he interpreted Japan's modern history as a century-long confrontation with the West. Starting with Commodore Perry's visit to the bay of Uraga in 1853 and culminating in the American occupation of post-war Japan, Hayashi saw Japan in a continuing military struggle for independence. This was not a struggle, however, fought only for

[23] Prominent examples of this tendency are the interpretations put forward by the 'Association for a liberalist view on history' (*Jiyūshugi shikan kenkyūkai*) led by Fujioka Nobukatsu.

[24] The revisionists pitting Japan against the 'West' are usually politically right-wing, and the discussions below will be limited to this approach. Nevertheless, there have also been attempts from within the Marxist camp to interpret Japanese history in the light of the confrontation with the 'West'. For an early example see Shibahara Takuji, 'Ajia shakai no henkaku to rekishigaku no ninmu', *Rekishigaku kenkyū*, 253 (1961), 60–6. Here Shibahara interpreted the Meiji Restoration as part of a national war of defence against encroachments from abroad. Revealingly, Shibahara did not use the term 'seiyō' that implicitly associated the 'West' with an advanced civilization but preferred the term 'the powers' (*rekkyō*). See also Nagahara, *Rekishigaku josetsu*, 124–7.

Japan's sake. The purported deeper meaning behind this clash was the Japanese mission to liberate Asia from Western dominance. 'The Greater East Asian War was the fate with which Japan was burdened in the course of these 100 years.'[25] Employing a terminology that reminded some of his readers of wartime propaganda, Hayashi envisioned modern world history as a giant struggle between Japan and the West.[26]

A similar interpretation had already been proposed in 1961 by the philosopher Ueyama Shumpei. Ueyama, who was employed at Kyoto University's Institute for Human Sciences (*Jinbun kagaku kenkyūjo*), was repeatedly involved in the historians' debates of the time. For Ueyama, likewise, the Pacific War against the USA was not an expression of Japan's failure to act according to the laws of world history. This, to be sure, had been the perspective of the majority of critical historians in the 1950s: Japanese fascism and its wars of aggression were seen as the result of Japan's deviant path, of its fatal turn against the West. For Ueyama, however, as for Hayashi Fusao, it was, conversely, the logic of world history, or 'fate' in their parlance, that had forced Japan on to a path that eventually led to military encounter with the West. After Perry and after the Meiji Restoration, Japan had allegedly passed the point of no return. 'The decision to open the country implied with almost logical necessity a course of development that had to lead—via the dissolution of feudalism, the industrial revolution, and the invasion of lesser developed countries—to collision with the progressive countries.'[27] This interpretation, like Hayashi's, encompassed an explicit endorsement of the war against the USA; the decision to resist colonization in the nineteenth century 'left no other way than war'.[28]

What is interesting here is not so much the fact that a kind of rhetoric that seemed to have vanished with Japan's surrender in 1945 now re-emerged on the discursive stage. It was striking, however, that Ueyama defined Japan's position in the world in a manner that would have been inconceivable a decade before.

[25] Hayashi Fusao, *Daitōā sensō kōteiron* (Tokyo, 1971), 140.

[26] See also Wolfgang Seifert, *Nationalismus im Nachkriegs-Japan: Ein Beitrag zur Ideologie der völkischen Nationalisten* (Hamburg, 1977).

[27] Ueyama Shumpei, 'Daitōa sensō no shisōshiteki igi', *Chūō kōron* (Sept. 1961), 98–107, at 106.

[28] Ibid. 106.

For him, the necessities of world history did not lead to an ever closer convergence of Japan with the modern West; rather, historical development produced and reinforced a dichotomy along the East–West divide. As part of this interpretative move, Japan was 're-Asianized', albeit in a very peculiar way: in the revisionist version of history, Japan was both the epitome of and the leading force within Asian culture. In essence, it was the Japanese mission to liberate the Asian nations from the West, and to lead them to a sense of Asian identity. Rather than being part of Asia, Japan in fact represented Asia.

Ueyama is interesting in this context in yet another respect. Unlike the figureheads of post-war modernism such as Maruyama Masao, he was an advocate of the era of national seclusion, of *sakoku*. In his recent 'History of Japanese Civilization', published in the 1990s, Ueyama underlined the central importance he attributed to the Edo period (1600–1868). For him, the politics of national isolation were not a sign of stagnation or backwardness, but rather initiated a necessary period of cultural digestion. After a long history of massive Chinese influence, both cultural and political, a period of seclusion seemed necessary to appropriate what had been acquired over the centuries. National isolation, from this perspective, was a strategy to turn foreign borrowings into things Japanese.[29]

The Edo period, in this interpretation, was a phase of purification, of the reaffirmation of a national essence. Ueyama's concern for the essentials of Japaneseness was not new: two decades ago, he had found the unchanging nature of Japan in the so-called Jōmon culture of the period before the second century BC. This was a period before the history of cultural borrowing began—not only before the influx of Chinese civilization, but even before the import of rice cultivation. In this pristine epoch of Japan's history, Ueyama saw the Japanese characterized by an eagerness to learn, by simplicity in their way of life and aesthetic style, and by an inherent peacefulness. All militarism and expansionist drive, therefore, had to be the result of foreign influences.[30] Now, in the 1990s, Ueyama again

[29] Ueyama Shumpei, *Nihon bunmeishi no kōsō: Juyō to sōzō no kiseki* (Tokyo, 1990). See also Tessa Morris-Suzuki, 'The Invention and Reinvention of "Japanese Culture"', *Journal of Asian Studies*, 54 (1995), 759–80.

[30] Ueyama Shumpei, *Daitōa sensō no isan* (Tokyo, 1972).

praised the benefits of a phase of seclusion, of abstinence from exchange. He idealized the Edo period as a phase of adaptation and Japanization, a phase in which Japan's individuality (*kosei*) finally re-emerged. His view implied that also at the end of the twentieth century, after yet another phase of cultural borrowing (this time, from the West), a new period of seclusion might be advisable.

2. *Modern World System* v. *Closed-Country System*

Ueyama was by no means alone in his idealization of the Tokugawa period. During the 1990s, public interest in the legacy of Edo rose significantly and led commentators to speak of an 'Edo boom' (*Edo būmu*). Symptomatic of this recurrent valuation was Irie Takanori's call for a universalization of the principles of the Edo period, for an 'Edonization of the world' (*sekai no Edoka*).[31] The intellectual historian Bitō Masahide re-evaluated Tokugawa Japan as a period of early modernization, long before intensified contact with the West. In his book 'What was the Edo period?', Bitō found the indigenous roots of modern Japan in the customs and mentalities that emerged in the Tokugawa period.[32] This resurgent interest in Japan's pre-Meiji history was not, however, confined to the academic sphere. The success of the new Edo-Tōkyō museum in Tokyo, for example, testifies to the popular base of the 'Edo boom'.[33]

It is in this context that we have to situate Kawakatsu Heita's attempt to arrive at a new understanding of the history of the Edo period. He presented the politics of seclusion as a key to an alternative modernity, as a way out of world history as defined in the West. Kawakatsu is an economic historian at Waseda University. He received his doctorate in 1984 from Oxford University for a study of 'International Competition in Cotton Goods in the Late Nineteenth Century'. Although largely couched in econometric and technical terms, this early work already reveals some of the culturalist convictions that Kawakatsu would popularize in the 1990s. In his dissertation, he argued that the early Japanese cotton industry competed not so

[31] Irie Takanori, *Gurōbaru herenizumu no shutsuge: Sekai wa 'edoka' suru* (Tokyo, 1990).

[32] Bitō Masahide, *Edo jidai to wa nani ka: Nihonshijō no kinsei to kindai* (Tokyo, 1992).

[33] See Carol Gluck, 'The Invention of Edo', in Stephen Vlastos (ed.), *Mirror of Modernity: Invented Traditions of Modern Japan* (Berkeley, 1998), 262–84.

much with the British textile industry, but rather with the other Asian nations. Contrary to contemporary predictions, the influx of British cotton goods did not have devastating effects on the Japanese cotton industry. In fact, there was hardly a market for British textiles in Meiji Japan. Kawakatsu explained this by a specific Japanese demand for thick cloth that could not be met by the fine, thin Lancashire products. The difference in cultural background between England and East Asia was so peculiar that different demand curves—and consequently, different spheres of trade—developed.[34]

In his later works, Kawakatsu has expanded his scope and has arrived at broad generalizations about Japanese culture and its position in the world. In this, he was strongly influenced by Ueyama Shumpei's theory of civilization. Ueyama had defined 'civilization' as both a temporal and a spatial category: while, on the one hand, 'Western civilization' was different from 'Chinese civilization', on the other hand, all civilizations in the course of their history underwent a transformation, or modernization. Ueyama introduced a three-stage scheme of a 'natural' society of hunters and gatherers, of an agricultural society, and, finally, of an industrial society which he saw emerging in Japan around 1900.[35] Kawakatsu combined this theory of civilization with the idea of 'habitat segregation' (*sumiwake*), a concept he borrowed from the naturalist Imanishi Kanji. Imanishi (1902–92), who was associated with the so-called Kyoto school, argued against Darwin's theory of natural selection in which the fittest survives, and instead propagated the mutual and peaceful coexistence of different species.[36] Kawakatsu transferred this notion of peaceful coexistence in separate spheres to the human history of different ethnicities. This operation owed much to the earlier attempts to

[34] For a summary of this argument, see Kawakatsu Heita, 'International Competition in Cotton Goods in the Late Nineteenth Century: Britain versus India and East Asia', in Wolfram Fischer *et al.* (eds.), *The Emergence of a World Economy 1500–1914. Papers of the IX. International Congress of Economic History, Part II: 1850–1914* (Wiesbaden, 1986), 619–43. The importance of intra-Asian trade has become a favourite theme in Japanese economic history since the epoch-making issue of the journal *Shakai keizai shigaku*, 51/1 (1985) with articles by Sugihara Kaoru, Hamashita Takeshi, Kawakatsu Heita, and Tsunoyama Sakae.

[35] Ueyama, *Nihon bunmeishi*. See also Tessa Morris-Suzuki, *Re-Inventing Japan: Time, Space, Nation* (London, 1998), 143–5.

[36] Kawakatsu Heita, *Nihon bunmei to kindai seiyō* (Tokyo, 1991), 152–82. See also id., 'Imanishi's View of the World', *Journal of Japanese Trade and Industry*, 18/2 (Mar. 1999), 14–18.

establish an 'ecological view of civilization' by Umesao Tadao. Umesao had in the 1950s introduced an analogy beteween natural and human history: 'Just as the theory of the succession of life-forms has enabled us to understand the history of the natural communities of animals and plants in a more or less lawful manner, we may likewise be able to understand the history of mankind . . . up to a certain degree in its lawful course.'[37] Combining this belief in the regularities of development with the notions of civilization and 'habitat segregation', Kawakatsu produced his own version of Japan's role in world history.[38]

Kawakatsu's view of the world explicitly competes with other variations of world history. His aim is to arrive at an 'image of the world which in all respects will rival the dominant image of world history in modern Western society'.[39] In Immanuel Wallerstein's world systems theory, for example, development since the age of exploration is essentially interpreted as a process of increasing incorporation of different regions of the globe into a European-dominated system of exchange. The Wallersteinian course of history, then, consisted in the gradual expansion of European influence, and the successive attempts of the 'periphery' to catch up with the industrialized West. For Kawakatsu, this is only one half of the picture. In his version of world history, the 'world system' represents only one of (at least) two paths into modernity.[40] While he admits Wallerstein's theory to be an accurate description of modern European history, it does not help to understand the decisively different course on which Japan had embarked.

To prove this, Kawakatsu goes back to the fifteenth and

[37] Umesao, 'Bunmei', 43.

[38] The strong influence of Umesao's work on Kawakatsu is obvious. However, their interpretations differ in at least two important respects, thus reflecting the different historical contexts in which they originated. While for Umesao, European modernity figures as the *telos* of development, Kawakatsu is looking for alternatives to the European paradigm. These different points of departure, accordingly, result in competing interpretations of the Tokugawa period as well. While Umesao sees the policy of *sakoku* as a decisive obstacle on the path of Japanese modernization, Kawakatsu praises the period of national seclusion as a catalyst that helped Japan to embark on its specific and unique path of development. For a concise summary of Umesao's views, see Umesao Tadao, *Nihon to wa nanika* (Tokyo, 1986).

[39] Kawakatsu, 'Imanishi's View', 14.

[40] Kawakatsu prefers the concept 'second-stage civilization' to the term 'modernity'.

sixteenth centuries to show that European industrialization was only one possible answer to a common problem. In this period, both Europe (mainly England) and Japan significantly increased contact and trade with the older Asian civilization, with China at its core. As a result, Europe underwent a virtual revolution in lifestyle, sparked by the import from East and South-East Asia of sugar, porcelain, tea, and cotton, that first were status symbols for the rich before becoming daily necessities. Likewise, exchange between Japan, the China Sea, and the Indian Ocean intensified from the late fifteenth century, when so-called *wakō* pirates and regular merchants introduced new goods to the Japanese archipelago. In both Europe and Japan, these imports became enormously popular and were soon an indispensable part of culture and daily life. At the same time, the luxury goods trade forced Europeans and Japanese into an ever-increasing economic dependence upon the Asian market. What was more, imports had to be paid for largely with silver and gold (and in addition, in the Japanese case, copper). A growing share of the gold and silver brought to Europe from the Americas, for example, was directly reinvested in the China trade. Thus, the import of cotton and sugar caused a serious outflow of bullion, a monetary drain that was seen both in Europe and in Japan as a dangerous threat to national strength and independence.

As a response to this shared predicament, Kawakatsu now argues, England 'invented' the industrial revolution. 'The process of the industrial revolution in England was, to a large extent, the process of developing domestic textiles as a substitute for imports from India.'[41] It was not the industrial revolution alone, of course, that alleviated England's dependence on China and India. At the same time, the newly colonized islands of the West Indies were used to grow sugar and coffee and thus contributed to the English economy. But the industrial revolution, soon exported to other countries to constitute a 'world system', was the most important contribution to ensuring England's autonomy from Asia. Japan, on the other hand, chose a different path: the path of national seclusion. It closed its borders, prohibited trade and intercourse with other countries, and isolated itself from the world for more than two centuries.

[41] Kawakatsu Heita, 'The National Seclusion Policy Reappraised', *Japan Echo*, 19/2 (1992), 67–76, at 70.

The absence of an industrial revolution in pre-Meiji Japan should not lead us to deduce, Kawakatsu assures us, that in Japan the economy remained unproductive and stagnant. Following the economic historian Hayami Akira, Kawakatsu speaks of an 'industrious revolution' in Japan during the Edo period. As a result, the outflow of specie came to an end, and formerly imported goods, like cotton cloth, were now produced at home. From 1600 to the 1850s, Japan led a life of isolation, with hardly any contact with the outside world. Faced with the common problem of increasing dependence on the Asian mainland, then, Europe and Japan chose two very different solutions: while England developed the industrial revolution, Japan opted for a policy of *sakoku*.[42]

Both Japan and Europe thus underwent a production revolution and advanced from the stage of agrarian societies to industrial/industrious societies. Both civilizations developed in very different and incompatible ways, but both reached a kind of modernity of their own. 'Industrial society does not represent the only possible form for civilization's second stage.' Kawakatsu, accordingly, differentiates between two different forms of 'second-stage civilizations'. On the one hand, there was the industrial West, now connected to other parts of the globe in the modern world system of Wallersteinian dimensions; 'the other type of second-stage civilization has its roots in ancient China, and it came into being when Japan asserted its independence from the Chinese sphere. When I speak of the closed-country system, this is the significance I attribute to it.'[43]

3. *The 'Wisdom of Internal Focusing'*

This revisionist interpretation of the period of national seclusion has, in recent years, found a considerable following among scholars who aim for a fundamental change in Japanese historiography. This objective is most closely connected to the project of propagating a 'liberalist view of history' (*jiyūshugi shikan*) associated mainly with Tokyo University historian Fujioka Nobukatsu and the specialist in German literature, Nishio Kanji. This loose

[42] See Kawakatsu, *Nihon bunmei*, 113–29.

[43] Kawakatsu, 'Seclusion Policy', 76. For a critique of Kawakatsu's version of economic history, see Sugihara Kaoru, 'Kindai Ajia keizaishi ni okeru renzoku to danzetsu', *Shakai keizaishigaku*, 62 (1996), 370–92.

group, who have mustered many high school teachers but have so far failed to gain substantial support from within academia, has set itself the goal of liberating Japan from what they call a 'masochistic view of history'.[44] According to Fujioka, post-war Japan has been under the spell of the 'Tokyo War Crimes Trial interpretation of history' (*Tōkyō saiban shikan*), an interpretation of the past allegedly forced upon the Japanese by the American occupation. In its stead, Fujioka pleads for a version of the Japanese past that allows the Japanese to feel pride in their history and culture. He thus connects to central tenets of the nationalist historiography of the 1960s, and Fujioka and his associates are therefore sometimes labelled 'neo-nationalists'. However, their project to revise Japanese history differs in important respects from the approach of Hayashi Fusao, for example, and has to be contextualized in the post-Cold War years of the 1990s. In particular, the search for an independent kind of modernity and the attempt to interpret the Japanese past as part of Asian history characterize the 'liberalist' approach and make it an integral part of a postmodern discourse on a globalized world.[45]

A central element in the widely publicized campaign to revise national historiography is the attempt to establish new school books to inculcate the new gospel in the next generation.[46] Part of this endeavour, part of the 'crusade for a revision of Japanese history', is the foundation of a 'Society for the production of new history textbooks' (*Atarashii rekishi kyōkasho o tsukuru kai*).[47] In its name, Nishio Kanji has published a voluminous survey of the 'History of the Japanese People' (*Kokumin no rekishi*) with the explicit objective of securing for Japan 'an appropriate position in world history'.[48] A seminal chapter in this book contains his

[44] For an overview of this 'liberalist' revisionism, see Ricki Kersten, 'Neo-nationalism and the "Liberal School of History"', *Japan Forum*, 11 (1999), 191–203; Steffi Richter, 'Nicht nur ein Sturm im Wasserglas. Japans jüngster Schulbuchstreit', *Internationale Schulbuchforschung*, 23 (2001), 277–300.

[45] See Aaron Gerow, 'Consuming Asia, Consuming Japan: The New Neonationalistic Revisionism in Japan', in Laura Hein and Mark Selden (eds.), *Censoring Histoy: Citizenship and Memory in Japan, Germany, and the United States* (London, 2000), 74–95; Narita Ryūichi, '"Rekishi" o kyōkasho ni egaku to iu koto', *Sekai* (June 2001), 69–77.

[46] See e.g. Fujioka Nobukatsu, *Kyōkasho ga oshienai rekishi* (Tokyo, 1996).

[47] Nishio Kanji, 'Eine Neufassung der Geschichte Japans und der Welt', *Japan Echo*, 24/2 (1997), 100–6, at 106.

[48] Nishio Kanji, *Kokumin no rekishi*, ed. by Atarashii rekishi kyōkasho o tsukuru kai (Tokyo, 1999), 768. For a critique see Kyōkasho ni shinjitsu to jiyū o' renrakukai (ed.), *Tettei hihan: Kokumin no rekishi* (Tokyo, 2000).

interpretation of the Edo period, which he rehabilitated as the decisive phase of Japan's modernization. To this end, Nishio draws on the work of historian Arano Yasunori to show that 'seclusion' (*sakoku*) inadequately describes the realities of the Edo period. In fact, there was never an order to close the country. And, as Arano's research shows, during the seventeenth and eighteenth centuries Japan was by no means shut off completely from the outside world. Contact with Korea and China was intensive; and through trade with Holland, Japan was able to gather information about the European world. What is more, the term *sakoku* itself was an invention of the nineteenth century, only popularized in the Meiji period; during Tokugawa days, the Japanese people had no consciousness of living in a 'closed country'. As Nishio argues, the ideology of the period of seclusion, firmly tied to notions of stagnation and backwardness, was itself a product of contact with the West.[49]

While there was no seclusion, the Edo period was nevertheless characterized by extensive regulations and limitations on trade as well as a strictly enforced prohibition on leaving the country. However, according to Nishio, this cannot be interpreted as 'seclusion', but rather as a form of conscious withdrawal while keeping up contact and a necessary level of trade. 'Some people refer to the phenomena of this period in Japan by the term "closed country" (*sakoku*), but I prefer to call it the "wisdom of internal focusing" (*jiko shūchū no chie*). . . . Thus, in an epoch of turbulent dynastic changes and internal revolts in Asia, Japan was able to keep a long period of peace, calmly to collect energies for the development of the arts, technology and productivity, and to mature.'[50] Japan in the Edo period focused almost entirely on internal development; the 'wisdom of internal focusing' served as an incubator for an indigenous version of modernity. And here, for Nishio, the world-historical significance of the Edo period becomes obvious: while the modernization of the West hinged on expansion, slavery, and colonization by force, Japanese civilization confined itself to internal trade within an inherently peaceful society. This version of a peaceful modernity

[49] Nishio, *Kokumin no rekishi*, 402–7. See also Arano Yasunori, *Kinsei Nihon to higashi Ajia: Shohan* (Tokyo, 1988); Arano Yasunori, Ishii Masatoshi, and Murai Shosuke (eds), *Ajia no naka no Nihon shi*, 5 vols. (Tokyo, 1992–3).

[50] Nishio, *Kokumin no rekishi*, 406.

(only discarded, one surmises, after exposure to Western military threats since the Meiji period) is presented as an alternative path in world history.

The example Nishio gives is the famous case of the abolition of guns in the Edo period. Indeed, firearms had come to Japan with the Portuguese in the sixteenth century, and they were soon copied, replicated, and widely used. By the end of the century, Japan had emerged as the world's largest producer of guns. But with the beginning of the Tokugawa period, the production and use of firearms was severely restricted, and Japanese warfare reverted to the sword. Guns, then, were intentionally given up. 'Japan turned into a country that valued internal peace more than anything else. This tradition is still alive today. None of the civilized countries of the world match Japan in terms of stability and safety.'[51] While Marxist historians had long described Japan's modern history as the history of militarism, Nishio and Kawakatsu see Japan as inherently peaceful and non-expansionist. The 'liberalist view of history' dismisses whatever militarism there might have been as the unfortunate result of Western influence since the Meiji period.[52] At the end of the nineteenth century, Japan was forced to adopt a policy of industrial and military prowess, epitomized by the ubiquitous slogan 'enrich the country, strengthen the army' (*fukoku kyōhei*). Kawakatsu Heita now concludes that, at the beginning of the twenty-first century, it is high time to abandon this fateful path and return to the Japanese path of modernization, in order to 'enrich the country and advance virtue' (*fukoku yūtoku*).[53]

[51] Ibid. 410. See also Noel Perrin, *Giving up the Gun: Japan's Reversion to the Sword, 1543–1879* (Boston, 1979), a book that is also mentioned by Kawakatsu.

[52] It is interesting to note that the idea of militarism as the result of foreign influence was by no means new. In the immediate post-war period, conservative historians like Tsuda Sōkichi and Marxists like Toma Seita both supposed an original state of Japanese peacefulness that was contaminated by the impact of cultural borrowings from abroad. But while Kawakatsu and Nishio relegate all militarism to the 'West', in the atmosphere of the 1950s, the image of Europe and the USA was still largely unblemished. For Tsuda or Toma, not the West, but China was the villain. See Sebastian Conrad, *Auf der Suche nach der verlorenen Nation: Geschichtswissenschaft in Westdeutschland und Japan 1945–1960* (Göttingen, 1999), 174–6.

[53] Kawakatsu Heita, *Fukoku yūtokuron* (Tokyo, 2000). Apart from the peaceful character of the Japanese, Kawakatsu notes a series of other legacies of the Edo period that he wants to see revived. Among them is the Japanese attitude to work, an attitude he regards as threatened by the global migration of workers seen today; here, too, he advocates the adoption of a closed-country system that inhibits infringements on Japanese culture.

III. *Conclusion*

Within this ambitious paradigm of revisionist historiography, the Edo period was rehabilitated and interpreted as a pivotal moment in Japanese history. Kawakatsu and Nishio no longer consider the phase of national seclusion/concentration a dead-end street producing backwardness. Rather, they see it as an epoch of internal development and progress. At the same time, Japanese history has been re-Asianized: Edo-period Japan is now represented as an integral part of Asian civilization. In the very policy of seclusion, historians such as Asao Naohiro have detected fundamental commonalities with other Asian countries; the strict regulation of exchange with the outside world was a feature common to the national policies in East Asia at the time, and was also adopted by China and Korea.[54] As a result of its policy of 'internal focusing', Japan was able to liberate itself from a Chinese-dominated order and establish a new hegemony in Asia, now centred on Japan.

This project to reframe the narratives of modern Japan is an attempt not only to reinterpret change and development, but also to define what has not changed but has remained stable. The 'liberalist view of history' relies on a strong notion of unchanging 'Japaneseness', running like a constant thread through the Japanese past. Within this paradigm, the Edo period figures as a retreat from the world that enables the constant traits of the nation to come into full bloom; for Ueyama, Japan asserted its individuality (*kosei*) by temporarily cutting all contact with the outside world, thus adapting all cultural imports to a Japanese essence.[55] Kawakatsu, too, refers to the notion of a continuous 'Japaneseness' (*wa*) which is preserved across the centuries.[56]

Against this substantivist view of Japan, scholars such as Amino Yoshihiko and Nishikawa Nagao have recently begun to question the assumptions of a unified 'Japanese history'. Amino, a historian of medieval Japan, has engaged in a search for diver-

[54] Asao Naohiro, *Nihon kinseishi no jiritsu* (Tokyo, 1988).

[55] Ueyama Shumpei, *Juyō to sōzō no kiseki* (*Nihon bunmeishi no kōsō*, vol. i) (Tokyo, 1990), 238.

[56] Kawakatsu, *Nihon bunmei*, 246.

sities in the Japanese tradition, and in the process has attempted to 'deconstruct "Japan"'.[57] Nishikawa Nagao, a specialist in French literature and history, has looked into the process of nation-state formation and the consequent construction of 'national cultures'; for him, likewise, notions of immutable 'Japaneseness' are ideological constructs that tend to ignore diversity and heterogeneity.[58]

These approaches from less essentializing quarters may very well pose a more sophisticated challenge to received interpretations. The revisionist narrative, in other words, by no means represents the only threat to an established discourse that still largely rests on some kind of reformed historical materialism or modernization theory. Nevertheless, the civilization theories put forward by Ueyama, Kawakatsu, and Nishio have generated strong resonance and broad media coverage. Support, including financial, in political and business circles is strong, and popular works of revisionist leanings are selling millions of copies. In the academic world, too, the project to establish a 'liberalist view of history' has elicited numerous commentaries. Although most of these are highly critical, their very number reveals the scale of the perceived threat.[59]

While the revisionist challenge is both political and historiographical, it also rests on a different view of world history. Within the *kaikoku* paradigm that flourished in the 1950s and 1960s (and remains influential with many academic historians to the present day), 'world history' (*sekaishi*) was the principal frame of reference within which Japan was interpreted. The analytical claims rested on an intricate relationship between the spatial and the temporal aspects of an allegedly universal development.

[57] See e.g. Amino Yoshihiko, *Nihonron no shiza: Rettō no shakai to kokka* (Tokyo, 1990). See also his 'Deconstructing "Japan"', *East Asian History*, 3 (1992), 121–42.

[58] See Nishikawa Nagao, *Kokkyō no kōekata* (Tokyo, 1992); id., *Kokumin kokkaron no shatei: Aruiwa 'kokumin' to iu kaibutsu ni tsuite* (Tokyo, 1998); id. *et al.* (eds.), *Kokusai chitsujo to kokumin bunka no keisei* (Tokyo, 1999). See also Komori Yōichi and Takahashi Tetsuya (eds.). *Nashonaru hisutorī o koete* (Tokyo, 1998).

[59] For a critical view of the project of the 'Association to promote a liberalist view of history', see e.g. Fujiwara Akira, *Kingendaishi no shinjitsu wa nanika* (Tokyo, 1996); Sato Nobuo (ed.), *Ima manabitai kingendaishi* (Tokyo, 1997); Nara rekishi kenkyūkai, *Sengo rekishigaku to 'jiyū shugi shikan'* (Tokyo, 1997); Yoshida Yutaka, *Gendai rekishigaku to sensō sekinin* (Tokyo, 1997); Nakamura Masanori, *Kingendaishi o dō miru ka: Shiba shikan o tou* (Tokyo, 1997); Tawara Yoshifumi, *Kyōkasho kōgeki no shinsō: 'Ianfu' mondai to 'jiyū shugi shikan' no sakujutsu* (Tokyo, 1997); id., *Tettei kenshō-abunai kyōkasho* (Tokyo, 2001).

In most accounts, the 'world' was essentially identified with an idealized picture of the 'West'; European modernity served as the yardstick by which to measure Japan. This geographical bias notwithstanding, there was a clear tendency to treat 'world history' not so much as a spatial but rather as a temporal category. The developmental scheme of explanation suggested that the 'modern' societies in Europe and the USA represented a future that Japan, as a 'late-comer', would eventually reach. World history, from this perspective, appeared as something that Japan was not so much influenced by, but rather hoped to 'catch up with'.

The temporal aspects remain central to Ueyama's and Kawakatsu's theories of world-historical development.[60] Both refer explicitly to various stages of civilization that can be observed universally: according to this scheme, a society of hunter-gatherers is superseded by an agricultural society and, finally, by an industrial society. Transition to the more advanced stages, marked by agricultural and industrial revolutions respectively, occurs at different moments in the history of the various civilizations. Ueyama places the advent of industrial society in Japan around 1900, while Kawakatsu sees the 'industrious revolution' of the late Edo period as the moment of departure. While a concern with the temporal dimension of world history thus continues to play an important role, the *sakoku* faction has at the same time inscribed their view of history into a decidedly spatial order. For Ueyama and Kawakatsu, world history consists of the development of separate civilizations, clearly bounded and progressing largely according to a logic of their own. Indeed, the privileged position accorded to the Edo period in both their accounts suggests the need for times when all foreign influences are shut out. The desirability of a new age of seclusion, then, is one of 'the lessons . . . for our present and future' to be drawn from the Japanese past.[61]

The shift from *kaikoku* to *sakoku*, from a unified and universal paradigm of world history to a theory of distinct civilizations, was thus accompanied by a tendency to replace the leading temporal metaphors with categories of space. World history no

[60] See also Morris-Suzuki, 'Invention', 773. For a polemical reply to Morris-Suzuki's interpretation, see Kawakatsu, *Fukoku yūtokuron*, 118–26.

[61] Kawakatsu, 'Seclusion Policy', 76.

longer appeared as a matter of chronology and periodization, but of separation and demarcation. The reaction against the universalist narratives in the modernist vein has thus produced a nativist discourse stressing spatial boundaries, cultural essences, and Japanese uniqueness. In the early Meiji period and again in post-war Japan, when the impact of the West was obvious and reached deep into everyday life, the Japanese adaptations to a Western world order were seen not as succumbing to foreign influence, but—in universalist parlance—as overcoming a time lag. At the end of the twentieth century, however, revisionist historians depicted world history as evolving differently in different regions, each 'civilization' carving out a space of its own. The increase of exchange and interaction has thus replaced a universalist discourse with notions of cultural particularity that serve to veil the actual entanglements that have produced it. At a historical juncture when the rhetoric of globalization abounds, and clearly in reaction to it, Kawakatsu therefore calls for the establishment of an 'ecological niche' where Japanese can 'live in their own familiar lands', undisturbed by migrant workers, isolated from the world.[62]

[62] Kawakatsu, *Nihon bunmei*, 247–50.

Notes on Contributors

MICHAEL ADAS is Professor of History at Rutgers University, New Brunswick. He is the author of comparative studies on the impact of colonialism, peasant protest movements, and the impact of technology on European and American expansionism. In addition to a number of edited volumes and co-authored textbooks on world history, he has written *Machines as the Measure of Men: Science, Technology, and Ideologies of Western Dominance* (1989). He is currently completing a book on *Dominance by Design: Technological Imperatives and America's Civilizing Mission* for Harvard University Press.

JERRY H. BENTLEY is Professor of History at the University of Hawaii and editor of the *Journal of World History*. He is the author of *Shapes of World History in Twentieth-Century Scholarship* (1996); *Old-World Encounters: Cross-Cultural Contacts and Exchanges in Pre-Modern Times* (1993); *Politics and Culture in Renaissance Naples* (1987); and *Humanists and Holy Writ: New Testament Scholarship in the Renaissance* (1983). His current interests include processes of cross-cultural interaction and cultural exchanges in modern times.

MICHAEL BENTLEY is Professor of Modern History at the University of St Andrews. He is the author of an introductory volume on *Modern Historiography* (1999), as well as several books about modern British politics, most recently on Lord Salisbury, and in 1997 he edited *Companion to Historiography*. He is currently preparing the Wiles Lectures for 2003 on British historiography in the age of Butterfield and Namier.

THOMAS M. BOHN studied History and Slavonic Studies at the University of Hamburg and has been Assistant Professor (*wissenschaftlicher Assistent*) in the Department of History at the Friedrich Schiller University in Jena since 1995. His publications include *Kollektivität und Individualität: Der Mensch im östlichen Europa* (co-ed., 2001); *Studienhandbuch Östliches Europa*, ii: *Russisches Reich und Sowjetunion* (co-ed., 2002); and *Russische Geschichtswissenschaft von 1880 bis 1905: Pavel N. Miljukov und die Moskauer Schule* (1998). He is at present working on the city of Minsk and urbanization in the Soviet Union after 1945, and his research interests include the history of Russian historiography, urban history in eastern Europe, and the history of south-eastern Europe in the nineteenth and twentieth centuries.

SEBASTIAN CONRAD is Assistant Professor (*wissenschaftlicher Assistent*) in the Department of History at the Free University of Berlin. His publications include *Die Nation schreiben: Geschichtswissenschaft im internationalen Vergleich* (co-ed., 2002); *Jenseits des Eurozentrismus: Postkoloniale Perspektiven in den Geschichts- und Kulturwissenschaften* (co-ed., 2002); and *Auf der Suche nach der verlorenen Nation: Geschichtswissenschaft in Westdeutschland und Japan 1945–1960* (1999). He is currently working on a study provisionally entitled 'Globalization and National Identity: "German Work" and the Mobility of Labour in Germany, 1880–1914'.

ARIF DIRLIK is Knight Professor of Social Science, Professor of History and Anthropology, and Director of the Center for Critical Theory and Transnational Studies at the University of Oregon. His most recent book-length publications are *Chinese on the American Frontier* (ed., 2001); *Places and Politics in an Age of Globalization* (ed. with Roxann Prazniak, 2001); *History After the Three Worlds* (ed. with Vinay Bahl and Peter Gran, 2000); and *Postmodernity's Histories* (2000).

ANDREAS ECKERT is Professor of African History at the University of Hamburg. He has published numerous articles on nineteenth- and twentieth-century African history and historiography. His books include *Herrschen und Verwalten: Afrikanische Bürokraten, staatliche Ordnung und Politik in Tanzania, 1920–1970* (2003); *Grundbesitz, Landkonflikte und kolonialer Wandel: Douala 1880 bis 1960* (1999); and *Die Duala und die Kolonialmächte* (1991).

ECKHARDT FUCHS is Assistant Professor (*wissenschaftlicher Assistent*) in the Department of Education at the University of Mannheim. His main field of research is modern American and European intellectual history. Currently he is working on the history of scientific internationalism. He has widely published in these fields, e.g. *Across Cultural Borders: Historiography in Global Perspective* (co-ed. with Benedikt Stuchtey, 2002); *Weltausstellungen im 19. Jahrhundert* (ed., 1999); *Macht und Geist: Intellektuelle in der Zwischenkriegszeit* (co-ed. with Wolfgang Bialas, 1995); *Geschichtswissenschaft neben dem Historismus* (co-ed. with Steffen Sammler, 1995); *Henry Thomas Buckle: Geschichtsschreibung und Positivismus in England und Deutschland* (1994); and, with Günther Fuchs, *'J'accuse!': Zur Affäre Dreyfus in Frankreich* (1994).

VINAY LAL is Associate Professor of History at the University of California at Los Angeles. He has published widely on Indian history, historiography, popular Indian cinema, the global politics of culture, terrorism, the Indian diaspora, and the politics of knowledge systems. His most recent publications include *Of Cricket, Guinness and Gandhi: Essays in Indian History and Culture* (2002); *Empire of Knowledge: Culture and Plurality in the Global Economy* (2002); a special issue of the journal *Futures* on 'End of Disciplines?' (February 2002); *Open Futures, Dissenting Knowledges: The Multiple Selves and Strange Destinations of Ashis Nandy* (ed., 2000); and a special issue of the journal *Emergences* on 'Islands' (November, 2000).

RICARDO K. S. MAK, who earned his Ph.D. in History from the University of Regensburg, is Associate Professor of History at the Hong Kong Baptist University. Specializing in modern Western intellectual thought and Sino-German relations, he has published a dozen articles and reviews on related topics in academic journals in China, Taiwan, Hong Kong, and the United States. He is co-editor of *Sino-German Relations since 1800: Multidisciplinary Explorations* (2000); and the author of *The Future of the Non-Western World in the Social Sciences in Nineteenth Century England* (1999).

PATRICK KARL O'BRIEN FBA was formerly Director of the Institute of Historical Research at the University of London, and is currently Centennial Professor of Economic History at the London School of Economics, where he lectures on the School's innovatory masters' programme in global history. He has written numerous books and articles on British, European, Middle Eastern, and latterly global economic history.

LUTZ RAPHAEL is Professor of Contemporary History at the University of Trier. His publications include *Recht und Ordnung: Herrschaft durch Verwaltung im Europa des 19. Jahrhunderts* (2000); *Die Erben von Bloch und Febvre: 'Annales'-Historiographie und 'nouvelle histoire' in Frankreich 1945–1980* (1994); and *Partei und Gewerkschaft: Die Gewerkschaftsstrategien der kommunistischen Parteien Italiens und Frankreichs seit 1970* (1984). He is currently working on the following research projects: 'State and Nation at Village Level: Case Studies in Rhenania, the Palatinate, Luxembourg, and Lorraine 1815–1880'; 'Psychologists in West German Industrial Enterprises, 1949–1980'; 'Poverty in the Countryside: Rural Areas in the Age of the Welfare State (1880–1960)'; and 'Mediterranean Migrants in the Mining and Steel Regions of Belgium, France, and Luxembourg (1946–1980)'.

BENEDIKT STUCHTEY joined the German Historical Institute London as a Research Fellow in 1995 after studying in Münster, Freiburg, and Trinity College Dublin. He has edited, with Eckhardt Fuchs, *Across Cultural Borders: Historiography in Global Perspective* (2002); and with Peter Wende, *British and German Historiography, 1750–1950: Traditions, Perceptions, and Transfers* (2000); and is the author of *W. E. H. Lecky (1838–1903): Historisches Denken und politisches Urteilen eines anglo-irischen Gelehrten* (1997). He is on the editorial committee of *European Review of History. Revue Européenne d'Histoire.* His main research interests are the history of historiography and of European imperialism, and he is currently working on anti-colonialism in a comparative perspective.

JULIA ADENEY THOMAS was educated at Princeton, Oxford, and the University of Chicago and is now Associate Professor in the History Department at the University of Notre Dame. She is currently working on the issue of art—particularly photography—and democracy in post-war Japan. She has published several essays from this project, including the award-winning 'Photography, National Identity and the "Cataract of Times"' in the *American Historical Review* (1998). Her earlier research concerned concepts of nature and modernity. In *Reconfiguring Modernity: Concepts of Nature in Japanese Political Ideology* (2001), awarded the John K. Fairbank prize by the American Historical

Association, Thomas argues that 'nature' is a dynamic political concept. She has also published articles on concepts of nature in the Meiji period (1868–1912) and in the thought of political theorist Maruyama Masao.

Index